Spanish and English literature
of the 16th and 17th centuries

Spanish and English literature of the 16th and 17th centuries

❖

Studies in discretion, illusion and mutability

❖

EDWARD M. WILSON

Formerly Professor of Spanish
University of Cambridge

CAMBRIDGE UNIVERSITY PRESS
CAMBRIDGE
LONDON   NEW YORK   NEW ROCHELLE
MELBOURNE   SYDNEY

Published by the Press Syndicate of the University of Cambridge
The Pitt Building, Trumpington Street, Cambridge CB2 1RP
32 East 57th Street, New York, NY 10022, USA
296 Beaconsfield Parade, Middle Park, Melbourne 3206, Australia

© Cambridge University Press 1980

First published 1980

Printed in Great Britain by
Western Printing Services Ltd
Bristol

British Library Cataloguing in Publication Data
Wilson, Edward Meryon
Spanish and English literature of the 16th and
17th centuries.
1. Spanish literature – Classical period,
1500–1700 – History and criticism
I. Cruickshank, Don
860′ .9′003   PQ6064   79-41612

ISBN 0 521 22844 1

CONTENTS

	Preface	vii
	Sources and acknowledgements	ix
	A list of the publications of Edward M. Wilson	xiii
1	The four elements in the imagery of Calderón	1
2	Fernando: the Constant Prince	15
3	On *La vida es sueño*	27
4	The discretion of Don Lope de Almeida	48
5	Towards an appreciation of *El pintor de su deshonra*	65
6	The cloak and sword plays	90
	Plate: Frontispiece of *Psalle et sile*, first edition *facing page*	105
7	A key to Calderón's *Psalle et sile*	105
8	Calderón's dramatic poetry	116
9	Images and structure in *Peribáñez*	130
10	'Quando Lope quiere, quiere'	155
11	The exemplary nature of *El caballero de Olmedo*	184
12	A Hispanist looks at *Othello*	201
13	Tragic themes in Spanish ballads	220
14	Spanish and English religious poetry of the seventeenth century	234
	Notes	250
	Index of names and titles of works	271

PREFACE

In 1973 Edward Wilson retired from the chair of Spanish in the University of Cambridge. For some time he had been thinking of publishing a collected volume, in English, of his critical essays, and hoped (in vain) that his retirement would leave him free to prepare it. He began in 1974 to assemble suitable articles, but the final contents had still not been settled at his death in November 1977. He left three draft lists: one dated December 1973, the others undated but clearly later. I feel that my main obligation is to respect the intention of the two later lists (as far as they can be reconciled); but I also believe that the author's death puts the whole volume in a different perspective. For this second reason I have included two previously unpublished articles which do not appear in any of the draft lists.

One of these unpublished articles, on Calderón's comedies, was written as part of a book (never completed) on Calderón; it would have joined the articles on *El príncipe constante*, *La vida es sueño* and Calderón's dramatic poetry. These were published separately when the Calderón book was abandoned, and it seems fitting to bring them all together at last. His many friends and colleagues were disappointed that what promised to be a major work on Calderón was never finished; the present collection of Calderón articles is perhaps as near as we are likely to get to it. The unity of the planned original will be clear to anyone who reads the collection as a whole. It will be clear, too, that the unity is provided by Wilson's own view of Calderón as a thoroughly consistent dramatist, constantly returning to the themes of *discreción* and *desengaño*, discretion and need to rid oneself of worldly illusions.

The other unpublished article, on Lope's *El caballero de Olmedo*, would certainly have represented an important contribution to the study of the play twenty years ago, when it seems to have been written. If it now appears a little conservative, this is no reason for omitting it: Wilson had a healthy contempt for what was 'fashionable' in literary criticism. Indeed, it can be looked on as a valuable counterweight to the present critical trend, coming as it does from a scholar who was perhaps more familiar than anyone with the play's literary antecedents. Again, readers will notice how the three Lope articles are unified by what Wilson saw as a unifying theme in Lope's work: discretion, and the dangers of its opposite, rashness; in his article on *Peribáñez* he describes discretion as 'one of the main concerns of the seventeenth century'.

My editorial intervention has been as minimal as possible. Some previously published articles were left in a state of partial revision, with footnotes omitted; this was also true of some footnotes in the unpublished ones. These I have supplied [thus], in some cases with the help of Dr Cecilia Bainton, like myself, a former pupil of Wilson's. Dr Bainton subedited the volume, and it owes a great deal to her painstaking efficiency. The article on *Peribáñez*, originally published in French, was only half translated, and I completed the translation. The article on *El caballero de Olmedo* had evidently been composed in Spanish, and resisted translation into straightforward English. I am grateful to my colleague Martin Cunningham for his help here, but I must be blamed for inelegancies that remain. Finally, I must thank Michael Black and Professor A. A. Parker for their help and advice.

University College, Dublin D. W. Cruickshank
August 1979

SOURCES AND ACKNOWLEDGEMENTS

'The four elements in the imagery of Calderón' derives from Wilson's doctoral dissertation (i.e. it dates from the early thirties) and was first published in 1936 in *Modern Language Review*. He revised some footnotes for this reprint, which is produced by permission of the editor of *Modern Language Review* and the Modern Humanities Research Association.

'Fernando: the Constant Prince' was written as a chapter in Wilson's projected Calderón book, and must date from the late thirties. It was published in *Modern Language Review* in 1939 as one of the two articles in 'Calderón's *Príncipe constante*: two appreciations' (W. J. Entwistle wrote the other). Wilson revised his text for this edition, taking account of Entwistle's views and defending his own. It is reprinted by permission of the editor of *Modern Language Review* and the Modern Humanities Research Association.

'On *La vida es sueño*': also planned as a chapter in the Calderón book, it first appeared in 1946, some eight years after it was first written, as '*La vida es sueño*' in the *Revista de la Universidad de Buenos Aires*; it is now reprinted with the editor's permission. Wilson made some slight revision for an English version in 1965, and again for this volume.

'The discretion of Don Lope de Almeida': planned as a chapter in another book on the theme of marital honour and wife-murder; written in the late forties and published in 1951 as 'La discreción de don Lope de Almeida' in *Clavileño*. Wilson himself prepared an English version for publication in 1973, but he did not revise it again.

'Towards an appreciation of *El pintor de su deshonra*': contemporary with, and in the same category as the previous article, but not published until 1970, when it appeared in *Ábaco* as 'Hacia una interpretación de *El pintor de su deshonra*'. Wilson translated the Spanish text for this volume, making minor additions and revisions; it is published by permission of Editorial Castalia.

'The cloak and sword plays': unpublished. Planned as a chapter in the Calderón book, so possibly first drafted in the nineteen thirties, although the most recent work referred to in the notes is dated 1941.

'A key to *Psalle et sile*': first published in 1959 in *Hispanic studies in honour of I. González Llubera*. Wilson added a note and made one or two minor changes for this edition.

'Calderón's dramatic poetry': planned as an early chapter of the Calderón book; the original Spanish version was delivered first as one of the Archer M. Huntington lectures at the University of Madrid on 10 April 1964. It was published in 1968 as 'La pocsía dramática de don Pedro Calderón de la Barca' in *Litterae hispanae et lusitanae: Festschrift zum fünfzigjähren Bestehen des Ibero-Amerikanischen Forschungsinstituts der Universität Hamburg*. This version is Wilson's own translation, with fuller notes; it is published by permission of Max Hueber Verlag.

'Images and structure in *Peribáñez*': first published in 1949 as 'Images et structure dans *Peribáñez*' in *Bulletin Hispanique*; it was a by-product of Wilson's interest in the theme of marital honour, and was also prompted by the publication of the Hachette edition of the play (edited by Aubrun and Montesinos). The English original was lost, and this translation is part Wilson's, part mine. It is published by permission of the editors of *Bulletin Hispanique*.

'Quando Lope quiere, quiere': another intended chapter in the wife-murder book, it first appeared in 1963 in *Cuadernos Hispanoamericanos* in Spanish. Wilson revised his original English typescript for this edition, which is published by permission of the editor of *Cuadernos Hispanoamericanos*.

'The exemplary nature of *El caballero de Olmedo*': unpublished, and evidently not planned as part of any book. Typed on Wilson's Hermes 3000 (i.e. 1959 or later). Possibly dates from the early nineteen sixties.

'A Hispanist looks at *Othello*': another result of Wilson's interest in the wife-murder theme. Part of it was published as '*Othello*, a tragedy of honour' in *The Listener* in 1952, but this, the complete version, is unpublished. Wilson kept and revised slightly his original typescript. He had a particular fondness for this article, and it appears in all three of his draft lists of articles for this volume.

'Tragic themes in Spanish ballads': first published in 1958 as the eighth in the *Diamante* series. A characteristically Wilsonian piece, which perhaps only he, with his exceptional knowledge of the 'popular' literature of both

Spain and Britain, could have written. Cambridge University Press gratefully acknowledges the permission of the Hispanic and Luso Brazilian Council to reprint the article.

'Spanish and English religious poetry of the seventeenth century': published in the *Journal of Ecclesiastical History* in 1958. Not merely contemporary with the previous item but also akin to it in the way in which it finds similarities and differences in a distinct but related genre.

A LIST OF THE PUBLICATIONS OF EDWARD M. WILSON

The first list of Wilson's publications appeared in his *Festschrift: Studies in Spanish literature of the Golden Age presented to Edward M. Wilson*, edited by R. O. Jones (London, 1973), pp. 3–8. It contained ninety-nine entries, even though it excluded reviews and review articles. It has been possible, adopting the same criteria, to add some thirty works which were not in print when the *Festschrift* went to press, as well as a few which were omitted from it. The important memoir of his friend Don Antonio Rodríguez-Moñino was included in the first check-list; Wilson himself included other such memoirs in a list he made in 1963. For these reasons memoirs are included in the list below.

ABBREVIATIONS

BH	*Bulletin Hispanique*
BHS	*Bulletin of Hispanic Studies*
BRAE	*Boletín de la Real Academia Española*
Comedias	Pedro Calderón de la Barca, *Comedias*, a facsimile edition prepared by D. W. Cruickshank and J. E. Varey. 19 vols. London, 1973. Vol. 1: Edward M. Wilson and D. W. Cruickshank, *The textual criticism of Calderón's 'comedias'*, ed. D. W. Cruickshank. Vol. XIX: *Critical studies*, ed. J. E. Varey
Entre las jarchas	Edward M. Wilson, *Entre las jarchas y Cernuda: constantes y variables en la poesía española*. Barcelona, 1977
HR	*Hispanic Review*
MLN	*Modern Language Notes*
MLR	*Modern Language Review*
NRFH	*Nueva Revista de Filología Hispánica*
PQ	*Philological Quarterly*
RABM	*Revista de Archivos, Bibliotecas y Museos*
RFE	*Revista de Filología Española*
RP	*Romance Philology*
TCBS	*Transactions of the Cambridge Bibliographical Society*
TCWAAS	*Transactions of the Cumberland and Westmorland Antiquarian and Archaeological Society*

The solitudes of Don Luis de Góngora, translated into English verse by Edward M. Wilson. Cambridge, 1931; 2nd edn, New York, 1965 (a piracy, with unauthorised revisions); 3rd (authorised) edn, Cambridge, 1965

'Two modern Spanish poets' [Federico García Lorca and Jorge Guillén], *Bookman* (September 1931), 288–9; to be reprinted in *Modern Iberian literature*, ed. I. Stern and M. J. Schneider

'Note on a sonnet of Rioja's', *HR*, II (1934), 155–7

'El texto de la "Fábula de Píramo y Tisbe", de Góngora', *RFE*, XXII (1935), 291–8; revised and reprinted in *Entre las jarchas*, pp. 333–42

'Sobre la "Canción a las ruinas de Itálica" de Rodrigo Caro', *RFE*, XXIII (1936), 379–96

'The four elements in the imagery of Calderón', *MLR*, XXXI (1936), 34–47; reprinted in *Calderón de la Barca*, ed. Hans Flasche, Wege der Forschung, vol. CLVIII. Darmstadt, 1971, pp. 112–30; and in *Comedias*, vol. XIX, pp. 191–207. Also reprinted as 'Los cuatro elementos en la imaginería de Calderón' in *Calderón y la crítica: historia y antología*, ed. M. Durán and R. González Echevarría, Madrid, 1976, pp. 277–99. (A translation only subsequently approved by the author.)

'Some extinct Kendal customs', *TCWAAS*, N.S., XXXVIII (1938), 164–79

'Calderón's *Príncipe constante*: two appreciations' (with W. J. Entwistle), *MLR*, XXXIV (1939), 207–22

'*La vida es sueño*', *Revista de la Universidad de Buenos Aires*, IV (1946), 61–78; revised and reprinted as 'On *La vida es sueño*' in *Critical essays on the theatre of Calderón*, ed. Bruce W. Wardropper. New York, 1965, pp. 63–89; and in *The great playwrights: twenty-five plays with commentaries by critics and scholars*, chosen and introduced by Eric Bentley. 2 vols. New York, 1970, vol. I, pp. 866–88. Also reprinted in *Calderón y la crítica: historia y antología*, ed. M. Durán and R. González Echevarría. Madrid, 1976, pp. 300–28. (A reprint of the Spanish original, only subsequently approved by the author.)

'Cervantes and English literature of the seventeenth century', *BH*, L (1948), 27–52

'Did John Fletcher read Spanish?', *PQ*, XXVII (1948), 187–90

'*Rule a wife and have a wife* and *El sagaz Estacio*', *Review of English Studies*, XXIV (1948), 189–94

'Images et structure dans *Peribáñez*', *BH* LI (1949), 125–59. Reprinted as 'Imágenes y estructura en *Peribáñez*' in *El teatro de Lope de Vega: artículos y estudios*, ed. José Francisco Gatti. Buenos Aires, 1962, pp. 50–90; 2nd edn, 1967

'The poetry of João Pinto Delgado', *Journal of Jewish Studies*, I (1949), 131–43; reprinted as 'La poesía de João Pinto Delgado' in *Entre las jarchas*, pp. 221–44

'The Spanish protest against "A game at Chesse"', (with Olga Turner), *MLR*, XLIV (1949), 476–82

'Edmund Gayton on Don Quixote, Andrés and Juan Haldudo', *Comparative Literature*, II (1950), 64–72

'La discreción de don Lope de Almeida', *Clavileño*, II, no. 9 (1951), 1–10; reprinted as 'The discretion of Don Lope de Almeida' in *Comedias*, vol. XIX, pp. 17–36

'Gerald Brenan's Calderón', *Bulletin of the Comediantes*, IV, no. 1 (1952), 6–8

'La estrofa sexta de la canción *A la flor de Gnido*', *RFE*, XXXVI (1952), 118–22

'*Othello*, a tragedy of honour', *The Listener*, XLVII, 5 June 1952, 926–7

'Family honour in the plays of Shakespeare's predecessors and contemporaries', *Essays and Studies*, N.S., VI (1953), 19–40
'Frederick Alexander Kirkpatrick', *Atlante*, I (1953), 163–4
'On Góngora's *Angélica y Medoro*', *BHS*, xxx (1953), 85–94
Quevedo, Francisco de, *Lágrimas de Hieremías castellanas*, ed. Edward M. Wilson and J. M. Blecua, *Revista de Filología Española*, anejo LV. Madrid, 1953. Revised edition of Quevedo's text to appear in *Obras* of Quevedo, ed J. M. Blecua, vol. IV
'Felix Persio Bertiso's *La harpa de Belén*', *Atlante*, II (1954), 126–36
'Modern Spanish poems: I: Guillén and Quevedo on death', *Atlante*, I (1953), 22–6; 'Postscript', II (1954), 237–8; reprinted as 'Guillén y Quevedo, sobre la muerte' in *Entre las jarchas*, pp. 299–309
' "Ora vete, amor, y vete, cata que amanece" ', *Estudios dedicados a Menéndez Pidal*, 7 vols. in 8. Madrid, 1950–62, vol. V, pp. 335–48
'Henry John Chaytor 1871–1954', *BHS*, XXXII (1955), 113–14
'La edición príncipe de *Fieras afemina amor* de don Pedro Calderón', *Revista de la Biblioteca, Archivo y Museo de Madrid*, XXIV (1955), 327–48; reprinted as 'The first edition of Calderón's *Fieras afemina amor*' in *Comedias*, vol. I, pp. 183–200
'Quevedo for the masses', *Atlante*, III (1955), 151–66; reprinted as 'Quevedo para las masas' in *Entre las jarchas*, pp. 273–97
'Samuel Pepys's Spanish chap-books', Part I: *TCBS*, II, no. 2 (1955), 127–54; Part II: II, no. 3 (1956), 229–68; Part III: II, no. 4 (1957), 305–22
'Some poems from Samuel Pepys's Spanish chap-books', *BHS*, XXXII (1955), 187–93
'Frozen words' (with Peter Rickard), *The Polar Record*, VIII (1956), 95–108
'Some Calderonian "pliegos sueltos" ', *Homenaje a J. A. van Praag*. Amsterdam, 1956, pp. 140–4
'Tradition and change in some late Spanish verse chap-books', *HR*, XXV (1957), 194–216
'Una *Ensalada de romances* impresa a Barcelona', *Estudis Romànics*, VI (1957–8), 75–93
'Memoir – John Brande Trend, 1887–1958', *BHS*, XXXV (1958), 223–7
'Notes on the text of *A secreto agravio secreta venganza*', *BHS*, XXXV (1958), 72–82; reprinted in *Comedias*, vol. I, pp. 95–106
'Spanish and English religious poetry of the seventeenth century', *Journal of Ecclesiastical History*, IX (1958), 38–53
'Thomas Stanley's translations and borrowings from Spanish and Italian poems' (with E. R. Vincent, who writes on the Italian sources), *Revue de Littérature Comparée*, XXXII (1958), 548–56: I: Edward M. Wilson, 'Polyphemus and other translations from Spanish', pp. 548–51
Tragic themes in Spanish ballads. Diamante, VIII. London, 1958; reprinted 1965, also reprinted as 'Temas trágicos en el Romancero español' in *Entre las jarchas*, pp. 107–29
'A key to Calderón's *Psalle et sile*', *Hispanic studies in honour of I. González Llubera*. Oxford, 1959, pp. 429–40
An exhibition of Spanish books and books of Hispanic interest. The University Library, Cambridge. 21 March 1959 (with other hands). Cambridge, 1959
González de Godoy, Pedro, *Discursos serio-iocosos sobre el agua de la vida*, ed. Edward M. Wilson. Sociedad de Bibliófilos Españoles, tercera época, II. Madrid, 1959

'On the Pando editions of Calderón's *Autos*', *HR*, xxvii (1959), 324-44
'The text of Calderón's *La púrpura de la rosa*', *MLR*, liv (1959), 29-44; reprinted in *Comedias*, vol. i, pp. 161-82
'The two editions of Calderón's *Primera parte* of 1640', *The Library*, series v, xiv (1959), 175-91; reprinted in *Comedias*, vol. i, pp. 57-77
'Calderón's *Primera parte de autos sacramentales* and Don Pedro de Pando y Mier', *BHS*, xxxvii (1960), 16-28
'Dos memorias de los libreros de Madrid a mediados del siglo xvii', *El Libro Español*, iii, no. 26 (1960), 52-4
'Las *Dudas curiosas* a la aprobación del Maestro Fray Manuel de Guerra y Ribera', *Estudios Escénicos*, vi (1960), 47-63
'Notas sobre algunos manuscritos calderonianos en Madrid y en Toledo', *RABM*, lxviii (1960), 477-87
'Textos impresos y apenas utilizados para la biografía de Calderón', *Hispanófila*, ix (1960), 1-14
'An early rehash of Calderón's *El príncipe constante*', *MLN*, lxxvi (1961), 785-94
'Calderón and the stage-censor in the seventeenth century: a provisional study', *Symposium*, xv (1961), 165-84
'Fray Hortensio Paravicino's protest against *El príncipe constante*', *Ibérida: Revista de Filología*, vi (1961), 245-66
'La estética de don García de Salcedo Coronel y la poesía española del siglo xvii', *RFE*, xliv (1961), 1-27; reprinted in *Entre las jarchas*, pp. 157-93
'An early list of Calderón's *comedias*', *Modern Philology*, lx (1962), 95-102
'¿Escribió Calderón el romance *Curiosísima señora?*', *Anuario de Letras*, ii (1962), 99-118
'Further notes on the Pando editions of Calderón's *Autos*', *HR*, xxx (1962), 296-303
'On the *Tercera parte* of Calderón – 1664', *Studies in Bibliography*, xv (1962), 223-30; reprinted in *Comedias*, vol. i, pp. 107-15
'Some Spanish verse chap-books of the seventeenth century', *TCBS*, iii, no. 4 (1962), 327-34.
'"Cuando Lope quiere, quiere"', *Cuadernos Hispanoamericanos* (1963), 265-98
'Miguel de Barrios and Spanish religious poetry', *BHS*, xl (1963), 176-80
'Seven *aprobaciones* by Don Pedro Calderón de la Barca', *Studia philologica: homenaje ofrecido a Dámaso Alonso*, 3 vols. Madrid, 1963, vol. iii, pp. 605-18
'*La Iglesia sitiada*: a Calderonian puzzle', *MLR*, lix (1964), 583-94
Poesías líricas en las obras dramáticas de Calderón: citas y glosas (with Jack Sage). London, 1964
'Folk traditions in Westmorland', *Journal of the Folklore Institute*, ii (1965), 276-93
'Spanish dawn songs', in *Eos*, ed. A. T. Hatto. The Hague, 1965, pp. 299-343; revised and reprinted as 'Albas y alboradas en la Península' in *Entre las jarchas*, pp. 55-105
'Calderón's enemy: Don Antonio Sigler de Huerta', *MLN*, lxxxi (1966), 225-31
'Nuevos documentos sobre las controversias teatrales: 1650-1681', *Actas del segundo Congreso internacional de hispanistas*. Nimega, 1967, pp. 155-70
Some aspects of Spanish literary history. The Taylorian Lecture, delivered on 18 May 1966. Oxford, 1967; adapted and reprinted as 'Algunos aspectos de la historia de la literatura española' in *Entre las jarchas*, pp. 15-54
'The *Cancionero* of Don Joseph del Corral', *HR*, xxxv (1967), 141-60

'A Cervantes item from Emmanuel College Library: Barros's *Filosofía cortesana*, 1587', *TCBS*, IV, no. 5 (1968), 363–71
'Florence Spencer Street (1921–1967)', *BHS*, XLV (1968), 42–3
'La poesía dramática de don Pedro Calderón de la Barca', *Litterae hispanae et lusitanae: Festschrift zum fünfzigjähren Bestehen des Ibero-Amerikanischen Forschungsinstituts der Universität Hamburg*. Munich, 1968, pp. 487–500
'Notes on a sonnet by La Ceppède', *French Studies*, XXII (1968), 296–301
'Some unpublished works by Don Pedro Calderón de la Barca', *Homage to John M. Hill: in memoriam*. Bloomington, Ind., 1968, pp. 7–18
'Variantes nuevas y otras censuras en las *Obras en verso del Homero español*', *BRAE*, XLVIII (1968), 35–54
Calderón de la Barca, Pedro, *Obras menores (siglos XVII y XVIII)*, ed. Edward M. Wilson. El ayre de la almena, vol. XXIV. Cieza, 1969
'Calderón y Fuenterrabía: el *Panegírico* al Almirante de Castilla', *BRAE*, XLIX (1969), 253–78
'"Coplas contradictorias": the perils of double-edged verses', *HR*, XXXVII 1969), 228–37
Two Spanish verse chap-books: Romançe de Amadis (c. 1515–19) and Juyzio hallado y trobado (c. 1510) (with F. J. Norton). Cambridge, 1969
Buendía, Fray Ignacio de, *Triunfo de llaneza*, ed. Edward M. Wilson. Madrid, 1970
'De un memorial a Felipe IV de don Pedro Calderón de la Barca', *Hacia Calderón: Coloquio anglogermano Exeter 1969*. Berlin, 1970, pp. 9–12
'Hacia una interpretación de *El pintor de su deshonra*', *Ábaco*, III (1970), 49–85
'History of a refrain: "De la dulce mi enemiga"' (with Arthur L.-F. Askins), *MLN*, LXXXV (1970), 138–56; reprinted as 'Historia de un estribillo: "De la dulce mi enemiga"' in *Entre las jarchas*, pp. 131–56
'Shakespeare and Christian doctrine: some qualifications', *Shakespeare Survey*, XXIII (1970), 79–89
'Un romancero tardío y desconocido', *NRFH*, XVIII (1970), 443–52
'Calderón and the *Décimas a la muerte*', *BHS*, XLVIII (1971), 301–313
'Calderón', chapter 6 of Edward M. Wilson and Duncan Moir, *The Golden Age: drama 1492–1700*, vol. II of *A literary history of Spain*, ed. R. O. Jones. London, 1971
Translations of poems by Cernuda in *The poetry of Luis Cernuda*, ed. Anthony Edkins and Derek Harris. New York, 1971, pp. 51–65, 87
'Un memorial perdido de don Pedro Calderón', *Homenaje a William L. Fichter*. Madrid, 1971, pp. 801–17
'Antonio Rodríguez-Moñino (1910–1970)', *RP*, XXV (1972), 298–310
'Cernuda's debts', *Studies in modern Spanish literature and art presented to Helen F. Grant*. London, 1972, pp. 239–53; reprinted as 'Las deudas de Cernuda' in *Entre las jarchas*, pp. 311–31
'Poesías atribuidas al Conde de Salinas en el *Cancionero* de don Joseph del Corral', *Homenaje a Casalduero*. Madrid, 1972, pp. 485–91
'Una obra menor de don Pedro Calderón' [*Tono, loa y baile al Santísimo Sacramento*], *Studia hispanica in honorem R. Lapesa*, 3 vols. Madrid, 1972–5, vol. I, pp. 597–608
'Un romance ascético de Calderón: "Agora, Señor, agora..."', *BRAE*, LII (1972), 79–105

'Adiciones a la bibliografía de *Psalle et sile*' (with D. W. Cruickshank), *Hacia Calderón: segundo Coloquio anglogermano Hamburgo 1970*. Berlin, 1973, pp. 13-26

'Calderón's *autos*: eighteenth-century *sueltos* and *relaciones*', Arnold G. Reichenberger *septuagenario praeclaro magistro litterarum universarum testimonium amoris, gratitudinis, et admirationis* (*Hispanic Review*, XLI, special issue (1973)), pp. 331-45

'Calderón y el Patriarca', *Studia iberica: Festschrift für Hans Flasche*. Bern-Munich, 1973, pp. 697-703

'*Comedias sueltas*: a bibliographical problem', *Comedias*, vol. I, pp. 211-19

'Inquisitors as censors in seventeenth-century Spain', in *Expression, communication and experience in literature and language: proceedings of the XII Congress of the International Federation for Modern Languages and Literatures*, ed. R. G. Popperwell. London, 1973, pp. 38-56; reprinted as 'Inquisición y censura en la España del siglo XVII' in *Entre las jarchas*, pp. 245-72

'José F. Montesinos', *RP*, XXVII (1973), 189-202

Poems from the 'Cancionero' of Don Joseph del Corral (Phillipps MS. 22216). Exeter Hispanic Texts. Exeter, 1973

'Un manuscrito español de la Biblioteca de St Catharine's College de Cambridge' (with C. C. Smith), *RABM*, LXXVI (1973), 487-519; 'Post-scriptum', LXXVII (1974), 783-4

'A Calderón collection in Dr Steevens' Hospital, Dublin' (with D. W. Cruickshank), *Long Room*, IX (1974), 17-27

'El texto de la "Deposición a favor de los profesores de la pintura" de don Pedro Calderón de la Barca', *RABM*, LXXVII (1974), 709-27

'Note by E. M. Wilson on the Spanish and Portuguese portion of the library [of Robert Southey]', in *Sale catalogues of libraries of eminent persons*, vol. IX: *Poets and men of letters*, ed. Roy Park. London, 1974, pp. 80-2

Smith, James, *Shakespearian and other essays*, ed. Edward M. Wilson. Cambridge, 1974

'The Cambridge copy of the *Imagen del Antechristo*' (with A. Gordon Kinder), *TCBS*, VI, no. 3 (1974), 188-94

'Una obra sacro-cómica atribuida a don Pedro Calderón', *Homenaje a Guillermo Guastavino*. Madrid, 1974, pp. 361-74

'A defence of the "British critics" of the *comedia*', *Hispania*, LVIII (1975), 481-2

'Carlos Clavería (1909-1974)', *BHS*, LII (1975), 143-6

'*El Auto de la confusión de San José*, suprimido en 1588 por la Inquisición' (with Antonio Rodríguez-Moñino), *Ábaco*, IV (1975), 9-53

'Richard Leake's plague sermons, 1599', *TCWAAS*, LXXV (1975), 150-73

'Un "fin de fiesta" atribuible a don Pedro Calderón de la Barca', *Homenaje al Instituto de Filología y Literaturas Hispánicas 'Dr Amado Alonso'*. Buenos Aires, 1975, pp. 441-51

Antonio Rodríguez-Moñino, *La transmisión de la poesía española en los siglos de oro*, ed. with a prologue by Edward M. Wilson. Barcelona, 1976

'On the *Romanze que dize mi padre era de Ronda*', *Medieval Hispanic studies presented to Rita Hamilton*. London, 1976, pp. 267-76

'Return of the Spanish travellers', *Times Literary Supplement*, 30 July 1976, 964

'Three printed ballad texts from Birmingham', *TCBS*, VI, no. 5 (1976), 339-45
'Addenda to *Poesías líricas en las obras dramáticas de Calderón: citas y glosas*' (with Jack Sage), *Revista Canadiense de Estudios Hispánicos*, I (1977), 199-208
'Ambigüedades y otras cuestiones en los poemas de San Juan de la Cruz', *Entre las jarchas*, pp. 203-19
'Enrique Moreno Báez (1908-1976)', *BHS*, LIV (1977), 329
Entre las jarchas y Cernuda: constantes y variables en la poesía española. Barcelona, 1977
'La estructura simétrica de la "Oda a Francisco Salinas"', *Entre las jarchas*, pp. 195-201
'Marginalia and other notes on "Barnabees Journall"', *Notes and Queries*, CCXXII (1977), 536-41
'Las *Obras* de D. Jacinto Issola, caballero de Génova', in *Libro-homenaje a Antonio Pérez Gómez*, 2 vols. Cieza, 1978, vol. II, pp. 275-87
'Ralph Tyrer, B.D., Vicar of Kendal, 1592-1627', *TCWAAS*, LXXVIII (1978), 71-84
'Samuel Pepys and Spain', *TCBS*, VII, no. 3 (1979), 322-37
Samuel Pepys's Spanish plays (with D. W. Cruickshank), to be published by the Bibliographical Society (1980)
'Calderón y Cervantes', to be published in *Hacia Calderón: quinto Coloquio anglo-germano Oxford, 1978*
Descriptions of Calderón *comedias sueltas* collected by Edward M. Wilson, to be published in vol. III of the *Calderón-Handbuch* of K. and R. Reichenberger
'Some Spanish Dick Turpins, or bad men in bad ballads', to be published in *Hispanic Review*

I
The four elements in the imagery of Calderón

This paper is intended as a contribution to the study of Calderón's diction. It can hardly be supposed that the process described in it has never been noticed by scholars and critics, but as far as the author is aware, it has never before been set out in full. Northup and others in their editions of single plays have illustrated the use of some parts of the system, as when they have noted the frequent equation of horses, birds and boats. They do not seem, however, to have grasped it as a whole. Other aspects of Calderón's imagery would probably lend themselves to a similar treatment.

I have made liberal use of quotations to illustrate the procedure. I could have added very many more, but it is not necessary. Once the system has been pointed out, the reader will come across many more examples whenever he rereads Calderón. My text has usually been the editions of Keil or the Biblioteca de Autores Españoles for the *comedias*, and those of Valbuena, Pando and the volume in the Biblioteca de Autores Españoles for the *autos sacramentales*.

THE ELEMENTS

The elements, fire, air, earth and water, were fundamental in the conception of the mediaeval world. Their order was fixed, and it was their equilibrium alone which differentiated the established world from chaos. This was the doctrine of the ancient world, and it was incorporated into the scholastic system. Ovid's is perhaps the best-known description, at the beginning of the first book of the *Metamorphoses*. Substantially his account was held as a belief by other ancient authors. It could also be reconciled with the account given in the first chapter of the book of Genesis, and accepted as Christian natural science. Probably it was considered theologically useful by Calderón and his contemporaries, as a revelation of physical law. Useful, but imperfect. Although this passage from Ovid culminates in the creation of Man, it is not clear that Man is the central (as opposed to the most important) figure, and that the elements are his servants, the instruments for his salvation. That was the Christian position.

There is a most interesting account of Calderón's scientific ideas in a brief essay by Picatoste.[1] He thus summarises the poet's position:

> Los elementos quedaron constituídos con existencia propia e individual y con cualidades opuestas, lo suficiente para su coexistencia dentro de una gran unidad... Hay pues en la creación dos momentos, dos actos; uno del Poder y otro de la Sabiduría. El sumo Poder distinguió los elementos; y luego entró la Ciencia a disponerlos para que el mundo distinga ambas cosas, y era que el arbitrio es obra exclusiva de la Ciencia.

These ideas are dramatised in some of Calderón's *autos*, notably in the *auto* of *La vida es sueño* and in *La inmunidad del sagrado*. In *La vida es sueño* we are shown the conflict of the elements before creation, and their subsequent harmony, in fine and powerful scenes. In the other play we find this stage direction:

> Salen los quatro Elementos asidos a una cadena, que les unirá a todos quatro, y el Mundo en medio del globo que forman, y él se aparta de ellos, quedando formado el globo.

This symbolises the dependence of the stability of the world on the equilibrium of the constituent elements. After Man's creation they are his servants, but after the Fall he is delivered to them for imprisonment. In a sense they are still his servants, but they are also his gaolers, and the World gives them orders as to how the prisoner is to be treated:

Mundo.   Tierra.
Tierra.   ¿Qué quieres?
Mundo.   Que no tributas
                                         desde oy al Hombre tus frutas,
                                         en que hago embargo.
Tierra.   No dudes
                                         que desde oy de mí no tenga
                                         en mis haveres más útil
                                         que comer de lo que afane,
                                         y beber de lo que sude.

Similar instructions are also given to the other elements.

But as they can bring pains and penalties, so also can they bring redemption. In the *auto* of *El jardín de Falerina* Lucifer tells Culpa how divine signs promise Grace to Man in all the different elements. The lily grows from stubborn ground, accompanied by the rose, cedar, palm and cypress. The stream turns from a serpent to a clear mirror. The air grows calm, and an eagle flies past. Fire is reduced to a star, which steers the wandering ship to harbour. And after all these happy omens 'Glory to God in the Highest' is sung on all sides.

CREATURES OF THE ELEMENTS

With the elements went naturally the idea of four orders of creatures that could dwell only in their respective elements. Also that of inanimate bodies native to them. So Ovid:

> Illic et nebulas, illic consistere nubes
> iussit et humanas motura tonitrua mentes
> et cum fulminibus facientes frigora ventos...
> Neu regio foret ulla suis animalibus orba,
> astra tenent caeleste solum formaeque deorum,
> cesserunt nitidis habitandae piscibus undae,
> terra feras cepit, volucres agitabilis aër.

The same idea was expressed by Spanish poets and dramatists of the Golden Age:

> Ni en este monte, este aire, ni este rio
> corre fiera, vuela aue, pece nada...[2]

> Ni el pez, aborto de la blanca espuma,
> ni el ave, a quien matiz la dió su pluma,
> ni de la salamandra la fe ardiente,
> ama tan firme ni con tal firmeza
> al mar, al viento, al fuego, a la aspereza,
> como yo del esquivo dueño mío
> la perfección adoro y desvío;
> porque mi amor excede ya se sabe,
> al pez, al bruto, salamandra y ave.[3]

> Fuego, tierra, ayre y agua,
> luces, flores, aves, pezes...
> quantas luzes rayos vibren,
> quantos picos plumas peynen,
> quanta espuma perlas sude,
> quanta flor ámbar bosteze...[4]

> Ave, que se calza viento,
> pescado, que el mar fecunda,
> fruta, que guarda la tierra,
> no perdonó; porque en suma,
> sirviendo tres elementos
> lucieron las mesas suyas
> la tierra, el viento y la mar,
> en peces, aves y frutas.[5]

In these passages we may observe three stages of the treatment of the elements. There is the element, or the synonym of the element, then there is the creature or inanimate object that is native to that element, and finally a specific quality or characteristic of the creature or object. Thus for the air we have the series: *aire, viento; ave; matiz, pluma, pico*. For water: *agua, mar; pez, sierpe, pescado; vidrios, espuma, perla*. For earth: *tierra, montes; escollo; fiera, bruto; flores, fruta; piel*. For fire: *fuego; salamandra, volcán; luces, rayos*. This process is fundamental to what follows in this paper.

CONFUSION OF THE ELEMENTS

Picatoste continues later in his essay:

Todos los grandes trastornos, los más asombrosos fenómenos de la naturaleza, reconocían por causa la confusión violenta de estos elementos penetrándose unos a otros. Calderón lo indica muchas veces llamando motines, rebeliones y confusiones de los elementos a los rayos, terremotos, erupciones, exhalaciones, etc.[6]

Often, however, Calderón let the confusion of the elements tell their own story, merely letting the creature or attribute of one element be that of another. So we find the description of terrible natural phenomena in the first part of *La hija del aire*:

Irene.
Los montes contra los aires
volcanes de fuego escupen,
y ellos pájaros de fuego
crían, que los golfos sulquen;
el gran Tigris encrespado,
opuesto al azul volúmen,
a dar asalto a los dioses,
gigante de espuma, sube.

Or this from the *auto* of *Las órdenes militares*:

Segundo Adán.
El tren de la artillería,
que disparaban los cielos,
también soldado del mar
restauré, quando los vientos
amotinando las ondas
en su azul campo me vieron
vencer baterías de rayos,
de relámpagos y truenos.

Other passages might be quoted, especially from such plays as *El mágico prodigioso* and *Los dos amantes del cielo*, in which the conflict is due to the intervention of the supernatural.

VISUAL EXCHANGE OF ELEMENTS

I propose to place in this category those metaphors of exchange of elements that are due to visual impressions, as opposed to others in which there also enters the idea of motion or violent action. Nearly all my examples are concerned with mountains or flowers.

Calderón's conceits of mountains resemble a beautiful couplet from one of Pope's *Pastorals*:

> Here where the mountains, less'ning as they rise,
> Lose the low vales, and steal into the skies.[7]

The mountain is so high that it reaches up into the skies, in the region of the clouds, where it is indistinguishable from the clouds. So at the opening of *La selva confusa* Fadrique describes a mountain:

> Aquí que de esmeraldas
> componen estas sombras
> colgaduras al monte, al valle alfombras,
> siendo en tantas colores
> gigante de zafir, pira de flores,
> pues, vello Adlante, hasta los cielos sube
> a convertirse ufano,
> si no en pardo dosel, en verde nube.[8]

This was a mild and moderate conceit. The region of the air is next to that of the earth. To give the idea of a high mountain this was not enough; the mountain must reach the heavenly regions. The mountain then becomes a pillar for the palace of the moon or for the moon itself to rest upon, or a support for the shafts of the firmament. So Luis in *Luis Pérez el gallego* talks of:

> Este monte eminente
> cuyo arrugado ceño, cuya frente
> es dórica coluna
> en quien descansa el orbe de la luna
> con majestad inmensa.

Sometimes, however, the two conceits are combined; the Queen thus describes Granada in *La niña de Gómez Arias*:

> Bellísima Granada,
> ciudad de tantos rayos coronada,
> cuando tus torres bellas
> saben participar de las estrellas,
> y a cuyos riscos liberal se atreve
> tu sierra altiva a convertir en nieve,
> cuando eminente sube
> a ser cielo, cansada de ser nube.

When the mountain itself enters the heavenly regions it did not need a very wide stretch of imagination to consider its flowers as stars. This happens in many descriptions, such as the following from *La hija del aire*:

> Adonde colocados tus pensiles [i.e. of Babylon],
> al cielo se han llevado tus Abriles,
> y con sus flores bellas,
> a rayos equivocan las estrellas.

This last example is really only a particular and better motivated one of a more general practice. Flowers are the stars of earth, stars are the flowers of heaven. Over and over again we find such lines as the following (taken from *El alcaide de sí mismo*) in the works of Calderón:

> Margarita bella,
> que fué del cielo flor, del campo estrella.

Among more complicated examples, we may quote Leonor in *Con quien vengo vengo*.

> Este cuadro (que es dosel)
> de la hermosa primavera,
> pues las rosas que hay en él
> estrellas son de otra esfera,
> cuyos muertos resplandores
> a las estampas y huellas
> del sol dicen entre olores:
> 'si esta noche sois estrellas
> mañana seremos flores'.

In *El mágico prodigioso* the device becomes poetry in Cipriano's magnificent *décima*s when he talks of:

> El clavel que en breve cielo
> es estrella de coral.

And also we would quote Calderón's ode to St Isidro, built up as it is on the mixture of the terrestrial and celestial landscapes. Such is Isidro's piety that heaven and earth are confused:

> Los campos de Madrid ya cielos bellos,
> y los cielos del sol campos hermosos.

It is all a particular case of a more general system. Flowers and stars are the equivalent, in their respective elements, of feathers and foam in theirs. So in *El mayor encanto amor*:

> Neutral la vista duda
> cual es la yerba, o el agua,
> porque aquí en golfos de flores
> y allí en selvas de esmeraldas,
> unas mismas ondas hacen
> las espumas y las matas.

In *La selva confusa*:

> Pues abes que la pueblan de colores
> flores de pluma son, abes de flores.

In the beautiful incantation of Aura in *Celos aun del aire matan*:

> Ven, Aura, ven.
> Ven, y con cláusulas sumas
> muevan trinados primores
> inquietos golfos de flores,
> blandos embates de plumas.
> Tus penachos las espumas
> sean, y el ámbar también.
> Ven, Aura, ven.

To this class of conceit also belong those lines that point out the similarity of land and water under certain conditions. This is to be seen in the passages where Góngora's line

> Montes de agua i pielagos de montes[9]

is quoted or remembered.[10] There is the same deliberate confusion in the following passage from *Afectos de odio y amor*:

> Y cuando así sea que no hay quilla que corte
> los helados carámbanos del norte,
> ni tropa que se acerque
> al erizado ceño con que el Merque,
> más que el Tanais helado,
> le impiden el rodeo, pues cerrado
> uno y otro horizonte
> peñasco el golfo es, piélago el monte.

HORSES, BIRDS AND BOATS

These three sets of beings are united in that they all move with speed and power, and each is particular to its own element. Calderón, expressing the baroque feeling for force and violence, referred to each in terms of the others. We have seen that he had, roughly speaking, three categories for each element: the element itself, its creature, and a special characteristic, either of the creature or of the element: e.g. the sea, fishes, scales and foam. A land creature that was to be compared to a fish could be called either a fish of the land, a fish with the special characteristics of the land or of the land creature, a land creature of the sea or with sea or fishy characteristics, or simply as a scaleless fish. This formula covers a large part of Calderón's imagery. So we find him calling ships: *ave del mar, caballo del mar, neblí del mar, delfín del viento, pez del viento, volcán del agua; pájaro de espuma, escollo que navega, velera ave; monte de velas, uracán de lino, selva de jarcias;* and *pájaro sin pluma, pez sin escama.* Two passages will serve to illustrate this, the first from *La Sibila del oriente*:

> En un delfín que es pájaro sin plumas,
> en un águila que es pez sin escama,
> . . .
> aré los campos de cristal y nieve,
> donde bebe en carámbanos la aurora
> la blanca espuma, que en aljófar llueve,
> y el argentado humor, que en perlas llora
> el viento, a cuyo son las plantas mueve
> ese del mar caballo.

The second from *El castillo de Lindabridis*:

> Seguirla quise, y sobre riza espuma,
> huésped ya del cerúleo pavimento,
> viví un bajel, que, sin escama y pluma,
> águila fué del mar, delfín del viento.
> Mas porque Amor de ciego no presuma,
> a la venganza Júpiter atento,
> fuego introdujo ardiente en nieve fría
> y el bajel volcán de agua parecía.

Once at least this practice was given a rational dramatic motivation. In *La aurora en Copacabana* the natives saw a ship for the first time, and one of them, Guacolda, thus described it to her comrades:

> Si digo que es
> un escollo que navega
> diré mal; pues para escollo
> le desmiente la violencia;
> si digo preñada nube,
> que a beber el mar sedienta
> se abate, diré peor;
> porque viene sin tormenta;
> si digo marino pez...
> velera ave...

Horses also were described in terms of more than one element. In *Lances de amor y fortuna* we are shown the horse of Rugero:

> Todos los cuatro elementos
> hicieron un mapa en él,
> tierra el cuerpo, mar la espuma,
> viento el alma, y fuego el pie.

There is even more elaboration in Irán's horse, in *La Sibila del oriente*:

> Un veloz caballo, cuyo aliento
> geroglífico ha sido de la guerra,
> sierpe del agua, exhalación del viento,
> volcán del fuego, escollo de la tierra,
> caos animal, pues con tan nuevo modo,
> no siendo nada desto, lo era todo.

Usually the metaphor is that of a ship or bird, and was sometimes the cause of a long part-by-part analogy. Such is the description of the horses on which the troops of Coriolanus crossed the Tiber in Calderón's first act of *El privilegio de las mujeres*:

> Al abreviado piélago se entregan,
> donde por rumbos fáciles navegan
> en los brutos bajeles y vivientes;
> que, espolones las frentes,
> el cuello proa, viento las espuelas,
> remos los brazos y los crines velas,
> jarcia el arzón más alto de la silla,
> el jinete piloto, el viento [*sic*: ?vientre] quilla,
> jarcias las riendas y timón la cola,
> y si el Tíber crespo se enarbola,
> áncoras breves siendo los estribos,
> pasó terrestre flota en leños vivos.

Birds of prey, and their prey, also follow the same procedure, but they are also referred to in terms of the celestial fiery region. So (in *Polifemo y Circe*) Ulysses tells Circe of the flight of the heron, 'árbitro igual' between the wind and fire, frozen and burned as it fell and rose in its flight:

> Geroglífico era
> la garza entre la una y otra esfera.

In *Luis Pérez el gallego* the falcon is called 'cometa sin luz ni fuego', and in *La puente de Mantible* the heron is called 'rayo de pluma'. Continued metaphors of the same kind that we have just examined are also to be found here, e.g. from *El mayor encanto amor*:

> Hechos remos los pies, proa la frente,
> la vela el ala, y el timón la cola.

Vélez de Guevara also used this type of metaphor; the following passage from his *Auto del nacimiento* is not without charm:

> Mirad cubiertos los vientos
> de nueuas lucientes plumas,
> cuyas doradas espumas
> inundan los elementos.

> Mirad como están atentos
> essos Argos celestiales
> a las batallas nauales
> de tanto alado baxel,
> que en piélagos de clavel
> son clarines de cristales.[11]

Other objects also called forth the same type of conceit. So Phaethon in *El hijo del sol,* driving in the sun's chariot, says:

> Etéreos campos corro,
> siendo en piélagos de plata
> luciente bajel de oro.

In *El castillo de Lindabridis* the flying castle is a problem; which element does it really belong to?

> En África alcancé aquel prodigioso
> castillo, que a su arbitrio se pasea,
> porque los elementos litigioso
> pleito tuvieron, sobre cuyo sea.
> El fuego le examina luminoso,
> la tierra sus campañas hermosea,
> en su estancia le ven mares y vientos;
> y así le traen por lid cuatro elementos.

Part of Calderón's vocabulary is directly due to this type of imagery. I refer to his fondness for words describing monsters and semi-mythical creatures, which express in their names the confusion of two or more opposing characteristics. So he calls rivers: *centauro indiano, centauro de hielo, hipogrifo de cristal*; a horse: *hipogrifo violento, caos animal de cuatro elementos*; a ship: *monstruo de dos especies,* etc. Also we may note his fondness for words that show doubt between two elements, or the strife and boundaries between them: *horizonte, árbitro, neutral, equivocar, promontorio, escándalo, asombro, geroglífico, guerra,* etc.

SCHEME OF THE ELEMENTS IN CALDERÓN'S IMAGERY

In the following list I include most of the ingredients that Calderón used in these metaphorical recipes. The list is probably not complete or watertight, but it will help to make the process clear.

Earth
Element: tierra, campo, jardín, campañas, arena, yerba, peñas, montes.
Inanimate creatures: monte, pirámide, torre, alcázar, montaña, escollo, selva, muro, coluna, sierra, risco, ciudad, pira, roca, peñasco.
Animate creatures: caballo, elefante, gigante, Atlante, hormiga, flores.
Attribute of element: flores, matas, polvo, fruta, rosa, clavel.

Attribute of creatures: verdores, perlas, piedra, ramos, pie, anca, cola, etc.
Water
Element: mar, agua, río, golfo, ondas, piélago.
Inanimate creatures: nave, bajel, galera.
Animate creatures: delfín, pez, sierpe, cisne, pescado, sirena.
Attribute of element: sal, hielo, nieve, espuma, cristal, coral, aljófar, zafir, plata, ámbar.
Attribute of creatures: escama, velas, pino, jarcias, lino, timón, remo, etc.
Air
Element: aire, viento, cielo.
Inanimate creatures: nube, uracán, exhalación.
Animate creatures: ave, pájaro, águila, neblí, etc.
Attribute of creatures: plumas, penachos, picos, alas, etc.
Fire
Element: fuego, cielo, firmamento, empíreo, incendio.
Inanimate creatures: sol, cometa, astro, lucero.
Animate creatures: fénix, mariposa, salamandra, Apolo, Faetón, comunero.
Attributes: luz, rayos, relámpagos, llama, humo, ceniza, pavesa, centellas, oro (and azul, celestial, cerúleo, etéreo).

PRECEDENTS

Calderón did not invent this metaphorical procedure, but standardised it. He probably derived it from a study of the works of Góngora, which show a less academic use of the same method. I shall now quote examples of its use before Calderón, mainly from Góngora, but also one or two from the court plays, *La gloria de Niquea* of the Count of Villamediana, and *Querer por solo querer* by Antonio Hurtado de Mendoza.

The conceit of a mountain's sustaining the heavens occurs as a simile in Góngora's *Panegírico al Duque de Lerma*:

> Su ombro illustra luego suficiente
> el peso de ambos mundos soberano,
> qual la estrellada maquina luciente
> doctas fuerças de monte, si Africano.[12]

The equation of stars, flowers, feathers and foam occurs with some frequency:

> Ia en nueuos campos vna es oi de aquellas
> flores que illustra otra mejor Aurora,
> cuio caduco aljofar son estrellas.[13]

> No todas las voces ledas
> son de Syrenas con plumas,
> cuias humidas espumas
> son las verdes alamedas.[14]

> Por seis hijas, por seis deidades bellas,
> de el cielo espumas i de el mar estrellas.[15]
>
> Tres vìòlas del cielo,
> tres de las flores ia breues estrellas.[16]
>
> De el cielo flor, estrella de Medina.[17]

We also find it in Villamediana:

> Eres en el cielo flor,
> y entre las flores estrella.[18]

The metaphors of birds of prey, and birds generally, either in that they are like ships, or that they have heavenly qualities, are also frequent in Góngora:

> ...el aue Reina...
> raio con plumas.[19]
>
> Qual en los Equinoccios surcar vemos
> los pielagos de el aire libre algunas
> volantes no galeras,
> sino grullas veleras.[20]
>
> El Nebli, que relampago su pluma,
> raio su garra.[21]

The figures of the bull and the goat recall their constellations in the zodiac:

> ...el mentido robador de Europa
> ...
> en campos de zaphiro pasce estrellas.[22]
>
> ...Promontorio...
> de cabras estrellado,
> iguales, aunque pocas,
> a la que, imagen decima del cielo,
> flores su cuerno es, raios su pelo.[23]

The idea of the elements composing a horse we find expressed by Lupercio Leonardo de Argensola in his tragedy of *Isabela*:

> Un caballo te espera tan gallardo,
> que dirán que nació de vivo fuego,
> y que de viento sólo se mantiene;
> tanta velocidad y fuerza tiene.[24]

Góngora, besides reminding us of the mythological conception of the foals of Andalusia, also uses this idea occasionally:

> Cauallo...
> arogante, i no ia por las que daua
> estrellas su cerulea piel al dia.[25]

> Ia centellas de sangre con la espuela
> solicitaua al trueno generoso,
> al cauallo veloz, que embuelto buela
> en poluo ardiente, en fuego poluoroso.[26]

We also find it in *Querer por solo querer*:

> Ave lo nombra lo veloz, lo ardiente
> rayo le aclama, el nombre generoso
> cisne galán que entre la blanca espuma
> es de nieve Faetón, bajel de pluma.[27]

The confusion of land and sea is almost more frequent in Góngora than in Calderón himself:

> ...vna Libia de ondas.[28]

> Montes de agua i pielagos de montes.[29]

> Al que, ia dèste o de aquel mar, primero
> surcò labrador fiero
> el campo vndoso en mal nacido pino.[30]

> Montes de espuma.[31]

And in Villamediana again:

> Que admiracion natural,
> que en dos rios se desata
> una montaña de plata
> y una selva de cristal.[32]

These examples are all taken from works written before Calderón's style had matured. We find in them quite remarkable resemblances to Calderón's own devices, and it was by these passages and by their like that Calderón must have been influenced. Few such examples can be found in sixteenth-century poetry, and where they are most noticeable is in the great *culto* poems of Góngora. They are a striking example of the rise of the baroque spirit in literature, with its emphasis on force and passion, and its tendency to overflow the natural bounds. But like so much that is baroque it is founded on an old harmony. Góngora was not its inventor in all probability, but he found it a convenient method for the construction of his superb metaphors and imagery. He was not a slave to it, he was always moderate and imaginative in its use; Calderón abused it by too frequent repetition and stylisation.

We have followed Calderón through the varieties of this metaphorical procedure. Each element in its bounds is stable and fixed, but if it overflows these bounds primaeval chaos is reproduced. So storms could be described as a mutiny against the order of creation. And so the effect of violence and motion could be enhanced by comparing it to a mixture or confusion of the elements. And Calderón had a fondness for violent action comparable to that of the baroque painters.

In Góngora also we find many cases of this confusion of the elements, especially in the great *culto* poems. Nevertheless it is not obtruded on our attention as it is by Calderón. Rather it is implied, and we do not often find ourselves thinking that such or such an effect is arrived at by mixing the elements of, say, sea and sky. For Góngora seldom relies wholly on doing this; the gulls in the *Soledad primera* are compared to flying galleys, but then, immediately we are borne on to the lovely comparison with waxing and waning moons. Calderón has borrowed from Góngora passages where their usage seems to coincide, but Góngora is almost always more subtle, less tabulated than Calderón.

There can be no doubt that Calderón was deliberate in this use of imagery, and many critics will consider it a serious defect in his work. Gerardo Diego for instance has already written:

> Calderón reduce a cuatro o seis moldes, agotados genialmente, algunos de los hallazgos gongorinos; simetriza lo que en Góngora era equilibrado pero libre. Da la forma para adquirir un culteranismo de bazar a precio único; y en suma, convierte la sorpresa en tópico, la forma en molde y lo clásico vivo en académico muerto.[33]

There remains something to be said on the other side. We have considered only a part of Calderón's technique when we draw attention to these devices; it may be that Calderón made use of a formula here in order to concentrate on other things that interested him more. Again, each play was written for a separate performance, not to make up a collected edition; and here we have formed a judgement after reading a large number of plays. The method of this paper, the only possible method, was to tear passages from their contexts and to put them side by side; in a successful work of art any passage must lose by such treatment. Isolation, though, is often a useful test, and there has been some good writing even in some of the passages quoted above.

Nevertheless such a system for turning out images to a pattern must be considered a defect. In Calderón it produced much writing of an inferior quality, and it lent itself to assimilation by his imitators: men who found here a means of covering paper without thinking or feeling for themselves.

2
Fernando: the Constant Prince

El príncipe constante is the story of a saint. What is the point of the play? It is, I think, that the man who follows out his beliefs sincerely to the end is superior to his fellows. Every character in this play has good feelings – even the Moorish King is only villainous when he is thwarted – but Fernando rises above all of them. He is measured successively against the other figures; none of them comes up to him.

Fernando is introduced to us as the Christian soldier. In the first act he is more the soldier than the Christian; he is a gentleman. The first to set foot on African shore, he captures the bravest of the Moors and sets him free – as Don Rodrigo de Narváez is said to have done – and he does not surrender to the Moors until further resistance would have been useless; then he has the officer's satisfaction of surrendering to the King himself. We meet a chivalrous man of action, whose battle-cry is 'Avis y Cristo'. His Catholicism is obvious; he is a crusader and not frightened by auguries as his brother is – he is prepared to die for the true faith. He is a soldier who may develop into a saint, but he is above all a soldier.

When Fernando is taken prisoner the Moorish King says that he cannot consider releasing him except in exchange for Ceuta. On hearing this Fernando shows that however much of a hero he may be, he is only human after all. In his farewell speech to Enrique he says:

> Enrique, preso quedo,
> ni al mal, ni a la fortuna tengo miedo.
> Dirásle a nuestro hermano
> que haga aquí como Príncipe cristiano
> en la desdicha mía.   (I, xix)

A brave beginning. But how is the Christian Prince to act? In the light of later scenes we know that his duty would be to keep Fernando a prisoner and to save Ceuta for Christianity. But might not this request also mean that the Christian Prince should sacrifice one of his possessions in ransom for a Prince of the Blood? So at least Enrique seems to understand him, for he replies:

> ¿Pues quién de sus grandezas desconfía?   (I, xix)

King Duarte will not be afraid of making this generous exchange. Thereupon Fernando repeats his request:

> Esto te encargo y digo
> que haga como cristiano. (I, xix)

He is still not quite explicit, but the first meaning seems to be uppermost now. Finally he says to his brother:

> Dirásle al rey... mas no le digas nada,
> si con grande silencio el miedo vano
> estas lágrimas lleva al rey mi hermano. (I, xix)

Has self-interest repressed altruism, or altruism self-interest? We cannot say. But these lines seem senseless unless they convey that Fernando at once wishes to be free, and feels that it would be unworthy to be free at such a price (the loss of weaker souls to Mahomet). The Fernando of the later acts would have given no uncertain answer to his brother. And though we may take the later Fernando to be speaking here, he has been misunderstood by Enrique; Fernando must have seen that he was being misunderstood, yet does not undeceive Enrique. Fernando has shown human frailty, and this makes his later saintliness all the more convincing.

This moral uncertainty of Fernando's is continued into the second act. Enrique enters with the Portuguese embassy, dressed in black. Fernando, not knowing that Duarte is dead, takes the mourning to be a sign of his own captivity.

> ¡Ay, don Juan, cierta es mi muerte! (II, vi)

he exclaims. Now, however, he is a different man; it has only been a momentary shock. He is able to rise superior to his last meeting, going on to say:

> No llores: que si es decirme
> que es mi esclavitud eterna,
> eso es lo que más deseo;
> albricias pedir pudieras
> y en vez de dolor y luto,
> vestir galas y hacer fiestas. (II, vii)

This was all he needed to become a saint. When it appeared that the Portuguese were willing to sacrifice Ceuta for him – and in no other way, except by another expensive military expedition, could he have hoped to become free – he utterly refused to have anything to do with it. Now he became indeed the Constant Prince. Henceforth he will be remarkable for his fortitude and humility, not for the more showy virtues of chivalry and courage.

Entwistle noted that there is a similar struggle later in the play:

> It is the same with succeeding trials. The Prince is on the point of accepting Muley's offer of escape, and does not do so because it becomes clear that Muley could not honourably make the offer. This is a secondary consideration really; the primary one is that to have run away would have left his task undone, and the justification of Faith incomplete. What is characteristic of Faith, however, is the ability to recognize the ultimate right in each situation and to grow in clearness of vision.[1]

There does, however, seem to be a difference between the two incidents. In the earlier one Fernando is unsure of himself; in the second, he would have been justified in escaping with Muley's aid *before* Muley became his gaoler. The first struggle is one of duty and inclination; in the second Fernando sees his duty clearly throughout.

The foil to Fernando in the first act is Enrique, the historical Prince Henry the Navigator. Enrique comes ashore bravely, but trips up as he lands (I, vii). We take this as an omen, and so does Enrique; it foretells the failure of the expedition and shows that Enrique is not his brother's equal. Fernando is right, though, when he reproves Enrique for his superstition in paying attention to it as an omen; this is not Christian, and though neither knows it, through the failure of the expedition, Fernando will finally triumph. The omen is both true and not true, and it has dramatic value either way. Enrique fights bravely in the battle, but he never outshines Fernando; he merely has better luck.

Later Enrique returns with the embassy: King Alfonso will exchange Ceuta for Fernando, and it is Enrique who bears the message (II, vii). Again the weak prince contrasts with the strong prince, for Fernando could not have brought such a message. And when he hears Fernando's determination to stay on he can only exclaim: '¡Qué desdicha!' '¡Qué desventura!' '¡Qué llanto!' But at last he promises to return with an armed force which shall free Fernando.

Enrique's part also becomes important in the last scenes of the play when he returns with King Alfonso and the army. Symmetry is given to the whole by Alfonso's taking on the attributes of Fernando displayed in Act I, but Enrique is still the foil. After Fernando's miraculous apparition, Enrique exclaims:

> Dudando estoy, Alfonso, lo que veo. (III, xi)

To which Alfonso's reply is such as Fernando might have made:

> Yo no, todo lo creo;
> y si es de Dios la gloria,
> no digas guerra ya, sino victoria.

But doubting Thomas has his place among the disciples.

We must now consider Fernando in relation to the Moorish characters. The absence of rancour towards the Moors in this play is very notable. Here there is no brutal husband who tortures his wife, no cruel king who takes away his subjects' property and orders them to be flogged when they protest; the element of caricature that can be found in Lope and in Cervantes is absent.[2] The King of Fez is not wantonly cruel; Muley and Fénix are sympathetic. The Moorish court is first and foremost a court; it might be the scene of a *comedia palaciega*. Calderón does not make his adversaries into ridiculous monsters of iniquity; avoiding crudity he shows them as worthy human beings, often moved by generous impulses.

> Pues no es el vencedor más estimado
> de aquello en que el vencido es reputado.[3]

We may consider the play as the story of the conflict of two wills: Fernando's against that of the King of Fez. Both are actuated by high motives; Fernando wishes to save a Christian town, the King to add to his domains. In Calderón's day the act of conquest was considered noble, and the King's desire a justifiable one. He acts strictly within the law and shows no signs of having a particularly cruel nature. While the negotiations respecting Fernando's release are proceeding, the King presses Fernando to see a tiger fight, an offer which Fernando greatly appreciates:

> Señor,
> gustos por puntos inventas
> para agradarme: si así
> a tus esclavos festejas,
> no echarán menos la patria.   (II, v)

Words that are indeed ironical in the light of future events. The King replies:

> Cautivos de tales prendas,
> que honran el dueño, es razón
> servirlos de esta manera.

No, the King has a due sense of his obligations and he strives to fulfil them. When he hears of the death of King Duarte he shows at least conventional grief.

At last there arrives the moment when the two men are driven into opposition. Fernando refuses to resign Ceuta and delivers himself up to life-long slavery. The King is able to attack him for his ingratitude:

> Desagradecido, ingrato
> a las glorias y grandezas
> de mi reino,   (II, vii)

and goes on to show that he is piqued in his kingship:

> si en mi reino gobiernas
> más que en el tuyo.

Then he proceeds to assert his ownership of Fernando (who obediently kneels at his feet before the Portuguese envoys) and appeals to law:

> Siendo esclavo tú, no puedes
> tener títulos ni rentas.
> Hoy Ceuta está en mi poder;
> si cautivo te confiesas,
> si me confiesas por dueño,
> ¿por qué no me das a Ceuta?

Whereupon comes Fernando's famous answer:

> Porque es de Dios y no es mía.

But the King is not satisfied and continues to appeal to man's abstract principles:

> ¿No es precepto de obediencia,
> obedecer al señor?
> Pues yo te mando con ella,
> que la entregues.

Fernando appeals to the law of God:

> En lo justo
> dice el cielo, que obedezca
> el esclavo a su señor;
> porque si el señor dijera
> a su esclavo, que pecara,
> obligación no tuviera
> de obedecerle; porque
> quien peca mandado, peca.

After this the King can only do what a tyrant would have done at first, threaten him. Fernando has forced him to become a cruel tyrant, when he was in no way vindictive by nature. From now on he can, and does, always claim, with reason, that he is not cruel to Fernando; the Prince is cruel to himself. The Moorish King cannot be expected to understand the workings of a Christian conscience directed *ad majorem Dei gloriam*. The battle is between a man of this world and one of the next; but this world has not an unworthy representative.[4]

Muley is the typical Calderonian hero of a *comedia palaciega*. He has all Fernando's military virtues and can be his foe in battle and friend in captivity. In battle he is defeated by Fernando; afterwards Fernando makes him decide rightly in his struggle between loyalty and friendship –

a struggle that again reminds us of the *comedia palaciega*. He is a conventional figure, but he plays his part in the play; a virtuous man, he shows how much more virtuous Fernando is. The convention is well exploited in the pattern of the play.

We are still left with the captives and Fénix. The first scene gives us their respective relationships. Zara, Fénix's maid, tells the captives to sing in order to please her mistress. The dialogue is worth a lengthy quotation:

Cautivo 1.	¿Música, cuyo instrumento son los hierros y cadenas, que nos aprisionan, puede haberla alegrado?
Zara.	Sí; ella escucha desde aquí. Cantad.
Cautivo 2.	Esa pena excede, Zara hermosa, a cuantos son; pues sólo un rudo animal, sin discurso racional, canta alegre en la prisión.
Zara.	¿No cantáis vosotros?
Cautivo 3.	Es para divertir las penas propias, mas no las agenas.
Zara.	Ella escucha, cantad pues. (1, i)

This passage was probably suggested by Psalm 137:

> For there they that carried us away captive required of us a song; and they that wasted us required of us mirth, saying, Sing us one of the songs of Zion.
> How shall we sing the Lord's song in a strange land?

We are given an indication, not only of the intolerable pain of lack of liberty, but also of the relation of Christian and Infidel. The speeches of the three captives bring this home, and they also prepare us for the melancholy of Fénix, which is one of the undercurrents of the play. She, who could command the services of the best musicians to sing to her, takes pleasure in the singing of the slaves. They are not so much resentful as puzzled. What can be the matter with the Infanta? They have cause to sing of their troubles; they have real sufferings, hers can only be imaginary. And they make the position clear by drawing two distinctions: the first, between the animal that sings merrily in captivity because it does not understand what captivity is, and man; the second between the man who sings to give pleasure to others and the man who sings because of his own misery. The simplicity of the diction, added to this intellectual analysis, is enough to make us feel deeply the plight of the captives. It is quite unnecessary to introduce references to hard tasks, cruel masters and all the apparatus of local colour that we find in Cervantes; here we know the essence of slavery. The scene, too, prepares us for what is to happen to Fernando later on.

Then the slaves are sent away. Fénix comes in

> a dar vanidad
> al campo con su hermosura. (1, ii)

Her request for a mirror, the flattery of her maids, cannot help her. What is the matter with Fénix?

Fénix. ¿De qué sirve la hermosura
(cuando lo fuese la mía),
si me falta la alegría,
si me falta la ventura?
Celima. ¿Qué sientes?
Fénix. Si yo supiera,
¡Ay Celima! lo que siento,
de mi mismo sentimiento
lisonja al dolor hiciera;
pero de la pena mía
no sé la naturaleza;
que entonces fuera tristeza
lo que hoy es melancolía.
Sólo sé que sé sentir,
lo que sé sentir no sé,
que ilusión del alma fué. (1, iii)

Here a nineteenth-century critic might have accused Calderón of quibbling. But there is a real distinction between her use of *tristeza* and of *melancolía*, and the play on the words *sentir* and *saber* is, though almost epigrammatic, terse and justified. It is like the distinctions of the first scene: poetry that arises from the analytical statement of the situation.[5] From now on one of the principal contrasts in the play is clearly situated: Fernando will rejoice in his unhappiness, Fénix will be melancholy in her good fortune.

The cause of her melancholy is not precisely stated. We learn afterwards of her love for the then absent Muley; but absence would have been a cause for *tristeza*, and she is melancholy. Nor can it be that she is upset because her father wishes her to marry Tarudante, for she has not yet heard of it. It is a more deep-rooted trouble; though she has cause to be genuinely unhappy later on, here there seems to be only her almost neurotic sensibility to make her miserable.

At the beginning of the second act Fénix reappears in a strangely excited condition to relate to Muley the story of the old African woman's prophecy. This incident is a parallel to Enrique's stumble on landing in Africa.

The stumble was an omen of misfortune which did not fall on Enrique himself; the prophecy also was one that was not to affect her adversely, although she fears it will. The woman had said to her:

> ¡Ay infelice mujer!
> ¡Ay forzosa desventura!
> ¿Que en efecto esta hermosura
> precio de un muerto ha de ser? (II, i)

She and Muley both take the 'muerto' to be Muley; she is agitated, but he takes the affair calmly and with serenity. She does not realise that Fernando, and not Muley, is the 'muerto', and like the earlier Enrique she worries about the omen that does not refer to her lover. The Inconstant Princess, thrown out of balance by the words of an old woman, provides the contrast to the Constant Prince.[6] Yet she is beautiful and pitiful, good as far as anyone can be who lacks emotional stability.

This scene is followed by the touching scene between Fernando and the captives which includes the reflections on captivity that prepare us for Fernando's final constancy:

> Temo venir desde aquí
> a más miserable estado;
> que si ya en aquéste vivo,
> mucha más distancia tray
> de infante a cautivo, que hay
> de cautivo a más cautivo. (II, iv)

The plot continues through the scene with Muley to the entrance of the envoys and Fernando's decision to defy the King of Fez by becoming his slave. Fénix witnesses this scene but takes little part in it. It is not until the famous scene in the garden that she once more becomes of importance in the play.

She enters the garden, having asked for flowers to be brought to her, and meditating upon this disturbing forecast. Who can the dead man be, she wonders, and 'Yo', answers Fernando unconsciously but truly, in a typically Calderonian *coup de théâtre* (II, xiv). This upsets her, although she cannot understand its meaning. She had asked for the flowers to make her forget her fear of her own destiny. Fernando has accepted his destiny by becoming the slave who brought her the garland. They converse together about his change of fortune, and he recites the famous sonnet 'Estas que fueron pompa y alegría'; in this he shows her that her destiny is foreshadowed in the very distraction she had hoped to find. The sonnet has more than the poetic value which is apparent in it when we meet it in the anthologies; it has a dramatic purpose as well. Fénix finds herself face to face with her fears again; the dialogue proceeds:

Fénix.	Horror y miedo me has dado,
	ni oirte ni verte quiero;
	sé el desdichado primero
	de quien huye un desdichado.
Fernando.	¿Y las flores?
Fénix.	Si has hallado
	geroglíficos en ellas,
	deshacellas y rompellas
	solo sabrán mis rigores.
Fernando.	¿Qué culpa tienen las flores?
Fénix.	Parecerse a las estrellas. (II, xiv)

Here we have a very telling scene. The last line in particular is fine in a style of which Calderón is the master: flowers in the element of the earth are the equivalent of stars in the heavenly element.[7] But here the similarity is given force because, like the stars, flowers can reveal the terrors of the future. So Fénix in return pronounces a sonnet (to my mind a disappointing one) and goes off. Now we can see perhaps the cause of her trouble. She is afraid of death, and she has not the resources of Christianity on which Fernando can draw, to enable her to overcome her fear.

In the last act Fénix pleads for the life of the noble captive as we might expect any Calderonian lady to do. She pleads in vain; the King is resolute (III, ii). And then, in Fernando's last hours, the Prince and Princess are brought together again, when he is lying stinking on the dunghill, visited by the King who wishes to show Tarudante his power. There is a powerful scene of the conflict of wills between King and Prince, the King remaining solid as a rock, completely justified in his own mind in his cruelty. The King and Tarudante move away; Fénix remains helpless before the horror of the dying man.

Fernando.	Si es alma de la hermosura
	esa divina deidad,
	vos, señora, me amparad
	con el rey.
Fénix.	¡Qué gran dolor! (III, vii)

Then the last touches are laid on. Fernando with religious cruelty lays bare Fénix's emotional inadequacy, giving her the last, terrible revelation:

Fernando.	Hacéis bien; que vuestros ojos
	no son para ver enojos.
Fénix.	¡Qué lástima! ¡Qué pavor!
Fernando.	Pues aunque no me miréis
	y ausentaros intentéis,
	señora, es bien que sepáis,
	que aunque tan bella os juzgáis,
	que más que yo no valéis,
	y yo quizá valgo más. (III, vii)

Notice how deliberately Fernando's trenchant criticism is contrasted with her vague expressions of pity: burning moral indignation against her inadequate sympathy. Finally she is brought to realise her plight, and losing even this feeling of charity she exclaims:

> Horror con tu voz me das,
> y con tu aliento me hieres.[8]
> ¡Déjame hombre! ¿qué me quieres?
> *Que no puedo sentir más.*

Fénix goes off, Fernando dies. The most important part of the play is over, but there are still a few points to notice in the last scenes.

With regard to the last scenes Entwistle wrote: 'The play reaches its climax in the lines

> En el horror de la noche,
> por sendas que nadie sabe,
> te guié.

In this way Fernando, after his death, leads the Portuguese army to the victory which he failed to achieve in his material body.' The lines quoted are fine, but unfortunately they are not supported by a very impressive context. They tell us much about the whole play but do not, to my mind, atone for the relatively poor verse of the rest of the scenes. Calderón is relying on the miracle to carry the attention of the audience and has not attempted to support it with any poetic re-creation. The verse is deliberately heightened in tone to contrast with the poignancy of the scene before, but the expression is cold and conventional (II, xi). Fernando's apparition is theatrical, probably very effective on the stage, but that is all. Then in the last scene we find that Fénix has become the prisoner of Alfonso, balancing, as it were, the imprisonment of Fernando by the King of Fez, and she is to be exchanged for Fernando (III, xiii). The King has to confess what the Christians already know, that Fernando is dead. Alfonso exclaims:

> Rey de Fez, porque no pienses
> que muerto Fernando vale
> menos que aquesta hermosura,
> por él, cuando muerto yace,
> te la trueco. (III, xiii)

Again Alfonso has taken over the attributes of Fernando: he continues to point out the inferiority of her beauty over Fernando's holiness. The truth at last dawns upon Fénix and she exclaims:

> Precio soy de un hombre muerto;
> cumplió el cielo su homenaje.

But she is rewarded for her attempts at generosity when Alfonso insists that she shall marry Muley. For me the finest parts of the play are the scenes in which this contrast between Fernando and Fénix is displayed. It has often been said that Calderón was at his worst in his depiction of women; have none of the critics read this play?

In reading and criticising this play we must avoid the hunt for characters which is the favourite pastime of so many writers on literature. We have here a number of almost conventional figures, all moving in the same world of courtly behaviour but with certain conflicts of loyalties and divisions of religion. What Muley is in himself is a matter of no importance whatever; we have met him many times before if we have read more than a few plays of Calderón. In this play, though, he is of great importance for he is used to set off Fernando. It is the same with the others. With Fénix there is more attempt at a psychological study, but not until she has been placed near Fernando can we see her in proportion, and then we are surprised at the revelation. Chivalry and pity are fine enough emotions, but here they are powerless to help the victim, not so much of evil, as of blindness (the King of Fez is wise in his own conceit) believing itself to be right. Saintliness, by their side, shows that they are entirely inadequate.

El príncipe constante is a study of how a good man becomes a saint, as *La vida es sueño* is a study of how an animal man becomes a good man. That does not necessarily mean that in order to appreciate this play we must accept the Catholic, even the Christian, values. (To justify the ending this would perhaps be necessary.) The figure of Fernando stands for any man who carries through his devotion to a belief to the end and sacrifices to it himself and all his interests. Such a man has integrity of character, a quality that is rare in these days when so many are well-intentioned. The value of this magnificent play lies in Calderón's concern for that quality.

NOTE

I wrote this article in the late thirties and sent it to W. J. Entwistle, then the Romance editor of the *Modern Language Review*. He sent me a reply, and after some discussion we agreed to publish my article and his reply in that journal. I added a final note to our joint effort in which I criticised two aspects of his approach: (1) Entwistle looked at the play in terms of an imaginary *auto sacramental*; he was preoccupied with the scheme of it as it existed in Calderón's mind, whereas I tried to state the way in which I was moved by the play itself. I found his approach too schematic, but he may well have thought that I did not carry mine far enough. The play is not an *auto*; what we make of it is more important than the original conception which we can only guess at. (2) Entwistle looks on the last scenes of Fernando's triumph as the climax of the play. Though I ought to have noticed the lines: 'En el horror de la noche ...' in my original version of this essay, they did not seem to me to atone for the verse in the remainder of the final scenes. To me it seems that Calderón was relying overmuch on the miracle to carry the attention of the audience and had not tried to support it with much poetic re-creation. The ending shows us the fulfilment of the prophecy about Fénix; Fernando might as well be lying in his grave, his soul in Heaven. He preserved his integrity, and that is enough.

I have revised slightly the text of the original article. The most important modifications consist in the adoption (with acknowledgements) of details mentioned by Entwistle which I had not originally noticed. I have, however, let my original case stand. It has not been completely accepted by the later critics mentioned below. I therefore commend to the reader the following articles on the play, conveniently collected in two different volumes: B. W. Wardropper, *Critical essays on the theatre of Calderón* (New York, 1965) contains: Leo Spitzer, 'The figure of Fénix in Calderón's *El príncipe constante*', pp. 137–60, and A. G. Reichenberger's 'Calderón's *El príncipe constante*, a tragedy?', pp. 161–3; *Critical studies of Calderón's 'comedias'*, ed. J. E. Varey, vol. XIX of Pedro Calderón de la Barca, *Comedias*, a facsimile edition prepared by D. W. Cruickshank and J. E. Varey with textual and critical studies (London, 1973), contains: B. W. Wardropper, 'Christian and Moor in Calderón's *El príncipe constante*', pp. 85–96, R. W. Truman, 'The theme of justice in Calderón's *El príncipe constante*', pp. 97–109, and W. M. Whitby's 'Calderón's *El príncipe constante*: Fénix's role in the ransom of Fernando's body', pp. 111–16. Finally, in R. O. Jones's compilation entitled *Studies in Spanish literature of the Golden Age presented to Edward M. Wilson* (London, 1973), there is a most interesting essay by P. N. Dunn, '*El príncipe constante*: a theatre of the world', pp. 83–101.

3
On *La vida es sueño*

To attempt a new interpretation of *La vida es sueño* may well appear a rash undertaking.[1] The play is so well known, so much has been written about it, that any novelty seems likely to be merely the result of a perverse desire for originality or at best a wrong-headed modification or distortion of what someone else has already said. Nevertheless I undertake this task because, despite the interesting studies of Ángel Valbuena Prat, the criticism of seventeenth-century dramatic literature is still conducted with nineteenth-century criteria. And the appraisal of the merits of *La vida es sueño* has seemed to me to suffer particularly for this reason.

My primary objection is to the way in which modern critics employ the notion of character. They do not realise that the idea that character is the be-all and end-all of drama was not that of the eighteenth century even, let alone of the seventeenth. The lack of a Spanish equivalent of the *New English dictionary* (now at last being repaired) raises difficulties for us when we try to follow the history of the word *carácter* in Spanish dramatic criticism; as far as I am aware, it was first used as a critical term by Ignacio de Luzán (*Poética*, III, x), who explained to his readers that 'lo que otras naciones llaman Charácter, proprio de cada persona' was 'algún género de costumbres o inclinaciones'. Aristotle had defined character as 'that which reveals moral purpose, shewing what kind of things a man chooses or avoids' (*Poetics*, VI, 17); Luzán's 'género de costumbres' may have a similar sense, like that used by other neoclassic critics who followed him. The nineteenth-century senses of the word were far less precise. But the age of Philip IV seems to have ignored the word as a dramatic term, though they might have picked it up from Aristotle. In these circumstances, though we can hardly omit the word 'character' altogether from our critical vocabulary, we must be careful when we use it of seventeenth-century plays. Calderón certainly thought about the disposition of his plot, the problems of verse communication, the moral questions raised by his presentations and, perhaps, how certain men might be expected to behave in certain conditions. He did not set out to make Pedro Crespo the living incarnation of the Spanish peasantry or to make Segismundo into 'a living character'.

On the first reading *La vida es sueño* appears to most people as an important but puzzling play. Its obvious power, the striking scenes in the tower and in the palace, at once move the reader deeply. No one can fail to be impressed by the horror and atrocity of Segismundo's plight in the first scene, his savagery when he finds himself in authority in the palace, his expression of the vanity of life when he finds himself back in the tower. If the verse of the first soliloquy is confused we need not worry too much, for the refrain is a statement of the contrast between man and brute which could hardly be more powerfully expressed:

>   ¿y teniendo yo más alma,
>   tengo menos libertad?   (131–2)[2]

The famous second soliloquy in the tower is immediately convincing in its simplicity:

>   el mayor bien es pequeño;
>   que toda la vida es sueño,
>   y los sueños sueños son.   (2185–7)

The plain statement has seldom done its work so well.

Nearly all critics of the play will admit the truth of these judgements. This play has something not to be found in ordinary versions of the folktale of the Sleeper Awakened, such as the story of Abu Hassan in *The Arabian nights* or of Christopher Sly in *The taming of the shrew*. The play expresses a view of life, and so does the title. Some critics have too easily assumed that Calderón ought to have made us believe that all life is unreal, that no one can rely on anything, that we are all like Don Quixote, who mistook windmills for giants and a barber's basin for Mambrino's helmet. Instead of blaming Calderón for not doing what he never intended to do, I shall try to find out some of what he did. I shall look at the sub-plot as well as at the main plot, at the third act as well as at the first two acts. I shall not assume that the title means what others would like it to mean. I shall try to point out how and why Segismundo is converted, how and why life is a dream, what I think the play as a dramatic whole means.

The great nineteenth-century critic Marcelino Menéndez y Pelayo judged *La vida es sueño* according to his criteria. He claimed that:

La drámatica, tal como todas las escuelas la han entendido, tal como ha aparecido en todas las civilizaciones del mundo, vive de pasiones, de afectos, de caracteres humanos; no es más que la vida humana en acción y en espectáculo.[3]

This statement is not wholly untrue, but it is too general and too sweeping. The schools of drama to which he refers have indeed represented human life, passions, characters and feelings, but their aim has often been far more than the mere exposition of a single character or of a group of characters. From such generalisations as this he went on to assume that the more individual the character the better the play. But Aristotle, the theorist of not a minor school of drama, said that tragedy could exist without character but not without plot (*Poetics*, VI, 14). Don Marcelino passed over the many good plays in which the characters are stock types; he placed too much emphasis on character in itself, not enough on plot, construction and diction.

When he discussed the *auto* of *La vida es sueño* (which of course is a refashioning of the *comedia*) he said – or at least implied – that it suffered from one great weakness: 'El protagonista no es hombre llamado Segismundo, sino el hombre en general'.[4] He meant this criticism of the *auto* to apply also to the *comedia*, for later on, after mentioning Tirso's Don Juan, he remarked: 'Calderón no alcanza nunca a crear un tipo de esta universalidad [i.e. la de don Juan]. Segismundo *no es más que* un símbolo.'[5] It is necessary to criticise these opinions. The assertion that a dramatic figure is a kind of Everyman is not necessarily a fault in the play in which he is found; how can Don Juan, a particular figure, be more universal than Segismundo, whom the critic takes to be the symbol of all mankind? As it stands the statement seems contradictory. Presumably Menéndez y Pelayo meant that in some way, because he was a particular figure and not a general type, Don Juan was superior to Segismundo. The opposite view is equally reasonable. But our purpose is not to compare characters but to analyse a play; even if we wanted to compare *La vida es sueño* with *El burlador de Sevilla*, it would not suffice to set Don Juan against Segismundo; we should also have to compare the plots, the construction and the diction of the two plays. I shall therefore disregard Menéndez y Pelayo's general criticism of this play.

Don Marcelino also pointed to two defects in the play's plan. First he said: 'En Calderón hay un salto mortal desde el Segismundo siervo y juguete de la pasión hasta el Segismundo tipo del príncipe perfecto, que aparece en la tercera jornada.'[6] He also described the sub-plot as: 'Una intriga extraña, completamente pegadiza y exótica, que se enreda a todo el drama como una planta parásita.'[7] The following pages will seek to confute these two judgements.

The Italian Hispanist Arturo Farinelli also criticised this play. He cited parallels to the story from all over the world, gave an account of Calderón's view of life and finally criticised the play itself. His examination is to be taken seriously, and his book, diffuse and sometimes prejudiced though it is, contains much valuable information. His most important adverse criticism of the play may be summarised as follows: *La vida es sueño* is founded on a contradiction. In it there is a sceptical thesis and a religious one. The sceptical thesis is that contained in the title, *Life is a dream*; the religious one that, as good works are necessary to salvation, so they are necessary to the reform of Segismundo. The theses contradict one another, because, if life is a dream, how can a man choose the good rather than the bad? Man cannot be held morally responsible for what he does in his dreams. Calderón avoided this difficulty by inventing a particular type of dreaming, what he called 'soñar despierto' in the *auto*. But this was a compromise; Calderón had deliberately subjugated the work of art to the improving moral lesson.[8]

At first sight this view seems plausible enough, but on further examination it does not provide a justifiable ground for criticism. Farinelli complains that Calderón's play is inconsistent because his analogy breaks down to some extent; because *all* life is not a dream in this work, but only some aspect of life, he censures it. Let us, however, imagine a work in which the analogy held absolutely, in which man was in no way morally responsible for his actions and in which he was no more the free agent than we are in our dreams. Such a work might contain powerful descriptions of scenes and events, it might provide us with interesting analyses of states of mind, but it could lead only to negation. If the statement 'Life is a dream' is pushed to its logical conclusion it means nothing is profitable; it seems unfair to Calderón to criticise him for rejecting this idea as pernicious or superficial.

Farinelli carried his arguments further. Calderón's thought went one way, the dramatic action another. Finally he changed the drama of *Life is a dream* for that of *Honour restored*. Majesty and pomp are wafted away, but no breeze or dream can remove honour. Honour, loyalty, obedience to authority, breeding, courtesy, social usages, order, deference to the ties of family and state, moderation: these things remain amid the vain phantoms that constitute earthly life.[9]

Again the previous objections apply. Because Calderón considered that certain things were more valuable than others, he is criticised for being illogical! That honour should appear as a positive virtue in the play is, perhaps, surprising, but we may find later on that there was some reason for it. Farinelli was so obsessed with his own idea of the logic of the title that he could not see how Calderón in fact applied it. I hope to show that the play is of a piece, logical, consistent and skilfully executed, and that its importance was not merely for one particular country or century.

To understand *La vida es sueño* we need not follow Farinelli's researches through the literatures of Europe and Asia in the track of the tale of the Sleeper Awakened, or those of Father Olmedo in sixteenth-century sermons and seventeenth-century Jesuit dramas. Doña Blanca de los Ríos unearthed ten other Segismundos who occur in other *comedias* by Calderón, and Ángel Valbuena Prat suggested (more fruitfully) that such figures are also to be found in the *autos sacramentales*; useful though these studies may be for other purposes, they are not essential to our present one. Even to compare our *comedia* with the *auto sacramental* (as did L. P. Thomas) may mislead us, for when we return to our play we may merely reread the *auto* at greater length.[10] Instead I shall examine the play in isolation to see what it can tell us. To do this I shall trace the parts played by the different persons, beginning with Segismundo; I shall bear in mind the two detailed criticisms of Menéndez y Pelayo as well as the more general objections of Farinelli.

Segismundo describes himself or others describe him as: *monstruo humano* (209) – *un hombre de las fieras, y una fiera de los hombres* (211-12) – *un monstruo en forma de hombre* (672) – *víbora humana del siglo* (675) – *un compuesto de hombre y fiera* (1547) – *un hombre que de humano no tiene más que el nombre* (1654-5). There is a terrible pathos in his first soliloquy, for his envy of the animal or of the inanimate almost expresses itself as a wish that he might lose his humanity. He suffers poignantly, through no fault of his own, and his suffering merely makes him violent. Clotaldo's teaching has remained external to him; every impulse immediately masters him. He tries to murder Rosaura, but her gentleness subdues him; he tries to resist Clotaldo and is shut up to rant in vain at the Heavens. He is an animal, uncontrolled. Calderón has not drawn him as a 'character', a being with a private individuality, but as a man in whom the animal, rather than human, nature is dominant: a man such as any of us might have been had we passed our early years chained up in a tower in the desert.

In the palace Segismundo is ungovernable. In his brief spell of power he insults the whole court from the King down, makes love outrageously to two women, throws a servant out of the window and tries to murder his former tutor. In this portrayal Calderón not only describes a man who is paying off old scores; the man is also shown as over-confident and proud.[11] He accepts his own power without question and takes as permanent a state of affairs that could have been permanent only if he had acted very differently. His pride shows itself in his assumption that he could do as he liked and in his manner of speech whenever he opens his mouth. There was pride in his defiance of the Heavens in the first act, and his pride is underlined continually in the second.

Nevertheless Segismundo is a man who has revealed certain possibilities of redemption. When Rosaura overheard his complaints in the tower, she offended his pride by learning his weakness; but although he threatened her, her plea moved him to pity. In the first soliloquy, in some speeches in the palace, in the earlier parts of his conversations with Estrella, and with Rosaura, he shows wit; wit is a human attribute that the beasts do not possess. Even if he expresses his aspirations too proudly some are not ignoble. If his manner is always harsh, the matter of his speeches is sometimes correct enough:

> En lo que no es justa ley
> no ha de obedecer al Rey. (1321–2)

Most significant of all, perhaps, for his subsequent change of heart is his exclamation in confusion on waking up in the palace:

> Dadme, cielos, desengaño. (1239)

Although the wish to know is soon stifled ('¿Quién me mete en discurrir?': 1245) and his appetites immediately resume their hold upon him, these phrases hint that Segismundo is not entirely degraded. Like King Baltasar in the *auto* he is a personification of *tesoro escondido*, as is every man whose animal nature dominates him.

During the palace scene there are two moments in which Segismundo has to face the possibility that he may be only a figure in a dream. Basilio warns him of this; so does Clotaldo. Together they have planned to take him back to the tower if his behaviour in the palace is unpromising. So that they speak with a double meaning, but he can only understand one. The first moment occurs after Segismundo's unfilial outburst to Basilio:

Basilio.   Mira bien lo que te advierto:
que seas humilde y blando,
porque quizá estás soñando,
aunque ves que estás despierto.
Vase
Segismundo.   ¿Que quizá soñando estoy,
aunque despierto me veo?
No sueño, pues toco y creo
lo que he sido y lo que soy. (1528–35)

He trusts to his senses and relies on his nature ('un compuesto de hombre y fiera') to carry him through to the throne. Later, when Clotaldo interposes to preserve Rosaura, the following dialogue ensues:

[*Clotaldo.*]   Y no, por verte ya de todos dueño,
seas crüel, porque quizá es un sueño.
Segismundo.   A rabia me provocas,
cuando la luz del desengaño tocas.
Veré, dándote muerte,
si es sueño o si es verdad. (1678–83)

On *La vida es sueño* 33

In the first passage Segismundo makes clear his assurance, his belief in his own powers and in the world in which he is placed; in the second his confidence has turned to hysteria and violence. 'La luz del desengaño' is a strange phrase to find on his lips; is he fighting against what he knows is the truth?

Overconfident after his first confusion, proud of his cruelty, Segismundo is thwarted and taken back, drugged, to his tower. There Clotaldo easily persuades him that all his experience in the palace was a dream. There are, however, certain associations with the tower itself that underlie the process of his conversion.

Rosaura's first impressions of the tower were not very pleasant. She criticised its architecture and added:

> La puerta
> (mejor diré funesta boca) abierta
> está, y desde su centro
> nace la noche, pues la engendra dentro.   (69–72)

When she sees Segismundo chained up inside she calls it:

> una prisión oscura
> que es de un vivo cadáver sepultura.   (93–4)

Later she mentions its 'bóvedas frías' (178). Segismundo says:

> que cuna y sepulcro fue
> esta torre para mí.   (195–6)

And he describes himself in the same speech as an 'esqueleto vivo' and an 'animado muerto' (201–2). When he wakes up again in the tower he exclaims:

> ¿No sois mi sepulcro vos,
> torre? Sí.   (2084–5)

The tower is associated with the idea of death, and for Calderón the fear of death often represented an essential preliminary towards a new life; properly realised, the idea of man's mortality will lead men to walk along the true path of virtue. 'La memoria de la muerte' sometimes saves the figures of Man from the devil in the *autos*; because Baltasar does not heed Daniel's reiterated warnings he is damned, and in *No hay más fortuna que Dios* the worldly figures are saved after Beauty has been changed into a skeleton. The tomb-like tower is here a reminder of death; this idea may escape a careless reading of the play, but it underlies Segismundo's change of heart.

Moreover, with Calderón, death often represents the final end of disorder. And disorder has been the dominant feature of Segismundo's life up to the moment of his awakening. The portents that attended his birth, the cosmic upheavals and the death of his mother showed Basilio almost as clearly as did the evil horoscope what was to be expected. In the first act Segismundo wanted to murder Rosaura for an almost frivolous reason, and, though he pined for freedom, he showed himself unfit for it by his behaviour when the guards separated him from his new source of consolation. In the palace he behaved wrongly towards every one he met: to his father he was unfilial, he rejected the servant's advice for the flattery of a buffoon, he was discourteous to Astolfo, he paid too much attention to Estrella and he showed criminal impulses in his conduct towards Rosaura and Clotaldo. He not only stopped at nothing; he was also imprudent. When free he could use his freedom only in a misdirected and distorted way. So he wakes up in a tower that is a tomb:

> Sí, hora es ya de despertar. (2091)

Back in the tower Segismundo dreams that he is still posturing in the palace; his real dream is a continuation of his waking life. He awakes, and Clotaldo easily persuades him that all that had happened in the palace was part of the same dream, a dream that had been inspired by the talk about the king of birds which preceded the first drugging. In dreams one does not act but is 'acted upon'; in the palace Segismundo acted as his passions, not his reason, dictated: he might as well have been dreaming. For while we are awake there are objective laws outside us to which we must conform; to know these laws and how to apply them is what gives life its reality. If they are neglected man becomes the creature of his passions, he is 'acted upon' and his life is no more real than a dream is. So that the palace scene became twice a dream for Segismundo: it was an unreal experience, and while it lasted he had merely acted on impulse in a dreamlike way. There was, however, one moment in which his higher nature was aroused: he loved a woman, and that memory was the one thing that seemed real to him.

Segismundo awakes then to find that what had seemed real was now unreal, that what he had thought was life, was, must have been, a dream. Clotaldo's explanation of the dream convinces him; it was a dream provoked by a conversation about an eagle. Clotaldo then adds:

> que aun en sueños
> no se pierde el hacer bien. (2146–7)

And Segismundo replies:

> Es verdad; pues reprimamos
> esta fiera condición,
> esta furia, esta ambición
> por si alguna vez soñamos. (2148–51)

Clotaldo's statement seems surprising, and so does Segismundo's reply to it. What Clotaldo says does not apply to ordinary dreams in which man is not responsible for his acts. But it does apply to Segismundo's life in the palace, for if he had acted more wisely he would not have found himself once more in the tower. In some way he seems to understand this, to realise that his 'dream' life was a continuation of his former life in the tower, and to accept the fact that by curbing his instincts he could save himself from similar disappointments in the future. Calderón does not expressly state, but he implies, that the Prince now sees that life is not an end in itself, nor is it something that he can control. It is something with which he must come to terms. That is to say, he is not yet fully converted; he has realised that evil does not pay and should be avoided for that reason.[12] His motives are not of the highest, but they are leading him in the right direction.

Segismundo is not acting from the highest motives when he decides to turn away from impulsive and passionate action. But the turning away prepares for the true conversion that will follow in the third act. Death is an awakening from the dream of life; Segismundo wakes from his life's dream in a tomb-like tower which almost unconsciously puts him in mind of his latter end. Having realised that he has been in error he utters the famous soliloquy in which he equates his experience with other types of worldly experience: the king's, the rich man's, the beggar's, the merchant's and the brawler's. He now knows that life is a dream; all life as the worldly know it. The expression is general: his dream is as real as his life is now that he is awake – and therefore all life is like that. He is still the dupe of Basilio and Clotaldo; he has still to understand that he was awake all the time that he thinks he was dreaming. Only then shall we be able to talk of him as truly converted.

Perhaps it is not idle to point out that the soliloquy itself establishes the nature of the dream of life. Its words are really the complete answer to the criticism of Farinelli:

> Y la experiencia me enseña
> que el hombre que vive sueña
> lo que es hasta despertar.
> Sueña el rey que es rey, y vive
> con este engaño mandando,
> disponiendo y gobernando;
> y este aplauso, que recibe
> prestado, en el viento escribe. (2155–62)

The emphasis is on what one is; the king dreams in his kingship, the rich man in his riches, and so forth.[13] The word *sueño* applies, not to the fact that one *is*, but to *what* one is. Before, Segismundo had refused to believe

that he was dreaming because he could feel what he was; now he sees that
what seemed real has only the reality of a dream. The palace, his attempts
to satisfy his passions, his seeming power were all untrustworthy and short-
lived. Calderón here has taken the Stoics' distinction between the things
that are in our power and those that are not. Our health, our property, our
position are not in our power; our judgement and our power of choice are.
If we live only for the things that are not in our power we are no more
free than is the dreamer in his dream who cannot exercise his powers of
choice, for the outside things, things not in his power, rule him. The king's
life is real; but his power and honours are only *prestados*. The Stoic, so
regarding them, would have him avoid them as far as possible; the
Christian would have him use them for good ends but live by them, not
for them. External events are also outside our power, and Segismundo had
wrongly assumed that he could shape them as he would. But instead,
events led to his awakening in the tower. In his dream he had flouted the
pagan precept: 'Require not things to happen as you wish, but wish them
to happen as they do happen, and you will go on well',[14] as well as the
Christian petition: 'Thy will be done.'

In the third act Segismundo is a man alternately swayed by passion and
by his newly acquired prudence. When the soldiers invite him to be their
king he at first takes them to be dream-figures whom he tries to drive
away. He only consents to lead them when they tell him that his 'dream'
foretold his present glory; nevertheless when he accepts he is carried away
by the passion of conquest. This in turn gives way to the cautious aside
just before Clotaldo's entrance:

> Mas si antes desto despierto,
> ¿no será bien no decirlo,
> supuesto que no he de hacerlo? (2383–5)

Until half way through the act he does not know whether he is asleep or
awake; there is a continual battle between the new Segismundo and the
old. Passionate impulses keep bursting out and are as often repressed.
One such moment occurs when Clotaldo declares:

> Yo aconsejarte no puedo
> contra mi Rey, ni valerte.
> A tus plantas estoy puesto;
> dame la muerte. (2407–10)

Segismundo replies:

> ¡Villano,
> traidor, ingrato! [*Aparte*] Mas ¡cielos!
> reportarme me conviene,
> que aún no sé si estoy despierto. (2410–13)

Segismundo is determined to march on to victory against his King and father and no less determined to do good lest all should be a dream. He is engaged in a treasonable act, yet his actions and words often belie it. His new attitude, though preferable to his earlier uncurbed violence, is not only inconstant; when he corrects it the selfish impulse peeps out again:

> Mas, sea verdad o sueño,
> obrar bien es lo que importa.
> Si fuere verdad, por serlo;
> si no, por ganar amigos
> para cuando despertemos. (2423-7)

A few lines before Rosaura comes onto the battlefield he appears, dressed in skins, and glories in the fact that he is a *fiera* in charge of an army (2660).

Rosaura's entrance brings him to his senses. In her appeal she tells him that they have seen each other three times, and the scales fall from his eyes, for, he says:

> que no es posible que quepan
> en un sueño tantas cosas. (2924-5)

With this comes his last struggle, from which the new Segismundo appears trampling down the old. All his life had been a dream, and each time that he had seen Rosaura before, he had lusted for her; why not make the most of this opportunity?

> Pues si es así, y ha de verse
> desvanecida entre sombras
> la grandeza y el poder,
> la majestad y la pompa,
> sepamos aprovechar
> este rato que nos toca,
> pues sólo se goza en ella
> lo que entre sueños se goza.
> Rosaura está en mi poder,
> su hermosura el alma adora.
> Gocemos, pues, la ocasión;
> . . .
> Esto es sueño; y pues lo es,
> soñemos dichas agora,
> que después serán pesares.
> Mas con mis razones propias
> vuelvo a convencerme a mí.
> Si es sueño, si es vanagloria,
> ¿quién por vanagloria humana
> pierde una divina gloria? (2950-71)

Then comes his final triumph of disillusion, perhaps the finest statement of it in the play:

> ¿Qué pasado bien no es sueño?
> ¿Quién tuvo dichas heroicas
> que entre sí no diga, cuando
> las revuelve en su memoria:
> 'sin duda que fue soñado
> cuanto vi'?
>
> (2972-7)

From now on he is the reformed prince, and 'acudamos a lo eterno' (2982) is his motto. He has triumphed over his lust, and he has found a justification for his treason: he will restore Rosaura's honour. The conflict of his action and his situation has been resolved. Rosaura is the instrument of his conversion; however we may criticise the sub-plot we must admit that it cannot be separated from the main plot without our misunderstanding the latter. Rosaura completed what Clotaldo began: the new Segismundo. After this his words and his conduct are harmonious and speak for themselves. He sacrifices his passion for Rosaura to the redemption of her honour and forgives his conquered father.

In this analysis I hope that I have to some extent answered Menéndez y Pelayo's objections against the rapidity of Segismundo's change of heart, which after all takes place in two stages. Perhaps the scene with Clotaldo in the tower is too much compressed; but the palace scenes hinted that such a change was possible, and the developments in the last act are very well worked out. The fact that Segismundo is a symbol does not hurt the play. His experience is a representation of Man's awakening from the life of the senses to that of the spirit.

Segismundo's experiences are reflected in those of other persons in the play. He trusted in his senses and in his newly found powers when he was allowed to be a prince for a few hours; he woke up, disillusioned, in the tower. Pride comes before a fall, and from the fall the proud man may become humble and prudent. Segismundo is not the only man to be humbled; Clarín, Basilio, Astolfo, a servant and the rebel soldier have also to learn how to submit to the inevitable. They all undergo a disillusion that is less strikingly presented than Segismundo's, but which, none the less, is important to them and to the development of the plot. Each man expresses too much confidence in his own powers, deeds or position, and each is humbled. In their different ways they too have been dreaming.

Clarín is something more than a *gracioso*, a *figura de donaire* of the common sort. He is cowardly, humorous; he puns on his own name. But his function is not merely to give comic relief but to add to the moral lessons of the play. His vices are funny, but they are also vices. There is little hint of this at first – in the scenes with Rosaura by the tower he seems

On *La vida es sueño*

only true to type. Gradually he reveals his true nature. Despite the blows of the halbardiers he forces his way into the palace; he must see what is going on, and he relies on his impudence and lack of shame. He finds Clotaldo and obtains a situation from him by blackmail; he has guessed the relationship between Clotaldo and Rosaura:

> Y hay que, viniendo con ella [Rosaura],
> estoy yo muriendo de hambre,
> y naide de mí se acuerda,
> sin mirar que soy Clarín,
> y que si el tal Clarín suena,
> podrá decir cuanto pasa
> al Rey, a Astolfo y a Estrella.[15] (1205-11)

But to be Clotaldo's servant is not enough for him; he immediately attempts to curry favour with Segismundo, whose temporary grandeur he looks upon as permanent.

> Señor,
> soy un grande agradador
> de todos los Segismundos. (1337-9)

His behaviour in the palace needs no further comment. He makes Segismundo's error. The sycophant succeeds over a short term.

Disaster follows. Clarín, proud of his cleverness, falls through being too clever. He has threatened Clotaldo before; now Clotaldo can shut him up out of the way, and he does so. A 'Clarion' that knows secrets is dangerous. Segismundo learns a lesson from his imprisonment, but Clarín, though his dreams might have warned him, can – for his imprisonment – give only a frivolous explanation. The moment called for more than puns about the Council of Nicaea or the invention of burlesque saints in a new calendar. He is interrupted by the soldiers who mistake him for Segismundo. He is puzzled, but he accepts the first solution that his ready wit supplies, an ingenious, but totally false, explanation of their conduct:

> ¡Vive Dios, que va de veras!
> ¿Si es costumbre en este reino
> prender uno cada día
> y hacerle príncipe, y luego
> volverle a la torre? Sí,
> pues cada día lo veo;
> fuerza es hacer mi papel. (2242-8)

> ¿Segismundo dicen? Bueno.
> Segismundos llaman todos
> los príncipes contrahechos. (2263-5)

He remains the clever self-seeker, and his self-seeking cannot save him from disaster. His very cleverness continually leads him astray. A minor example of this occurs when Clotaldo begs for his life from Segismundo, after the latter has been acclaimed by the rebel soldiery. Clarín, leaping to a false conclusion, murmurs to himself:

> Yo apuesto
> que le despeña del monte. (2389–90)

Segismundo, however, does not throw Clotaldo down the mountain but pardons him.

After these earlier errors Clarín's death can be seen as a natural consequence of his too superficial cleverness. He meets his end by trying to escape it. The scene is among the most powerful in the play, and we shall have to return to it when we examine Basilio's part. Here again Clarín appears in the double role of *gracioso* and of a man whose moral failings are to be exposed. The speech in which he declares his intention of hiding safely until the battle is over is a good example of humorous writing in the comic convention; but it is also an expression of cynicism and pride which deserves punishment:

Dentro unos.	¡Viva nuestro invicto Rey!
Dentro otros.	¡Viva nuestra libertad!
Clarín.	¡La libertad y el Rey vivan!
	Vivan muy enhorabuena,
	que a mí nada me da pena,
	como en cuenta me reciban;
	que yo, apartado este día
	en tan grande confusión,
	haga el papel de Nerón
	que de nada se dolía.
	Si bien me quiero doler
	de algo, y ha de ser de mí;
	escondido, desde aquí
	toda la fiesta he de ver.
	El sitio es oculto y fuerte
	entre estas peñas. Pues ya
	la muerte no me hallará,
	dos higas para la muerte. (3042–59)

Clarín is then killed by a random shot. His dying speech makes it clear that he has at last understood where true wisdom lies:

> mirad que vais a morir,
> si está de Dios que muráis. (3094–5)

All through his life he had been a clever, short-sighted opportunist; death alone could teach him the necessary lesson. Clarín dreamed he was clever and did not wake up until a few minutes before his death.

Basilio, hailed by the rival princes as the wise Thales and the learned Euclid, reveals his own defects as well as his good intentions in his long speech in the first act:

> Ya sabéis que yo en el mundo
> por mi ciencia he merecido
> el sobrenombre de docto. (604-6)

He is proud of his astrological ability and so certain of his powers of prediction that he acts upon them. Although he recognises that:

> la inclinación más violenta,
> el planeta más impío,
> sólo el albedrío inclinan,
> no fuerzan el albedrío, (788-91)

yet he had assumed that, as his prescience was so great, it could not be mistaken. He knew that his son's will was free, but at the same time he assumed that it would be forced. He therefore had him reared in circumstances that made it virtually impossible for him to make wise choices. Basilio considers that he can mould another man's life as he pleases, and at the same time he neglects the fact that this man's will is free. So he makes two mistakes: one of presumption, the other of ignoring an important human truth. The consequence is that he enables the prediction to be fulfilled by the very means that he hoped would avoid that conclusion. His motive was partly a good one – to save Poland from civil war – but nevertheless his conduct was wrong, and he involved Poland in the war he wished to avoid. He was rash to assume that by wisdom he could control the decrees of Heaven; he was wicked to bring up a young boy as though he were a caged beast.

At the same time Basilio's wisdom is not confined to astrology. He at least feels compelled by a rather belated Christian charity to grant Segismundo a chance to redeem himself. Not only that; he explains to Clotaldo how the chance is to be given in such a way that Segismundo shall not be too much shocked if the experiment fails; he will then see that life is a dream, for, Basilio says:

> Podrá entender que soñó,
> y hará bien cuando lo entienda;
> porque en el mundo, Clotaldo,
> todos los que viven sueñan. (1146-9)

These words were to prove true, as we have already seen.

Clarín meets his end by trying to escape it; Basilio finds humiliation by trying to avoid it. Both were too confident, but Basilio profited from Clarín's example. Basilio had never admitted that he had been unwise and unjust to Segismundo when they met in the palace. His son's behaviour outraged and grieved him, but he never recognised his responsibility for it. All this was reversed after Clarín fell wounded before him to give his dying warning:

> que no hay seguro camino
> a la fuerza del destino
> y a la inclemencia del hado.
> Y así, aunque a libraros vais
> de la muerte con hüir,
> mirad que vais a morir,
> si está de Dios que muráis. (3089–95)

Not only had Basilio announced his intention of fleeing; he has also looked upon his earlier 'camino' as 'seguro'. The voice that spoke from the dead man's wounds made him see the truths that he could not learn before:

> que son diligencias vanas
> del hombre cuantas dispone
> contra mayor fuerza y causa. (3105–7)

The futility of his conduct is now obvious to him; only God can decide the course of a man's life. He therefore submits, waits for his son and humbles himself before him. Basilio dreamed in his wisdom and only awakened when his schemes were defeated.[16]

Astolfo's position was rather different, but he also put too much trust in appearances. He relied on being able to escape from the workings of the law of honour by trusting to his position and to his own personal merits; his false self-confidence was thus a double source of error. Notwithstanding his bravery and loyalty, Calderón made his faults exemplary too. He wronged Rosaura. When he thought he had left her for ever he set about planning his political marriage to Estrella, purely to further his ambition by securing his rather doubtful right of succession to the Polish throne. When he handed Rosaura's portrait to Estrella he made clear that he was wronging Rosaura knowingly:

> Perdona, Rosaura hermosa,
> este agravio, porque ausentes,
> no se guardan más fe que ésta
> los hombres y las mujeres. (1774–7)

Although he knows the wrong he does her he never troubles to think of the consequences of his action; he does not see that retribution may overtake him because of it. He is too sure of himself to think about such things; he trusts to the distance that he supposes lies between them (that is, perhaps, the world in its most literal sense!) to carry him through, while he justifies himself because other men act in the same way. He wrongs Rosaura. He trusts to appearances in the hope of marrying Estrella and gaining a kingdom. Afterwards Segismundo defeats him in battle and compels him to marry Rosaura, not Estrella. He too is a dreamer; he dreams in his position and in the belief that he could escape the consequences of his past actions.

Two minor characters meet disaster also through their presumption. They are the second servant and the rebel soldier. The servant is not afraid to speak his mind, and he reproves Segismundo for his evil ways. He is a good man, but as soon as he displays confidence and pride, disaster overtakes him:

Segismundo.	También oíste decir que por un balcón, a quien me canse, sabré arrojar.
Criado 2.	Con los hombres como yo no puede hacerse eso.
Segismundo.	¿No? ¡Por Dios, que lo he de probar! (1422–7)

The soldier who headed the revolution is confident that he will receive a good reward for his treason. When he asks for it Segismundo sends him to be imprisoned in the tower:

> que el traidor no es menester,
> siendo la traición pasada. (3300–1)

Segismundo, Astolfo, Basilio, Clarín, the servant and the soldier all trusted too much to the things of this world and all were thwarted. Some at least, by meeting disillusion and realising what it meant, were able to rise again after their downfalls. All were rudely awakened from their dreams.

Rosaura and Clotaldo do not appear to enter into the scheme. Moral considerations dominate both of them, and these make disillusions unnecessary. Loyalty dictates all Clotaldo's actions, honour Rosaura's. The sub-plot is the story of the conflict of these motives. Each person is swayed to some extent by the feelings of the other, but each is right in remaining true to an ideal. So Clotaldo is willing to sacrifice his daughter's honour rather than be disloyal to Basilio and to Astolfo; Rosaura to fight against her father in order to vindicate her honour.

Yet the sub-plot is still in part a reflection of the main plot. The difference is that Clotaldo and Rosaura recognise confusion when they see it, whereas the others either do not recognise it as confusion (e.g. Clarín in the tower) or trust overmuch to their own abilities to solve it. Clotaldo and Rosaura trust instead in principles of conduct, not in worldly importance, self-conceit or mere cleverness. Segismundo's confusions in the palace, in the tower, on the battlefield are echoed in their doubts and conflicts. By realising the difficulties of life and by putting their trust in loyalty or honour they find their way through the labyrinth in which the others are thwarted or even destroyed. Confusion, though, is always stressed. Clotaldo, when Rosaura shows him the sword, exclaims:

> ¡Válgame el cielo! ¿Qué escucho?
> Aun no sé determinarme
> si tales sucesos son
> ilusiones o verdades. (395–8)

After Rosaura has revealed her sex he says:

> ¿Qué confuso laberinto
> es éste, donde no puede
> hallar la razón el hilo? (975–7)

And Rosaura sees clearly her difficulties when Estrella tells her to bring the portrait:

> ¿Qué haré en tantas confusiones,
> donde imposible parece
> que halle razón que me alivie,
> ni alivio que me consuele? (1824–7)

In his moments of trial Clotaldo is moved neither by fear of death nor by love of his daughter; Rosaura risks putting herself into Segismundo's hands in the hope of removing her dishonour. Through plot and sub-plot runs the theme of confusion; only devotion to virtue enables men and women to overcome the difficulties around them. Clotaldo and Rosaura know this from the beginning; the others have to learn it by a hard road. The sub-plot has therefore a logical justification in the plan of the play.

There is one scene in the sub-plot which particularly stresses these facts. It occurs in the last act when Clotaldo and Rosaura are brought into conflict with one another. Each is right in the course of action he or she has decided to pursue. Clotaldo has had to change his attitude towards her because Astolfo saved his life when Segismundo tried to kill him. For Rosaura the moral situation has not changed: Astolfo is still faithless, even if he rescued her father. She is therefore able to quote back at her father his earlier words: 'Vida infame no es vida' (910), when she says:

> De ti recibí la vida,
> y tú mismo me dijiste,
> cuando la vida me diste,
> que la que estaba ofendida
> no era vida. (2592–6)

The civil war is of the greatest importance to Clotaldo; to Rosaura, in comparison with her private problem, it means nothing. The confusions of the world are such that father and daughter can both be right in taking opposite sides and in pledging their loyalty to rival factions. Here is an illustration of the way in which each Christian soul has to work out his own salvation for himself.

There is another point to note in Clotaldo's part. He is loyal to his King because he is King; his loyalty asks no questions. Another author might have made him an inhuman executioner of Basilio's cruel decrees. Calderón does not attempt to palliate the enormity of Basilio's decisions, but neither does he blame Clotaldo for putting them into effect. Clotaldo is the faithful servant of an unjust master, but as the master had authority to govern, he obeyed him scrupulously. Had the servant questioned the decisions of his master he might have appeared presumptuous – like the second servant. Instead Calderón makes him loyal and humble.

The play is a carefully constructed whole. Segismundo's adventures are reflected in those of Basilio, Clarín, Astolfo and two unnamed characters; they are contrasted with those of Rosaura and Clotaldo. (Estrella is a figure who merely serves to help the plot; I do not see how her part exemplifies a moral lesson as do the others.) There is a close correspondence between the behaviour of the characters and their fortunes and misfortunes. In this way Calderón shows how virtue and vice earn their rewards, and the plot clearly represents the workings of God's providence – except that the rewards and punishments of the future life appear in this.

We may summarise the play thus: Segismundo is a compound of pride and passion, the satisfaction of which is thwarted; so he learns to subdue his passion and to see that pride is useless in a world in which nothing is certain. He turns to follow moral precepts, at first for selfish reasons, but later for purer motives. Clarín is clever and proud of his cleverness; his early efforts meet with success, and he assumes that he can gain whatever he may want by his wits. He ignores the warning that his imprisonment might have given him and, still sure of himself, he at last meets his end by trying to avoid it. Basilio is wise and proud of his wisdom. He assumes that he can alter the decrees of the stars and that he can ignore the free will of the only man who could alter them. He is defeated in battle (which deprives him of power) and witnesses Clarín's death, which convinces him of man's impotence and his own error. Astolfo trusts to his position to evade the responsibility; but the revolution overthrows his position, and he has to right the wrong he did to Rosaura. All were proud in one way or another. All trusted to their abilities, took as permanent what was transient, thought that they could control the future in accordance with their own desires; they thought that life was too simple. In a word, all were dreaming. Clotaldo and Rosaura subordinated their lives to principles; they saw that they had difficulties to face and that the world was confusing and untrustworthy. They faced their problems with constancy, unselfishness and prudence. For this reason they did not ride to a fall as the others did.

Plot and sub-plot depict different aspects of the same teaching. Plot and sub-plot are united also by Rosaura's part in Segismundo's conversion. When these two facts are clearly seen Menéndez y Pelayo's criticism that the sub-plot is a 'parasitical growth' that has no connection with main plot is seen to be worthless.

The structure of the play is complex. We have already seen some ironies that come true or are proved false by the progress of events. Clotaldo imprisons Clarín for being a 'Clarion'; Clarín had hoped to feather his nest for the same reason. Rosaura turns on Clotaldo the arguments that he had earlier used on her. Segismundo, at the end, can reprove his father, as his father had before reproved him. These are the most striking instances, but others that are hardly less so can easily be found. No detail in the play is idle. A mere compliment may serve to hint at the vanity of a king or the pride of a prince; asides show the wit and lack of judgement of a clown.

In general earlier criticism of this play has emphasised its fine dramatic moments. I do not wish to deny their merit or to minimise their importance. What I have tried to do is to prove that they cannot safely be isolated without serious misunderstandings. Literature teaches us both to feel and to order our feelings. In *La vida es sueño* the ordering of feelings is as important as the expression of the feelings themselves. Calderón expresses magnificently the misery of mankind[17] or the ferocity of an artificially repressed brutality, disillusion with the world or the death throes of a repentant self-seeker. Even more magnificent is the organisation of the whole play.

The details are accessible to all. Can the play as a whole mean anything to those who do not share the religious outlook of the author? I think it can. We may not all be able to value all the positive qualities that Calderón holds up to us. Rosaura's honour is for us but of historical interest; Clotaldo's loyalty appears servile; Segismundo's treatment of the rebel soldier seems unnecessarily vindictive. Yet these are types of – they stand for – other feelings that we can respect. Clotaldo's loyalty is the type of fidelity to a just cause; Segismundo's justice represents true justice; Rosaura's honour stands for a determined self-respect. We are not yet able to feel that there is no conflict between our impulses and our reason; we have still to come to terms with the world in which we live. Calderón was conscious of these problems, he stated them, and he gave us a solution of them. His statement is of the greatest importance to us, whatever we think of the solution.

NOTE

This article was written in 1938–9. It owes much in its arrangement to James Smith, who held the chair of English Language and Literature at the University of Fribourg, Switzerland; Professor A. A. Parker suggested some sentences in the account of Segismundo's first conversion. In 1946 Don Enrique Moreno Báez translated the article into Spanish, and we added some paragraphs and deleted others in order to make it more appropriate to Hispanic readers. I have now revised slightly the original English version, added some passages from the Spanish translation and rephrased a number of sentences. I hope that the changes I have made may clarify my original interpretation without distorting it.

POSTSCRIPT

I wrote the above note for the publication of this essay in B. W. Wardropper's *Critical essays on the theatre of Calderón* in 1964. The text of my essay, except for one sentence, remains unchanged from that printing. A. K. G. Paterson in 'The traffic of the stage in Calderón's *La vida es sueño*', *Renaissance Drama*, new series, IV (1971), 155–83 (p. 179, n. 30), pointed out a mistake I made in all the earlier printings of this essay: on p. 38 I wrote that Segismundo 'sacrifices his passion for Rosaura to the redemption of her honour and *restores his conquered father to the throne of Poland*'. Dr Paterson rightly criticised the words I have italicised; I have replaced them by 'forgives his conquered father'. My essay has provoked a spate of amplifications, qualifications and criticisms too numerous to enumerate here. I confine this postscript to three: A. A. Parker, 'The father–son conflict in the drama of Calderón', *Forum for Modern Language Studies*, II (1966), 288–99; R. Pring-Mill, 'Los calderonistas de habla inglesa y *La vida es sueño*', *Litterae hispanae et lusitanae: Festschrift zum fünfzigjährigen Bestehen des Ibero-Amerikanischen Forschungsinstituts der Universität Hamburg* (Munich, 1968), pp. 369–413; L. Abel, *Metatheatre: a new view of dramatic form* (New York, 1963), pp. 59–72.

4
The discretion of Don Lope de Almeida

The action of *A secreto agravio, secreta venganza* takes place in Portugal during the reign of the unfortunate Don Sebastian. As far as I am aware, the question why Calderón chose this setting has never been discussed. Calderón often used his historical material freely, and for that reason, perhaps, critics have paid little attention to his choice of settings for particular plays. This has sometimes led to misunderstandings of his intentions in plays in which historical material is incidental. In this play Sebastian's part is not particularly interesting in itself, and the setting in Portugal, at first sight, hardly seems particularly significant.

Don Lope and Don Juan are Portuguese; Doña Leonor and Don Luis are Castilians. Don Lope is Doña Leonor's husband, Don Luis, her former lover. Lope tells Juan early in the first act:

> Yo me he casado en Castilla,
> por poder, con la más bella
> mujer. (290b. I, iii)[1]

Leonor weeps before she crosses the frontier, and, though her tears are the result of her passion for Luis, her husband's old uncle attributes them to her grief at leaving her native land:

> aunque no es gran maravilla
> que con sentimiento igual
> a vista de Portugal
> te despidas de Castilla. (291a. I, iv)

Luis, when he is disguised as a diamond-merchant, tells the travellers that he is journeying from Lisbon to Castile (293a. I, vii). Later on he is referred to, or addressed as, 'caballero castellano' (298a. II, vi; 304a. II, xvii), or simply as 'el castellano' (305b. III, i), and he tells Lope that he was an exile from Castile who had fled to Lisbon for safety after he had killed a rival in a duel (303b. II, xvii). Just before, he had pleaded with Leonor to love him still,

> que en Toledo, nuestra patria,
> (perdonadme) os quise bien. (301b. II, xi)

The discretion of Don Lope de Almeida

And, when the lovers were interrupted by the husband, Leonor told Luis:

> podrás irte, no a Castilla. (302a. II, xi)

Obviously the difference between Castile and Portugal is significant; why the two regions should be precisely those two, rather than – say – Naples and Barcelona,[2] is not apparent from any of the foregoing quotations.

In an edition of two plays of Tirso de Molina the editors remark that: 'Por toda la literatura clásica abundan los portugueses "derretidos de amor" hasta convertirse en *sebo* y no quedar más que *pabilo*... La arrogancia, la cortesía y el valor portugueses fueron reconocidos por Tirso cumplidamente.'[3] There is nothing *seboso* about Don Lope or his friend, but the rapid growth of his love for Leonor in the first scene might possibly be taken as a typically Portuguese trait. Luis, in one of the most dramatic scenes, is forced to recognise the 'portuguesa arrogancia' of his enemy (304b. II, xvii), and Juan's account of his part in the expeditions in the East Indies – with the appeal to the authority of 'el gran Luis de Camoens' (288b. I, iii) – bears witness to Portuguese bravery. Bravery, arrogance and even susceptibility as a lover were not looked on as being exclusively Portuguese; the enquiry must be pursued a little further.

In Tirso's play *El amor médico*, the second and third acts of which are set in Portugal, there are allusions to the care with which women were guarded in that country, how gallantry was less tolerated there than in Castile, how Portuguese men were more jealous than Castilians and how they were even more punctilious.[4] Don Francisco Manuel de Melo, some years after Calderón's death, also mentioned that the Portuguese were stricter with their women than the Castilians were;[5] and earlier in the century, Pinheiro da Veiga had noted that there was a greater freedom of behaviour in the Spanish court at Valladolid than there was in Lisbon.[6] Similar ideas seem to lie behind the situation in *A secreto agravio*; they are explicit when Leonor sends her message to Luis by Sirena:

> Dile a don Luis...
> que una mujer...
> le suplica que su amor
> olvide; que maravilla
> cuidado en la calle tal,
> y no sufre Portugal
> galanteos de Castilla. (296a. II, ii)

Also Calderón makes Lope reprove Leonor for speaking smooth Spanish compliments and flatteries and tell her that the Portuguese prefer blunt truths or silence:

> ¡Qué castellana que estáis!
> Cesen las lisonjas, cesen

> las repetidas finezas.
> Mirad que los portugueses
> al sentimiento dejamos
> la razón, porque el que quiere,
> todo lo que dice, quita
> de valor a lo que siente.
> Si en vos es ciego el amor,
> en mí [es] mudo. (296b. II, iii)

Calderón seems to have set his play in Portugal in order to contrast the stricter sense of honour and the more reserved character of Lope with the superficial effusiveness of Leonor and the sly gallantry of Luis. A Castilian author shows how Portuguese virtue overcomes Castilian treachery and weakness.

King Sebastian makes three appearances in the play. His part is not, superficially, very important. In the final scene he does not officially ratify Lope's acts of vengeance; he remarks to Juan that they are justified. He does not play the traditional kingly role as do the Catholic Kings in *Fuente Ovejuna*, Henry III in *Peribáñez*, Philip II in *El alcalde de Zalamea* or even Peter the Cruel in *El médico de su honra*. These sovereigns represent justice; they make legal the technically illegal acts of vengeance they have to judge. Sebastian also represents justice, but he merely receives a verbal report of a vengeance he makes no attempt to declare legal. It almost appears as if Calderón introduced him to fulfil the traditional royal duty and forgot to make him do so. Such a view would not be appropriate to this play. If the outrage is secret and the vengeance is also secret, the king has no need to do anything, because the perpetrator will be safe whatever happens. Calderón perhaps implies that the King has a right to be told of the acts of vengeance after they have been committed – a king is after all the father of his subjects; consequently Juan, who has guessed the truth, tells him about it, and Sebastian agrees, secretly, that the action was fitting:

> Es el caso más notable
> que la antigüedad celebra,
> porque secreta venganza
> requiere secreta ofensa. (315b. III, xx)

Sebastian's name is invariably linked with the disaster of Alcazarquivir, in which he and his army were slaughtered and through which Portugal lost her independence a few years later. Calderón's Sebastian also has these associations. The preparations for the expedition do not allow Sebastian to act as 'padrino' at Lope's wedding (287b. I, i). Later in the play Lope wants to be one of the throng of nobles who are joining up (296b, 297a. II, iv and v), and Leonor advises him to do so (297a. II, iv) whereas Juan tells him not to do so (II, v). Sebastian, though he tells Lope that his sword would bring victory in Africa, advises him to stay at home now he is a married man (307a. III, v). As we shall see later, the preparations for the expedition directly affect the plot. There was no need to remind the playgoers of the sixteen thirties that Sebastian and his army perished; nevertheless, Calderón occasionally dropped a hint to remind them of the fact:

Lope. No queda en toda Lisboa
fidalgo ni caballero
que ser no piense el primero
que merezca *eterna loa*
con su muerte (296b. II, iii)

and

Leonor. Servid hoy a Sebastián,
cuya vida el cielo aumente;
que *es la sangre de los nobles*
patrimonio de los reyes. (297a. II, iii)

Sebastian himself is unconsciously explicit after his entrance in the last act. He pauses with the Duke of Braganza to meditate on the beauties of the seascape. Then he is carried away by an irrational pride in his own future victories:

Adiós, dulce patria mía,
que en él espero que vuelva
(puesto que es la causa suya)
donde ceñido me veas
de laurel entrar triunfante
de mil victorias sangrientas,
dando a mi honor nueva fama,
nuevos triunfos a la Iglesia,
que espero ver...

Voces Dentro. ¡Fuego, fuego! (314a. III, xvii)

Such an expression of pride could only go before a fall. Even the expression of pride could not be completed, except by the terrible appropriateness of the voices off, who, terrified by the fire in Lope's summer-house, unconsciously warn Sebastian of the fate that awaits him in Africa. The shout of '¡Fuego, fuego!' completes the sentence, and suggests the earthly destruction of the royal boaster. After this incident, Lope's action of enlisting in Sebastian's army becomes acceptance of death, if not an act of suicide. The audience all knew what happened to the army; the audience had also heard, and presumably understood, the speech just quoted. Calderón did not trouble to produce a psychological study of Sebastian; instead he used his presence to suggest the disaster with which his name will always be associated. By this means the dramatist suggested that the fate of Lope was that of Sebastian, that the careers of the two men to some extent ran parallel. The play is called a 'tragicomedia' – in it the comedy is confined to the clownish servants. The avenger, as well as his victims, met an end that can almost be described as tragic:

> Con vos iré, donde pueda
> tener mi vida su fin,
> si hay desdicha que fin tenga. (315b. III, xx)

Some years ago I drew attention to the way in which Calderón built up a system of imagery by referring to an object typical of one element in terms of another. Foam, flowers and stars were interchangeable; horses were ships of the earth, ships were birds of the sea, and so forth.[7] In this play Lope kills Luis by water and Leonor by fire. Fire may destroy or purify; water may drown or wash clean. After he has drowned Luis, Lope declares he will use all four elements in his secret vengeance:

> Mis intentos
> sólo los he de fiar,
> porque los sabrán callar,
> de todos cuatro elementos.
> Allí al agua y viento entrego
> la media venganza mía; [i.e. the death of Luis]
> y aquí la otra mitad fía
> mi dolor de tierra y fuego.
> . . .
> Sacaré acendrado dél [i.e. el fuego]
> el honor que me ilustró,
> ya que la liga ensució
> una mancha tan cruel;
> y en una experiencia tal,
> por los crisoles no ignoro
> que salga acendrado el oro
> sin aquel bajo metal
> de la liga que tenía
> y su valor deslustraba.
> Así el mar sus manchas lava
> de la gran desdicha mía;
> el viento la lleve luego
> donde no se sepa della;
> la tierra ande por no vella,
> y cenizas la haga el fuego;
> porque así el mortal aliento
> que a turbar el sol se atreve,
> consuma, lave, arda y lleve
> tierra, agua, fuego y viento. (313b. III, xvi)

The passage explains itself in its context. It also refers back to other earlier passages in the play in which the elements had been used to express the intensity of feeling of both Leonor and Lope.

Love affects the soul directly; under its influence tears issue from the lover's eyes, sighs from his mouth. Calderón sometimes described this by talking of fire in the soul, water in the eyes, air in the mouth. Early in the play Leonor used these metaphors when she described her unhappiness:

> Pues salga mi pena (¡ay Dios!)
> de mi vida y de mi pecho.
> Salga en lágrimas deshecho
> el dolor que me provoca,
> el fuego que al alma toca,
> remitiendo sus enojos
> en lágrimas a los ojos
> y en suspiros a la boca. (291b. 1, v)

In these lines only one element has been mentioned; in the lines that follow she assumes that sighs are air, tears water, only to show that her tears and sighs, through the intensity of her grief, burn like fire:

> Y sin paz y sin sosiego,
> todo lo abrasen veloces,
> pues son de fuego mis voces
> y mis lágrimas de fuego.
> Abrasen, cuando navego
> tanto mar y viento tanto
> mi vida y mi fuego cuanto
> consume el fuego violento,
> pues mi voz es fuego y viento,
> mis lágrimas fuego y llanto. (*ibid.*)

There is disorder as well as intensity in Leonor's grief; the intrusion of fire into the domains of air and water echoes this disorder.

Leonor's unhappiness is displayed in the lines that follow shortly after those in which Lope naïvely expresses his joy at having married Leonor by proxy. He indulges in conceits about flying with Love's wings through waves of fire and air to show the intensity of his happiness:

Lope.	¡Felice yo si pudiera volar hoy!
Manrique.	Al viento igualas.
Lope.	Poco aprovecha, que el viento es perezoso elemento. Diérame el amor sus alas, volara abrasado y ciego, pues quien al viento se entrega, olas de viento navega, y las de amor son de fuego. (288a. 1, ii)

and

> (Suspiros,
> ofreced viento a las velas,
> si es que en los mares del fuego
> bajeles de amor navegan.) (291a. I, iii)

Such language is indeed hyperbolic for a man who has not even seen the woman he is so happy to have married.

Later in the play, when Lope is consumed by the feeling that he has lost his honour, he again refers to fire to express his feelings:

> esta pena, esta rabia y este fuego. (307a. III, v)

And in one of his most agonised soliloquies, he asks:

> ¿No fuera mejor castigo,
> ¡cielos!, desatar un rayo
> que con mortal precipicio
> me abrasara, viendo antes
> el incendio que el aviso
> de la palabra de un Rey
> que grave y severo dijo
> que yo haré falta en mi casa?
> ¿Pero, qué rayo más vivo,
> si, fénix de las desdichas,
> fuí ceniza de mí mismo? (307b. III, vi)

Some of these speeches will be referred to again later in this essay. For the moment, however, we may notice that the four elements are used externally and internally, to bring about the punishment of Leonor and Luis, and to describe the feelings of Lope and Leonor. Fire works in the soul of the woman whose body is later to be burned; fire works also in the soul of the man who burns her. Lope's fire consumes Leonor's fire by fire.

The first scene in the play shows how Sebastian congratulates Lope de Almeida on his marriage. Lope asks for permission to retire from soldiering in order to marry; the King grants his request. There is a reference to the African expedition which was afterwards to lead to the disaster of Alcazarquivir: a hint that the military expedition and the marriage would both turn out badly. Lope is left with his servant and expresses his joy in conventional hyperboles. 'Abrasado y ciego' he wants to fly on Love's wings rather than tread on solid earth. His servant Manrique reminds him that there is a world of fact in which men must move cautiously:

> ¿Y no miras que es error
> digno de que al mundo asombre
> que vaya a casarse un hombre
> con tanta prisa, señor? (288a. I, ii)

The quatrain is to be taken seriously, though it is spoken by the *gracioso*.

The discretion of Don Lope de Almeida

So, in a different way, is his next remark – a not very good joke which helps to prepare the reader for the misfortunes that follow:

> Si hoy, que te vas a casar,
> del mismo viento te quejas,
> ¿qué dejas que hacer, qué dejas
> cuando vayas a enviudar? (*ibid.*)

The slight foundation for Lope's happiness is shown in the imagery with which he himself describes it; his lack of prudence in marrying in a hurry is the subject of comment by his servant.

Don Juan de Silva then comes in, poorly dressed. Lope recognises his old friend and hears how he has met misfortune through avenging an insult. Lope adopts him, welcomes him as a friend, pities his misfortunes and approves his actions which befitted a gentleman:

> Sólo dichoso
> puede llamarse el que deja,
> como vos, limpio su honor
> y castigada su ofensa. (290a. 1, iii)

Lope's admiration for his friend's sacrifice of wealth to honour prepares us for his own sacrifice in the last act. Except for a brief scene in which he welcomes Leonor, here is the Lope of the first act: a generous man, too eager to marry, appreciative of the fulfilment of the code of honour. Calderón has also dropped more than one hint of the misfortunes that were to follow.

In the second act Lope enters tormented by the thought that he too ought to go to the wars. Leonor enters, he reproves her for being too effusive in her greetings (as we have already seen). He then asks her whether she will allow him to serve the King. To his surprise she readily consents, whereas Juan advises him to stay at home. Left alone, Lope thinks aloud and at length. There can only be one explanation for this extraordinary situation. After a struggle he admits that he is jealous, that he suspects the Castilian whom he has seen too often in his street and in church. He would have preferred Leonor to have given him the same advice that Juan had given him; what she had said would have been understandable if Juan had said it. Still, perhaps Leonor had encouraged him to go for the sake of his reputation, and Juan had told him to stay because he wanted his friend's marriage to be a happy one. Leonor is noble and virtuous but ... he is left in doubt. The only possible course is to be silent, prudent, alert, careful until he can see the truth, and, if necessary, act:

> que yo sabré proceder
> callado, cuerdo, prudente,

> advertido, cuidadoso,
> solícito y asistente,
> hasta tocar la ocasión
> de mi vida y de mi muerte:
> y en tanto que ésta se llega,
> ¡valedme, cielos, valedme! (299a. II, vi)

He has not to wait long. Juan surprises Luis in the house and Lope arrives just after Luis has hidden. Consequently, as the room is dark, the friends fight one another until a light is brought in. Both the friends learn the truth later on, but Lope now tries to persuade Juan that he was the intruder. Juan is puzzled, but Lope has at least concealed the fact that he now knows that his honour is compromised. He sends Juan to search the house and himself discovers Luis. The latter tries to excuse his presence with a cock-and-bull story about taking refuge after a street fight. Lope is sceptical, but pretends to believe Luis. He takes Luis out of his house by a garden-door so that, he says, Luis's honour should not in any way be suspect. At the same time he warns Luis of the vengeance he would take if anyone were to prejudice his own honour:

> Y si llegara a creer...
> ¿Qué es creer? Si llegara
> a imaginar, a pensar
> que alguien pudo poner mancha
> en mi honor... ¿Qué es mi honor?
> en mi opinión y en mi fama
> y en la voz tan solamente
> de una criada, una esclava,
> no tuviera, ¡vive Dios!,
> vida que no le quitara,
> sangre que no le vertiera,
> almas que no le sacara,
> y éstas rompiera después
> a ser visibles las almas. (304b. II, xvii)

These lines may be criticised as so much bombastic fustian; their purpose is not to inspire the reader with admiration for their particular poetic beauties, but to make a theatrical audience realise that Lope is an angry man who has almost lost control of himself when he finds his enemy in his grasp. Read in this way, the speech is skilfully written; the rhetorical questions, the interrupted sentences, the interjection and the monstrously absurd hyperboles at the end are carefully designed for their dramatic effect. Luis trembles and follows him out. Lope returns to Leonor who excuses herself too much. He pretends to believe her, but reflects:

> Desta manera,
> el que de vengarse trata,

> hasta mejor ocasión
> sufre, disimula y calla. (305a. II, xix)

In the last act Juan adds to Lope's suspicions by bringing up the question: can a man tell his friend that his friend's honour is compromised? Lope replies no, but in his heart he sees that his own honour is implicated. Still more strongly does he see it when King Sebastian tells him, significantly, that he ought not to go to the wars because he is needed in his own house. Lope again soliloquises: what has he done to deserve this? he has always behaved as a gentleman should. But he realises the uselessness of complaining of the usages of the world. No, he will go to the wars, and when he returns he will execute the vengeance that will astound his fellows and the generations that will follow him.

He is interrupted by Juan. Juan, who had thought he had wiped out the insult he had received by killing the man who insulted him, now finds the insult repeated because his public revenge had made it more notorious. Such is the way of the world. Juan has silenced his slanders for the time being, but the lesson is not lost on Lope. Public vengeance is no use; it will merely broadcast the original fault. He must await his opportunity with dissimulation, endurance and silence until at last he can act.

Soon afterwards he is at the riverside and calls for a boat to take him over to his summer-house. Luis, who also wishes to cross because he has an assignation with Leonor, comes on to the stage reading her letter. Lope realises that his opportunity is at hand; before he addresses his rival he says to himself:

> Rigor,
> disimulemos, y dando
> rienda a toda la pasión,
> esperemos ocasión
> sufriendo y disimulando;
> y pues la serpiente halaga
> con pecho de ofensas lleno,
> yo, hasta verter mi veneno,
> es bien que lo mismo haga. (309b–310a. III, x)

A double-edged conversation between husband and lover follows, and Lope invites Luis to accompany him. They embark, and the boat breaks adrift from its moorings. Lope has his opportunity; he overturns the boat, murders Luis and swims ashore. On his arrival Leonor and Juan welcome him. He tells them that Luis met his death accidentally; Leonor faints, overcome by grief. Lope, now convinced of the justice of his suspicions, decides to kill Leonor too. He sets the house on fire and she perishes; he has satisfied the demands of honour and at the same time kept secret the fact that his honour had been compromised.[8] The others – Juan, King

Sebastian and the court – will merely think that she has perished in an accidental conflagration. Lope kills her and makes his final entrance, bearing her charred body in his arms and feigning grief at her early death.

The play began with Lope's requesting King Sebastian to allow him to leave soldiering in order to marry. Later, the King told him he should not rejoin the army because he was needed in his own house. Now that Leonor was dead he could once more serve the King. He offers his services and his life. We have already noted what this implied for the audience of Calderón's day. Calderón in fact condemns Lope to death by making him march off with Sebastian on the fatal African expedition. There is no reason why we should not interpret these facts as a suggestion that, not only has Lope now nothing else to live for, but also he ought not to live any longer. We have seen how Calderón hinted that his marriage was an imprudent act that ended in disaster; his later conduct was much more discreet, but even there there are hints that Calderón disapproved of some of his thoughts and actions. Lope has told us how he would tear souls to pieces, has compared himself to a serpent that caresses before it strikes; the violence of this language is deliberately crude and shocking, and it implies a condemnation of the anger and deceit it expresses. Lope is not so much to be looked at as a pattern of conduct for the injured husband to follow, as a tragic hero, who struggles valiantly and even prudently against his fate, but who nevertheless perishes through his own frailty. I think that in this play at least, Calderón's attitude towards the secret vengeance was more detached than has often been thought.

Don Juan is the foil to Don Lope. He is as much a man of honour as his friend, but – the difference is important – he is less prudent. After he had been called a liar, his vengeance was open for all the world to see; the world remembered that he had been called a liar. He nearly made public Lope's plight when he found Luis in the house, and Lope had to deceive him to overcome his excessive zeal. When he put the case of honour to Lope at the beginning of the third act, Juan could not conceal from his friend that the two of them were the persons involved. Lope had occasion to reflect:

> ¡Oh, cuánto a un hombre daña
> un ignorante amigo!
> ¡Que no puedan los cuerdos, los más sabios
> celar de un necio amigo los agravios!   (303a. II, xv)

Juan is brave, a good friend, punctilious – but he is hasty and unthinking.

In Leonor there is a struggle between love and honour. Before she meets her husband she exclaims:

> Hasta las aras, amor,
> te acompañé; aquí te quedas,
> porque atreverte no puedas
> a las aras del honor.   (292a. I, v)

So she said, but that was while she thought that Don Luis de Benavides was dead. Afterwards this remark is seen to be ironical. In the same way that Lope's unreasonable joy was reproved by Manrique, her purposeless grief is censured by her maid Sirena:

> Tu inútil queja esuchando
> estoy.   (291b. I, v)

Calderón implies that she is luxuriating in her emotions when she ought to be preparing herself for her future duties as a wife, or perhaps she ought not have married at all, for she tells Sirena a little later that she is:

> muerta sí, casada no.   (292a. I, v)

At the same time that we are shown the purposelessness of her grief, we are also made aware that she is an object of pity by the images in which she describes her feelings:

> y con acento süave
> se queja una simple ave
> del que la cogió a traición,
> y en la [dorada] prisión
> así aliviarse pretende,
> que al fin la queja se entiende
> si se ignora la canción.   (*ibid.*)

When she first appeared on the stage she was unable to conceal her grief, but she was able to conceal its cause from her husband's old uncle. We see how she has made a wrong choice, but is determined to abide by it and act honourably; we also see her emotional instability and her ability in deceiving other people.

A little later she discovers that Luis is still alive because he comes in disguised as a diamond-merchant. She has sufficient notion of honour to refuse to take the jewelled hearts, clasps and Cupids that her disguised lover offers for sale. She recognises Luis in his disguise and replies to his double-edged speeches in the same terms, but with a refusal. She carries out her belief in honour and acts deceitfully as she does so. Luis offers her a diamond – the emblem of constancy – and her struggle between love and honour begins. The dialogue is carried on in metaphors which the poor old uncle cannot understand because he takes the figures of speech literally. The ingenuity and verbal dexterity of this scene are continued into the next in which Leonor, while patently addressing Lope, is really speaking to

Luis. Her speech is purposely ambiguous, for though the sonnet she recites cannot be taken as meaning that she will allow Luis to continue to court her, it does, none the less, encourage him to do so. Its ambiguity is double (it is repeated by Luis after Leonor has left the stage): it is spoken to the husband for the lover; it can be read as either encouraging him or discouraging him. It shows either duplicity or indecision or a combination of both qualities. In other words, Leonor is playing with fire.

At the beginning of the second act Leonor decides to break off all communication with Luis. She tells Sirena to tell him that all is over:

> Ya vuelvo determinada.
> Esto, Sirena, es forzoso;
> declárese mi rigor,
> porque mi vida y mi honor
> ya no es mío, es de mi esposo. (296a. II, ii)

Her message appeals to Luis's sense of honour; a lady begs him to return to Castile and to trouble her no more. The scene is followed by that in which Lope reproves her for her too great effusiveness, and she arouses his suspicions by her ready consent to his proposal to serve the King. There is a connection between these two scenes; if Leonor shows herself to be so insincere now, can we take her rejection of Luis any more seriously? When the maid returns from her errand, Leonor has not enough strength of mind to burn the letter from Luis, and after a little persuasion from the servant – not for nothing is she named Sirena – she reads it. From now on her passion has won the battle over the sense of honour; honour which, although rather weakly, she tries to preserve. She relies on her honour to carry her through, but it is weaker than her feelings. She has to travel along a dreary road of shame, deception and self-justification until at last she suffers death at her husband's hands. The stages of her degradation are made so obvious by Calderón that we need only summarise them. She sees Luis; when they are interrupted, she tells him to go away, but not too far away; she lies to Lope about Luis's presence in the house, and she excuses herself too much after he has left it. Finally we hear a terrible confession from her lips when she is talking to Sirena outside the summer-house in the conflagration of which she would shortly perish:

> perdí, Sirena, el miedo
> que a mi propio respeto le tenía,
> pues si escaparme puedo
> de lance tan forzoso, la osadía
> ya sin freno me alienta;
> que peligro pasado no escarmienta. (311b. III, xiii)

She is no longer afraid for her honour, because she thinks all the dangers

The discretion of Don Lope de Almeida 61

of the discovery of Luis in the house are gone: Don Juan was deceived, Don Lope shows himself more loving than ever before.

> Y pues para mi vida
> hoy sigue al Rey don Lope en la jornada,
> escribo que don Luis a verme venga,
> y tenga fin mi amor, porque él le tenga. (312a. III, xiii)

Her letter led Luis to his death; she fainted when she heard of it, thus confirming Lope's suspicions. Her moral guilt was certain; she had reconciled herself to the act of adultery. No one can claim that in this play Calderón sacrifices an innocent life to a punctilious quibble.

The Castilian, Don Luis de Benavides, is a man who refuses to learn the lessons of experience. He acts as though he never realised that Leonor has married Lope. He nourishes his old love affair and makes no attempt to conquer his old feelings, whereas Leonor tries, if vainly, to restrain and conquer hers by her appeals to her honour. He deliberately rejects honour, as we see in his violent speech at the end of the first act:

> sea mi loca esperanza
> veneno y puñal dorado.
> Si ha de matarme el dolor,
> mejor es el gusto, ¡cielos!
> Y si he de morir de celos,
> mejor es morir de amor.
> Siga mi suerte atrevida
> su fin contra tanto honor,
> porque he de amar a Leonor
> aunque me cueste la vida. (295b. I, x)

He emphasises his acceptance of all the chaos that honour held in check, and his deliberate rejection of honour itself. Judged by the code of honour, his speech is equivalent to Satan's 'Evil, be thou my good.'[9] His love is antisocial, and he defies the conventions with his eyes open. Better than resign himself to grief or jealousy, he will seek pleasure and love; if it is unsuccessful, he may lose his life, but even that, in his present state of mind, will not matter. Nor does he care that Lope's honour will suffer. When he first met Leonor after her marriage, he addressed her violently; his reproaches did not become a man of honour:

> ¿Qué me podrás responder,
> mujer tan fácil, liviana,
> mudable, inconstante y vana,
> y mujer, en fin, mujer,
> que pueda satisfacer
> a tu mudanza y tu olvido? (294b. I, viii)

Leonor, it may be noted, takes him to be a gentleman of honour; she tells Sirena:

> Dile a don Luis que, pues es
> principal, noble y honrado,
> por español y soldado
> obligado a ser cortés... (296a. II, ii)

The mistake in the judgement of his character leads ultimately to her downfall. Luis is honour's enemy, anti-honour. That is how he sees himself, and how the others see him too. Lope, when his suspicions are first aroused, says that the Castilian

> es girasol de mi honor,
> bebiendo sus rayos siempre. (298a. II, vi)

And Leonor, after she has read Luis's sonnet, confesses:

> Este hombre ha de obligarme,
> con seguirme y ofenderme,
> a matarme y a perderme
> (que aun fuera menos matarme),
> si no se ausenta de aquí. (300b–301a. II, ix)

He rejects any consideration external to his passion, which he cultivates for its own sake. In his furtive interview with Leonor in Lope's house, he invokes their past pleasures even before he pleads with her and explains the rumour which led her to think that he was dead. When he was surprised in the house, Lope warned him of the dangers he ran if he compromised Lope's honour; at the time he was impressed, but the warning was soon forgotten. This is made clear in the scene with Lope in the last act: before he begins the conversation with his enemy, he revels in the thought of the future pleasures which he believes will soon be his. Then the two men have a double-edged conversation while they are waiting to embark. This is followed by a series of asides by each of them, which is perhaps the culminating scene in the play:

Lope.   Llegó
                           la ocasión de mi venganza.
Luis.   ¿Cuál hombre en el mundo alcanza
                           mayor ventura que yo?
Lope.   A mis manos ha venido
                           y en ellas ha de morir.
Luis.   ¡Que me viniese a servir
                           de tercero su marido!
                           ...
Luis.   ¿Quién ha visto igual ventura
                           Él me lleva desta suerte
                           adonde a su honor me atrevo.

Lope.	Yo desta suerte le llevo	
	donde le daré la muerte.	(311b. III, x)

Lope is filled with the spirit of vengeance; Luis has almost forgotten the pleasures he expects to enjoy in the thought of the means by which he seems likely to get them. He dwells on the insult to Lope's honour, not on the favours of Leonor. He rejoices in the fact that Lope acts as his bawd, Lope is helping him to ruin Lope's honour. The most important feature of this striking and famous scene is that it clinches the contrast between the libertine and the avenger and brings out clearly the libertine's defiance of the code of honour.

We have seen how Manrique reproved Lope for his unreasonable joy in getting married, how Sirena told Leonor that her grief was futile and purposeless. There is also a third servant, Celio, who tries to make Luis see reason during the only scene in which he takes part. The three servants all have the same function in the first act with regard to their respective masters or mistress. In addition Sirena helps her mistress in her affair and influences her to follow her passion rather than her sense of honour. Manrique is the comic anti-hero; he is happy when his master is sad, sad when he is happy (296b. II, iii); the thought of war terrifies him; he is inconstant in love, imprudent in love also; loquacious, cowardly and of course a wine-bibber. The sub-plot of the ribbon given him by Sirena has not much point, and Manrique himself is not even a very humorous *gracioso*. The servants, however, help on the action, they throw into relief the attitudes of their masters and mistress, and the burlesque affair between Manrique and Sirena is an example of a low, coarse business in which all idealism, honour and gallantry are absent. The fact that the servants themselves and the sub-plot in which they take part are largely conventional, does not mean that they and it are to to be entirely passed over by reader or hearer. They are a reminder that to many people the values of civilised behaviour, which are implicit in the main plot, mean nothing at all.

The main plot contrasts the behaviour and motives of four people. Don Lope de Almeida believes in honour, subjugates his passions to honour and uses discretion to make sure that his honour has in fact been outraged, and, after that, to see that his vengeance shall be secret. His faith in honour controls his feelings, his discretion controls his judgement and actions; he is honour's saint. Don Juan de Silva believes in honour, but, as his discretion is less, he cannot guard it completely; he is something less than Lope. Doña Leonor believes in honour, but is carried away by her feelings; she is honour's sinner. Don Luis de Benavides deliberately rejects honour and believes only in the satisfaction of his passion; he is honour's apostate.

In this analysis I have not scrupled to summarise the play as a sort of *comedia de santos* in disguise. Such a statement may well seem paradoxical; nevertheless, that is how, I think, Calderón conceived it. In *A secreto agravio* Calderón seems to say, let us take a worldly code of conduct and develop it to its logical conclusion: let us rigorously exclude all religious views that may conflict with it,[10] let us see the code as it is, and what it involves; let us imagine a man who believes in it and who carries it out to the letter, another who follows it less perfectly, a woman who believes in it but has not the strength to live up to it and a man who rejects it completely. There are Lope, Juan, Leonor and Luis. What are the acceptable moral values of the code? Fidelity and generosity in friendship, submission of sensual and personal feelings to some kind of order, courtesy, earnestness to find out the truth at all costs, discretion in the enquiry and in the action that follows it. These qualities are admirable enough. On the other side there is dissimulation, revenge and murder. Dissimulation is not always necessarily evil, and revenge here is not of a common sort, like 'getting your own back' in everyday life; it is justified only in so far as it is part of the code. If my interpretation of the play is acceptable, Calderón shows how revenge is followed by the death of the revenger.

That this interpretation is not completely fanciful is, I think, borne out by the fact that at no time does Calderón stress the fact that Luis and Leonor are sinning. The only mentions of religious belief are purely incidental; there is no attempt to place the words or actions of those taking part against the background of eternity. Calderón is exact in this delimitation. Had he been preaching that all men who found themselves in Lope's position ought to act as Lope did, that the laws of the code of honour were universally valid and true, he would surely have added that adultery was a mortal sin and that marriage was a sacrament. Nowhere in the play is such an idea expressed.

The fundamental idea behind the play is the necessity of prudence in man's everyday life. Had Lope and Leonor considered their marriage more carefully before they embarked upon it, the later situations would never have arisen. Lope learns prudence through the pressure of circumstances; Juan and Leonor try vainly to be prudent, and Luis throws prudence – and every other moral value – out of the window. Prudence is one of the cardinal virtues which it is every Christian's duty to cultivate. In *A secreto agravio secreta venganza* Calderón's main emphasis is on the prudence with which the code of honour is applied, rather than on the morally ambiguous prescriptions of the code itself.

5
Towards an appreciation of
El pintor de su deshonra

In his defence of the Spanish theatre against the attacks of some theologians Don Francisco Antonio de Bances Candamo (1662–1704) made a curious allusion to *El pintor de su deshonra*. Moralists had attacked Spanish stage plays for their encouragement of sexual immorality; Bances pointed out that the plays that ended with a vengeance of honour were anything but an incitement to adultery. He added:

> Desde que Don Pedro Calderón atendió al aire y al decoro de las Figuras, no se pone adulterio que no sea sin culpa de la muger, forzándola y engañándola. Y en su primorosa Comedia de *El Pintor de su deshonrra* hace que el galán robe a una muger casada, sin culpa de la infeliz, y se mantiene intacta en el poder de el galán, y, no obstante, por la duda, mata a los dos el marido. Pues ¿qué pluma, por seuera que sea, dirá que podrán las mugeres casadas hallar más a mano en ésta el deseo del adulterio que el horror del castigo, dándole a beuer el vno junto al otro? Y, si lo hallaren, maldad será de los ojos que miran, y no intrínseca malicia de el objecto, quando todo el discurso de la Comedia puede ser escuela de los buenos casados, y el fin terror de los malos.[1]

For modern readers the play requires quite a different justification. The last criticism they would level against it is that it makes adultery seem a pleasure. Bances's observations are interesting in that they suggest that one of the reasons why Calderón wrote plays of honour and vengeance was to condemn adultery: not his only reason, of course, as that expert dramatist Bances himself would certainly have acknowledged. But his statement that the heroine's innocence makes the play more exemplary should not be passed over; it tells us how an intelligent man, who may even have known Calderón personally, saw the play. We shall look differently at the play from the way Bances discussed it; but his observation reveals an obviously true fact in it which is easily forgotten.

The husbands' vengeances are secret in *El médico de su honra* and in *A secreto agravio secreta venganza*. In *El pintor de su deshonra* Don Juan Roca, disguised as a painter, shoots his wife and her supposed lover; the fact is discovered by her father, by the lover's father and sister, by the Prince of Ursino, by a gardener and by the comic servant. The vengeance, then, is public. A secret vengeance would have had no point. Secret vengeances punished secret outrages and kept them secret. When a man was publicly dishonoured – and Don Álvaro's abduction of Serafina was witnessed by a considerable crowd of masqueraders – his vengeance also had to be public in order that he might reinstate himself in the good opinion of his fellows. A public vengeance was the natural sequel to a public outrage.

This play is later than the other two. It may well date from the sixteen forties. Obviously the play is more stylised, less naturalistic than the two plays of secret vengeance. The way in which supposedly casual stage effects (guns fired off-stage, etc.) coincide with the dialogue, the expert arrangement of entrances and exits, the relevant glosses of songs that seem to be sung accidentally, the repeated parallels of dialogue and situation – all these features make it appear artificial, theatrical, even operatic; but once the reader has accustomed himself to Calderón's practice in *coups de théâtre* he can see that they are used purposefully. Realism is sacrificed to a sort of symbolism that employed theatrical conventions to exemplify old truths about human nature. If we want to understand Calderón we must not condemn those conventions as false, untrue to life, artificial, until we have seen their exact purpose in the particular play we happen to be studying.

At the end Porcia says:

> Porque en boda y muerte acabe
> *El pintor de su deshonra.*
> Perdonad yerros tan grandes.   (III, xxvii)

What relation exists between the respective marriage and death of the sister and brother? Generally speaking in Calderón plays the persons get their deserts at the end of them.[2] Here Porcia marries the Prince; Álvaro dies in his father's arms; his murderer is forgiven. The two plots are joined together by a series of links; did the author intend a contrast between them? The story of Porcia's affair with the Prince is not very interesting unless it adds something to the other one. Then it might be interesting, even though the two plots contradicted one another. To examine the sub-plot about the two lovers who stayed in Italy may throw some light on that of the others whose tragedy was precipitated by an accidental fire that broke out in the course of one of the Carnival festivities for which Barcelona was so well known.[3]

We first meet Porcia as Don Luis's virtuous daughter. She does not reveal her inner feelings, except for her friendship with Serafina. We see her as a good housekeeper to her father, who is ostentatiously hospitable. She hears Serafina's confession. When Serafina faints, Porcia's desire to help her friend is even stronger than her joy at hearing that her brother

Towards an appreciation of *El pintor de su deshonra* 67

Álvaro has arrived safe and sound in Naples. Of course she is glad to learn that her brother is still alive, but she is also conscious that her first duty is to her friend who is in distress. Even when she greets her brother, the knowledge of her friend's plight continues to dominate her words and actions. A brief scene between her and the Prince of Ursino follows; in it she reproaches him for his long absence. Serafina interrupts them, but Porcia is still able to arrange a rendezvous with her lover for that night. We see her again at the end of the first act when she hears her brother's recriminations and Serafina's grief. Like Henry of Trastámara's page she exclaims: 'ni quito ni pongo amor' (I, xxii); she will act like a sister and as a sentinel for the two of them. But she also says to her brother:

> Quéjate, suspira, llora,
> pues no tienes más fortuna. (I, xxii)

She withdraws, and when the time comes, she enters again to tell them her brother and Serafina must part. In Act I we see Porcia as daughter, sister, friend and a loved one; in each of these capacities she behaves prudently. The laws of hospitality must be obeyed as her father wills; she keeps watch while Don Álvaro talks with Serafina; she does all she can to help Serafina in her fainting fit; she reproves her brother without breaking with him; she continues to maintain her relation with the Prince.

In her scene with the Prince in Act II Porcia has to hide him from her father Don Luis. She arranged with him beforehand that he might approach her when she sang about love, but he must withdraw when her songs were about jealousy. For Porcia this symbolised the conduct of true lovers, but the Prince commented that he knew a lady who came forward when she was jealous and repelled her suitor when she was loved. Porcia then tells him that they must talk to music; Don Luis is still working and thinks that she is strumming and singing only to amuse herself. She informs the Prince that she and her father are going off to the country; the father approaches, and the Prince retires. Her father leaves again, so she is able to tell the Prince that they can easily meet one another if he goes hunting near Belflor, Don Luis's country house. Her father then calls her to go to bed; she sings a song about absence, the scene ends with a separation. The general effect of it is a little precious, but under the elegant affectation we are shown a prudent young lady who can control a situation that might have proved disastrous to a more impulsive woman.

In the third act the situation is more complex, more difficult to summarise. Porcia reconciles her father with her brother, sees her brother and contrives to get him away from the summer-house in which she has hidden the Prince. Now she and Don Álvaro are playing the same game; each is ignorant of the fact that either his beloved (Serafina) or her lover (the Prince) is hidden in the same place. Her stratagem causes a meeting which, had she known of it, she would have tried to prevent; yet it caused no bad consequences to her own private life. She never learns that the Prince has sighed after Serafina, that her jealousy (I, xv; II, ix) was in fact justified. She returns to the summer-house and witnesses the deaths of Don Álvaro and Serafina. Then she accepts the Prince's offer of his hand and the play closes. Porcia has difficulties to overcome. She faces them calmly. She knows what she has to do and does it.

The Prince of Ursino has a more complex part. He is successively the protector of Don Álvaro and of his murderer, that unknown painter whose real name was Don Juan Roca. Ursino is in love with Serafina, but at the same time he courts Porcia, who really loves him. He is frank with Celio about this double life, but one can hardly admire the man who admits:

> ¿Qué importa, Celio, ver a Porcia bella
> si de mi pena no es la causa ella?
> Este divertimiento
> es no más que engañar el pensamiento.   (II, xi)

And later he will confess to himself that his conduct towards Porcia is a means of overcoming his feelings for Serafina:

> Miento; que aun dura en mi pecho
> aquel incendio pasado;
> pero así, loca memoria,
> si no te venzo, te engaño.   (III, ix)

This subtle unfaithfulness, which Serafina never encourages and he tries to control, helps to bring about the final catastrophe. If he had not decided to have Serafina's portrait painted, Don Juan would never have been hidden in the summer-house in which he killed her. The Prince, however, did not force his attentions on Serafina. He sees her, is impressed by her beauty and her conversation; Don Álvaro tells him who she is; he cherishes the memory of her – and then, through a series of coincidences, he finds himself face to face with her. She asks him to keep secret the fact that she is in Italy – and to go away at once. He obeys her, but he also sends his painter secretly to paint her likeness. The Prince acts cautiously. He does not allow his feelings to dictate to him his actions. He respects Serafina's request. He is attentive to Porcia, even when he is in love with her friend. He controls feelings that other men find hard to check, and at the end he marries Porcia, by which act the ambiguity of his early behaviour is perhaps excused. Most modern readers of the play will prefer Don Álvaro's impulsive frankness to the carefully concealed feelings of the Prince; Calderón, fully assured of the dangers of impulse, shows how one man avoided, and

Towards an appreciation of *El pintor de su deshonra*

the other sought out, such dangers. The basic passion of both men – love for the same married woman – was the same; one risked and lost everything, the other, by his caution, saved a good deal from the wreckage.

At one moment in the play the Prince (as was noted in the last paragraph) revealed his passionate feelings to Celio. He can never forget Serafina's brief appearance to him. Celio remembered the occasion and pointed out that 'ese día se fue también'. Then the Prince attempted to prove that such moments are as much a part of life as more permanent conditions are:

> No porque al primer paso,
> antes de ver las sombras del ocaso,
> tal vez el sol en nubes se obscurece,
> podremos decir dél que no amanece;
> no porque al primer susto
> del relámpago y trueno
> tal vez se desvanezca el rayo, es justo
> decir que no fue rayo de iras lleno;
> no porque de su seno
> nazca tal vez, orilla
> del mar, a breve edad la fuentecilla
> donde su cuna en su sepulcro vea,
> dirán que su cristal cristal no sea;
> no porque ardiente llama
> al primer resplandor con que se inflama
> expirase tal vez de un soplo herida,
> se dirá que no tuvo ser ni vida;
> y no porque tal vez en el primero
> albor la flor examinase el fiero
> hielo que su esplendor adormeciese,
> se dirá de la flor que flor no fuese.
> Luego no porque hallase en un momento
> la nube, el mar, el soplo, el hielo, el viento,
> mi amor recién nacido,
> sol, rayo, fuente, llama y flor no ha sido.   (II, xi)

If, when we read speeches like this, we see them only in terms of rhetoric, we shall mistake their sense. The sense here lies in the fact that the Prince is trying to emphasise what is permanent in what is transitory. Clouds that hide the sun, streaks of lightning, streams swallowed by the sea, flames extinguished and flowers nipped by the frost are all old metaphors that have repeatedly been used in meditations upon the brevity of life and the inevitability of death. The Prince, anxious to convince Celio that his passion is natural, contradicts his intention by using comparisons that run counter to what he is trying to say. Calderón, by making him speak in this way, shows that the Prince is in conflict with the natural order of things, for he seems to be affirming that the past is still present. And this, as we shall see, is Don Álvaro's primary mistake.

Celio was not convinced by his master's eloquence:

> Bien argüir pudiera
> contra aquesa razón, si ya no oyera
> en el jardín, sonoro, el instrumento
> que es la seña de Porcia. (II, xi)

His remark underlines the falsity of the Prince's comparisons.

After the Prince has returned from Italy and before he has seen Porcia, he had had another conversation with Celio, this time about love in general. Celio's theory about love was simple; when asked whether he had been in love, he replied:

> Yo
> mirón del amor he sido;
> y a pagar de mi dinero,
> a la que me quiere, quiero,
> y la que me olvida, olvido. (I, xiv)

The Prince then explains why lovers' actions must appear absurd to one who never truly loved:

> Quien ve de lejos danzar
> al que más airoso ha sido,
> como no oye el dulce ruido
> de la música, en juzgar
> que está loco, juzga bien,
> pues sin compás las acciones
> parecen desatenciones:
> lo que no sucede a quien
> de cerca oye la armonía,
> que es el alma de su primor.
> Así el que ignora de amor
> una y otra fantasía,
> a cuyo compás quien ama
> se mueve, estar loco puede
> juzgar: lo que no sucede
> a quien la dulzura inflama
> que le negó la distancia;
> pues atento al blando son
> no oye, no mira acción
> que no le haga consonancia.
> Acércate, pues, un poco
> al ruido de amor; verás
> que está danzando a compás
> el que piensas que está loco.[4] (I, xiv)

Celio hints at the reply he would have given had not the arrival of Porcia interrupted him:

> Bien pudiera replicar
> que en quien se acerca o se aleja,
> aun siendo a compás, no deja
> de ser locura el danzar.
> Pero no es tiempo, pues vi
> que a verte Porcia salió. (I, xiv)

The Prince says that love is the hidden music to which his actions and words conform. Celio implies that although a lover's actions may accord with the love he feels, there are other criteria in life besides those proper to a good lover. Really, however, a general reference is intended here to all men who are in the grip of a passion that entirely governs them. If we fail to bear in mind their passion their acts remain inexplicable. In order to satisfy his passion for Serafina the Prince is in his heart unfaithful to Porcia, and he makes rhetorical speeches about it all to his gentleman-in-waiting. Another man, to satisfy a similar passion for the same woman, carried her inert body out of Barcelona and kept her against her will at Belflor. A third man, moved by a different passion – the desire to vindicate his lost honour – isolated himself from his fellows and took service with the Prince in Naples as his painter. Both the Prince and Celio are right. You cannot follow the dance if you do not hear or at least imagine the music; the dance may have harmony and beauty, or it may turn out to be a series of wild, incoherent movements.

There are similarities between the Don Álvaro of this play and Don Luis de Benavides in *A secreto agravio*. For Don Álvaro, like him, cannot recognise the fact that things have changed as a consequence of the marriage of his former love, whom he continues to court as though she were still single. He refuses to learn from experience. He cherishes his old feelings towards her and makes no effort to conquer his passion. This is the music he dances to. He differs from Don Luis in that his love does not degenerate into a perverse desire to take away another man's honour. Calderón has some sympathy for Don Álvaro. Just before he carries away Serafina's body he exclaims:

> porque es tanta
> la fe con que a Serafina
> ha querido y quiere el alma,
> que si a su vida le importa
> mi muerte, es justo buscarla. (II, xvi)

And when she is in his power at Belflor he never tries to take advantage of her. He tries to win her by abducting her, and he fails; but his manners are otherwise (at least in the last act) those of a gentleman, though his conduct had been inexcusable and his soliloquies, asides, confidences and entreaties are painful.

Don Álvaro acts on impulse. After he has survived the shipwreck he comes home to find that Serafina is now Don Juan's wife; whereupon, without reflection and against his father's will, he quickly decides to return to Spain, with the excuse that his father's affairs need his presence there, but really in order to follow the woman he so rashly loves. In the two scenes he has with her in Naples he refuses to allow her marriage to be an obstacle in his path, and he tries to persuade her that, in spite of it, she still loves him. In the course of the second of these scenes he takes offence and calls her 'aleve, falsa, perjura' (I, xxii), words that reveal his own loss of self-control as well as discourtesy (to put it no more strongly) towards her. In Barcelona he impetuously enters Don Juan's house in order to see her; he mentions his respect for her and her reputation ('opinión'), but he refuses to go away when she asks him to leave. In the Carnival he repeats his imprudence by dancing with her before her husband's eyes. And finally, when the fainting Serafina is delivered into his care, he is swayed by a momentary impulse to carry her off. Later he acknowledges that he acted badly, but he also hoped that by acting badly the very extravagance of his deed would impress her:

> [Pensé]
> que por el mismo paso
> que fue tan desesperada
> mi acción, fueran tus agrados
> menos crueles; pues vemos
> que amor en lo temerario
> vive, y disculpa no tiene
> un error enamorado,
> como no tener disculpa:
> tanto ama el que yerra tanto. (III, v)

Don Álvaro's impetuosity was the result of his lack of confidence in himself and in his fortune. He is a *desconfiado*:

> Crean mis desconfianzas
> de una vez que ya este bien
> se perdió. (II, xvi)

He continually deplores the brevity and fragility of human happiness:

> Poca dicha es de un ausente
> hallar su dama durmiendo. (I, x)

> Pues nadie mejor que yo,
> aleve, falsa, perjura,

Towards an appreciation of *El pintor de su deshonra*

> te podrá decir cuán breve
> es la edad de la ventura. (I, xxii)

> La dicha de un desdichado
> siempre de un acaso nace. (III, xxv)

Every reverse makes him despair:

> ¿De qué sirve andar en busca
> de alivio? Que lo peor
> no debe dudarse nunca;
> y es echar a mal la queja
> lisonjear con la duda. (I, xxi)

> De ver cuán vanas
> para mi imposible amor
> son todas mis esperanzas... (II, xvi)

'Estoy perdido' (II, v), he exclaims when he has almost been discovered by Don Juan in the house in Barcelona. He sees everywhere signs of his own death:

> Desdichas, no me matéis. (III, xvii)

> ¿Qué es esto que miro, cielos?
> ¡Serafina se ha casado,
> y viéndola yo en ajenos
> brazos, no pierdo la vida! (I, xii)

> Cierta es mi muerte, pues es
> cierta la mudanza suya. (I, xxi)

Of course these premonitions are fulfilled when he is killed, but they are also symptoms of the fears he suffers from. Twice was his fear caused by casual shots that coincide with the mention by Serafina or by him of a thunderbolt (I, xxii; III, iv) and once by the mere sight of the man who later would kill him:

> temor...
> ...de haber visto
> la verdad de cuán valiente
> es en su casa un marido. (II, vii)

The combination of rashness in his actions and of lack of self-confidence in his words is manifest in all that Don Álvaro does and says. He is a rash man who refuses to see things as they are; in his feelings he lives in the past. He never stops to think about the consequences of his acts. He offers an obvious contrast to the Prince of Ursino: both men feel a similar love; but the one acts with foresight, the other on impulse.

There are series of correspondences between what happens to Don Álvaro, what he says and does, and what happens to Don Juan Roca, what he says and does. At times, even, they use the same or very similar words on similar occasions. When Don Álvaro awakens Serafina after her first swoon, he calls her: 'Mi bien, mi dueño, mi esposa' (I, x); Don Juan uses the same words in the same order a few lines later when he sees her for the first time after her recovery from it (I, xii). When Don Juan suspects that his honour is in danger because a stranger (Don Álvaro, of course) is in the house, he exclaims:

> Apuremos, corazón,
> todo el veneno al peligro. (II, ix)

When Don Álvaro realises that his father knows about Don Juan's dishonour, he exclaims:

> Apuremos, corazón,
> toda la malicia al lance. (III, xvii)

Serafina's words also echo this pattern when she recovers from her first and from her third swoons. In the first she murmurs:

> Déjame; por Dios te ruego,
> don Álvaro, no me mates. (I, x)

and in the other:

> Don Juan, esposo, señor,
> aguarda, espera: no manches
> tu noble acero en mi vida.
> ¡No me mates, no me mates! (III, xxiv)

Early in the play Don Luis tells Don Juan that they suppose that Don Álvaro has perished at sea (I, i); towards the end of it Don Luis tells Don Álvaro that they suppose that Don Juan also has been lost at sea. In the first act Don Álvaro describes his poverty in Barcelona (I, xx); in the last Don Juan's conversation with Juanete reveals his poverty in Naples (III, xiv). In Barcelona Don Álvaro appears disguised as a sailor: '*Sale don Álvaro de marinero*' (II, iv); in Naples Don Juan is also in disguise 'en este traje de pintor' (III, xiv). Don Álvaro makes his first appearance as a protégé of the Prince; later in the play the Prince is Don Juan's patron. Early in the play the Prince tells how Don Álvaro was rescued from the sea after the shipwreck; an unnamed correspondent informs Don Luis that: 'arrojándose don Juan desesperado al agua, de donde lo sacaron casi muerto algunos que acudieron a favorecerle' (III, i). When Don Álvaro snatches Serafina from Don Juan in Barcelona, there is a more violent parallel to Don Juan's action in Naples when – in all innocence – he deprived Don Álvaro of Serafina. Such parallels cannot be accidental. Calderón used them to show that there were strong links to bind together the lives of these two men.

Towards an appreciation of El pintor de su deshonra

They both love Serafina. Her feelings towards them are clearly defined. She loved Don Álvaro; now it is her duty to love Don Juan whom she respects and admires. She tells Porcia that Don Álvaro, before he disappeared, 'palabra me dio de esposo' (I, viii); in other words he was almost her husband before her marriage to the other man. (Here, of course, is another parallel between them.) Her honour prevents her from expressing her love for her former suitor, but at bottom she knows that he is the man she really loves. In her long speech to Porcia she says:

> Muy pocas mujeres, Porcia,
> o ninguna, se ofendieron
> de ser amadas: quien más
> llore su aborrecimiento,
> a los desaires atienda
> de su dama, y verá en ellos
> que aunque el valor los anima,
> andan en visos y lejos
> rebozados los favores
> a sombra de los desprecios. (I, viii)

And when she has received his verbal promise she admits that then:

> fue el desdén el embozado
> y el favor el descubierto. (*ibid.*)

We must remember this double interpretation of lovers' language later in the play when we hear her conversations with Don Álvaro and with Don Juan. Her words obey what her duty orders her to feel rather than what she truly feels. Her husband believes the words she utters; her lover continually tries to make them mean what he suspects must be her deepest feelings. Both men are deceived: Don Álvaro cannot realise that her words are provoked by her consciousness of her duty; Don Juan cannot understand that they do not come from her heart.

The parallels and correspondences noted in the last few paragraphs do not mean only that the two men are in love with Serafina. There is yet another strong link between Don Álvaro and Don Juan. Though the causes are different, both of them are rash in the decisions they make, in the actions they pursue. Don Álvaro is timid and impulsive; Don Juan is brave and over-confident. His bravery needs no illustration; he himself admits his over-confidence: 'Matóme mi confianza' (II, xix). He wades out into the sea and watches the boat that is carrying his wife towards Naples.

Don Juan's marriage was an imprudent act; he was a middle-aged man who chose a young woman to be his bride. When first he saw her and Don Álvaro together, he was so full of uxorious passion that he did not note either her confusion or the presence with her of the other man. When he first tried to paint her portrait he attributed his lack of success to her beauty rather than to his own deficiencies of skill. He admitted, though, that he had been 'loco, altivo, vano' (II, i) in even attempting to portray her. To distract himself from that failure he left the house, and Don Álvaro took advantage of the opportunity to enter it. Don Juan discovered that an unknown man had made his way into the house, and his suspicions of Serafina began; nevertheless he went on with his project of taking her the following day to the Carnival. During those festivities Don Álvaro asked Serafina to dance with him; she refused, but Don Juan insisted that she should accept this dangerous invitation. When the dance was over, she wanted to go home; but Don Juan took her instead to a friend's house where they might enjoy themselves longer and more privately. The tent caught fire; he bravely rescued her, but incautiously he left her in the care of some sailors (among whom was the disguised Don Álvaro) while he impetuously went back to the flames to see whether he could rescue some other person. Don Álvaro made the most of this opportunity and abducted Serafina. Don Juan returned to find that his honour had been publicly ruined by his own over-confidence and lack of caution.

His public dishonour demanded a public vengeance on the innocent Serafina and on her guilty lover. He could not face his friends until his honour was restored, so he went again to Italy and worked as the Prince's painter until he had an opportunity to avenge himself. In Naples we hear his outbursts about the 'escrupulosa condición del honor' in terms that ultimately derive from Juan Rufo's *romance* about the Commanders of Cordoba.[5] In his conversation with Juanete he reveals that he can no longer consider himself a gentleman, and when he talks with the Prince he addresses him as a painter, almost as an artisan (*oficial*) talks with a patron. He draws a lively picture of himself as he describes his painting of the jealous Hercules:

> Fuera de la tabla está,
> y aun estuviera más fuera
> si en la tabla no estuviera
> el Centauro tras quien va. (III, xv)

The obvious parallel of the two attempts to paint Serafina's portrait is brought out when he tells the Prince how once he failed to portray a 'beldad tan superior' (*ibid.*). The Prince gives the painter his task and tells him to trust in his master's protection. Don Juan's reply shows that adversity has not changed his nature; he remains confident:

> Digo, gran señor, que iré
> en tu palabra fiado,
> y después en mi valor. (*ibid.*)

Towards an appreciation of *El pintor de su deshonra*

He accepts the Prince's order without knowing whither it may lead. Then he tells Juanete to put a pair of pistols as well as paint-brushes into the box he will carry with him. The last lines of the scene, in which he calls himself the painter of his dishonour (III, xiv), point towards the final catastrophe and to the fact that now he feels his action will be well concluded.

The same determination (or is it rashness?) is shown in the short scene between him, Belardo and the Prince:

> Guiad vos; que obedecer
> me toca, no hacer examen.
>
> ¿Temor?
> Mal, señor, mi valor sabes;
> que no acobardan peligros
> a quien no matan pesares. (III, xx)

He has surrendered his will to the Prince. He no longer decides for himself. Then Belardo locks him into the summer-house 'por más seguridad' (III, xxii); he is not his own master; now he is physically a prisoner. Serafina's arrival prevents any further talk with Belardo. She goes to sleep. Don Juan recognises her and utters an agonised soliloquy. Jealousy will paint the portrait that love could not complete. His situation is dangerous. Vengeance now seems impossible:

> que es la sobra de valor
> tal vez falta de cordura. (III, xxiv)

He will wait until the facts are clearer; then he will avenge his honour decisively and completely:

> Pues sufrir, temer, penar,
> corazón, hasta tomar
> por entero la venganza. (*ibid.*)

Don Álvaro's arrival reveals his enemy's identity. Serafina's plea to her old lover convinces Don Juan of her guilt. So he forgets all considerations of prudence and kills them both:

> (*Aparte*) (Ya, cielos,
> no hay sufrimiento que baste.
> Cuantas razones propuse
> aquí para reportarme,
> al verla en sus brazos, todas
> es forzoso que me falten.)
> ¡Muere, traidor, y contigo
> muera esa hermosura infame! (III, xxv)

He is physically imprisoned and at the mercy of his passion. He cannot hold himself back. An automatic murder follows an automatic abduction: both have an innocent victim. He shoots in despair to kill a guilty man and a virtuous woman. He hopes that the others will kill him. But the Prince comes to his aid; the others forgive. The presentation is completely objective. A credulous husband finds himself in such a situation that he cannot refrain from murdering his wife. Calderón shows us that Don Juan is partly to blame for his own dishonour and that his act of vengeance is its automatic consequence. A man like Don Juan could not have been expected to act otherwise; he rejects all 'sufrimiento', all 'razones para reportarme'. The witnesses of his crime do not kill him because they either know or can guess his motives. The double murder was the sequel to his earlier imprudence; it was committed in defiance of caution and reason. Don Juan danced to the music of love and of the jealousy of honour. That is all that can be said in his favour.

Serafina was remarkable for her beauty and her intelligence. The Prince described her as 'discreta'; Don Luis and Don Álvaro praised her 'ingenio singular'. When the Prince is introduced to her, she is mistress of the situation, despite her emotional crisis (I, viii); she is resourceful when in Barcelona she has to conceal the presence of Don Álvaro from her husband. In her long speech to Porcia she describes her own feelings with great psychological penetration. She is intelligent, perhaps, rather than prudent. She has also considerable will-power, but not quite enough to keep her strong affections in check. She knows what her duty is, she tries to do it, and she fails.

We have already seen how well she understood that when she expressed disdain she took a secret satisfaction from her suitor's advances (I, viii). At first she felt guilty at having betrayed Don Álvaro; she expressed this guilt when she recovered from her first swoon by pleading that he should not kill her. Later on she was to feel equally, perhaps even more, guilty about Don Juan. In her first scene with Don Álvaro she could express only her grief at having lost him, but in the second one we see her resolution to be a good wife to Don Juan and to fight back her earlier, her first love. Grief, she tells us, causes tears; honour dries them (I, xxii). Don Álvaro had some justification for his assumption that he could still awaken again her old affections. Despite her intentions she gave him some hope even after she had married Don Juan.

In the first scene of the second act she poses while her husband attempts to paint her portrait; she talks affectionately to him, and, when he has left her, she is glad that she had been able to repress the tears that her love had hitherto made her shed. Her composure is threatened by Don Álvaro's intrusion. She tells him to go, but he stays on. She tells him of her constancy, her love for her husband, her honour. He glosses some lines on mutability by Luis

Vélez de Guevara;⁶ she replies, reminding him of the changed situation he refuses to admit. She mentions 'mi honor, mi altivez, mi brío' (II, iv) and asks him to respect these qualities in her as he did before. Don Juan's return interrupts the conversation; she must now deceive her husband in order to facilitate Don Álvaro's escape.

At the Carnival she refuses to dance with the disguised Don Álvaro until her husband makes her do so. While they dance she tells him to go away. Again he disobeys her. Generally during the second act Serafina appears firmer in her intentions than she seemed to be in the earlier scenes. There is, however, a slightly hysterical tone in the emphasis which she lays on her declarations of her honour as a married woman. Her will has not completely won the battle against her affections.

An accident allows Don Álvaro to carry Serafina off. In the boat she weeps ceaselessly, and in Belflor she does nothing but grieve and weep. Her tears now have another source; before she wept at the loss of Don Álvaro; now she weeps at her own dishonour. She refuses to encourage her lover. When they talk together she begins with a long rhetorical question: can he really think that honour means so little to her that she can throw it aside merely because he has carried her bodily away from her husband? He replies with the excuse: 'Amor en lo temerario vive.' She rejects such an excuse, as it deserves, and in her passionate grief calls him: 'ingrato,...aleve...fiero,/traidor, injusto, tirano' (III, iv). Then she pulls herself together. All is lost. What has happened cannot be mended. She suspects that Don Juan is everywhere. She cannot accept Don Álvaro. Don Juan will overtake and find them soon. Her only escape can be into a convent. Her lover stops her. He cannot hear of such a plan. A casual shot coincides with his declaration that he would rather a thunderbolt slew him. The omen of his death is obvious.

Then we see Serafina's tears once more, her sleep and awakening outside the house. She has had a bad dream: that her husband was killing her. Don Álvaro comes up to comfort her and asks what causes her distress. She replies:

> Haber
> visto entre sueños la imagen
> de mi muerte. Nunca fueron
> tus brazos más agradables.   (III, xxv)

For a moment only, when she woke up from her terrifying dream, her instinctive love for Don Álvaro overcame her duty to her husband. Unfortunately Don Juan was nearby, with his pistols loaded. He fired at her, and she died calling on Heaven to help her and making a kind of confession of her guilt to her father, Don Pedro:

> Llegar, infelice padre,
> muerta a tus brazos, porque
> no tengas tú que matarme. (III, xxvi)

So ends Serafina, overcome by her instinctive love after a long, difficult struggle against it. Calderón depicted her with sympathy; she is as innocent as Doña Mencía in *El médico*, except for the small but fatal error that she made just before her death. Her fall was prepared by her earlier struggle and in the analysis of her own feelings that she made to Porcia. According to the code of honour she was an innocent victim; but her strong feelings and her final – if accidental – imprudence helped to bring on the tragedy. We can see, perhaps, that Bances's description of her part was a little too simple.

Fire and water are important in the imagery and in the action of the play. Fire from Don Juan's pistols kills Don Álvaro and Serafina. Don Álvaro carries Serafina over the water to Italy. Don Juan saves Serafina from fire and plunges into water when she is taken away from him. There is no hint that water cleanses or that fire purifies. Both elements are dangerous in themselves, dangerous to the persons in the play and represent dangerous feelings in the human heart.

An unexpected salvo from ships in port interrupts, at the beginning of the play, the courtly talk of Don Juan, Porcia, Don Luis and Serafina. It announces the arrival of the Prince, with whom is Don Álvaro (I, v). At the end of the first act another salvo interrupts Don Álvaro's pleas that Serafina should return to his love:

Don Álvaro. Serás mía.
Serafina. ¿Yo ser tuya?
Un rayo... ¡Válgame el cielo!
(*Disparan dentro.*)
Don Álvaro. ¡Ay de mí! ¡Cuánto me asusta
que el aire ejecute el trueno,
cuando tú el rayo pronuncias! (I, xxii)

In the last act a casual shot, off-stage, from Porcia's gun interrupts another conversation of the same couple:

Don Álvaro. Suspende el labio.
No prosigas: que primero
que yo viva sin ti, un rayo
me mate... ¡Válgame el cielo!
(*Disparan dentro un arcabuz.*)
Serafina. ¡Ay de mí!, que ya este acaso,
segunda vez sucedido,
mi muerte está pronunciando.
Don Álvaro. No; no temas; que yo, aunque
me asusto, no me acobardo. (III, v

Finally Don Juan fires on them both. The second salvo and Porcia's shot are both warnings to the lovers and a hint to the audience about how the play will end. So also, perhaps, is the fire from which Don Juan rescues Serafina. The coincidences of the mentions of thunderbolts and death forge a link with the destruction brought about by fires. Destructive fire appears also in the images used in speeches by the Prince, by Don Juan, by Serafina and by Don Álvaro.

All her lovers associate Serafina with fire. Don Juan describes her as a

> beldad que compuesta está
> de sol, aire, luz y fuego. (II, i)

For the Prince she was a 'monstruosa exhalación de fuego y nieve' (II, xi), and his love for her was in his breast 'aquel incendio pasado' (III, viii). Don Álvaro recalls how, in the old days:

> fuiste girasol, que al vivo
> rayo de amor abrasado
> enamoraste sus visos. (II, iv)

We must not regard these images as a part of the conventional language of seventeenth-century lovers; they fit too precisely into the general symbolism of the play.

Fire represents also the avenger of outraged honour and appears specially associated with Don Juan. Don Álvaro describes how his enemy rescues Serafina from the conflagration in Don Diego de Cardona's pavilion:

> Entre pavesas y llamas
> (monstruo de fuego, humo y polvo)
> un caballero a una dama
> saca en los brazos. (II, xvii)

And when Don Juan paints his own emotions in his picture of Hercules and Dejanira, he adds to it the motto:

> 'Quien tuvo celos primero,
> muera abrasado después.' (III, xv)

Fire consumes Serafina's admirers and herself also; fire burns in Don Juan's jealousy of honour and finally destroys his wife and his enemy.

We are twice told that Serafina was the daughter of the Castellan of St Elmo (I, i; I, xviii). St Elmo's fire (or the corposant) was associated with storms at sea. Calderón often uses seriously such plays upon words or folk etymologies of proper names in order to create an allegory or even an isolated symbol.[7] If Serafina's name denotes her innocence, her father's title, deliberately repeated, may imply that her life would be tempestuous and ill-fated. St Elmo's fire presages storms in water. Serafina kindles fire in others, but she in her turn – at least after her abduction – ceaselessly weeps; Don Álvaro tells us:

> Desde el instante
> que desmayada en mis brazos
> pasó del golfo de fuego
> a incendios de agua, trocando
> del un extremo a otro extremo
> dos elementos contrarios,
> no se enjugaron sus ojos. (III, iv)

Before that her tears were shed for the sake of Don Álvaro; now she must weep for her own misfortunes. Water, then, comes to be associated with her old love and with her lost reputation. Don Álvaro's actions are particularly associated with water: water nearly caused his death when his affair promised well; he crossed the water to persuade Serafina to return to him; he intrudes into Don Juan's house disguised as a sailor; in that disguise he carries her away from Barcelona. Apparently slight references in the dialogue strengthen these associations. Serafina tells Porcia how she gave her heart to Don Álvaro:

> una noche que yo acaso
> estaba tomando el fresco
> a una reja que caía
> sobre el mar, pudo encubierto
> llegar a hablarme. (I, viii)

And when she firmly rejected his advances:

> el trato, el gusto, el cariño
> me han trocado de manera,
> que robusta encina, fijo
> escollo será más fácil
> a los embates continuos
> del mar, o a los destemplados
> soplos del ábrego frío
> moverse, que mi fineza,
> al contrastarse mi brío
> todo el mar lágrimas hecho,
> todo el aire hecho suspiros. (II, iv)

And before the abduction, Don Álvaro, having been rejected, thinks of leaving by sea:

> porque vayan
> por agua y viento mis dichas
> a buscar sus esperanzas. (II, xvi)

Water, then, stands for the unhappiness of Serafina and its causes: her former lover, his importunity and his rashness.

Fire and water are literally and symbolically present in the scene of the abduction:

> ¡Cielos! Tanta
> la violencia es del incendio,
> que en un instante a ser pasa
> volcán del mar. (II, xvii)

We have seen how Serafina is saved from the 'gulf of fire' to be plunged into the 'conflagration of water'. Don Juan saved her from fire to lose her on the water. We can then see that he implicitly mentions past, present and future when he cries out:

> Espera, ladrón pirata
> destos piélagos; que yo
> contra el fuego y contra el agua
> lidiaré igualmente. Dadme
> ¡cielos! o muerte o venganza. (II, xx)

Metaphors of fire and water are an integral part of the action of the play. Calderón's technique is more elaborate than some critics imagine.

Play is also made with disguises, both physical and metaphorical. At the Carnival Don Álvaro, already disguised as a sailor, puts on a mask and a party cloak. Don Juan takes vengeance on him disguised as a painter. We have seen how Serafina described the disguise of disdain that hides a kind of favour:

> rebozados los favores
> a sombra de los desprecios
> . . .
> fue el desdén el embozado
> y el favor el descubierto. (I, viii)

Such observations parallel those of Don Álvaro:

> y una palabra en amor
> tanto los sentidos muda
> que aunque es una en quien la dice,
> siempre es otra en quien la escucha. (I, xxii)

The quatrains that form the skeleton of the dialogue between Don Álvaro and Serafina in Don Juan's house imply a disguise that Time has put on to the ruins of a building:

> Escollo armado de hiedra,
> yo te conocí edificio,
> ejemplo de lo que acaba
> la carrera de los siglos.
> De lo que fuiste primero
> estás tan desconocido,
> que de ti mismo olvidado
> no te acuerdas de ti mismo.[8]

Serafina conceals Don Álvaro's presence from her husband by offering to show him the dress she will wear at the Carnival, though she had bought it for a different reason (II, vi). Don Álvaro and Serafina take advantage of a dance lyric heard by everybody present to conceal their conversation. Porcia conceals her conversation with the Prince by the pretence that she is singing to herself. Serafina hides Don Álvaro from Don Juan; Don Álvaro hides Serafina from Porcia; Porcia hides the Prince from Don Álvaro; the Prince hides Don Juan from Serafina; Don Álvaro hides from Don Luis the fact that he has dishonoured Don Juan by swearing to take vengeance on Don Juan's enemy. The Prince hides from everyone except Serafina herself and his man Celio his love for her. What are we to make of all this?

The play echoes the confusion of life. Confusions are caused by deliberate deceptions, by judging life by false standards, by the effects of Time, which turns fine buildings into ivy-clad rocks. So there are purposeful deceptions, hidden passions that break out at unexpected moments, deep changes that lie under apparently placid surfaces. Don Álvaro manages to deceive his father, but he deceives himself when he takes a rock to be the building it once was. Serafina thinks she has vanquished her tears, but she weeps through the last act. Don Juan never thought the rock could be other than a rock, until it was too late. Even Juanete thinks the masked man is a friar until he finds out that he is a sailor. Don Juan, Don Álvaro and Serafina commit fatal mistakes; Porcia and the Prince contrive by prudence to stop the consequences of such errors as they have made.

The minor characters deserve a word or two. We have noticed that Celio corrected, or added to, two important speeches by the Prince; he has little other interest. Fabio and Julia are servants; Don Álvaro and Porcia talk to them, but they add nothing to the total effect. Flora is more prominent. She helps Don Álvaro to escape from Don Juan's house – in other words she helps Serafina to deceive her husband – and she perishes in the fire from which Don Juan rescues Serafina. Serafina does not know of Flora's death; indeed she thinks that Flora will still be alive and that through Flora Don Juan will be aware of all that passed between her and Don Álvaro. This has its importance in the plot, because therefore Serafina remains terrified of Don Juan, and her fear makes her see his vengeance as inevitable, unless she can become a nun. Flora's posthumous life helps to preserve Serafina's innocence.

Belardo is a comic figure. Everyone expects him to give his help in the difficulties that surround them. He comments wryly on the situation and the little that he gains for his trouble.[9] The humour in his part is good, if not very original. When his comments are not purely personal they show that at least one man knows exactly the relations of those who play the principal parts in the play:

> Sólo eso faltaba ahora;
> que estuviese enamorado
> el amante de la hermana,
> de la dama del hermano.   (III, xi)

Here is the master of the situation, who knows almost everybody's secrets and keeps the key of the summer-house. He tells the Prince and Serafina when they are free to leave it without fear of discovery; he locks Don Juan into it for (whose?) greater safety. He knows also how to smoothe away the difficulties that cause Porcia's jealousy and to place Serafina so that Don Juan can paint her portrait. He does what he can in the difficulties that face him. His part is small, but crucial in the development of the action.[10]

Juanete stands out more prominently than any of the other servants do. He tries to show off by telling (or trying to tell) funny stories. He finds Don Álvaro in his master's house and tells him of it. He follows the masked man whom he had seen with Serafina at the Carnival and finds he is a sailor. He watches also her abduction by the sailor and tells his master that too. But his discoveries are always incomplete. He touches Don Álvaro's beard but cannot catch hold of it. He identifies the masked man with the sailor, but he fails to observe that the sailor is Don Álvaro in disguise. So his discoveries never affect the action of the play. He is a commentator, not an agent.

His comments take the form of humorous tales that reflect situations in the play. They do not always amuse their hearers. 'Deja locuras' says Porcia on hearing one (I, iii); Don Juan calls another a 'locura' and exclaims: '¡Oh, qué tema tan cansado!' after it is told (II, ii). The stories are sometimes so inopportune that he has to begin one three times before he can finish it. For Juanete is what his name means – a bunion – someone who may annoy everybody present. His master thinks he is a faithful but tiresome servant.

In themselves the tales are well told, moderately funny. They help to lighten the darkness of the play in which passion, treachery, violence and murder threaten us so closely. But this is not their sole function. From time to time Juanete's stories accentuate the folly, vanity or fortune of the characters that surround him. The relation of tales to plot is not always precise, but they emphasise details we might otherwise pass over, details that are less trivial than at first they appear. Here is a brief summary of them and an attempt to relate them to the whole play.

1. Soldiers are to be billeted in a village. One peasant asks for two

soldiers. The neighbours enquire why he wants two, if no one else wants any. He replies that he does so because he will be doubly glad to see them go. Juanete here mocks the ostentatious hospitality of Don Luis, who has just said:

> Mi contento
> es festejar a quien pasa. (I, ii)

Hospitality is a noble virtue, but Don Luis exaggerates it without seeing that his generosity may cause difficulties to the guests he seeks to please. Had he not insisted that Don Juan should stay longer in his house, Serafina would not have seen Don Álvaro again, nor would she have met the Prince.

2. A man is given cold chicken and warm wine at a meal. He puts the chicken into the wine to see whether the chicken will cool the wine or the wine warm the chicken (I, iii). Juanete explains the moral of his anecdote:

> Lo mismo me ha sucedido
> en la boda, pues me han dado
> moza novia y desposado
> no mozo: con que habrá sido
> fuerza juntarlos [al] fiel,
> porque él con ella doncella,
> o él la refresque a ella,
> o ella le caliente a él. (I, iii)

He hints at the imprudence of the marriage of a middle-aged man to a young wife.

3. A poor woman dies. A coach bears her corpse to the funeral. The coach makes her so happy that she comes to life and orders the coachman to drive her along the Prado, 'que después me enterrarán'. Juanete supposes that Serafina is happy because she will travel by coach; in fact she is disconsolate because she grieves over the supposed death of Don Álvaro. (This story may also be intended as a vague hint of the final catastrophe.) When Juanete has done Don Luis asks:

> ¿A quién tu lengua perdona
> con aquesos cuentecillos? (I, iii)

4. One morning a man wakes up to find himself deaf. He cannot hear what the others say to him, so he thinks that everyone else is talking in too low a voice. Juanete tells the tale just after Don Juan has attributed the failure of his attempt to portray Serafina to her great beauty rather than to his own lack of skill. The impertinent servant applies this anecdote to his master:

> Tú así
> presumes que no está en ti

> la culpa; y aunque te pese,
> es tuya, y no la conoces,
> pues das, sordo, en la locura
> de no entender la hermosura
> que el mundo la dice a voces.   (II, ii)

5. Serafina observes that women know more about their husbands than husbands know about themselves. Juanete then tells a story of how an angry priest calls a parishioner a cuckold; the man's wife thereupon accuses the priest of betraying the secrets of the confessional. The word *cornudo* is not directly pronounced; Juanete uses a euphemism that involves an ingenious play upon words:

> que empezando en *cor*-tesano
> viene a acabar en des-*nudo*.   (II, ii)

Don Juan may be considered a courtier in the early part of the play: when it ends he is – if not naked – dressed as a poverty-stricken painter. The joke concerns a man who is called a cuckold as he might have been called a rogue or a rascal, but who really is a cuckold. In the last act Don Juan considers himself a cuckold, though in fact he is not one, and no one reproaches him with that insulting word.

6. Juanete tries three times to tell the story about the three, four or five children in Barcelona and the cat. Each time either other events interrupt him or he is ordered to keep quiet (I, iii; I, xii; II, ii). Finally he is able to tell it to the Prince (III, xxi) who gives him a chain as a reward. The anecdote would have had no point had Juanete told it on the occasions when he started to tell it. The repetitions and interruptions are theatrical jokes, but they also let us see how a long wait is sometimes necessary to obtain even a trivial objective. Don Álvaro waits in vain for Serafina to return his love; Don Juan waits to avenge his honour; Juanete waits... to tell rather a stupid little story. When it is told it contrasts him with Belardo and shows the Prince's generosity to those who wait. The delay in telling the tale is more important than the tale itself.

Such are some of the elements in this complex play about murder and marriage. The main plot and sub-plot are deliberately contrasted. Porcia and the Prince talk to music at Belflor; the conversation of Don Álvaro and Serafina follows the music at the Carnival. Serafina asks the Prince to leave, and he goes; she asks Don Álvaro to leave, and he stays on. The world of impulse, temerity and despair is counterbalanced by another of caution and prudence. The threads are drawn together at the beginning and at the end, separated in the middle. Over and through the incidents that occur there are signs of catastrophe that are wrongly interpreted, ignored or defied: swoons, salvoes, shots, even funny stories. Emotions are depicted in terms of fire and water. Men disguise themselves and their feelings. The tragedy is shown in outward and visible signs of the inner mistakes, conflicts and presentiments of the different persons. Sometimes they seem to be impelled by exterior forces: Serafina, victim of circumstances; Don Álvaro, a prisoner of his unreflecting despair; Don Juan, brave, overconfident and blind. But they have themselves brought about their own powerlessness. Don Juan cannot escape from the summer-house because he allowed the Prince to lead him to it and Belardo to lock him up in it. If Serafina had been firmer in her first scene with Don Álvaro, if Don Álvaro had learned the difference between past and present, if Don Juan had noticed Don Álvaro's attentions to Serafina... And even in lesser matters too. If Don Luis had been less ostentatiously hospitable, if Don Pedro had waited longer before marrying off his daughter, if the Prince had checked his desire to have a portrait painted of Serafina... the play would not have ended in tragedy. Calderón shows us a world in which men are responsible for their actions and are too easily deceived. By the signs and portents as they occur, by the dramatic consistencies of images and meanings, he hints at the existence of a Power who controls all and who devises a coherent pattern from the mistakes, as well as from the harmonies, of the human comedy. *El pintor de su deshonra* is not perhaps one of Calderón's most famous plays; it deserves more study than it has so far received.

NOTE

This essay appeared in Spanish in *Ábaco*, III (1970), 49–85. The English original was lost, so I have translated the Spanish text for this volume. I wrote the first version of the essay in the early fifties. At that time I had not seen B. W. Wardropper's 'The unconscious mind in Calderón's *El pintor de su deshonra*', published in the *Hispanic Review*, XVIII (1950), 285–301. Professor A. A. Parker saw the early draft of my essay, and the version now published owes something to his criticism. Since then he has published an article entitled 'Towards a definition of Calderonian tragedy' in the *Bulletin of Hispanic Studies*, XXIX (1962), 222–37, which contains pertinent remarks about this play. The following year A. I. Watson published in the same journal '*El pintor de su deshonra* and the neo-Aristotelian theory of tragedy', reprinted in B. W. Wardropper's *Critical essays on the theatre of Calderón* (New York, 1965), pp. 203–23. Two later studies by A. K. G. Paterson are also interesting: 'The comic and tragic melancholy of Juan Roca: a study of Calderón's *El pintor de su deshonra*', *Forum for Modern Language Studies*, V (1969), 244–61; 'Juan

Roca's northern ancestry: a study of art theory in Calderón's *El pintor de su deshonra*', *Forum for Modern Language Studies*, VII (1971), 195–210. I recommend these articles to those interested in the interpretation of this magnificent play. I have not revised my essay to take account of their observations.

6
The cloak and sword plays

The comedies of Calderón, by which I mean the plays that set out above all to entertain, enjoy less popularity now among critics than they did a century ago. The religious and philosophical plays share the first place with *El alcalde de Zalamea*; the tragedies of honour and jealousy are often mentioned, sometimes with approval; there are signs that the mythological theatre may become a minority cult – but the cloak and sword plays and palace plays of Calderón are less appreciated than similar plays by Lope and Tirso, in which the human interest is more obvious. My purpose is not to claim that *La dama duende* is as important as *La vida es sueño* or that Calderón's palace plays are better than Tirso's; I merely want to try to find out what claim these plays of his have on our attention. The text-books point out that their action is rapid and complicated, their plots ingenious, their diction relatively free from gongorism, but their characterisation is stereotyped and monotonous. This kind of praise could hardly convince the early nineteenth-century critic who complained: 'However astonishing may be the variety of the situations which he [Calderón] has created out of this uniformity of plan, yet they cannot long satisfy a cultivated taste which requires a nobler kind of variety.'[1] Nevertheless many men of letters from Calderón's time until our own have at least been entertained by them: Bances Candamo, Guerra, Luzán, Schack, Hartzenbusch, Menéndez y Pelayo, Valbuena Prat. Is there any justification for reversing their judgement?

In this chapter I mean to confine myself to the cloak and sword plays and to leave the palace plays on one side. Cloak and sword plays are easier to recognise than to define. In Calderón's hands they are about the adventures of two (or more) pairs of lovers, of high, but not the highest, rank, who have to overcome material and other difficulties before they are able to marry. The difficulties arise from many causes: mistakes in identity, fortuitous but unfortunate circumstances, jealousy, the laws of honour and so forth. Eventually the crooked is made straight and the plays end with a couple of happy marriages. The plots are intricate; the action is rapid.

Menéndez y Pelayo wrote of these plays: 'Ciertamente que sería vano buscar en ellas el pensamiento sublime de *La vida es sueño*.'[2] Perhaps the task is not so vain as this illustrious critic asserted. For in *La vida es sueño* we find a certain similarity of subject matter; there is confusion and difficulty there too. We have already seen how, in that play, the characters who put their trust in the confusions of the world are thwarted, but those who recognise them and rely on virtuous principles overcome their difficulties. May not something of the same kind occur in these plays? At least the theme of confusion (although it is not exactly of the same kind) is common to the two; the solution may also be similar. The Rosaura–Estrella sub-plot resembles incidents in some of these plays and I have shown that it has a deeper meaning in *La vida es sueño* than appears at first sight. In other plays Calderón shows himself a Christian and there is evidence of consistency of theme and treatment in all his theatre. I find it hard to assume that he wrote some plays in which he demonstrates the workings of God's providence, and others in which chance was supreme.

Nevertheless, as we shall see, several critics have held this opinion. Professor Atkinson has doubted whether the plays could have any justification but that of amusing 'an idle moment in their day'.[3] An earlier article by the same author makes more specific objections.[4] In this he gives a general account of the plays and an analysis of one of them: *No hay burlas con el amor*. He praises Calderón for his dexterity, allows that the play is readable, but also makes the following criticisms. Such plays, he says, reached maturity at a time 'when in literature men turned to *genres* which called rather for skill in manipulating old formulae than for inspiration drawn directly from the fulness of life'. This reminds me of Menéndez y Pelayo's strictures on Calderón. But even if Calderón's plays are less rich and varied in their subject matter than Lope's, we need not assume that therefore Calderón is not so great a dramatist. Invention is not synonymous with greatness; had Calderón done nothing but remake plays by his predecessors, there seems to me to be no reason for saying that he was, for that reason only, their inferior. Professor Atkinson continues: 'Such was the comedy of intrigue, admirably suited to entertain an artificial age with pictures of a society concerned only with courtly mannerisms and a hollow philosophy.' The condemnation is rather too severe. The 'courtly mannerisms' may represent something more than mere etiquette; the philosophy may be less hollow than appears at first sight. Professor Atkinson does not tell us directly what the philosophy was, but two sentences provide us with a clue: 'The chief role falls inevitably to chance' and 'we know that, whatever shabby tricks fortune may play, Chance, the only destiny that shapes their ends [the characters' ends], will bring all things right at last'. It would be surprising if the author of *La vida es sueño* had adopted such an inadequate view of life, even in a frivolous genre.

A somewhat similar view was brought forward last century by E. J.

Hasell. She, however, allowed that some notion of order was present in all the confusion wrought by coincidence. She wrote: 'Certainly in them circumstances seem stronger than man – design fails where accident succeeds: strong purpose comes to nothing, and some sudden incident precipitates the resolve which will shape the man's whole future course. An unseen Hand is divined throughout them (scarcely felt), moulding into form

> Our ends,
> Rough-hew them as we may.'[5]

Some kind of pattern is apparent behind the stage tangle. The question is whether this pattern is intended to appear purely as the work of chance (as Professor Atkinson claims) or whether order is dependent on the conduct of the characters themselves.

Superficially there is order in their construction. Many critics, including even the adverse neoclassics, praised the skill with which the plot is developed and the complications are finally disentangled. If the first impression is that of confusion, the second is that the confusion is well controlled. Unless we follow the plays with attention we shall be lost in their intricacies; but when they are read with care there is no difficulty in threading the labyrinth. The persons on the stage are in confusion, but we know the secret all the time; Calderón did not play the modern trick of mystifying the audience too. We are always able to see that mistakes are mistakes. The preparation and entanglement are put forward with an ability that is beyond all praise. The opening is often striking and, as we go on reading, each turn and accident of the intrigue surprises us still more. There are no irrelevant episodes; every detail prepares us for some later twist of circumstances: if Eugenia gives Clara her handkerchief, Félix mistakes her identity (*Guárdate del agua mansa*); a servant puts out the important papers so that he shall remember to pack them, he forgets them and his master has to return to Madrid, where he surprises the 'goblin lady' in his room. Each scene helps the action forward; no detail is idle. There is extraordinary technical dexterity.[6] Is there anything more? The plays deal with love and honour; perhaps an examination of Calderón's treatment of these subjects in these plays will help us to answer this question.

'La pasión dominante en las comedias de capa y espada, y sin la cual no existirían, es el amor.'[7] Love, which is in fact one of the compelling forces in these plays, is usually more than just physical passion. When love that is merely sensual is depicted Calderón contrasts it with love that is founded on other qualities. If a gallant remarks of his lady:

> que no tiene una mujer
> más que hacer que ser hermosa
> (Félix in *¿Cuál es mayor perfección?*, 1622a)[8]

because his lady is beautiful but stupid, her sister is admired for displaying

> en las burlas el buen gusto;
> en las veras la cordura;
> en lo que cuenta, el donaire;
> en lo que dice, el cariño;
> en lo que viste, el aliño;
> y en todo, en fin, el buen aire.
>
> (Leonor, *ibid.* 1621b–1622a)

In another play the lover says:

> ¡En mi vida vi mujer
> de igual ingenio, mezclando
> las licencias del buen gusto
> con las leyes del recato!
>
> (Juan in *Los empeños de un acaso*, 1050b)

And in yet another the lady admits that her lover enjoys her favour:

> por ilustre y por discreto,
> por valiente y por galán.
>
> (Leonor in *Con quien vengo, vengo*, 1128a)

In the same play Calderón expresses the idea that underlies all the lovers' relations in these plays:

> quien no tiene amor…
> no tiene entendimiento (Octavio, 1137b)

and

> quien
> ama sin entendimiento,
> sonar hace el instrumento,
> pero no que suene bien. (Octavio, 1138b)

Love, then, for Calderón, should be something that includes more than physical attraction; it is a means by which the physical may be subordinated to the more discerning part of man's nature. He does not often show us mere physical passion, although in one play (*No hay cosa como callar*) a man takes advantage of a woman's helplessness; yet he is forced to right the wrong that he does her. The play in which this scene occurs is powerful, but the incident is an exception among the plays of this genre. More representative is the attitude of Carlos in *No siempre lo peor es cierto*:

> que es hombre bajo, que es necio,
> es vil, es ruin, es infame
> el que solamente atento
> a lo irracional del gusto
> y a lo bruto del deseo,
> viendo perdido lo más,
> se contenta con lo menos.[9] (1455a)

Sometimes the action depends on the fact that one of the characters claims to be indifferent to love. A woman scorns men, or a man thinks only of his enjoyment. In these circumstances we find that the changes of fortune in the play correspond in some degree to the defects of those who take part in it. When a man is told:

> Como tú nunca has sabido
> qué es estar enamorado;
> como siempre has estimado
> la libertad que has tenido
> tanto, que a los dulces nombres
> de amor, fueron tus placeres
> burlarte de las mujeres
> y reírte de los hombres
>
> (Moscatel in *No hay burlas con el amor*, 494b)

we are not surprised when he finds he cannot maintain this attitude, and finally:

> En fin, el hombre más libre,
> de las burlas de amor sale
> herido, cojo y casado,
> que es el mayor de sus males   (*Ibid.* 524b–525a)

because he has had to marry a presumptuous and ridiculous woman. Something of the same kind occurs with Ángela in *Fuego de Dios en el querer bien* and with Antonio in *¿Cuál es mayor perfección?* The situation is often repeated: Don Félix in *Guárdate del agua mansa* is carefree and selfish:

> aunque ellas son bellas,
> me quiero a mí más que a ellas;   (1293b)

but he has as many difficulties to overcome as have the others; in *Mañanas de abril y mayo* Don Hipólito thinks that he can afford to carry on affairs with two women at once, for, he says:

> Yo tengo notable estrella
> con mujeres,   (581a)

but both women publicly humiliate him and his remark is quoted back at him ironically.

Of the group of plays in which a man or woman claims either to be indifferent to love or always to be successful, the most brilliant are *Mañanas de abril y mayo* and *No hay burlas con el amor*. Of the former an early editor wrote that it contained: 'dos amantes virtuosos y poseídos de una pasión verdadera. Al momento su [Calderón's] imaginación le sugeriría la idea de otros dos enamorados al uso, que se correspondieran por vanidad y cuyo mayor recreo fuese el de engañarse ... Fue un rasgo de genio hacer que las locuras del pisaverde y su querida ocasionasen mil penas a los verdaderos amantes.'[10] Such a presentation cannot be described as exemplifying the blind work of chance. In *No hay burlas con el amor* there is a continual battledore and shuttlecock of repartee between the characters. An inexperienced reader of Calderón might well look at this as an artificial kind of symmetry imposed by the author; nevertheless this apparently capricious device drives home the lesson of the play. At the opening Alonso threatens to dismiss his servant Moscatel because he is in love; later Moscatel threatens to find another master because Alonso is now in love. Early in the play Beatriz had priggishly reproached Leonor for her clandestine love affair; later Leonor uses the same terms when she surprises her sister in hers. Alonso makes Juan accompany him to court Beatriz by using similar arguments to those with which Juan had induced Alonso to go with him when he (Juan) was courting Leonor. Alonso and Beatriz had scorned love, whereas Juan falsely believed that Leonor was unfaithful to him. The parallelism of the situation underlines the false confidence of those who thought that their hearts could not be touched and the credulity of a man who too readily believed in appearances. In these plays at least success comes most readily to those that deserve it.

The confusion of the world is presented in these plays. Men are deceived by their senses; they believe too readily in appearances. Love may guide their actions to some extent, but that passion alone, however pure or comprehending it may be, can only regulate actions involving the loved one. It cannot tell a man how to behave to his rival, his lady's father or his own friends when they come to him because they are in difficulties or distress. If the polite usages of society are sufficient for ordinary social intercourse, something more is needed when passions conflict. In these circumstances the code of honour provided the required guide. Love and honour dictate the behaviour of the characters, but these qualities alone can help only the man who knows the truth about the situation in which he finds himself. After he has found out the true aspect that lies behind the apparent situation he must not only know how to act; he must also know when to act and how to choose what is right if several courses of action lie open to him. Besides love and honour, caution and prudence are necessary for right action. The nature of the code of honour, its essential violence, could easily bring disaster if men were carried away by impulse; rashness or a too hastily formed judgement might easily make a man of honour into a murderer. Just as a magistrate, though he may know what sentence he should impose for a given crime, must be certain that the crime has been committed and that the man in the dock is guilty before he can pass it, so the man of honour must make sure that his honour is in fact compromised and by whom, before he acts according to the rigorous prescriptions of the code. We have therefore to take into account both the nature of the code of honour that governs the moral world of the cloak and sword plays, and the degree of prudence with which it is acted upon in each particular case.

The plays represent the working out of a moral code. The phrase 'soy quien soy' is not repeated for nothing in so many of them; the concept of honour regulates all the actions of the gallants. We saw in the last two chapters how the code affected the relations of husband and wife; here we see it operating between man and man, lover and beloved, father and daughter, and brother and sister. We have already noted that the principle of honour involved respect for the pledged word, loyalty to a friend and the protection of those in misfortune. All these topics occur in some of the cloak and sword plays, but the aspect which is most frequent is that of the honour of the parent or guardian which is jeopardised by the conduct of the unmarried woman. Before marriage a woman's conduct affected the honour of her guardian, whereas after marriage his responsibility ceased and the duty devolved upon the husband, whose obligations to himself and society were correspondingly increased. With an unmarried woman the affront could be wiped out by her marriage to her lover, by her entering a convent or, of course, by the killing by the injured man of one or both of the guilty pair. Generally, as has been noticed already, the duel provides the solution when the woman is unmarried and, in these plays, we find only unmarried women: there are no mothers or wives, only ladies and servants. The lover, until his marriage can be arranged, is therefore the enemy of his lady's guardian's honour. Often her brother is the guardian and he may also be some other woman's lover; hence, partly, the involved plots of these plays – friendship, love and honour seem inextricably mixed until the final marriage declaration cuts the knot and the situation is regularised. The jealousy of the gallant was also in some degree caused by honour; he felt that any unfaithfulness, any suspicion of unfaithfulness, was not only an injury to his vanity but a slur on his reputation.

In the fourth chapter we saw the extent to which tragedies of vengeance conflicted with Christian ethics. In the cloak and sword plays there is also a divergence. No Christian of course would object to the principles of loyalty, fidelity, respect for hospitality and parental discipline. The most bigoted puritan could hardly complain of the conduct of Carlos in *No siempre lo peor es cierto* who protected a woman whom he had loved before, but whom he then hated because he thought her unfaithful. Difficulties, however, arise with the duel, which, as Calderón himself observed, had been condemned by the Council of Trent:

> Escríbase luego al Papa
> Paulo Tercero, que hoy

The cloak and sword plays

>   goza la Sede, una carta
>   en que humilde le suplique
>   que esta bárbara tirana
>   ley del duelo, que quedó
>   de gentiles heredada,
>   en mi reinado prohiba
>   en el Concilio que hoy trata
>   celebrar en Trento, siendo,
>   si en este duelo se acaban
>   los duelos de España, éste
>   *el postrer duelo de España.*
>   (Charles V in *El postrer duelo de España*)[11]

Nevertheless Calderón puts duel after duel into these plays and there is hardly another hint that he looked on the custom with much displeasure. Sometimes he even points out that fighting might have good results:

>   Hermano, llega;
>   que dos, que han reñido iguales,
>   desde aquel instante quedan
>   más amigos, pues ya hicieron
>   de su valor experiencia.   (Juan in *La dama duende*, 238b)

Only when you know that a man is brave can you rely on him; there is no way of finding this out that is as good as fighting him yourself! The most extreme case occurs in *Con quien vengo, vengo* – a play that shocked Menéndez y Pelayo and Rubió because of the following 'unnatural' situation. Ursino has to accompany his friend Sancho to the duelling ground; when they arrive there the former finds that his own son is Sancho's opponent. Whereupon he says to him:

>   Caballero, yo no sé
>   lo que decís; y admirarme
>   debo de que me tratéis
>   con respeto semejante.
>   Yo soy un hombre que vengo
>   al lado de quien me trae:
>   no conozco otro en el mundo
>   de quien yo deba acordarme,
>   que estando en esta ocasión,
>   yo nunca conozco a nadie.
>   Haced vos lo que debéis,
>   sin que os turbe ni embarace
>   nada; que yo me holgaré
>   de veros en esta parte
>   cumplir las obligaciones
>   que decís; que en semejante
>   caso un noble caballero
>   debe reñir con su padre.   (1162a)

The son protests, but the father continues inexorably:

> Cuando al lado de otro hombre
> el que es caballero sale,
> no ha de dar medio ninguno,
> porque él para nada es parte.
> Con Don Sancho vengo aquí;
> yo no soy mío este instante;
> bien hecho estará y bien dicho
> cuanto hiciere y cuanto hablare;
> si él riñere, he de reñir;
> haré paces, si hace paces;
> que yo con quien vengo, vengo,
> y aquí no conozco a nadie. (1162b)

The situation is perhaps rather absurd, but the verse is effective and the whole passage revealing. Honour can overcome the love of father to son. And as it can overcome love so also can it direct and control (if only Christianity can abolish) hatred. Your enemy must be attacked only with the sword and you may have to preserve his honour in order to prove to him that you can maintain your own:

> decidle...
> que soy quien soy, y que tenga
> entendido (esto más bajo)
> que sabré guardar mi honor,
> puesto que el ajeno guardo.
> (Luis in *Cada uno para sí*, 1693b)

> jamás con la lengua
> se vengó hombre bien nacido.
> (Félix in *Cada uno para sí*, 1687a)

> tengo por hombre infame
> quien ve a su enemigo en riesgo,
> y a su enemigo no vale.
> (Juan in *Los empeños de un acaso*, 1063a)

Calderón is once more using honour as a means to order. In these plays, as in the tragedies of vengeance, it is used, not as an end in itself, but as a means to an end. He felt that honour was something that could overcome any other feelings and thereby curb undesirable impulses:

> Perdone lo sucedido,
> amor, en esta ocasión,
> que primero es la opinión.
> (Juan in *Mañana será otro día*, 789b)

> Ninguno
> a costa de su honor trata
> sus conveniencias. (Félix in *Cada uno para sí*, 1674a)

There is no need then to justify Calderón's use of a system of conduct which, although it differed from that in which he believed as a Catholic, was superior to an undisputed world of self-seeking, lust and ambition. The code had many defects: it encouraged the secret vengeance, the duel and hence lawlessness in the purely social sense of the word; it tolerated some degree of deception, eavesdropping and lying. It was not Christian in that it allowed of no turning of the other cheek after the first blow had been struck; it was unsocial and unreasonable according to the ideas of the Enlightenment. Calderón used it because it was a check to man's inner lawlessness, because a man who attempted to live according to its ideals was more of a Christian than was the self-seeker. That he realised what were its limitations we have abundant proof; in almost every play we find laments about the unreasonable demands of honour and its extreme fragility. But he accepts the code for the purpose in hand and lays it before us as an example.

For the purpose of understanding the code of honour in the cloak and sword plays it may conveniently be summarised thus: remember who you are and what is expected of you; guard carefully the reputation of your word; be brave and loyal to your friends; and be prepared to sacrifice every other feeling and interest to these maxims.

The characters in the plays live in a world of unfortunate coincidence and confusion. As lovers they must put their ladies' good first: *antes que todo es mi dama*; as men of honour they have certain rules of conduct to follow. The two claims sometimes conflicted; how should a man choose between them? The lover and the man of honour know the rules of behaviour, but both men are likely to make mistakes through impulse. The lover may be carried away by his passion, he may even mistake the identity of his love; the man of honour may see an affront where none is intended and the more acute his sense of honour the more likely is he to act rashly. How can we avoid such evils? Only by using our wits, by examining every assumption, by never jumping to conclusions, by restraining our impulses, by recognising confusion where it exists and by taking counsel.

The most frequent mistake is to trust too much to the senses and not to realise their limitations. When a character says:

> Nada creo que me digas;
> sólo lo que miro, creo
>   (Félix in *Los empeños de un acaso*, 1048a)

the audience is convinced by his very assertion that he is deceiving himself. In another play a gallant says sarcastically to his love:

> Miente la noche, la reja
> miente también, finalmente

> mienten mis mismos oídos,
> y mis mismos ojos mienten:
> tú sola dices verdad.
>
> (Félix in *También hay duelo en las damas*, 1497b)

But we know from the circumstances that she is justified when she answers:

> Ni lo digas ni lo niegues;
> que todos mienten, y yo
> digo verdad. (Violante, *ibid.*)

We must remember that confusion is everywhere, the truth hard to find. The sun itself deceives us, so does the sky and glass; human beings are weak and inconstant.[12] But truth is eternal and will reveal itself at last:

> la verdad se prueba
> sin más testigos de abono
> que con ser la verdad mesma.
>
> (Ana in *Bien vengas mal, si vienes solo*, 616b)

When we have learned the truth of the situation, the rules of conduct are easy to apply:

> Las grandes dificultades,
> hasta saberse lo son;
> que sabido, todo es fácil.
>
> (Ángela in *La dama duende*, 250a)

In many plays we meet with a contrast between rashness and prudence. The rash man acts on impulse and is deceived by circumstances; the prudent man tries to probe the seeming contradictions that surround him. Lasso de la Vega noticed that this was the moral of *Casa con dos puertas*; there is a contrast between the attitudes of Lisardo and Félix:

> el primero es prudente y siempre discreto, y el segundo más valiente y dominado por sus celos, pero nunca desleal y desmerecedor de su noble amigo... *Casa con dos puertas* es, no sólo un agradabilísimo cuadro que deleita y excita un vivo interés por sus dramáticos y cómicos incidentes, sino una lección que prueba los peligros y disgustos que acarrea un antojo imprudente y una desenvoltura que, aunque no ofenda el decoro, lo arriesga en la opinión de los demás.[13]

In *Dar tiempo al tiempo* Leonor knows what is happening all the time, whereas her lover Juan is impulsive and continually mistaken. In *El maestro de danzar* the impetuosity of Enrique offsets the serenity of Leonor. In *Mañana será otro día* only Beatriz can see clearly; Juan, Elvira, Leonor, Fernando and Luis are in turn misled by events. In that play there is also a significant piece of dialogue which puts the need for caution clearly:

The cloak and sword plays

Capitán.	Mirad, Don Juan: si allí hicierais cualquier acción, disculpada fuera, porque lo improviso no dió lugar de pensarla; pero ya que los sucesos tiempo han dado a vuestras ansias, pensadlo, Don Juan, mejor.
Juan.	La puerta abren: allí aguarda.
Capitán.	Sí haré; mas quiero primero deciros una palabra. Estas cosas, advertid, del honor (la frase es baja, pero no importa) mejor se descosen que se rasgan. No tiréis dellas, sino poco a poco examinadlas. (768b)

Calderón is continually preaching such lessons in these plays. Remember that other men are like you:

> Yo he juzgado siempre
> el ajeno corazón
> por el mío.   (Félix in *Antes que todo es mi dama*, 901a)

Do not trust all to a single throw:

> es grande inconveniente
> querer arriesgarlo todo,
> sin que nada se remedie.
>   (Octavio in *La desdicha de la voz*, 941a)

Sometimes you must fight first, but advice is often as important:

> la primera instancia, en casos
> tan ásperos como éste,
> del acero es; la segunda,
> del consejo.
>   (Antonio in *¿Cuál es mayor perfección?*, 1653b)

Forewarned is forearmed; but cures are possible when prevention has failed:

> Yo no me espanto de nada.
> Mozo he sido, viejo soy:
> todo cabe en la edad larga.
> Escuelas son de la vida
> los años, en cuya sabia
> academia, la experiencia
> lee, en su cátedra sentada,
> aquella lición de que
> se ha de ir hacia la desgracia,

> antes, a que no suceda;
> sucedida, a remediarla.
>
> (Fernando in *También hay duelo en las damas*, 1502a)

More examples could easily be found, but these may suffice. Almost always they arise naturally from the situation in which they occur. I think that there can be no doubt that one of Calderón's chief aims in his cloak and sword plays was to inculcate prudence.

There is, however, one development of Calderón's ideas on this topic that must be noticed. Time makes all things plain, time and prudence in action will remedy many a difficulty. This notion lies behind the titles of *Dar tiempo al tiempo* and *Mañana será otro día*. Of the latter play Lasso de la Vega wrote:

> Falsas experiencias extravian y confunden a los personajes que en ella figuran. Una sola palabra o explicación del engaño que preocupa a todos, aclararía por completo la situación... El dicho vulgar que prueba la conformidad a los reveses que se espera remediar con el tiempo, *mañana será otro día*, es el que da satisfactoria solución al enredo de esta pieza.[14]

On time alone can Carlos and Juan rely in the midst of the almost insuperable difficulties from which they had to extricate themselves in *No siempre lo peor es cierto*:

> [*Juan.*] ¿Qué puedo hacer?
> *Carlos.* Resolveros
> a que el tiempo ha de decirlo,
> obrando en los lances, como
> se vinieren sucedidos.
> *Juan.* Pues si habemos de esperarlos,
> Carlos, no hay que prevenirlos;
> que ellos vendrán... (1469a)

And when time is unpropitious even knowledge is unavailing:

> *Luis.* Pues ¿cuándo el saber es malo?
> *Diego.* Cuando fué el saber sin tiempo.
>
> (*No hay burlas con el amor*, 498a)

The danger of rashness is that time is permitted no opportunity. In Calderón's eyes this was a worse fault than procrastination. Men try to forestall time, but success goes to those who allow it to help them.

Many illustrations of the notions of prudence and of reliance upon time could be taken from the works of political thinkers of Golden-Age Spain. The statement of Philip II (*the Prudent*) that time and he were a match for anyone, is well known. That he was not the only man to hold this opinion may be seen from the instructions that Antonio de Mendoza, the first and greatest viceroy of New Spain, left behind him: 'he told his successor that the secret of good ruling was to do little, and to do that slowly, since most matters lend themselves to that kind of treatment, and in that way alone can one escape from being deceived'.[15]

Calderón was not merely applying to private life a received political maxim. The same idea is also found in mediaeval devotional writers. Thomas à Kempis wrote:

It is an evidence of true wisdom, not to be precipitate in our actions, nor pertinacious and inflexible in our opinions; and it is a part of the same wisdom, not to give hasty credit to every word that is spoken, nor immediately to communicate to others what we have heard, or even what we believe. Always take counsel of a prudent and conscientious man; and choose rather to be guided by the advice of one better than yourself, than to follow the suggestions of your own blind will.[16]

And later on in the same treatise we read:

We generally judge of persons and things, as they either oppose or gratify our private views and inclinations; and, blinded by self-love, we easily lose sight of a right judgement...we are frequently drawn aside from truth and peace, by some apparent good or evil rising without. Many, indeed, secretly seek their own selfishness in everything they do, and perceive it not. These, while the course of things runs smoothly with their own sentiments and wishes, seem to possess all the blessings of peace; but when circumstances take an adverse turn, they are immediately disturbed, and become wretched.[17]

What might be taken as only a maxim of worldly wisdom had before been given the sanction of Christian thinkers. Calderón has used the cloak and sword plays as a means to broadcast the necessity for this kind of prudence. We have again to stress his debt to the heritage of European Christian teaching.

The very titles of some of the plays when put side by side summarise much of what I have already written in this chapter. The world is full of confusion and deception: mock astrologers, sham dancing-masters, goblin ladies, houses with two doors that are hard to guard, voices that betray. In attempting to meet the obligations of a coincidence, although it may appear that things are worse than they are, the worst is not always true. The lover may decide that there is no jesting with love and that his lady comes before all else; the man of honour remembers only that he is with his companion. In all difficulties we must remember that each must fend for himself and that silence is golden; we must give Time time to show us the way out of difficulties, for tomorrow will be another day that may bring their solution.[18]

I hope that I have shown that the plays did not merely amuse an idle moment in their day. They are more than artificial, if amusing, tangles of coincidence that are unravelled in the end. Chance does not reign supreme; nor does it alone shape the destiny of the characters, although it is an ingredient that tests their strength of purpose and subtlety. Other complications arise through mistaken action in the midst of temporary confusions. Rectitude of conduct and wisdom triumph over the confusion, whereas rashness and frivolity are deceived by it, although all may be well at the end. The characters may be divided into two classes: those who know how to act wisely and those who learn how so to act by their mistakes. The former are successful because they deserve success; if the latter finally gain what they seek, they do so as a rule for one of two reasons: either they have awakened from their deception, or the steadfastness and prudence of another has won the battle for them.

In this chapter I have stressed what seems to me to be the most serious aspect of these plays and I have omitted their more amusing features. The surprises, the humour of situation, the badinage and repartee, and the *graciosos* and *criadas*, who are more humorous than many critics lead us to suppose. All this is only one side of the plays; even when Calderón is most light-hearted, he is still serious. The moral lessons underlie *La dama duende* and *No hay burlas con el amor* as well as *No hay cosa como callar* and *No siempre lo peor es cierto*. To bring out adequately the particular moral purpose and value of each play a series of special studies would be necessary. All that I have been able to attempt here is to outline the characteristics of the plays as a group.

To conclude: the cloak and sword plays are worth more than the conventional praise that they generally receive. In them Calderón has given us a kind of allegory of the confusion of the world; a confusion which can be overcome not only by recognising the obligations of a moral code, but also by knowing how and when to apply it.

Engraved frontispiece of *Psalle et sile*, first edition, showing the railing of the choir of Toledo Cathedral

7
A key to Calderón's *Psalle et sile*

TO THE MEMORY OF
IGNACIO GONZÁLEZ LLUBERA

I suppose that very few people today take seriously the ideas about pure poetry that were fashionable twenty or thirty years ago. But a certain hankering after poetry that is self-contained, that is not subordinate to non-literary ends, still persists. The poet who writes because he was ordered to support a given cause or to embroider a given theme still seems likely to be adversely judged; and if his poetry attempts to persuade or to exhort, it is likely to be dismissed as rhetoric. Modern poems often stress a subjective, self-centred attitude to life which the reader is invited to share; a 'finalidad sin fin', to use the useful expression of Carlos Bousoño, such as:

> ¡Concentrarme, concentrarme,
> hasta oirme el centro último,
> el centro que va a mi yo
> más lejano,
> el que me sume en el todo!

Poetry which deals with personal religious (or political) feelings is often admired; but few modern readers of poetry seek out verses which preach at them, in which the poetical effects are carefully disciplined to help the sermon to give its message. The poem *Psalle et sile*, printed in 1662, is perhaps to be regarded as a sermon in verse. I regard it as an important work of literature.

The early editions of it (Madrid, 1662, 1741) are rare. It is included among some other poems by Calderón in the fourth volume of Hartzenbusch's edition of the *Comedias* in the Biblioteca de Autores Españoles and also in the volume of *Poesías inéditas*, edited by F. P. (Felipe Picatoste) in the Biblioteca Universal. These last two editions are inaccurate and unreliable, but the second is better than the first. The best modern edition is that of Valencia, 1936–9, begun by Leopoldo Trénor Palavicino (who died during the Spanish Civil War) and finished by Joaquín de Entrambasaguas. It is a facsimile reprint of the edition of 1662 and contains a useful *Noticia bibliográfica* by Trénor (which includes the transcription of the 1741 preliminaries) and a *Comentario crítico* by Entrambasaguas.

In 1653 Calderón became a 'Capellán de la Capilla de los Reyes Nuevos de Toledo'.¹ We are told that Cardinal Baltasar de Moscoso y Sandoval had seen the words 'Calla y reza' on the choir-screen in Toledo Cathedral and that he 'deseó que estas dos palabras, discernidas con alguna paráfrasis más libre que rigurosa, y comentadas con espíritu, promoviesen la devoción. Encomendó esta obra a don Pedro Calderón.'² This poem then was executed by Calderón at the orders of an ecclesiastical superior in order to excite the devotion of the faithful. It was printed with the title: *Exortación panegírica al silencio. Motivada de su apóstrophe Psalle, et sile* in 1662; but in the later edition the title was changed to: *Discurso Métrico–Ascético, sobre la inscripción Psalle et sile, que está gravada en la verja del Choro de la Santa Iglesia de Toledo*. The second title was popularised by Hartzenbusch's reprint, but it clearly has less authority than the other. Both titles stress the didactic aim of the poem.

Calderón's dedicatory letter to the Cardinal mentions the 'interior unión (que al primer viso opuesta) tiene entre sí Silencio, y Canto', but otherwise it sheds little on the poem. The writer of the approbation, Dr Don Francisco de Aranda y Mazuelo, to whom the Cardinal submitted the poem, praised it highly. He extolled 'el fervor, la elocuencia y discreción de don Pedro Calderón... sugeto bien conocido y estimado en toda Europa por sus numerosos escritos y por sus decentes, morales y celebrados poemas, que deben coronarse con este sagrado y provechoso asunto'. He implies, moreover, that its presumed readers – the Cathedral clergy – are probably not in need of its lessons, but none the less 'lo que no es reprehensión de lo que sucedió, es cuerda prevención a lo que puede suceder'. The Cardinal's biographer Fray Antonio de Jesús María said that Calderón 'compuso unas canciones reales de tal dulzura, que nadie comenzará a leerlas que las deje, y con tal devoción, que nadie las leerá sin mejorarse'. And the editor and the two writers of approbations for the edition of 1741 say much the same: the verses are excellent, the poem is most persuasive to virtue.³ The poem is successful because its intrinsic beauties make its readers take much more trouble about their devotions.

One of the eighteenth-century approbations, that of the Reverendísimo P. Joseph Félix Ibáñez de Mendoza, S. J., praises the poem for its morality, 'tan útil a todos; especialmente a los que, o por ministerio o por institución, se emplean en el sagrado ministerio de las divinas alabanzas en las horas canónicas y canto del coro'. And his fellow censor Dr Don Manuel López Aguirre also assumes that the poet had principally in mind the 'sagrado coro' while he was writing. Although the editor of the 1741 edition, Don Antonio Fernández de Azevedo, remarked that 'en ella habla con todos los fieles',⁴ there can be little doubt that the poem was primarily written for the Cardinal and the various members of the Cathedral clergy. Praises of the Sandoval family – the Cardinal's kith and kin – occur in lines 119–38,

A key to Calderón's *Psalle et sile*

and the marginal references, nearly all in Latin, point to borrowings from the Bible, St Ambrose, the Mozarabic liturgy, el Toledano, Chrysostom, Isidore of Seville and others. Although much of the poem was probably accessible to the ordinary faithful in his own day, the same can hardly be said of those of today. We have to learn or to learn up much that was then common knowledge. Here then is another difficulty for the modern reader: Calderón uses for his material theology, history and legends which no longer form any ordinary part of our culture. Without these references the ordinary reader is lost; with them he is confused. They are not the familiar reading of poetry lovers of today. But they do help to solve the difficulties of the poem. The first of them, to Reg. lib. 3, cap. 7 (i.e. I Kings, vii, 17), shows how a misinterpretation of a verse in the Vulgate supplied Calderón with a poetic relationship between his Cathedral and the Temple of Solomon.[5]

The work is polymetric. Several passages could be lifted out and anthologised, although, as I shall try to show, the poem is a single whole. Here is the scheme:

(a) 44 lines of *romance* – an introduction
(b) a sonnet in praise of the Cathedral
(c) 80 lines of *romance* – religious and historical associations of the Cathedral
(d) 3 *décimas* in praise of the image of the Virgen del Sagrario
(e) 32 lines of *romance* which bring the reader back to the motto
(f) 7 *octavas reales* about silence
(g) 13 nine-line stanzas about sacred music
(h) 48 lines of *romance* in which the seeming contradiction is resolved
(i) 13 *octavas* on the duty of those who sing in cathedral choirs.

Total: 525 lines in five different metres. The *romance* passages are assonanced in *a–a* throughout. This helps to bind together the different portions of the poem.

Perhaps the easiest way into the poem is to start by reading (f) and (g). Each of these passages is reasonably self-contained; the marginal references need not be consulted in order to follow the argument. Silence is extolled; chant is praised. In each passage we see the object of praise brought into relation either with morals (silence) or worship (chant). Silence is the mark of prudence; chant the expression of the Seraphim, David, Deborah, Barach and the Virgin herself. In the *octavas* there is a strange combination of impressive writing and moral commonplace, legend and erudition. One has met many of the thoughts before, but never in such company. The tone varies between the magnificent, and the deliberately direct, statement:

> Es el silencio, un reservado archivo,
> donde la discreción tiene su asiento;
> moderación del ánimo, que altivo
> se arrastrará sin él del pensamiento;
> mañoso ardid del menos discursivo,
> y del más discursivo, entendimiento;
> pues a nadie pesó de haber callado,
> y a muchos les pesó de haber hablado. (201–8)[6]

The shock of the two last lines is a calculated effect – a drop in intensity by means of verbal repetitions and a humble rhyme – after the opening metaphors, the *auto*-like glimpse of the third and fourth lines and the complex expression of the fifth and sixth. Here is a poetry that includes the prosaic as well as the sublime. But probably it did not shock Calderón's contemporaries as it may well shock some readers today. To get anything out of the poem we must conquer our aversion to verse which is unadornedly moral. This *octava* begins by being noble and ends in a deliberate bareness. Those who cannot enjoy this stanza had better avoid *Psalle et sile*.

The other six *octavas* contain similar effects. The dumb eloquence of sighs, the importance of blushes, silence as a symbol of modesty, the inviolability of silent fish from idolatry, the silence of the Universe when Michael fought Lucifer, silence in the *Thebaid* and in the school of Pythagoras ... in all these instances the poet provides a moral lecture, and the topics are stages in a lesson. He paraphrases sacred and secular authorities: Seneca, St Ambrose, Chrysostom, Socrates, Isaiah ... (the thoughts are old, only the combination of them is new) in carefully balanced, highly wrought *octavas*. It is superb rhetoric, poetry subordinated to its message. The whole passage is, in fact, an exploration by the understanding of what silence should mean in the moral life of man. Silence is prudence.

The 117 lines on chant open more engagingly. Here, in the distinction between sacred and profane music, are some effective seventeenth-century images:

> Es la blanda armonía
> (no hablo en común de aquella,
> que, áspid del aire en flores escondido,
> la fragrancia que envía,
> hubo quien dijo della,
> que era un hermoso estiércol del oído)
> de aquélla, sí, que ha sido
> el aura de la nube,
> en quien el humo del incienso sube. (257–65)

The old commonplace (Latet anguis in herba) is given new life by being transported into the air. The dung metaphor is from Chrysostom and very effective.[7] The magnificent end-couplet is Calderón's own working up of a thought in Psalm 141 (140 in the Vulgate). But all these metaphors are arranged so as to give point to the distinction between good sacred music and immoral worldly music rather than to be enjoyed for their own sakes.

The poet continues to explore the nature of sacred music. It is the outcome of inner worship, even of devout tears. Using Isidore's etymologies he goes on to consider the nature of *cántico* ('voz herida'), *himno* ('orar cantando') and psalm (from psaltery). Sacred music derives from Heaven where the Cherubim and Seraphim continually do cry Holy, Holy, Holy; whence it descended to Earth on the night of the first Christmas. After this he considers how music and worship became united, an innovation he attributes to David; even though Deborah and Barach had sung before he did, David brought music into the Temple, as – later – St Ambrose brought it into churches. All this is rather more austere writing than the opening stanza quoted in the last paragraph, but the passage contains some memorable lines, such as:

> al genio
> sigue el afán, que tras su imán le lleva;
> y nadie facilita
> trabajos al ingenio,
> sin que interior espíritu le mueva.   (330–4)

Finally the poet rounds off his praise of sacred music with the recollection that Mary had justified it once and for all when she sang the Magnificat.

It can, I hope, be seen from this bare summary how the poet uses his understanding to try to penetrate the essence of the expression *armonía*. This leads him through etymology and ecclesiastical history to the Virgin herself. Poetry aids an intellectual exploration of the nature of divine music, which ends in a religious mystery.

If the reader of the two sections on silence (f) and on chant (g) is sufficiently attracted by them, he should then turn back to the opening of the poem and begin to read it slowly and carefully. The first six *romance* quatrains offer no particular difficulties. They pose the paradox that is to be resolved: how are silence and singing to be reconciled? The only obscurity can be solved by referring to the Vulgate text of I Kings, vii, 17. The manner of these quatrains recalls that of passages in the *comedias* in which the *persona* states a doubt before he tries to resolve it. The mixture of metres is not the only sign that the author of this poem was a considerable dramatist.

The seventh quatrain beginning 'Ignorante peregrino/soy' is the start of the long digression which lasts from (a) to (e) and ends at line 193. This is the most puzzling part of the poem, and it contains the three *décimas* (d) which are very difficult to understand. In (a) the poet sees himself as a pilgrim who approaches the Cathedral which contains the famous image of the Virgen del Sagrario. He is not a native of Toledo (see also line 116), but he is drawn by devotion to her shrine, also by the sight of the tower among hills and other buildings and by the sound of the bells. The union of devotion (which takes first place), sight and sound in this passage is notable. The senses are subordinated, not obliterated. And when he reaches the Cathedral itself he utters a sonnet, which begins as a formal apostrophe and ends as a prayer.

The first line continues the exclamation which ended the first passage in *romance*:

> saludé el umbral, diciendo:
> '¡Salve, basílica sacra!
> ¡Salve, primer metrópoli de España!' (43-5)

The line is adapted from an address to Toledo by a character in Góngora's play *Las firmezas de Isabela*.[8] Calderón hails the Cathedral for its fame, splendour and glory: a symbol of faith in the midst of persecution. But it is also a storehouse of heavenly treasures, for even its gravestones are holy relics and tombs of saints. As he adores the footprint left by the Blessed Virgin when she gave the chasuble to St Ildephonsus, he adapts the words of one of St Ambrose's prayers: 'May my heart be less hard than was that stone which preserved her footprint.'[9]

The progression from external splendour through religious marvels to the heart of the pilgrim is triumphantly accomplished. And when we begin to read section (c) we find that another progression has also taken place: the pilgrim is now *inside* the Cathedral.

The next passage consists of a long evocation of the poet's reaction to the past wonders worked by God in the setting of the Cathedral of his own day. He begins by comparing his own feelings to the troubles of a storm-tossed ship (the metaphor arises from the double meaning of the word *nave*), because his thoughts of early saints and heroic kings, together with the architectural magnificence, bewilder him. After the evocation of the miracles, saints and conquerors, the storm is seen to have been an illusion:

> En cuya admiración (ya
> lo dije) absorta, y turbada
> la vista corrió tormenta...
> mas no, que todo es bonanza
> en puertos de María. (111-15)

Meanwhile, however, the dead histories have become living memories. He recalls SS. James, Torquatus, Eulogius, Julian, Leocadia and Ildephonsus;

Alfonso VI, his fanatical Queen and St Ferdinand. The allusions can easily be elucidated by referring to such works as Calderón's own *comedia*, *Origen, pérdida y restauración de la Virgen del Sagrario* (written before 1637), Cristóbal Lozano's gossipy *Historia de los Reyes nuevos de Toledo* (first printed in 1666) and the many accounts of St Ildephonsus by the Archpriest of Talavera, Lope de Vega, Góngora, etc. The imaginary storm of admiration is stilled by the thought of the Virgin, and the sign of the calm is seen in a rainbow of stars, formed by the shield of Cardinal Bernardo Sandoval y Rojas, a predecessor and collateral of Cardinal Baltasar de Moscoso y Sandoval, Calderón's own superior.

The lines contained by the two references to the storm (lines 70–110), which contain the record of so many saints and kings, are given unity by a continued metaphor of a tree: St James and Torquatus planted the first roots of the Cathedral on its present site, St Julian and Eulogius fertilised them, St Eugenius made them blossom and his homonym blessed them. The flowers turned to stars – when the Virgin and St Leocadia appeared to Ildephonsus; but only a little later Fortune turned her other face as Roderick the Goth stripped the blossom and leaves from the trunk, till Alfonso VI restored them, and the mosque again became a Christian temple. Then the tree was surrounded by laurels, cedars and palms (other churches arose in Toledo); the city became Europe's second Rome, Spain's primary see. Here again we can see the way in which the metaphors are used to bind the poem together rather than for their own sake.

All through this recollection of the past the poet keeps hinting at the double presence of the Blessed Virgin Mary and her statue in the Cathedral: she appeared there in her own person to St Ildephonsus and left her footprint on the stone; there too is the image of the Virgen del Sagrario, whose origin was mysteriously heavenly, which was miraculously preserved in troublous times and found by Bernardo Galvo after the reconquest. The poet entered the Cathedral by the 'gradas de perdón', and she had once entered the same way.[10] The building itself was dedicated to the mystery of the Assumption. Stars on the Sandoval shield surround the image because she is the Queen of Heaven. The double association has underlain all this section; it is developed strongly and almost paradoxically in the three *décimas* that compose section (d).

These three stanzas are the most difficult in the poem. Calderón addresses the image, the only true image of her, heavenly in origin, brought by angels to Toledo, as she herself once came. The image is addressed in the second person; the Virgin is referred to in the third. The appearance (of the image) guarantees the apparition (of the Virgin). This paradox is exploited in the first two *décimas*, the second of which ends with the words:

> Y si de ángeles traída
> fuiste, ¡o imagen celestial!,
> bien en premio del leal
> afecto que lo creyó,
> lo que tu origen calló
> nos dijo tu original. (153–8)

'And if, O heavenly image, thou wast carried here by angels as a reward to the loyal feelings of Ildephonsus who so believed, thy Original, the Virgin herself, told us what thy origin kept silent.' The stanza ends with the word *original*. Calderón continues:

> Original dije, y fiel
> al nombre me estremecí,
> pues supo dél para ti,
> sin saber para sí dél. (159–62)

The poet's shock is due to his having applied to her the word *original* when he – like nearly every Spaniard of his day – believed in the Immaculate Conception, that she was born free of original sin. She then knew of the original in order to inspire the creation of the image, without knowing of original sin in so far as she herself was concerned. The image, then, deserves Heaven as its canopy and the whole earth as its carpet;[11] so let us venerate the holy footprint.

The next section starts as though the *décimas* were to be continued:

> ¿Qué dijera más? Dijera...
> si a voces no me llamara
> aquella primera duda,
> que tras sus ecos me arrastra. (169–72)

The false start, paralleled so often in the *comedias*, is a recognition by the author that he has seemed to digress. The subject of the poem was the inscription on the choir-screen; but since line 25 he has been praising the more obvious glories and deeper religious mysteries associated with the Cathedral: the miracle that rewarded a Saint's devotion, the unknown origin of the statue and the devotion and heroism of the faithful during the intervening centuries. This, however, has not been an 'ocioso paréntesis': for the paradoxical inscription is part and parcel of the whole which he has dwelt on. In a sense the Virgin directed the graver's hand as he worked, and so the authority of the words is not to be doubted. It would have led to false interpretations had he isolated them from their context – the whole Cathedral, where she had worked such marvels. Even so, the words remain mysterious. He must give distinct eulogies of silence and song before he can go on to reconcile the two. Then starts the passage in *octavas*: 'Es e silencio un reservado archivo', which we have already discussed.

The two hundred lines of introduction have provided the setting of the inscription, its architectural and religious associations. When we have grappled with its difficulties we can see that it provides a lengthy and effective 'composition of place'. The memory here is the primary faculty involved, though there are lyrical outbursts also in the sonnet and *décimas*, and the understanding too has played its part. In fact we see that the poem is really a religious meditation after the Ignatian pattern. We have seen the memory at work; the octaves and *canción* provide material for the understanding, and the will comes into play after the solution of the difficulty has been given.[12]

The two passages in praise of silence and sacred song (f) and (g) stress the religious benefits of both. If silence and song are both so pleasing to God, then a reconciliation between them must be possible. The contradiction can only be apparent. The song of victory succeeded Michael's silent battle with Lucifer; that of the angels broke the silence on the night in which Christ was born. And in the Bible there must be a text which shows 'quanto se aman/silencio y voz'. Calderón might have here brought forward 'the still small voice' that spoke to Elijah, which in the Hebrew reads 'a sound of gentle stillness',[13] but instead a Vulgate reading from the eleventh chapter of St John's Gospel served his purpose: 'Et vocavit Mariam sororem suam, in silentio dicens: Magister adest, et vocat te.' God would have us pray to Him in silence. Silence and song are reconciled in divine worship. Góngora's oxymoron 'hablar callando'[14] becomes religiously significant.

The understanding has done its work. It now remains for the will to know its task. The purely didactic part of the poem (i) now begins, again in *octavas*. The choir must concentrate as they sing and as they wait. Spirit and voice must work in harmony. 'Si cor non orat, in vano lingua laborat.' The meaningful voice is heard in Heaven, not the merely tuneful one. The singer must not be merely a sounding brass or a tinkling cymbal. If we wish God to hear us we must speak to Him with comprehension. And the *octava* which describes the contrast between man's treatment of God and that of an earthly king comes straight from the first meditation of the second week from St Ignatius's *Ejercicios espirituales*.[15] This leads directly to what is perhaps the most remarkable thought in the whole poem:

> No tan de balde sirves que no sea
> logro tuyo lo que uno y otro gana;
> pues el soldado por tu paz pelea,
> y el labrador por tu sustento afana.
> Lo que hay de una tarea a otra tarea,
> mide, y verás: ¡cuánto es más soberana
> la de tratar y conversar al Cielo
> que arder al Sol y tiritar al hielo! (486–93)

Cathedral clergy owe a debt to their fellow men as well as to God. Their labour is supported by the farmer's and the soldier's. They are spared the exertions and privations that these men perform and suffer. To save themselves from reproach they ought to work with similar determination. The plea is put in such a way that it both enhances the privilege of the clergy and ennobles the labours of humbler men. Farmers and soldiers are their collaborators, and together they all form the commonwealth. Calderón testifies to the dignity of labour by pointing to the fact that society itself, of which the canons form the peak, depends ultimately on those who dig and those who risk death to serve it. The passage expresses in religious terms what Juan Crespo vainly tried to explain to Don Álvaro de Ataide.[16] Two more stanzas then elaborate this thought. Calderón finally introduces a more abstruse parallel of silence and chant to the three stages of the mystic way: chant corresponds to purgation, silence to illumination, the two together in harmony to mystic union. Silence and song provide a foretaste of Heaven.

This completes the analysis of the poem. The prologue is set in a particular place whose associations were better known then than they are now to us. Here the memory gathers them together to prepare the understanding for its task. This faculty then enters into the body of the meditation in general terms restricted to no one place. And the directions to the will in the last *octavas* are applicable to all Christians who meet together to pray and praise.

Psalle et sile is a difficult poem, written for a non-literary end and for a restricted circle of readers. It contains some fine images and well-wrought stanzas, but it does not seek to explore the unexplored or to express original ideas. Its originality consists in the organisation of what others have thought or felt according to the patterns of religious meditation that were frequently practised in the Spanish Golden Age. Memory helps in the composition of place, the understanding examines the subject, the will is urged to concentrate. However much such concepts may be said to have dated, the organisation remains self-consistent and impressive. Those who cannot accept Calderón's religious creed may still find here, if they will take a little trouble, a pattern of feelings that may impress them, as well as a number of powerful lines and images. This poem and the *Sueño* of Sor Juana Inés de la Cruz are, perhaps, the only considerable poems of some length composed in the Spanish world between 1650 and 1700.

NOTE

Antonio Rodríguez-Moñino, with his usual generosity, gave me a copy of the very rare first edition of this poem. He also showed me an unrecorded edition of it printed in Valencia between 1691 and 1694. This edition contains a long *aprobación* by Fray José Laguna, of the Order of St Francis of Paola, by whom sermons were printed in Valencia (1664 and 1673), Barcelona (1677), Valencia (1685 and 1692) (Félix Herrero Salgado, *Aportación bibliográfica a la oratoria sagrada española* (Madrid, 1971), nos. 527, 690, 746, 870 and 1000). This edition is described, and the *aprobación* reprinted, in Edward M. Wilson and D. W. Cruickshank, 'Adiciones a la bibliografía de *Psalle et sile*', *Hacia Calderón: segundo Coloquio anglogermano Hamburgo 1970* (Berlin, 1973), pp. 13–26. In this article Dr Cruickshank has also demonstrated that the first edition of *Psalle et sile* was printed by the Imprenta Real of Madrid. Since this article appeared in 1959 the poem has been republished in facsimile in a limited edition by Don Antonio Pérez Gómez of Cieza: Don Pedro Calderón de la Barca, *Obras menores (siglos XVII y XVIII)* (Cieza, 1969); it contains a short bibliographical note by E. M. Wilson.

8
Calderón's dramatic poetry

A number of poems by Calderón are to be found in various seventeenth-century printed books and manuscript compilations. Despite the efforts of earlier scholars many remain uncollected.[1] In a number of manuscripts in the Biblioteca Nacional at Madrid there are poems attributed to him which are ingenious and well-written. But they add little to the literary glory of the author of *La vida es sueño*. Some of the titles are revealing: *Décimas a una dama que desdeñaba y quería*, or *Romance probando ser mejor mudable que firme*. These are poems composed for competitions at a literary academy. One sonnet at first sight seems to be an extract from a cloak and sword play: *Una dama da satisfacciones a tres galanes a un tiempo*. The gallants are a Duke, Carlos and Enrique; these names occur in only one authentic play by Calderón, but the sonnet is not to be found in it. And in another manuscript I found another sonnet of the same kind and with the same title but by an anonymous author. So Calderón's poem seems also to have been written to fulfil such conditions. It is most ingenious: with different systems of punctuation either the Duke or Carlos or Enrique appears to be the lover favoured by the lady. It is composed for the eye, not for the ear, so it could not have been effective on the stage. It cannot be considered as one of the finest sonnets in Spanish. All the non-dramatic love poems attributable to Calderón seem to be ingenious trifles composed for academy competitions or at the request of a friend.[2] *Vers de société* or *Poésie précieuse*.

Other poems by Calderón – generally sonnets or *décimas* – are to be found in the preliminaries of books by his friends or acquaintances. Occasional poems like these seldom cross the frontier between the formal and the profound, though perhaps some by Don Luis de Góngora did. In 1663 the Most Reverend Father Master Fray Nicolás Baptista, of the Holy Order of our Lady of Carmel, Preacher to His Majesty, died of an abscess in his ear. Calderón wrote a sonnet in praise of him for the preliminaries of a sermon preached to commemorate the virtues of this religious. The poem begins with a mention of Mount Carmel and the prophet Elijah; it goes on to mention the death in life of this second St John the Baptist, whose excellences as an apostolic preacher equalled those of the last of the prophets. The sonnet ends with the statement that Fray Nicolás's death was his last sermon on that subject:

> al fervor de haberse a sí escuchado
> Vida le da la voz, muerte su oído.

All that we are told about the dead preacher is elegantly combined together in this sonnet: a Carmelite, that is to say a member of an order traditionally founded by Elijah, the double reference to St John the Baptist, the famous sermon subjects, the orator's eloquence. Skilfully constructed, it resumes the public life of the dead man and ends with a paradox which might have been profound in a different context. Here it is trivial. Calderón wilfully confined himself to praising Fray Nicolás's virtues as his sole object. He did not choose to write a meditation upon death. What was wanted was a short panegyric; Calderón supplied it.[3]

On the other hand there are also poems by Calderón in which he wrote poetry of meditation. In them the paradoxes are dominated by the whole, and the language is both powerful and sensitive. The *Décimas a la muerte* (if they are – as I think – his), the *romance* that begins 'Agora, Señor, agora' and above all the poem in a variety of metres entitled *Psalle et sile* are masterpieces of their kind.[4] Some of the same quality comes out in his elegies: the *décimas* on the death of Juan Pérez de Montalbán, the tercets to the Cardenal-Infante on the death of his elder brother Don Carlos. Here poetry is the handmaid to post-Tridentine Catholicism; the poet makes himself the tool of his religion in order to convert his fellow men. Sometimes he followed the meditative system of St Ignatius Loyola: composition of place, followed by bringing to bear on his subject the three powers of the soul: memory, understanding, will. The poet spoke as a believer in order that others might sincerely believe too. So, in these non-dramatic poems, it was all a question of the subject undertaken. If he had to write occasional poems he wrote them; the result fulfilled (if it did no more) the obligations of that occasion. When he undertook meditative poetry he wrote best. In both enterprises poetry was a means, not an end in itself. He did not allow himself unnecessary luxuries. The tailor measured his cloth before he cut out the suit. Sometimes he dressed a dwarf, sometimes a prince.

Few of Calderón's poems are included in anthologies. At most we find the famous sonnet ('Estas que fueron pompa y alegría') from *El príncipe constante* and perhaps some other, more light-hearted, extracts from other plays. Nevertheless lyric poetry is important for the mood or for the action in many of his *comedias* and in some of the *autos sacramentales*. At times the lyrics are undoubtedly his own compositions; for instance the one which begins the temptation of Justina in *El mágico prodigioso*, perhaps also the *romance* that foretells the death of Peter the Cruel in the last act of *El médico de su honra*. But often the persons in his plays sing, gloss or quote well-known poems by other poets – Góngora, Lope de Vega, Boscán, Silvestre – or by those of a later generation – Don Antonio de Mendoza, Bocángel, the Count of Villamediana and the Count of Salinas. (During the years in which Jack Sage and I began to study such borrowings[5] I felt tempted to compile an *Anthology of Spanish poetry selected by Don Pedro Calderón de la Barca*.) Once more the subjects dictated the poet's choice; if another poet had composed a good poem that would fulfil the dramatist's purpose in a given scene, why should he trouble to invent another one? I quote two or three examples. Mariene is shut in her tower because she knows that Herod hopes that she also will meet her death if he is killed. Her life is in danger, and she is no longer in love with the Tetrarch. In order to console her, her maids sing the adaptation made popular by Montemayor of an old poem by the Comendador Escrivá:

> Ven, muerte, tan escondida
> que no te sienta venir,
> porque el placer de morir
> no me vuelva a dar la vida.
>
> (*El mayor monstruo los celos*)

Queen Catherine of Aragon learns that Henry VIII loves her less than he used to do, so she glosses the following verse:

> En un infierno los dos
> gloria habemos de tener,
> vos en verme padecer,
> y yo en ver que lo veis vos.   (*La cisma de Ingalaterra*)

Henry appreciates the poetry, but he immediately forgets it when Ann Boleyn begins to dance a galliard before him. The verse was good, if old-fashioned, written – as Mr Sage discovered – by Pedro Liñán de Riaza, who died in 1607.

Don Álvaro, the former lover of Serafina, continues to court her after she has married Don Juan Roca. He wants to resume their old relations; she realises that her marriage has made their old friendship impossible. Don Álvaro lives in the past, she in the present. Disguised as a sailor Don Álvaro thrusts his way into Don Juan's house and begins to talk to her. They speak in *décimas*, at the end of each of which are quoted two lines of the following *romance*:

> Escollo armado de hiedra,
> yo te conocí edificio,
> ejemplo de lo que acaba
> la carrera de los siglos.

> De lo que fuiste primero
> estás tan desconocido
> que de ti mismo olvidado,
> no te acuerdas de ti mismo.   (*El pintor de su deshonra*)

These lines, the first two quatrains of a *romance* by Luis Vélez de Guevara (1579–1644), were famous in the seventeenth century. (They were alluded to by Don Antonio de Mendoza, Juan Ruiz de Alarcón, Álvaro Cubillo de Aragón, Miguel de Barrios and others.) In Calderón's play the theme of this gloss is the difference between past and present: the very subject of the dialogue between Álvaro and Serafina.

In the three instances just quoted verses by other poets bring out the significance of what happens on the stage. Those who saw the play already knew the lines quoted and could relate them to the situation they were watching. Calderón saw, perhaps, that the effect of other men's poems in such scenes would be greater than had the actors sung, glossed or quoted a new song or poem of his own. What looks like poverty of invention or lack of imagination was something else. As a dramatist he could have invented, but did not invent, a poem, when he found that another writer's work satisfied the given conditions. As an architect he could see that other men's statues fitted into, and adorned, the niches that he had so carefully fashioned.

Sometimes quotations of lyrics became 'proverbialised' – to use a term invented by Margit Frenk Alatorre;[6] elsewhere they provided a basis for allusions in the typically Calderonian constructions. I quote one example only, the successive adaptations of two lines, translated into Spanish, from the *Babel e Sião* of Luis de Camoens.

> Dijo el portugués Virgilio
> en una dulce canción:
> 'Vi el bien convertido en mal,
> y el mal en otro peor.'   (*Peor está que estaba*)

The quotation is almost a paraphrase of the title of the comedy in which it occurs; its date is uncertain, but 1630 seems probable. A year later Calderón wrote another play which reverses the earlier title to *Mejor está que estaba*, and he ended it with the opposite of Camoens's quotation:

> y pues tras tantos engaños
> el mal se convierte en bien,
> si es bien casarse, las faltas
> nos perdonad.

And in a late mythological play – perhaps written in 1673 or 1674 – both sentiments were expressed:

> ¡Ay de quien vio
> el bien convertido en mal
> y el mal en peor!
>
> Tened, parad, suspended el rigor:
> veréis a mi voz
> el mal convertido en bien
> y el bien en mejor. (*La estatua de Prometeo*)

Finally in another late play – also of uncertain date – one person says:

> ¡Qué mucho, si considero
> cuánto distantes están
> el bien y el mal para quien,
> en la porción de mortal,
> ve el bien convertirse en mal
> más veces que el mal en bien! (*Apolo y Climene*)

Calderón used the two octosyllables of Camoens to construct dialogue or lyrics in four different plays written during the span of at least fifty years. In such ways he used many works of his forerunners to obtain the effects he sought.

The poet who most influenced him was Don Luis de Góngora. One of Calderón's earliest poems – a sonnet in the preliminaries of a book by his uncle Juan Bautista de Sosa – is gongorist in style and vocabulary.[7] Besides many quotations and glosses of Góngora's *romances* and *letrillas*, some passages from the *Soledades*, the *Polifemo* and the beautiful description of Toledo in the third act of *Las firmezas de Isabela* (Góngora's only completed play) are found in many *comedias* of Calderón. Mr Sage and I found sixteen plays in which were mentioned the 'yawn' of Polyphemus's cave and the 'gag' of the boulder that closed it. In scenes of diabolic invocation in *auto* after *auto* are found typical gongorist latinisms. But Calderón's *culteranismo* has not Góngora's syntactical complications. The dramatist well knew that obscurity is impossible in theatrical dialogue, for the hearer cannot have a speech repeated if he has not understood it at the first hearing; a reader can return – if need be several times – to reread what was not originally clear. The *culto* passages in Calderón are often (I suspect) an obstacle to readers of his plays; many, perhaps, will share the opinion expressed by Gerardo Diego in 1927:

He aquí el enemigo. El que debe cargar con más de la mitad de las culpas que se le abonan en cuenta a Góngora. El peor gongorismo no es sino calderonismo. Calderón reduce a cuatro o seis moldes agotados genialmente por él, algunos de los hallazgos gongorinos; simetriza lo que en Góngora era equilibrado, pero libre. Da la fórmula para adquirir un culteranismo barato de bazar a precio único; y, en suma, convierte la sorpresa en tópico, la forma en molde y lo clásico vivo en académico muerto.[8]

These vigorous remarks of a distinguished twentieth-century poet need some qualification. But his adverse criticism has some justification if we look at Calderón's plays purely as poetry and ignore the drama. Amusing also was the attack by the elder Moratín (1737–80) on the opening lines of *La vida es sueño*:

> Yo quisiera saber, si una muger que cae despeñada por un Monte con un Cavallo, en vez de quexarse donde la duele, y pedir favor, le dice todas aquellas impropias pedanterias, que las entiende el Auditorio, como el Cavallo. Si algún su apassionado cayesse por las orejas, llamele Hypogripho violento, y verà como se alivia.[9]

That kind of verse in Calderón is rhetorical and at times bombastic. I suppose it pleased the audience of the court theatre of the Buen Retiro palace and the less refined public of the commercial playhouses. In itself it has little to interest us today. But such passages may have dramatic, if not poetic, value. The saints on the façade of a baroque church often seem poor stuff compared with those we see at Chartres; but the façade itself may impress us despite the poverty of the individual sculptures. And the presence in it even of inferior statues makes it better than if there had been no statues in it at all. We must take into account the total effect and not give too much importance to the details. Don Pedro was first and foremost a playwright; his poetry takes the second place.

Nevertheless he was also a poet, and we cannot fairly judge him if we consider only the weakest verses in his plays. There is much rhetoric in his verses, and many modern critics have scorned rhetoric and regarded it as trivial. But I cannot believe that poetry can never exist where we find rhetoric. If we reject all those works in which rhetoric supports poetry we discard a good number of plays and poems that are capable of giving us hours of enjoyment and artistic pleasure. When Cipriano describes Justina he recites a set piece carefully constructed in accordance with Calderón's own rhetorical recipes. The lines impress us when recited, but when we read them we see the tricks of the craftsman. Still there are beautiful details in Cipriano's picture, for instance:

> el clavel, que en breve cielo
> es estrella de coral.   (*El mágico prodigioso*)

The equation 'flower = star' occurs time after time in Calderón's descriptions. But here the flower is a carnation, and the star is also a particular star – 'of coral'. The 'brief heaven' can be a woman, as can be seen in numerous passages in his other plays, so that here also it represents Justina. These lines seem to me justified as poetry. The carnation in the garden, its brief earthly heaven, shines like a red star of coral; coral and carnation often do duty for the lips of the loved one, who is also a 'brief heaven'.[10]

Justina is shown to contain in herself the fair symbols of post-Renaissance nature: carnation, coral, star show how she can rise from earth to heaven.

Another example from the same play. Cipriano, before the devil appears to him, sees a terrifying storm, which he describes in violent, almost gongoristic, lines:

> ¿Qué es esto, cielos puros?
> ¡Claros a un tiempo, y en el mismo oscuros,
> dando al día desmayos!
> Los truenos, los relámpagos y rayos
> abortan de su centro
> los asombros que ya no caben dentro.
> . . .
> Todo nuestro horizonte
> es ardiente pincel de Mongibelo;
> ¡niebla el sol, humo el aire, fuego el cielo!

Then comes a surprising parenthesis that contrasts with the melodramatic metaphors I have just quoted:

> ¡Tanto ha que te dejé, filosofía,
> que ignoro los efectos de este día!

In an earlier soliloquy Cipriano had offered his soul that he might enjoy Justina; the devil accepted it, and the tempest followed. In these two lines Cipriano recalls his earlier studies in natural philosophy which revealed at least some of the secrets of nature to him; but from the time he fell madly in love with Justina he has forgotten all that he had learned. In themselves the lines quoted are trivial, but in their context they give us an important sign for the comprehension of the carnal lust of the man who would later become a Christian martyr. But now lust has blinded his memory and his understanding; his will may lead him anywhere. This couplet is an example of the poetry of plain statement; it is effective for dramatic, not for purely poetic, reasons.

Thanks to an excellent study by Dámaso Alonso, we have learned how some rhetorical devices used by Calderón, especially his correlations and summations, came to form part of the dramatic constructions themselves as well as occurring in single scenes and speeches.[11] I shall not repeat the words of one to whom I owe so much, words to be commended heartily to all those patient enough to read this essay. His article shows how in another way rhetoric is to be taken seriously, not only in the single passages of verse, but also in the way the different scenes are ordered. However, I shall quote one of the examples he used to show how the 'technique of a correlation in which there is no differentiation in its binary members' can also give us a key to interpret the role of King Basilio in *La vida es sueño*:

Estrella.	Sabio Tales...
Astolfo.	Docto Euclides...
Estrella.	que entre signos...
Astolfo.	que entre estrellas...
Estrella.	hoy gobiernas...
Astolfo.	hoy resides...
Estrella.	y sus caminos...
Astolfo.	sus huellas...
Estrella.	describes...
Astolfo.	tasas y mides...
Estrella.	déjame que en humildes lazos...
Astolfo.	deja que en tiernos abrazos...
Estrella.	hiedra de este tronco sea.
Astolfo.	rendido a tus pies me vea.
Basilio.	Sobrinos, dadme los brazos.

According to his contemporaries Calderón was considered a 'fino cortesano', and Gregorio Marañón called him a 'mejor administrador del incienso' than Lope de Vega was.[12] Here the dramatist piles flattery on flattery to show the adulation – as well as the rivalry – of Estrella and of Astolfo; Basilio accepts their absurd praises without a murmur. The correlation technique exposes the insincere flattery of the prince and princess and also the monarch's self-satisfaction. Then Basilio begins his long speech in which, along with much else, he prides himself on his astronomical learning:

> Ya sabéis (estadme atentos
> amados sobrinos míos,
> corte ilustre de Polonia,
> vasallos, deudos y amigos),
> ya sabéis que yo en el mundo
> por mi ciencia he merecido
> el sobrenombre de docto;
> pues, contra el tiempo y olvido,
> los pinceles de Timantes,
> los mármoles de Lisipo,
> en el ámbito del orbe
> me aclaman el gran Basilio.

The bimembration of the praises emphasises their flattery; Basilio proclaims his lack of modesty. The whole effect of these passages is calculated to produce a refined irony as well as to show Astolfo's rivalry with Estrella. These lines are not empty; they help us to detect the weaknesses both of the King of Poland and of his presumed heirs.

An exclusively formalist approach, then, cannot help us fully to comprehend Calderón's dramatic poetry. Very often the context is essential in order to reveal the interpretation of every aspect of a given passage. Let us now take a poem mentioned in the first paragraph of this essay. Let us suppose that in a cloak and sword play there is a lady called Lisi, who loves but also scorns (as in the poem of which I quoted the title) a gallant, whom we may call Don Félix; he has learned of her love and scorn for him. In these circumstances the four *décimas* of the poem might well come from his lips; they would be suitable and proper to the situation in such a play. Don Félix is alone with Lisi, and he says:

> Yo he visto en vaso dorado,
> Lisi, encubierto el veneno,
> y en campo, de flores lleno,
> el áspid disimulado;
> pero no he visto ni he hallado
> oculto el bien y el favor
> a la sombra del rigor;
> que fuera estar en tal caso
> el veneno antes del vaso
> y el áspid sobre la flor.

And when he has recited the other stanzas he concludes the last *décima* with the lines:

> que no es mucho bien el bien
> que tanto parece al mal.

The poem which in itself appeared well written and superficial could be appropriate enough in a given context. The poetry would arise from the dramatic situation and would compare favourably enough with other passages of lovers' preciosities, in which Calderón sometimes showed himself over-subtle or too ingenious. His love poems are rather like pictures that cannot reveal their merit until they are adequately framed.

Here I must pass over many fine examples of good poetry in plays and *autos* which are worth detailed analysis: that wonderful description by Muley in *El príncipe constante* of a naval battle, so justly praised by E. H. Gombrich;[13] the musical and poetic temptation of Justina; Segismundo's first soliloquy; those monosyllabically rhymed octaves in *La cena de Baltasar*; and other equally famous and notable specimens. I omit them in order to pay attention to another facet of Calderón's style which is less often noticed and is perhaps more profound. I repeat that he was a poet in the service of the theatre, and this kind of poetry can hardly be considered separately from the stage and from the dramatic context; it resumes a generalisation or a commentary on the scene as it takes place and also on human conduct in general; it is rooted in, supported by, the whole extent of the work in which it occurs. The best-known example is Segismundo's second soliloquy, pronounced when he wakes up in the

Calderón's dramatic poetry

tower after his one day's life as a prince. I need not quote these lines; they are well known. They convince us not only because they are tersely expressed and deeply moving in themselves, but also because they are supported by all that Segismundo suffered, endured and struggled against in the earlier scenes. The speech could well be isolated and figure in an anthology; but all who knew the play well would think when they read it printed separately of Segismundo's illusions and disillusions.

The same might be said of other lines – to me equally moving – pronounced by the same man in the course of his long soliloquy in the third act. Then – thanks to Rosaura's reappearance – he learned that he truly lived in the tower, in the palace and again in the tower; that he was then on the battlefield, in front of an injured woman, whose presence there and in the earlier scenes proved to him that he had lived his dream throughout. He repressed his savagery and lust to say:

> ¿Qué pasado bien no es sueño?
> ¿Quién tuvo dichas heroicas
> que entre sí no diga, cuando
> las revuelve en la memoria:
> sin duda que fue soñado
> cuanto vi?

Segismundo defined his own experience; the definition is exact, not only for him but for thousands of men who have outlived their worldly glories and their brave deeds. Is it an exaggeration to call lines like these useful? They help us to comprehend what is true and to clarify our values.

In 1881 the Catalan scholar Antonio Rubió y Lluch wrote of 'la multitud de observaciones y máximas aplicables a todas las situaciones de la vida, que a manos llenas derrama [Calderón] en sus obras'.[14] We shall now examine one such passage, which occurs in *El mágico prodigioso*, just after the poetic temptation of Justina mentioned in the last paragraph but one. The devil appears to her in person and begins his intellectual temptation. She had rejected the purely sensual one, but for a few moments she had felt inclined to succumb to it. So the devil says to her:

> En haberlo imaginado
> tienes hecha la mitad:
> pues ya el pecado es pecado,
> no pares la voluntad,
> el medio camino andado.

She had listened to the voice of her tempters; according to the enemy she has therefore sinned in thought. Why can she not admit the fact and go on to the enjoyment of what she had begun? Her innocence is lost; she would be foolish not to accept the consequences of that loss. She replies:

> Desconfiarme es en vano
> aunque pensé; que, aunque es llano
> que el pensar es empezar,
> no está en mi mano el pensar,
> y está el obrar en mi mano.
> Para haberte de seguir
> el pie tengo que mover,
> y esto puedo resistir;
> porque una cosa es hacer,
> y otra cosa es discurrir.

The devil begins by telling her that one cannot distinguish between an involuntary thought and an imagined sin. She acknowledges that she had had dangerous thoughts that might become sinful; but she would not sin unless she consented to the temptation and acted upon it, courses which she utterly rejected with all her will. Actions in their nature differ from thoughts: thoughts are often involuntary, whereas actions come under the dominion of the free will. Justina, then, makes distinctions of a scholastic sort, which at the same time have dramatic value on the stage and are useful to her hearers because they define and characterise the qualities of this and other temptations. Her contrasts between action and thought, moving and resisting movement, doing and thinking, are related to the capacity for good and evil of the hand and their instrument the foot. The hand controls; the foot obeys. The immediate result is that Justina routs the devil. In the mind of the reader or hearer these verses seem applicable to a multitude of other situations in life. A particular situation is analysed on stage; the analysis can be relevant to many other situations in almost any man's life.

The devil foments confusions between thinking and doing, between thought and action. Justina, guided by the truth, dispels them. There are confusions on all sides. The beauties of the natural world can be emblems of virtue or snares in the path that lies before us. As one of the Argensolas wrote:

> Porque ese cielo açul que todos vemos
> ni es cielo ni es açul.[15]

Calderón at least once repeated his paradox.[16] Even the titles of his plays can be so arranged as to preach similar lessons: In this life all is truth and all lies. Which is the greater perfection, beauty or discretion? The obligations of a coincidence. From one cause two effects. Getting ill through the remedy. On all sides there are things or persons who are not what they seem: here a mock astrologer, there a goblin lady or a phantom gallant; there a (gentleman) dancing master, a hidden man and a veiled woman. Sometimes we think that things are worse than they were, at others that the worst is not always true or that things are better than they were. The way out is to follow certain simple, almost proverbial rules: To know the difference between good and evil. Let no one tell his secret. Beware of still waters that run deep. There is nothing like silence. Give Time time. Because tomorrow will be another day. Let us use virtue combined with prudence as a golden thread in our labyrinth. For confusions are to be found both in the court of King Basilio and in that house with two doors which is so difficult to protect.[17] We must see the difficulties that surround us before we try to solve them; they can be solved if prudence and time can help us.

The recognition of life's confusions saves Rosaura and Clotaldo in *La vida es sueño*. The others must be disillusioned: Segismundo, Basilio, Astolfo, Clarín; but Clotaldo and Rosaura have already placed their trust in the solid principles of loyalty and honour, and, in a sense, they are already disillusioned when the play begins. We find the same theme in the cloak and sword comedies. In *Peor está que estaba* at one point Don César enters 'como a oscuras' and says:

> En notable confusión
> estoy, la puerta buscando
> sin discurso y sin razón,
> en las sombras tropezando
> de mi misma turbación.

Shadows surround him, and shadows dwell in his mind. The scene is comic; Don César manages for a few moments to hide from his enemies in a Sedan chair, which later is carried somewhere else, where fresh adventures overtake him. The lines he recites, however, can easily be adapted to other more difficult, and even tragic, situations by changing the word *puerta* to - say - *verdad*. And this too exemplifies Rubió's dictum about observations applicable to difficult situations in our own lives. It is unlikely that we shall have Don César's experience; but we all know what he means when he talks of how he is

> en las sombras tropezando
> de mi misma turbación.

And so we come to the great themes of Calderón's poetry. When his characters express the transience of earthly benefits, of the vanity of power or riches, of the 'large disillusions of Catholicism' (the phrase is Santayana's), of the omnipresent threat of death, then poet and dramatist are united in the man who took Holy Orders at the age of fifty-one and became a respected priest. In his youth (*El príncipe constante*), in his maturity (*La vida es sueño*), in his old age (*auto* after *auto sacramental*), these themes are repeated with equal intensity of expression and with all the resources of the baroque. Even in his own funeral he sought to give his fellow-men an edifying spectacle:

Primeramente pido y suplico a la persona o personas que piadosas me asistan que luego que mi alma, separada de mi cuerpo, le desampare dexándole a la tierra, bien como restituida prenda suya, sea interiormente vestido del hábito de mi seráfico padre San Francisco, ceñido con su cuerda, y con la correa de mi también padre San Agustín, y habiéndole puesto al pecho el escapulario de Nuestra Señora del Carmen, y sobre ambos sayales, sacerdotales vestiduras, reclinado en la tierra sobre el manto capitular de señor Santiago, es mi voluntad que en esta forma sea entregado al señor capellán mayor y capellanes que son o fueren de la venerable Congregación de Sacerdotes Naturales de Madrid, sita en la parroquial de señor San Pedro, para que usando conmigo, en observancia de sus piadosos institutos, la caridad que con otro cualquiera pobre sacerdote, me reciban en su caja (y no en otra) para que en ella sea llevado a la parroquial Iglesia de San Salvador de esta villa; y suplico así al señor capellán mayor y capellanes como a los señores albaceas que adelante serán nombrados, dispongan mi entierro, llevándome descubierto, por si mereciese satisfacer en parte las públicas vanidades de mi mal gastada vida con los públicos desengaños de mi muerte; y asimismo les suplico que para mi entierro no conviden más acompañamiento que doce religiosos de San Francisco, y a su Tercera Orden de hábito descubierto, doce sacerdotes que acompañen la cruz, doce niños de la Doctrina y doce de los desamparados.[18]

Such details help us to see that Calderón could express the transience of life with something like the same intensity as that shown in Jorge Manrique's *Coplas* or in Quevedo's moral sonnets. The *Décimas a la muerte* (or *a la nada de la vida*) – if they are Calderón's – have some of the same quality. To bring this chapter to an end I shall comment on a sonnet recited by El Hombre in the *Auto sacramental de la segunda esposa y triunfar muriendo*, written in 1648 (the year in which Calderón's bastard son Pedro José was born), three years before he was ordained priest. The sonnet appeared in Montoliú's anthology, and Ángel Valbuena Prat has praised it in several works.[19] We may call it *La antorcha de la vida*.

> Oh tú, Antorcha, que en esa breve, en esa
> tibia llama contienes sombras sumas,
> no por hermosa de inmortal presumas,
> pues puedes antes ser que luz, pavesa.
>   Si no ardes, mueres, pues tu lumbre cesa;
> si ardes, también, pues fuerza es te consumas;
> luego ardiendo, o no ardiendo, siempre ahumas
> las lóbregas paredes de la huesa.
>   ¡Qué luciente, y qué bella te creía,
> cuando cabal, no imaginé que pueda
> deslucirte la edad del primer día!
>   ¡Oh mortal! ¡Oh mortal! deshaz la rueda
> pues debida a merced de la agonía
> lo que te queda es lo que [aun] no te queda.[20]

The torch's flame is as weak and short as a man's life. We can even see in it the shadow of death. Although it is beautiful, it cannot pride itself on its immortality, for its weak flame can be put out by a mere puff of air. The flame, whether it continues to burn or not, consumes itself, and the smoke, whether the flame is burning or not, blackens the walls of the tomb. So man, whether he lives or dies, approaches in the same way the same goal. When the flame was fresh it appeared handsome and bright; never did I think that it could all vanish into shadows and smoke. We must come to terms with reality. We must not be like the peacock that furls out his splendid tail and forgets the hideousness of his feet. Let us cease to spread out our feathers and remember:

> pues debida a merced de la agonía,
> lo que te queda es lo que [aun] no te queda.

In isolation the sonnet is well wrought and moving. In its context it is dramatic and impressive. El Hombre, newly born, enters with his torch with six lights. After his meeting with Sin and with Death, after he has learned that the hand of Death is less to be feared than is the arm of God which controls it, he faces Death herself (La Muerte). Death brags of her strength and power and puts out the first light. The second is extinguished by hunger and thirst, the third by sickness, the fourth by anxiety, sadness, weariness and ambition, the fifth by pain, poverty and misery. So when El Hombre recites the sonnet the torch has only one flame and five smoking wicks. The lines embody the disillusion he has undergone and teach us the lesson he has learned. They tell us that our salvation may be reached if we recognise the fact of our mortality.

This example shows how poetry and theatre can mutually strengthen one another. The poem in itself is excellent and profound. Its dramatic setting, however clumsily I have summarised it, makes it even more excellent, more profound. Does poetry serve the theatre here, or the theatre poetry? Each reader must decide for himself when he reads through this noble sacramental allegory.

9
Images and structure in *Peribáñez*

At first sight *Peribáñez y el Comendador de Ocaña* seems a simple play. It has a single plot; there is no question of relating a sub-plot to the main plot or of interpreting the events in it as examples of moral error and disillusion. The case of honour is also simple and needs no explanation, for here there is nothing to shock modern sensibilities. The intrigue is straightforward, the poetry not conceited. The numerous difficulties to be overcome in reading Calderón are not to be found here. Part of its merit lies in the fact that it is easy for a modern reader to approach it.

In 1943 Charles V. Aubrun and José F. Montesinos published an excellent edition of this play with a brilliant introduction to it.[1] After considering the Golden-Age *comedia* in general they discussed the work itself: its date, sources, historical background; the genre – plays about overlords and their peasants; Lope's ideas about psychology and morals, about love; his depiction of minor figures in the play – e.g. Belardo, one of his pseudonyms; its style and versification. I have nothing to add about either sources or dates, nor do I propose to comment on their relevant comparisons of this play with others by Tirso de Molina, Luis Vélez or Lope himself.[2] My intention rather is to see whether an examination of its style (the words themselves) can lead to a better appreciation of its merits. To study a play as though it were a poem – which, as a poetic drama, it certainly is – can tell us as much as a study of sources, psychology, customs and depiction of characters. So I shall talk chiefly about single or repeated images and some more general features in order to see whether they affect our view of the work as a whole. I avoid the traditional procedure of examining a drama in terms of its characters, a point of view better suited to Victorian novels than to Spanish plays of the age of the Philips.[3]

Aubrun and Montesinos stressed the importance of Lope's *Arte nuevo de hacer comedias en este tiempo*[4] for the comprehension of his plays. This half-jesting *ars poetica* has its faults, but it is better than no guide at all. Lope's empirical procedure with metres and his remarks about imitation help us to guess his intentions. Unfortunately he says nothing about character in the modern sense of that word; instead he discusses the type of language which is most appropriate to the social rank of the person in question. Hence the reason why we should try to discuss his works in hi

Images and structure in *Peribáñez*

own terms rather than in those (like character) which today are used and abused. Lope spoke of the king, the old man, the lover, the lady in general; he never particularised or gave us rules for depicting a Peter the Cruel or the Knight of Olmedo. He sought less to make his personages individuals than the moderns do; that is no reason for censure. Rather should we try to see how he made them speak in different ways and whether the play gains or loses thereby. First I shall quote his own words; though the passage is well known it has not always been well understood:

> Si hablare el rey, imite cuanto pueda
> la gravedad real; si el viejo hablare,
> procure una modestia sentenciosa;
> describa los amantes con afectos
> que muevan con extremo a quien escucha.
> . . .
> Las damas no desdigan de su nombre.
> . . .
> El lacayo no trate cosas altas. (269–73, 280, 286)

Lope never tells us how a peasant should speak. In *Peribáñez* more than half the number of those who take part are peasants. Their way of speaking will be the first object of our enquiry.

Peribáñez portrays the relation between social classes. No one in it questions the difference between master and man, between peasant and overlord. Lope continually insists on the fact that Peribáñez and the Commander Don Fadrique belong to different worlds. The hero observes that the peasant takes the same pleasure in the bouquet of a wine that the lord receives from a rose's scent (59–60). Bartolo praises the Commander's generosity (251), and Casilda calls him the flower of Spain (291). Don Fadrique regrets that a coarse farmer has become her husband (342–3), but only a little later he vainly desires to exchange Ocaña for her house (552–7). She remarks that Peribáñez eats the simple food she gives him with the same relish that the Commander must have in his expensive banquets (742–5). Peribáñez does not scruple to ask his overlord to lend him suitable trappings (*repostero*) and rug (*alhombra*) for the family trip to Toledo (774–8, 855–74). He is overcome by gratitude at Don Fadrique's generosity to him, a mere peasant (844–6), and he stresses how in his own house the hangings are poor compared with those that adorn the castles of the nobility. When the Commander asks him whether he is happy, he replies that he would not exchange his rough working-clothes for the order that decorates his overlord's chest (875–82). Class differences are often commented on during the first act, but there is not a sign that they are considered unfair or unjust:

>   un villano
> por la paz del alma es rey.   (76-7)

Peribáñez is happy in his present condition; he neither resents, envies nor hates Don Fadrique. Casilda's famous outburst in the second act (1554–1617) is amply prepared by these and other observations in the first.

The opening scene brings out the harmony of Peribáñez's marriage with the natural and supernatural world. Inés and Costanza congratulate the lovers. The priest tells them such words are unnecessary, for the Church's blessings which he has just pronounced in the sacrament of marriage include all others (1–13). The effect is half serious, half humorous; if the reproach is pedantic, it stresses the fact that the marriage has won God's blessing as well as the villagers' approval. After a few quips about lovers' jealousy (19–25) Peribáñez sings Casilda's praises and she his (86–120) in parallel terms. The young people sing a marriage song, the style of which owes little to folk poetry; but all its imagery shows that the love of the young couple harmonises with the natural order. Let the alders grow taller, the flowering almond trees bear fruit, the lilies flower and the beasts climb the hills to graze on wild thyme; the frozen mountain and high cliffs, the ilexes and oaks will let the streams flow clearly from the snow slopes to the valley, while the nightingales tell their loves to the myrtles and the meadows become fertile for the happy pair. In other words, the young villagers beg Nature to follow her own ordinary course so that the life of the married couple may be happy and prosperous (126–65).

The lovers' praises of one another are worth a mention too. He compares her to an olive tree laden with fruit, to a flowering meadow, to a pippin, to shining olive oil. White wine forty years old smells less sweet than her lips; October grape juice, vine stocks cut in December for the hearth, the May showers and the August harvest provide less comfort than does her presence in the house in summer or in winter. Finally, as a countryman is happy as a king because his soul is at peace, so Casilda is a queen because the proverbial luck of an ugly woman will now pass to a beautiful one. So two homely proverbs round off a series of country images based on his own labours and their fruit. The details are familiar, the olive oil shines like gold in its earthen jars. He speaks like a countryman; he expresses his love in terms of the crops and fruits that will surround them both, which both of them will cultivate and gather. Half consciously he mentions that wine is to the peasant what roses are to the noble; nowhere else does he talk about roses. He knows his place and will keep to it.

In her reply Casilda uses another series of images. Peribáñez saw her in terms of his crops and daily work; she sees him in the amusements and adornments of country life. He pleases her more than the music she likes to dance to, than the shouts of the dancers, than the herbs gathered on Midsummer morning, than the sound of a tambourine or the sight of a processional banner. Love of him fits her better than a pair of new shoes; he is like an Easter cake, a bull, a new shirt laid on jasmines on a gilded tray, the Paschal candle or the marzipan at christenings . . . In short, he is comparable only with himself.

The two speeches are charming. Simple familiar images, brought to life by their specific details; the poetry of everyday life. Lope makes his rustic lovers talk naturally and gives them metaphors or similes proper to their labours or their pleasures. Their phrases are adapted easily to the rhythms of his verse without unnatural alterations of syntax. Wordsworth's poetic aims come naturally to the mind of an English reader:

> The principal object, then, proposed in these Poems was to choose incidents and situations from common life, and to relate or describe them throughout, as far as was possible, in a selection of language really used by men, and, at the same time, to throw over them a certain colouring of imagination, whereby ordinary things should be presented to the mind in an unusual aspect.[5]

What a contrast these two speeches make with the conventional lovers' language of the seventeenth century, with its flames, wounds, golden arrows, its suns, stars, flowers, jewels and precious metals! Lope makes his lovers express their feelings by metaphors drawn from their everyday surroundings. Furthermore the two speeches clinch the harmony previously indicated by the priest's blessing and reproof and by the marriage song of the younger men and girls. Casilda is the crown of the farmer Peribáñez; she sees him as the epitome of all the good things she has seen, heard and tasted.

The same spirit emerges in a later scene in the same act in which Inés, Costanza and Casilda talk about what they will wear on their excursion to Toledo (667–90); the details about their dresses recall those of Casilda's description of her husband. Later on, when he comes back from Toledo a second time, there is another list, now of the presents he has brought back for her (2002–13). Lope purposely associates Casilda, crown of the farmer's life, with the pleasures and finery of country people, carefully described and precisely named. Her conversation with Costanza and Inés leads to her charming account of her daily life with her husband. It is composed of everyday things: her embroidery frame, straw and barley for the mule, soup flavoured with garlic and onions shared by the two of them, grace after supper and bed-time. The same lyrical feeling for peasant life that we saw in the early scene is apparent here too. She also compares his life with that of the Commander:

> que no la come mejor
> el señor de muesa villa

as he had done before:

> que como al señor la rosa
> le güele al villano el vino

with the implication that the peasant is at least as fortunate as the noble. Later Peribáñez would tell Fadrique that his happiness was complete and hint that Casilda preferred the farmer to the noble.

Besides the rustic metaphors and comparisons, Lope from time to time put some dialect forms into the words spoken by the villagers, including Peribáñez himself. Unfortunately we have not Lope's autograph manuscript of this play so we cannot guarantee that these expressions may not sometimes be alterations made by the copyist or the printer; or perhaps copyist or printer smoothed out other such forms from the original manuscript. The modern editors (and I follow them) nevertheless assume that such forms as *güele* (60, Peribáñez speaks), *Bras* (174, Bartolo), *nueso* and *mueso* (186, 251, Bartolo again), *la nuestra cofradía* (1127, Benito), *Helipe* (1445, Mendo), *mala fuese la tu dicha* (1615, Casilda), *vuesa* (1867, Peribáñez), *her* and *hue* (2247, 2339, Belardo) are intended to indicate dialect forms, not accidental archaisms. Indeed such formations are more likely to be Lope's own than to come from a scribe or a compositor. Lope introduced a deliberate dialect flavour into some speeches by Peribáñez, by Casilda, by their neighbours and by their farm servants. As the action takes place in Toledo an exaggerated use of them would not have been appropriate to it. But the combined effect of them helps to hint at a communal unity to the spectators of the play. Lope did not use dialect to mock peasants and so to obtain an easy laugh from the urban public that would hear the play.

So dialect and country imagery unite Peribáñez's mode of speech with that of his neighbours. The harmony of the lovers goes beyond their home and their own daily life. When the parish council debate whether the statue of their saint should be replaced or merely repainted, Peribáñez decides the question and consents to act on their behalf (1125–99). Later he will tell the king that:

> Fui el mejor de mis iguales,
> y en cuantas cosas trataban
> me dieron primero voto,
> y truje seis años vara. (3036–9)

The pleasing scene between the harvesters shows how these hired men are anxious to please their master and mistress by the amount of wheat they can mow and by their happiness in their work,

Bartolo.	Al alba he de haber segado	
	todo el repecho del prado.	
Chaparro.	Si diere licencia el sueño.	
	Buenas noches os dé Dios,	
	Mendo y Llorente.	
Mendo.	El sosiego	
	no será mucho si luego	
	habemos de andar los dos	
	con las hoces a destajo,	
	aquí manada, aquí corte.	
Chaparro.	Pardiez, Mendo, cuando importe,	
	bien luce el justo trabajo.	(1425–35)
Llorente.	Seguidme todos, amigos,	
	porque muesama no diga	
	que porque muesamo falta	
	andan las hoces baldías.	(1648–51)

Peribáñez the peasant loves Casilda. He is respected by his companions and by the men who work for him and want to please him. He is *primus inter pares*.[6] The others, as Aubrun and Montesinos noted, provide a kind of extension of him, in their respect for him and in that they to some extent share his problems.[7] The source of this comradeship is their life in common expressed by the names of tools and crops that are natural to their daily life. All are united in their work and by their speech. The way they speak is almost as important – from a dramatic point of view – as what they indeed say. Lope is here supreme; no other writer has so acutely painted in concrete terms the ideals of country life so naturally and so vividly.

After the scene of the marriage and public rejoicing, after the hurly-burly caused by the bull's arrival, Luján and Marín carry on to the stage the unconscious body of the Commander Don Fadrique. Casilda is left alone with him, for the others have gone to look either for the priest, for a chair or for a glass of water. She laments what she takes to be the death of her overlord. But he recovers his senses and asks who she is. She tells him. He then begins to praise her beauty in the vague conventional manner of noble, seventeenth-century lovers:

> Estuve muerto en el suelo,
> y como ya lo creí,
> cuando los ojos abrí
> pensé que estaba en el cielo.
> Desengañadme, por Dios,
> que es justo pensar que sea
> cielo donde un hombre vea
> que hay ángeles como vos. (316–23)

She takes him literally, or pretends to do so:

Casilda.	Antes por vuestras razones
	podría yo presumir
	que estáis cerca de morir.
Comendador.	¿Cómo?
Casilda.	Porque veis visiones. (324–7)

He pays her more compliments, and she repeats the proverb her husband had recently quoted about 'la ventura de la fea' (341, cf. 84). He mutters that she is too handsome to be married to a peasant, describes her as a diamond set in lead (346–7), and, after Peribáñez has returned, declares that he has recovered his health by means of a precious stone fallen from heaven. Casilda's literal interpretation of his first speech of compliments contrasts with the gallant's courtly manner. The would-be seducer's precious language is very different from the homely metaphors of the lovers' earlier love-talk. Her husband saw in her the fruits of the earth that he tilled; the gallant calls her an angel, a diamond, a celestial jewel. So is the courtier's world differentiated from the peasant's; Casilda can hardly understand what he says to her. Her failure (or pretended failure – one can hardly tell which) to comprehend him is echoed by Luján not many lines later – and Luján is the Commander's most plebian servingman:

Luján.	¿Qué sientes?
Comendador.	Un gran deseo
	que cuando entré no tenía.
Luján.	No lo entiendo.
Comendador.	Importa poco.
Luján.	Yo hablo de tu caída.
Comendador.	En peligro está mi vida
	por un pensamiento loco. (378–83)

The aristocrat's manner of speaking, full of strange allusions, is not intelligible to the vulgar.

Aubrun and Montesinos did justice to the role of the Commander.[8] He is not a depraved monster but a man carried away by a guilty passion. But here I am less interested in what he is than in the way he talks. At home again he sends for Luján. While he is alone he recites a courtly poem in the Italian metres in praise of Casilda. She is more beautiful than the crimson dawn; she seems to have gathered all the flowers that Zephyrus engendered in Flora's lap; her feet made the green meadow display flowers – and green is the colour appropriate to hope. Then suddenly the metaphors change and the nobleman describes Casilda almost in Peribáñez's style:

¡Venturoso el villano
que tal agosto ha hecho

> del trigo de tu pecho
> con atrevida mano,
> y que con blanca barba
> verá en sus eras de tus hijos parva! (540–5)

Then he calls on the Sun and on Charles's Wain to lend him their chariots. And finally he announces that he would change his sword for Peribáñez's mattock, Ocaña for his house. The change of imagery in this lyrical soliloquy produces a dramatic effect. He briefly introduces country images to prepare us for his desire to become her equal. But the leopard cannot change his spots; he cannot fulfil that wish, so he calls on Luján, his servant, half lackey, half peasant. Their sordid dialogue follows; even so Don Fadrique cannot refrain from saying to his man:

> Como va el fuego a su esfera,
> el alma a tanta hermosura
> sube cobarde y ligera. (565–7)

Such expressions recur in later scenes. When he sees Casilda in Toledo he says:

> Como sombra voy siguiendo
> el sol de aquesta villana. (991–2)

He there tells the painter to portray her against a sky embroidered with clouds while she stands in a flowery meadow; when the painter complains that the light is fading, he replies:

> No lo temas, que otro sol
> tiene en sus ojos serenos,
> siendo estrellas para ti,
> para mí rayos de fuego. (1046–9)

When later on Luján relates how, disguised as a harvester, he had penetrated Casilda's room, his master exclaims:

> ¿Que has entrado a su aposento?
> ¿Que de tan divino sol
> fuiste Faetón español?
> ¡Espantoso atrevimiento!
> ¿Qué hacía aquel ángel bello? (1328–32)

And Don Fadrique, now also a pretended harvester, takes leave of Casilda thus:

> Señora mía,
> ya se va acercando el día
> y es tiempo de ir a segar.
> Demás que, saliendo vos,
> sale el sol, y es tarde ya. (1535–9)

Peribáñez sees Casilda in earthly symbols; the Commander sees her in heavenly ones.

There is another motif in Don Fadrique's part: his embarrassment when Peribáñez's name is mentioned. In the first act, after he has told Luján why he is using such a humble man as his agent, Leonardo – a servant superior to Luján – comes in to tell their master that Peribáñez wants to see him (820). The Commander suddenly grows confused and asks Leonardo to explain himself. The question is repeated. Leonardo, who does not yet know the truth, tells him who Peribáñez is, a peasant much respected by his fellows. Why, Luján then asks the Commander, has he gone pale? Does he not want to see the man against whose honour he has been plotting? The Commander recovers his poise and replies that his momentary confusion arose from his feelings towards Casilda, that he would see in Peribáñez the image of Casilda. Again, in the first scene of Act III, when Leonardo, who has learned the secret and become as much an accomplice as Luján, tells Don Fadrique that among the nobles at the Cortes at Toledo is a certain Periáñez; his master interrupts:

> Detente.
> ¿Qué Periáñez? Aguarda;
> que la sangre se me hiela
> con ese nombre.   (2164–7)

This revealing mistake starts a conversation in the course of which the plot against his vassal's honour is carried further. Both these scenes immediately precede the two meetings between the peasant and his overlord. In both the overlord favours the peasant whose honour he is attempting to ruin. The Commander's confusion and hesitations betray his guilty feelings. He admits to Leonardo that the honour he seeks to give Peribáñez is in fact lined with infamy (2191–3), and when the peasant-captain makes his ambiguous declaration as he leaves with his troops, Don Fadrique is further disconcerted (2294–2309). He knows and he admits that he is acting wrongly. So finally his behaviour at his death, the forgiveness granted to his murderer and his acceptance of the fate he has deserved (2850–85) are all a logical and pathetic development from the scenes that we have just summarised.

'*Hagan gran ruido y entre Bartolo labrador.*' The initial harmony of the wedding scenes was interrupted by the noise made by the men as they brought the bull to the village. Bartolo's words are intended to be comic; they have also an appropriate rustic flavour: *se ha vido, el nueso Comendador*; or they are natural to a cattlebreeder or to one used to village bull-

Images and structure in *Peribáñez*

fights: *tiznado, encintar, la yegua recién sacada del verde, cerrar a picarle, cintero*. He jokes coarsely about the mare's torn belly and about Tomás whose breeches have been ripped off by the savage animal (169–91). The very coarseness of his expressions (which does not worry Peribáñez, Casilda or the priest) is as typical, as appropriately rustic as the more poetic speeches of the bride and groom. When Bartolo describes the Commander as

> más gallardo que un azor,

as he prepares to meet the bull, his image has the same direct quality that was observed in the lovers' earlier conversation. The comic note is continued in the dialogue that follows, where the priest displays his fright and Costanza her childish faith in the efficacy of prayer (192–201). Humour also appears in the lovers' dialogue:

Peribáñez.	¿Tú quieres que intente un lance?
Casilda.	¡Ay no, mi bien, que es [el toro] terrible!
Peribáñez.	Aunque más terrible sea,
	de los cuernos le asiré,
	y en la tierra con él daré,
	porque mi valor se vea.
Casilda.	No conviene a tu decoro
	el día que te has casado,
	ni que un recién desposado
	se ponga en cuernos de un toro.
Peribáñez.	Si refranes considero,
	dos me dan gran pesadumbre:
	que a la cárcel, ni aun por lumbre,
	y de cuernos, ni aun tintero.
	Quiero obedecer. (208–22)

Peribáñez is tempted to display his strength and courage to the villagers. This gives the audience a hint of the courage he will show later in defence of his honour and of his care for his reputation. Casilda dissuades him by an appeal to his honour as a married man by a mild joke about horns. He follows her humour and confirms her plea by referring to a couple of proverbs. The play's main theme is introduced by some playful banter.

'*Ruido y voces dentro*.' Bartolo comes on stage and in a *romance* curses the bull. His curses recall those with which the Cid threatened Alfonso VI at the church of Santa Gadea at Burgos.[9] May this bull never find fresh grass in April; may his rivals always defeat him; may the streams deny him water; may he die, not by the golden sword or lance of a gentleman, but by goad-thrusts from a country mob, or the rusty steel of a lackey who attacks from behind! (226–45). Those on the stage as well as the spectators off it have no idea of the cause of Bartolo's vituperations. His deluge of curses breaks the harmony of the earlier scenes. The maledictions from an early ballad are a sort of parody of it, but, despite their comic effect, Bartolo gives in them a kind of prophecy of what was to come about later:

> [1] No te mate caballero
> con lanza o cuchillo de oro,
> mas lacayo por detrás
> con el acero mohoso,
> te haga sentar por fuerza
> y manchar en sangre el polvo! (240-5)

Casilda had already compared Peribáñez to a bull:

> Pareces en verde prado
> toro bravo y rojo echado. (111-12)

The bull's arrival had interrupted the marriage song and chased away the priest. We soon learn that it has nearly killed the Commander. Later Peribáñez curses it (389); Belardo alludes to it when he is a soldier in Peribáñez's troop (2476-7); and finally it provides the excuse for the Commander's serenade to Casilda:

> Cogióme a tu puerta el toro,
> linda casada;
> no dijiste: 'Dios te valga.'
> El novillo de tu boda
> a tu puerta me cogió;
> de la vuelta que me dio,
> se rió la villa toda;
> y tú, grave y burladora,
> linda casada,
> no dijiste: 'Dios te valga'.[10] (2718-27)

Peribáñez will slay his overlord the Commander. The lord will be slain by his former vassal. Is it pushing things too far to see a complex symbolism in this bull, which seems to stand both for the Commander's violent attack on Casilda's virtue and her husband's honour, and for the death of the Commander at the hands of his former peasant? The bull stands also, perhaps, for Peribáñez's Castilian sense of marital honour and his manliness. The bull's wounding of the Commander hints at the fate which will finally overtake him. The symbolism is both contradictory and implicit. The bull seems to stand for the violence of both Peribáñez and Don Fadrique, as it also stands for the violence that interrupts the peaceful marriage festivities. Peribáñez does not seek such violence, but when the Commander tries to gain his ends with force, the only way to check him is to kill him.

Bartolo's curses derive, as we have seen, from the *romancero*, and

Peribáñez thinks of a situation which relates them to the siege of Zamora in other *romances*:

> Repórtate ya, si quieres,
> y dinos lo que es, Bartolo;
> que no maldijera más
> Zamora a Bellido Dolfos. (246-9)

In the early version of this essay I tried to find in this allusion a further ambiguous symbolism. Professor Joseph Silverman politely corrected what can only be described as a mare's nest by a note in a later number of the journal in which my essay first appeared.[11] I withdraw my early suggestion now. The double associations of the oath at Santa Gadea and of the treachery of Bellido Dolfos merely add some appropriateness to the story of the defeat of treachery and necessary defiance of a local tyrant.

By the time the Commander, having recovered from his misadventure, leaves the lovers together, we have learned a great deal about the situation. Lope has not yet told us all he intended to describe and to develop, but he has shown us Don Fadrique's passion and the high value that Peribáñez places on his marital honour. Two men, from two different social classes, will come into conflict. The peasant speaks simply and uses metaphors drawn from everyday life; his manner of speech is echoed by his wife and even by Bartolo, a coarser, less poetic speaker. The Commander uses more rarified images and allusions; his hearers, even his personal attendants cannot always follow his thoughts. Vague hints of disaster have also been introduced into the narration of the nobleman's disaster and in the picturesque, half-comic curses that caused them.

Jealousy was mentioned in the first scene of the play. Peribáñez mentioned its dangers immediately after the ceremony; he and Casilda swear to one another never to be guilty of it (18-25). During their jokes about the bull's horns – I have already quoted them – the dangers of jealousy are perceptible behind the half-serious quips. He mentions it again at the end of his alphabet:

> Por la Z has de guardarte
> de ser zelosa, que es cosa
> que nuestra paz amorosa
> puede, Casilda, quitarte. (440-3)

When she is left alone with Inés after her husband has gone to Toledo, she declares that she is not jealous in her solitude (1396-1412). Such allusions prepare us for the hero's feelings when he finds his wife's portrait in the Toledan painter's studio.

In the studio Peribáñez and Antón discover Casilda's portrait. Antón perceives his friend's jealous fury (1692–3), but neither man reveals his feelings to the other while they are together. When the painter tells Peribáñez the truth about why he painted the portrait, he dissimulates his feelings, for when a man's honour is at stake he should not betray the fact, for then his honour would inevitably be compromised. Peribáñez remains outwardly calm and pretends merely to admire the painting. By hiding his emotions he comes to see that Casilda is innocent,[12] the Commander guilty. His dissimulation enables him to make this important discovery; by acting with discretion he has avoided what might have been an initial disaster.

When he is alone he soliloquises about his honour. The facts are obvious. His honour as a married man is at stake. The Commander, who ought to honour him, is taking away his honour. The normal relations of overlord to vassal are abolished. Woe to the humbly born man who seeks a beautiful wife! But his wife is virtuous; can they afford to go on living in Ocaña? How can they leave it? Such are the main themes of his speech. Perhaps its style is more important than its content. For now, instead of enumerating concrete details ('rubio y dorado aceite, conservado en la tinaja') he begins to generalise. His case is like that of other poor men married to pretty women. The Commander is referred to as 'la riqueza poderosa', Casilda, perhaps, as 'la virtud'.[13] The facts are assembled and argued in an almost judicial fashion:

> Basta que el Comendador
> a mi mujer solicita,
> basta que el honor me quita
> debiéndome dar honor.
> Soy vasallo, es mi señor,
> vivo en su amparo y defensa;
> si en quitarme el honor piensa,
> quitaréle yo la vida,
> que la ofensa acometida
> ya tiene fuerza de ofensa.   (1746–55)

When Peribáñez sees that his honour is endangered he no longer talks like a peasant. The threat to it makes him sharpen his wits. Honour is an aristocratic notion: its source is the King, it flows down through the nobility to the people. When he finds himself involved in a case of honour he begins, almost unconsciously, to talk like a gentleman.

He and Antón return to Ocaña. He sends Antón ahead, for he pretends to want to see how the harvest is progressing. Here he makes a moving speech, justly praised by Aubrun and Montesinos: 'Dans le passage qui commence "Estos son mi trigo y eras", Lope note avec une grande finesse comment Peribáñez ressent doublement l'affront, quand il contemple ces richesses qui lui créent une responsabilité sociale et morale' (p. xxxiv).

He admits his embarrassment at the idea of facing again his innocent wife. Then he exclaims:

> Estos son mi trigo y eras.
> ¡Con qué diversa alegría,
> oh campos, pensé miraros
> cuando contento vivía!
> Porque viniendo a sembraros,
> otra esperanza tenía.
> Con alegre corazón
> pensé de vuestras espigas
> henchir mis trojes, que son
> ahora eternas fatigas
> de mi perdida opinión. (1886-96)

These words express something more than their literal meaning, even a little more than the editors of the play include in their revealing commentary. For he sees Casilda in his fields and crops. Before he had compared her with 'la parva de trigo blanco' (65); and Antón had recently said to him:

> Y ¿no fuera mejor haza
> vuestra Casilda? (1863-4)

Don Fadrique had also used a similar metaphor before he declared that he wanted to change places with his tenant (540-5). Casilda was the crown of Peribáñez's life and work, as well as of his love. What he says about his harvest can also be applied to her if we look at other images and metaphors in the whole play.

The reapers' song reassures Peribáñez up to a point, although he realises that he must continue to be on his guard. Out of discretion, he hides from the men, his faithful servants, who have just confirmed his wife's innocence. He now returns home, where he is welcomed by Casilda and Inés. After telling her what presents he has brought back from Toledo, he begins to speak in the form of a parable. Casilda seems to take his words literally, but we cannot be quite sure from her answers that she does not appreciate their implications: after all, she has just rejected the Commander's advances. The parable illustrates Peribáñez's difficulties and enables him to find an excuse and a pretext for returning the *reposteros* to their owner. His own fall was an imaginary one, but his honour might suffer a fall if he did not take the necessary precautions. Casilda agrees with him about the *reposteros*. Then he declares with a hint of bitterness that aristocratic finery is out of place in a cottage. His language recalls Casilda's as she rejected her noble gallant. Peribáñez is just about to tell her the whole truth and the story of the portrait; but he restrains himself. The tone of the whole speech gives an idea of his anxiety:

> Pienso que nos está bien
> que no estén en nuestra casa
> paños con armas ajenas;
> no murmuren en Ocaña
> que un villano labrador
> cerca su inocente cama
> de paños comendadores
> llenos de blasones y armas.
> Timbre y plumas no están bien
> entre el arado y la pala,
> bieldo, trillo y azadón;
> que en nuestras paredes blancas[14]
> no han de estar cruces de seda,
> sino de espigas y pajas,
> con algunas amapolas,
> manzanillas y retamas.
> Yo ¿qué moros he vencido
> para castillos y bandas?
> Fuera de que sólo quiero
> que haya imágenes pintadas:
> la Anunciación, la Asunción
> ...
> y otras pinturas sagradas,
> que retratos es tener
> en las paredes fantasmas.
> Uno ví yo, que quisiera –
> pero no quisiera nada.
>
> (2038–58, 2063–7)

Peribáñez shows himself a peasant again. But there is bitterness in the adjectives *ajenas*, *inocente* and *comendadores*. Instead of light-heartedly comparing his life with that of the nobles, he defends, almost angrily, his own way of life. He almost goes too far when he speaks of the portrait, but he controls himself; his mention of the phantoms hanging on the walls, which means nothing to Casilda and Inés, reveals only to the spectators the cause of his anxiety. When Casilda is asked to prepare his bed, she even asks if he is ill.

Peribáñez is surprised by the arrival of Luján, who has to repeat to him the Commander's name. An identical situation occurred when the Commander was so troubled on the occasion of Peribáñez's visit to his palace. However, the hero soon recovers his outward calm, and, when Luján has given his message, he asks:

Peribáñez. ¿Eres tú aquel segador
 que anteayer entró en mi casa?
Luján. ¿Tan presto me desconoces?
Peribáñez. Donde tantos hombres andan,
 no te espantes.

Luján (*Aparte*).	Malo es esto.	
Inés (*Aparte*).	Con muchos sentidos habla.	(2076-81)

Peribáñez has been speaking 'con muchos sentidos' throughout the scene. Perhaps Casilda has grasped some of these meanings; perhaps she has understood nothing. Luján and Inés seem to have understood the last remark. The parallel is not quite exact, but might not Lope have been attempting, in these deliberate obscurities, in these litotes and parables, to give a kind of echo of the Commander's behaviour after he regained consciousness in Peribáñez's house? The Commander also talked in such a way that Luján did not understand him, and one could not say for sure whether Casilda grasped what was in his mind. Thus Peribáñez's speech tends to resemble that of the Commander before the latter makes him a captain. This growing artifice in his speech prepares us for his elevation in rank in Act III; it also shows how jealousy and a sense of honour can ennoble a man of common origin.

In the last act Peribáñez is made a captain. Before he is given his noble rank he shows some embarrassment in two speeches in which the rustic tone is predominant:

> Que [voy a servir] al Rey es justo, y también
> a vos, por quien tengo honor;
> que yo ¿cuándo mereciera
> ver mi azadón y gabán
> con nombre de capitán,
> con jineta y con bandera
> del Rey, a cuyos oídos
> mi nombre llegar no puede,
> porque su estatura excede
> todos mis cinco sentidos?
> Guárdeos muchos años Dios.   (2220-30)

> Pardiez, señor, hela [i.e. la espada] aquí.
> Cíñamela su mercé.   (2242-3)

The manner is rustic. When he reminds the Commander that his honour depends on him, he means two things: that the Commander is granting him honour in giving him that rank, and that that honour will be preserved only if the Commander gives up his designs on Casilda. Peribáñez is wearing proper captain's clothes. The Commander admits that both of them are equally well dressed (2232-3). And the captain turns round to address the other almost like an equal:

> Mi casa y mujer, que dejo
> por vos, recién desposado,
> remito a vuestro cuidado
> cuando de los dos me alejo.

> Esto os fío, porque es más
> que la vida con quien voy;
> que aunque tan seguro estoy
> que no la ofendan jamás,
> gusto que vos la guardéis,
> y corra por vos, a efeto
> de que, como tan discreto,
> lo que es el honor sabéis;
> que con él no se permite
> que hacienda y vida se iguale,
> y quien sabe lo que vale,
> no es posible que le quite.
> Vos me ceñistes espada,
> con que ya entiendo de honor,
> que antes yo pienso, señor,
> que entendiera poco o nada;
> y pues iguales los dos
> con este honor nos dejáis,
> mirad cómo le guardéis,
> o quejaréme de vos. (2266–89)

His words constitute a moral victory. The Commander is now quite puzzled by what Peribáñez has just said to him, and he is forced to admit (although only to himself) that he is behaving badly; he speaks of 'el pensamiento culpado' and refers to 'mi malicia' (2299–2300). He reassures himself only by counting on his greater influence and power. Peribáñez's speech, which implies much more than it states, expands what he had said to Casilda, Inés and Luján in the previous act. And this time his words are understood perfectly by the person to whom they are addressed. From now on Peribáñez is not merely a captain; he is also a *caballero discreto*.

At the head of his soldiers, Peribáñez bids his public farewell to Casilda. Their witticisms about soldiers and jealousy permit them to hold a conversation which reveals nothing to the characters who are listening to them. Aubrun and Montesinos remark of this passage: 'Peribáñez s'exprime dans un langage obscur et plein d'allusions que ses interlocuteurs ne peuvent ni ne doivent comprendre sur-le-champ.'[15] Casilda, however, seems to understand something, for her answer is quite pertinent:

Peribáñez.   Señora, voy a Toledo
a llevar estos soldados,
que dicen que son mis celos.
Casilda.   Si soldados los lleváis,
ya no ternéis pena dellos,
que nunca el honor quebró
en soldándose los celos.
Peribáñez   No los llevo tan soldados
que no tengo mucho miedo,

> no de vos, mas de la causa
> por quien sabéis que los llevo.
> Que si celos fueran tales
> que yo los llamara vuestros,
> ni ellos fueran donde van,
> ni yo, señora, con ellos.
> La seguridad, que es paz
> de la guerra en que me veo,
> me lleva a Toledo, y fuera
> del mundo al último extremo.
> A despedirme de vos
> vengo, y a decir que os dejo
> a vos de vos misma en guarda,
> porque en vos y con vos quedo,
> y que me deis el favor
> que a los capitanes nuevos
> suelen las damas, que esperan
> de su guerra los trofeos. (2367-93)

The farewell is courtly in style. This was deliberate on Lope's part, first because he wanted to demonstrate Peribáñez's new subtlety of expression, and second to explain how it came about. Peribáñez is now a *caballero*. He can speak just as well in his new language as he can in the old:

> ¿No parece que ya os hablo
> a lo grave y caballero?
> ¡Quién dijera que un villano
> que ayer al rastrojo seco
> dientes menudos ponía
> de la hoz corva de acero,
> los pies en las tintas uvas,
> rebosando el mosto negro
> por encima del lagar,
> o la tosca mano al hierro
> del arado, hoy os hablara
> en lenguaje soldadesco,
> con plumas de presunción
> y espada de atrevimiento!
> Pues sabed que soy hidalgo,
> y que decir y hacer puedo. (2394-2409)

Casilda explains that she cannot wholly follow this new manner of speaking, but she gives him the favour he asked her for.[16] It is a black ribbon:

> Es favor desesperado;
> promete luto o destierro. (2426-7)

He accepts it nevertheless (later the Commander will refuse a black cloak and insist on wearing a bright red one on the occasion of his last visit to

Casilda (2594-2606), although the first would have been more in keeping with a clandestine expedition).

The public farewell reinforces and accentuates several clues given in the scene where Peribáñez received his sword. The hero is still the Commander's inferior in rank; but he is more than the equal of that man of straw, Leonardo, as far as authority over the soldiers is concerned. And he no longer belongs to a different world. Lope has used all the means available to him to bring out the noble status of the new Peribáñez: he is as well dressed as his lord, he is a better leader of men than his master's lieutenant, he says the things that a captain says and in the way in which a captain says them. The change in social class shows through in his manner of speaking; but although he is a captain, he remains a peasant. He does not turn his back on the past; he has learned to play a superior role.

Peribáñez's next appearance on stage shows clearly this composite nature of his personality. He utters a soliloquy on honour into which he introduces a series of puns on the words *Oh caña* and *Ocaña*. One imagines that he has a reed in his hand. If the pun on this frail reed and the fragility of honour reminds us of the captain, what he says about his mare reminds us of the farmer. To be sure, the *conceptos* are more in keeping with the taste of the seventeenth century than with ours. Nevertheless they serve admirably Lope's dramatic purpose, which is to remind the audience that Peribáñez is at once a peasant and a captain:

> ¡Caña compuesta de ñudos
> y honor al fin dellos lleno,
> sólo para sordos bueno
> y para vecinos mudos!
> Aquí naciste en Ocaña
> conmigo al viento ligero;
> yo te cortaré primero
> que te quiebres, débil caña.
> . . .
> ¡Oh, bien haya la cebada
> que tantas veces te di!
> Nunca de ti me serví
> en ocasión más honrada.
> . . .
> Préciese de buena espada
> y de buena cota un hombre,
> del amigo de buen nombre
> y de opinión siempre honrada,
> de un buen fieltro de camino
> y de otras cosas así;
> que una bestia es para mí
> un socorro peregrino.   (2634-41, 2646-9, 2658-65)

Images and structure in *Peribáñez*

It is hard to say whether the prudent captain or the cunning peasant is uppermost in this man who makes his way into his house by his neighbour's door.

When at last he enters his house, it is the peasant who speaks. The tone of the monologue is almost plebeian. His cock sleeps securely in the midst of twenty or thirty hens, while he cannot be sure of the fidelity of one wife (2760-75). Formerly he saw his love in terms of country life, and now he also describes his outraged honour in these terms. The unrest among the animals seems to him to have the same cause (2788-95). Finally he gets into a sack of flour to hide. The prosaic – almost comic – details are provided to enhance, by way of contrast, the effect of the heroic vengeance he is about to take. Casilda and Inés enter. Inés is justly scolded. The Commander and Luján join them. While Luján takes Inés off stage, Casilda invokes her absent husband, a captain.[17] The vassal and the nobleman struggle for a moment in Peribáñez's mind before he asserts himself as he is:

> (¡Ay honra! ¿qué aguardo aquí?
> Mas soy pobre labrador,
> bien será llegar y haballe –
> pero mejor es matalle.)
> (*Adelantándose con la espada desenvainada.*)
> Perdonad, Comendador,
> que la honra es encomienda
> de mayor autoridad.
> (*Hiere al Comendador.*)   (2843-9)

The captain has just avenged the peasant.

When he appeals to the King, Peribáñez's language is direct. The fact that he is a captain is not stressed more than his status as a peasant. The comparison with the wolf and the lamb, which is perfectly conventional, could be used by anyone, of any social rank. When he asks Casilda to be given her reward for having handed him over, he acts as a good husband rather than as a captain. The King is struck by his humility; he pardons his crime and confirms his rank (3032-3122).

In *Peribáñez* Lope shows us the career of a man who rises in rank without ambition and who gives orders to others without pride.[18] His sense of honour is his most prominent characteristic and, if he betters his situation, it is because his whole life is subordinated to this principle. He is equally remarkable for his prudence and his discretion: they permit him to grasp the fundamentals of the situation in which he finds himself and to take appropriate action in any circumstances.

Peribáñez's promotion is reflected by the fact that the Commander is obliged to turn to Leonardo as well as to Luján in his attempts to seduce

Casilda.[19] One finds the same consistent values in the castle and in the cottages of Ocaña. The Commander is loyally served by his groom and by his gentleman-in-waiting. Luján is an inferior; he can pass for a reaper when it suits his master. When he speaks, he sometimes uses rustic metaphors or images in order to express himself:

Comendador.	Pues vamos, y buscarás
	el par de mulas más bello
	que él [Peribáñez] haya visto jamás.
Luján.	Ponles ese yugo al cuello;
	que antes de un hora verás
	arar en su pecho fiero
	surcos de afición, tributo
	de que tu cosecha espero;
	que en trigo de amor, no hay fruto
	si no se siembra dinero. (652–61)

The Commander explains that he is turning to a man of inferior rank because the object of his love is a peasant's wife (801–17). Luján is the tool he needs: he knows what peasants are like; moreover, he has himself plenty of the peasant cunning necessary to guide his master in this affair:

>   Si yo
> quisiera bien, con recato,
> quiero decir, advertido
> de un peligro conocido,
> primero que a la mujer
> solicitara tener
> la gracia de su marido.
> Éste, aunque es hombre de bien
> y honrado entre sus iguales,
> se descuidará también
> si le haces obras tales,
> como por otros se ven.
> Que hay marido que obligado,
> procede más descuidado
> en la guarda de su honor;
> que la obligación, señor,
> descuida el mayor cuidado.   (576–92)

However, each stratagem is a failure. The ownership of mules does not make of Peribáñez a man indifferent to his honour; the *reposteros* are returned to their owner; the pretended reaper does not manage to get his real master into the bedroom of his supposed one; and he is recognised by Peribáñez himself. Leonardo has no more scruples than Luján; his schemes are more successful – up to a point – but he also fails. The maliciousness of Luján, the deceitfulness of Leonardo and the effrontery of the Commander

Images and structure in *Peribáñez*

all come to naught before the prudence, integrity and determination of Peribáñez.

The idea of discretion underlies virtually all of the play. It is brought out, as we have seen, by the speeches and silences of Peribáñez, by his dissembling with the painter, his attitude towards Antón, towards the reapers, Casilda, Inés and Luján. The Commander, on the other hand, comes across as a rash man. Luján points this out to him:

> Ya que no fué tu amor, señor, discreto,
> el modo de tratarle lo parece. (818–19)

The Commander does not act only immorally and unjustly; he pursues his unwise intention with malice. He loves without discretion; but he appears prudent and, it seems, discreet in his enterprise. The word *parece* is full of meaning. Luján intends it as a compliment, but one can interpret it as a reprimand. When the Commander saw Casilda for the first time, he said:

> En peligro está mi vida
> por un pensamiento loco. (382–3)

What does this remark mean? That he has almost been killed because he imprudently attacked the bull which caused his fall? In fact he is referring to his desire for Casilda. The first time the Commander tries to gain access to Peribáñez's house, Mendo speaks of the 'atrevidos pies' of the nobleman. On the last occasion when he tries to do so, his insistence on wearing a scarlet cloak instead of a black one is an act of folly. And Luján tells him so (2594–2606). When he declares himself to Casilda, he says:

> Ya no puede mi afición
> sufrir, temer ni callar. (2814–15)

And Casilda herself pronounces his epitaph:

> Dios haya al Comendador.
> Matóle su atrevimiento. (2906–7)

His passion was unwise; in giving in to it, he meets his death. The wisdom of the vassal triumphs over the rash imprudence of his lord.

One can find other examples of prudence in the play. In this way Lope emphasised this idea to his audience. When the Commander approaches Peribáñez's house the two reapers Llorente and Mendo hear and recognise him in the darkness. Llorente suggests raising the alarm. Mendo thinks it would be better to say nothing:

> ¿No es mejor
> callar? (1508–9)

Llorente agrees and they remain silent. Lope does not explain why they think silence more appropriate. Is it due to cowardice on their part? There is no reason to believe that these two men, though they may be humble, are cowards. The fact is that there is nothing to be gained from crying out: if Casilda is innocent – as they suppose – they would ruin their master's honour by making her seem guilty. If she is not innocent, there would be no point in calling out. Here is an undoubted example of silence prompted by wisdom.

Antón, who is Peribáñez's colleague in the village council, as well as his friend and next-door neighbour, is wisdom personified. His interventions in the council chamber are timely. As Peribáñez's friend, he behaves very tactfully when they are together in the painter's studio. He admits that the portrait looks like Casilda, but he does not consider that he has the right to pronounce judgement on someone else's wife:

> Pedro, vos sois su marido;
> a vos os está más bien
> alaballa que no a mí. (1679–81)

Faced with the portrait, he realises that it is indeed of Casilda; but he is aware of Peribáñez's suppressed jealousy (1690–3). He gives nothing away: consoling a man whose honour is in danger would only increase that danger. He leaves his friend alone with the painter and goes off to saddle the horses. The two of them return to Ocaña almost equally aware of the situation. Peribáñez tells Antón that he wants to look at his fields before going home. Antón suggests that his friend has duties towards his wife; but Peribáñez invents a pretext to delay his arrival. Antón then mutters to himself:

> ¡Extraño caso!
> No quiero darle a entender
> que entiendo su pensamiento. (1870–2)

In the scene in the last act when Antón opens his door to Peribáñez, the two men appear to understand each other perfectly. Peribáñez speaks in hints. Antón grasps their meaning. Knowing that Casilda might be the innocent victim of outraged jealousy, he assures his friend of the innocence of his young wife, and will not let him into his house until Peribáñez acknowledges it too:

Peribáñez.	Por vuesa casa, mi Antón,
	tengo de entrar en la mía,
	que ciertas cosas de día
	sombra por la noche son.
	Ya sospecho que en Toledo
	algo entendiste de mí.
Antón.	Aunque callé, lo entendí;
	pero aseguraros puedo
	que Casilda –
Peribáñez.	No hay que hablar.
	Por ángel tengo a Casilda.
Antón.	Pues regaladla y servilda.
Peribáñez.	Hermano, dejadme estar.

Antón.	Entrad, que si puerta os doy,	
	es por lo que della sé.	
Peribáñez.	Como yo seguro esté,	
	suyo para siempre soy.	(2690–2705)

 Antón keeps quiet until the right moment. But when he can intervene effectively, he speaks. In fact Peribáñez does not need his advice. The course of events highlights Antón's tact and also reflects Peribáñez's wisdom. The audience's attention is therefore directed towards these two proverbs: silence is golden; look before you leap.

Peribáñez is one of the finest *comedias* of the Golden Age. Its excellence is not apparent if one judges the play merely from the point of view of the characters and from certain remarkable lyric passages. The action is simple, but its poetic texture is rich. Images and ideas are repeated on the lips of different characters. The critic will not appreciate them fully if he examines them in isolation. In the play Lope reveals attitudes common to all, and collective feelings, rather than purely individual temperaments. So we see that the villagers echo the language appropriate to Peribáñez and that the wisdom of Antón, Mendo and Llorente is a reflection of his wisdom. In the course of the play he undergoes a training for a kind of nobility by means of his cruel experience – so that there are numerous parallels between his attitude and language and those of the Commander: embarrassment when the name of the other is pronounced, indirect allusions, images and figures of speech.

 The play deals with several related subjects. It affirms the harmony of class relations;[20] for the perfidy of the Commander and the resultant violence of the hero lead us to assume that relations between lord and vassal are normally harmonious, provided that their differences are recognised and mutually respected.

 The play also concerns itself with the fundamental equality of all men. Peribáñez is a man as good, in the ordinary sense of the word, as his lord, and, in a strictly moral sense, he is better. Since the natural order of society is overthrown by the personal incontinence of the Commander, the struggle takes the ancient form of the alliance of the people with the king against the nobility. This, however, is a last resort, to which one has recourse only when the social hierarchy breaks down as a result of the bad behaviour of the lord. There is no reason to suppose that Lope would not have applauded an alliance of king and nobility against flagrantly rebellious rustics.

 The social order is harmonious because it is represented as a product of the land. The metaphors of the peasants are concrete, as if impregnated with earth. Peribáñez describes Casilda by comparing her to the fruits of his everyday labours. She is the crown of his farming life. Their love is part of the natural order of things, as are the faithfulness of servants and the affection of friends. This sense of idealised country life[21] – not the ideal of the Renaissance pastoral nor Rousseau's return to nature – is undoubtedly found in other works of the period; but it is expressed here with more fervour, so far as I can judge. It matters little whether such an idyllic state ever existed. It is an ideal which could perhaps be realised, because it took account of the hard manual labour and the physical risks of working in the fields. This ideal is not unrelated, in fact, to certain rustic ideas and aspirations, expressed from time to time in popular songs, proverbs, or even in the everyday gossip of ploughmen and farm servants. Lope has expressed it poetically, once and for all.

The images of the field of wheat and the bull recur constantly in the play. The field of wheat or the corn spread out on the threshing-floor represents in part Casilda herself, in part the life which she incarnates – and which she crowns. The bull is a more complex symbol. It interrupts the peace of the wedding, just as the Commander will later interrupt the peace of the married couple. Its horns are the image of what Peribáñez fears most, and against which he is induced to be on his guard. The bull is to perish at the hands of a lackey, a man of little worth, just as the Commander will later die at the hands of a rustic. It is a bad omen for both of them. Its strength is the strength of Peribáñez. It caught the Commander at Casilda's door, just as Peribáñez will later surprise the Commander in his own house. In fact the bull is the symbol of violence, the violence of the Commander and the counter-violence of Peribáñez. This complex function is skilfully suggested, but never directly expressed. It adds to the excitement and effectiveness of the play, although its meaning changes every time the bull is mentioned.

Finally *Peribáñez* is a didactic *comedia* in which virtue is rewarded and vice punished. Although it deals mainly with the concept of honour, it is also fundamentally Christian. The death of the Commander proves this, as does the absence of ambition and pride in the hero's speeches. But the most important thing is the idea of discretion or wisdom, often suggested or expressed directly by Peribáñez himself, by Antón, by the reapers and perhaps also by Casilda. Here Lope is in agreement with Cervantes, Calderón and Gracián: he expresses one of the main concerns of the seventeenth century. This idea here takes on a particular importance: Lope proves that wisdom can be as much a virtue of the common man as of the nobleman or the scholar. One's actions must be governed by wisdom: that is the principal moral lesson of the *comedia*. But for modern readers, its charm consists rather in the poetic image of a harmonious rustic society, happy in the knowledge that it is firmly rooted in the soil.

10
'Quando Lope quiere, quiere'[1]

El castigo sin venganza is one of the few Spanish tragedies of the seventeenth century. In it we are shown how a man's happiness is destroyed through his own fault, though it does not show his death. The play is the story of how the Duke of Ferrara brings about his own downfall as a private man, while he upholds his public position as the ruler of a state. It is thus both a tragedy and a *comedia palaciega*. The Duke's private failings destroy his private life, but his public life is finally vindicated. It is not a pure tragedy. We feel pity and fear for the Duke's victims, not perhaps for him. Nevertheless he is the hero of the play; his vices lead to his own undoing. And when his public virtue triumphs over his private vices, the victory is one of self-destruction. Not merely does he sacrifice all his private happiness; the sacrifice itself is shown as being a gesture that is admirable only in its public aspect. The failure of the private man is complete.

Conflicts between private inclinations and public duties were often repeated on the Spanish stage. The *comedia palaciega* specialised in such situations. In these plays we often see the heroic action of a ruler who subjugates his inclinations to his duty. Lope's play is remarkable because it gives us a ruler who virtually fails to do this. He never acts until it is too late. The inter-relation of public and private life is brilliantly depicted in the final climax. It is also to be remembered in all the earlier scenes. The Duke had his public functions to discharge; he also had private duties to his wife and son; and, further, there were his own inclinations that led him to commit sensual sins. The Duke's infidelities made his wife and son betray him. And the final 'punishment without vengeance', which killed wife and son and destroyed all his private happiness, was publicly a punishment of an invented rebellion and privately the vengeance of outraged honour.

In the course of this magnificent play we hear about the reactions of the ordinary Ferrarese, the ruled who occasionally influence the actions of the rulers and in whose thoughts the rulers' reputations lie. The Duke cannot afford to neglect his subjects because they are the keepers of his good name. In the opening scene he is afraid that they will recognise that he has played a practical joke or something worse (line 4), and he is deeply wounded when Cintia, a courtesan, says that he 'ha vivido yndignamente' (98) and that his 'viciosa libertad' (100) has been the common talk of the city. A few lines later he remarks how easily deceived are the vulgar, and how their judgements can easily go astray. He hopes, however, by his marriage, to silence the tongues of the malevolent (150–73).

The popular judgement uttered by Cintia is repeated in the palace itself. Batín talks to the Count of the Duke's

> proçeder vizioso,
> de propios y de estraños reprehendido.   (256–7)

The Count, in his reply, calls him 'mi vizioso padre' (291). The Duchess, even before she arrives in Ferrara, is much perturbed at having to share the bed of one of 'libre vida y condición' (604–5); and her love for the Count begins, as she more than once admits, because the Duke does not reform after his marriage.[2] The Duke married because it was his duty to guard his subjects against civil war after his death; but in marrying he had to go against his own tastes and the interests of his son (665–85). The Duchess repeats these facts in the second act (1344–7) when she tells the Count that he need not fear that she will bear the Duke children:

> Assí el Duque, la obedienzia
> rota al matrimonio santo
> va por mugerçillas viles
> pedazos de honor senbrando.
> Allí se dexa la fama,
> allí los laureles y arcos,
> los títulos y los nonbres
> de sus ascendientes claros,
> allí el balor, la salud
> y el tiempo tan mal gastado,
> haziendo las noches días
> en estos yndignos pasos.   (1366–77)

Up to the time that he leaves Ferrara for the battlefield, the Duke has stained his reputation as a respectable man in the eyes of his subjects, noble and common. He tries to preserve it by his marriage, and he fails. The attempt to preserve it and occasional remarks let fall, show that none the less he had wished to have succeeded and to have upheld the good of the commonwealth. When his son wished to accompany him to the wars, the Duke told him to stay behind because his house needed a governor: that is to say, that reasons of state forbade both Duke and Count to leave Ferrara at the same time (1700–7).

In this public world of Ferrara, the Duke fights a losing battle with

'Quando Lope quiere, quiere'

public opinion until he returns from the war. His private inclinations towards sensual indulgence and luxury are stronger than the obligations of marriage. He cannot conceal his licence from his wife, his son, his courtiers and his common subjects. His marriage seems meaningless to the wife with whom he slept only once during the month after his marriage (1034-5). The Duke married to please his subjects, and continued to live as though he had still been a bachelor. His married life was in fact, and even in appearance, a cloak to conceal his irresponsible love affairs from the eyes of his subjects. But his subjects, as we have seen, were not deceived.

Let us now examine the brilliant opening scene of the play. This scene is often quoted to illustrate Lope's literary and dramatic ideas; it has also importance in the interpretation of the play as a whole.

>   *El Duque de Ferrara, de noche; Febo y Ricardo, criados.*
> Ricardo.   ¡Linda burla!
> Febo.   Por estremo.
>   Pero ¿quién ymaginara
>   que era el Duque de Ferrara?
> Duque.   Que no me conozcan temo.   (1-4)

The play opens with these lines. What was the *burla*? No one tells us. The point of Febo's remark is that, whatever the *burla* was, it was not to be expected from the head of the state. The Duke's fear is natural enough. His reputation would suffer even if people laughed at what he might have done, had he been a private citizen, without censure. Perhaps it was not an innocent escapade but a serious offence that would have injured him even more in his subjects' eyes. After this Ricardo expatiates on the nature of disguises: elaborating on an idea of one of the Argensolas,[3] he says that Heaven itself is like a gigantic cloak on which moon and stars are clasp and orders (9-16). The Duke's uneasiness leaves him; he and his servants joke about the extraordinary metaphors of modern poets. Lope is not only poking fun at the devotees of *culteranismo* here; he also emphasises the prevalence of deception – a recurrent theme in the whole scene:

>   que la poesía ha llegado
>   a tan miserable estado,
>   que es ya como jugador
>   de aquellas transformadores,
>   muchas manos, ciençia poca,
>   que echan çintas por la boca
>   de diferentes colores.   (26-32)

The courtiers change the subject and discuss a beautiful woman who has an awkward husband. He too deceives. He takes money from his wife's lovers and then does not allow them to lie with her; he only pretends to be a cuckold! The mention of a devout mother with two daughters provokes the Duke's comment:

> Nunca de esteriores fío. (65)

Ricardo makes a joke about a lady called Cintia who lives near.

Duque.	Bamos allá.
Ricardo.	No querrá abrir a estas oras.
Duque.	¿No? y ¿si digo quién soy yo?
Ricardo.	Si lo dizes, claro está. (77–80)

Cintia, however, refuses to admit them. Ricardo cannot be accompanied by the Duke, she says. He is 'tan gran señor'; even if he has sown wild oats, he cannot conceivably go out to visit strange women when his wife is on her way from Mantua to Ferrara. Ricardo must have trumped up this story as an excuse to talk to her. Cintia is deceived because she refuses to believe that the Duke will sacrifice his reputation to curiosity or lust the night before his marriage. The Duke feels humiliated; Cintia told him what his conscience also told him, that his conduct was unfitting and imprudent. Febo tries to reassure him: many emperors have gone out into the streets as private persons to get away from court flatterers in order to hear what common citizens said about their way of ruling. The Duke cuts him short. The mob is fickle and easily deceived. He has done wrongly to act in this way. He will pull himself together and reform his ways by his marriage. Ricardo distracts him: they listen to the singers in the house of an *autor de comedias*. An actress speaks inside the wings. She compares past happiness to present misery. The Duke speaks his famous lines about how plays are the mirrors of life, and concludes:

> Basta, que oý del papel
> de aquella primera dama
> el estado de mi fama:
> bien claro me hablaua en él.
> ¿Que escuche me persüades
> la segunda? Pues no ygnores
> que no quieren los señores
> oýr tan claras verdades. (226–33)

He sees his honour in terms of the actress's lost happiness.

The scene as a whole tells us a number of things about the situation and the persons who take part in it. It tells us that the Duke is about to get married and that he has a bastard son Federico. It shows that the Duke, while engaged on nocturnal expeditions that are unbecoming to his position, is ashamed of his own behaviour. We are thus prepared both for the unfaithful husband of Act II and for the returning warrior of Act III who has done with evil courses. We learn about the marriage itself. But most important of all, we are given or hear about a series of shams, disguises, deceptions, illusions and contradictions.

A disguised Duke behaves like an ordinary citizen; a man just about to marry goes round the houses of courtesans. The sky is really a cloak. The modern poets are not poets but jugglers. The cuckold is not really a cuckold at all. The Duke is not recognised because his private actions do not accord with his public functions. A true fact is interpreted as a ruse to start an idle conversation. Flattering servants try to give a good colour to what the Duke recognises as his failings. The recital of a fiction makes the Duke realise a moral fact. A Duke admits that the gentry cannot bear to be told the truth about themselves. In all these instances we are shown how reality and appearance often conflict with one another. The theme recurs constantly as the play progresses.

We next see the Duke in a scene with Aurora, before the Duchess arrives in the palace. Like Lucindo and Albano in an earlier scene (337–9), he sees that his marriage must cause his son intense chagrin, because the Duchess's children will be the heirs to the Duchy. Aurora tells the Duke that she and Federico are in love, that their marriage will make him forget his disappointment at being deprived of the succession. The Duke believes this account of his son's emotional life – which the audience know was once, but is now no longer, true. This is his first misapprehension. He waits to receive his wife with the courtesy appropriate to the occasion, but his solicitude for her health does not reveal the ardent desire of a lover. In brief, polite phrases of welcome and compliment, he shows that Cassandra is unlikely to make him forget the pleasures to which he has for so long been accustomed.

In the scene with his son in the second act we see the consequences of his misapprehension. The two men enter together in earnest talk, immediately after Cassandra has expatiated to her lady-in-waiting on her husband's neglect. The Duke ignores, or does not see, her; she goes out threatening vengeance. The Duke says that he attributes his son's melancholy to his own marriage, but the Count refuses to admit that this is the true cause.

> La falta de salud se ve en mi cara,
> pero no la ocasión. (1123–4)

As the Duke brings forward the suggestion that his son marry Aurora, he again mentions the 'agrabios', the injury inflicted on his son by the marriage (1146). The dialogue continues:

Federico. Poca esperiençia de mi pecho tienen;
neçiamente me juzgan agrauiado,

> pues sin causa offendido me preuienen.
> Ellos saben que nunca reprobado
> tu casamiento de me voto ha sido;
> antes por tu sosiego desseado.
>
> *Duque.* Assí lo creo y sienpre lo he creýdo;
> y esa obediençia, Federico, pago
> con estar de casarme arrepentido. (1147–55)

Father and son are both lying. The Count had been angry at his father's marriage, but that was before he met his stepmother; the Duke admitted to Aurora in the other scene what he now denies. Perhaps neither man means the other to believe him. Conscious insincerity is part of the courtier's equipment, and it might even affect what father and son said to one another. When the Duke says that he has repented of his marriage, he is obviously speaking the truth; if Cassandra walked out hastily a few lines beforehand, we now see that she had some reason for doing so.

The scene ends in a quarrel. For reasons that the audience knows, but not the Duke, the Count is unwilling to marry Aurora. He therefore invents a pretended jealousy of the Marquis, lest he should 'escriuir sobre papel borrado' (1170). The Duke tells him that breath only appears to stain a mirror. He replies that water is used by blacksmiths to increase the intensity of their fires. Both similes show that appearances deceive: the Duke is defending a lady's honour, his son – her former lover – is casting doubts upon it. The Duke knows that Federico's aspersion is unjustified, so he angrily exclaims:

> Mui neçio, Conde, estás y ynpertinente.
> Hablas de Aurora, qual si noche fuera,
> con bárbaro lenguaje y yndecente. (1192–4)

The pun on Aurora's name is the Duke's diagnosis of the Count: he thinks white black. The Count has lied; he does not really believe that Aurora is playing him false. He has in fact deliberately made white black; unable to conceal his emotional distress, he was able to make the Duke think that it had a different cause. He deceived the Duke, and the reply of the latter had a hidden truth that was concealed from the speaker. The imagery of this scene – the stain of breath on a glass pane, the water on the smith's coals and the pun on Aurora's name – emphasises the Count's deception of his father and the other deceits and confusions with which all in Ferrara are surrounded.

If Cassandra had not been married to the Duke, she and Federico would have made a good match. The fact is implied in the scene in which he rescues her after the accident, and it is twice asserted by each of the two servants Batín and Lucrecia. Lucrecia tells Cassandra that she would be happier with Federico than with the Duke (589-90). And in the second act Lucrecia repeats, with greater emphasis:

> Conforme a naturaleza
> y a la razón, mexor fuera
> que el Conde te mereçiera
> y que contigo casado,
> asegurando su estado,
> su nieto le sucediera.   (1098-1103)

The marriage of Federico and Cassandra, if it could have taken place, would have been agreeable to nature and to reason. Batín says much the same thing to his master at the end of Act I (989-91), and previously he had exclaimed against the laws of the world – '¡pesia las leyes del mundo!' – which made this marriage impossible. These remarks are made without irony or flattery by the servants. Natural and reasonable love is thwarted by human acts; the lovers rebel against the laws of the world, and finally they are punished for their rebellion. Lope, as will be seen, does not condone the lovers' behaviour, but he makes its origin understandably human by these comments of the two servants, as well as by the early behaviour of the two lovers.

The Count Federico is proud of the way in which he can dissimulate. He tells the Duke that if he had been piqued at the prospect of not succeeding to the Duchy, he would have known how to conceal the fact (1120-2). Throughout his affair with the Duchess, he never lets anyone but the faithful Batín have an indication of his feelings, except, of course, the Duchess herself. Aurora finds out, because she spies on him, and one other man, the writer of the anonymous letter to the Duke, finds out somehow. When Federico welcomes the Duchess on her arrival the Duke – who believed his son was piqued at the marriage – remarks that 'es Federico discreto' (889). If the Duke speaks aloud so that the others hear him, this is just a pointless compliment; but if it is spoken as an aside, the Duke means that he is proud of the way in which his son can conceal his feelings under a mask of flattery and compliment. In the last act the Count shows some cunning in his plan to marry Aurora after all, so as to divert suspicion from his amorous relations with his stepmother. Federico is clever, but even a deceiver can be deceived, and he does not know how to thread his way through the labyrinth that surrounds him.

Federico's pique at the prospect of dispossession by his stepmother's children was genuine enough before he met her.

> De mí mismo quisiera retirarme;
> que me cansa el hablarme
> del casamiento de mi padre, quando

> pensé heredarle; que si voy mostrando
> a nuestra gente gusto, como es justo,
> el alma llena de mortal disgusto,
> camino a Mantua, de sentido ageno;
> que voy por mi veneno
> en yr por mi madrastra, aunque es forzoso. (247-55)

He tries to appear pleased in order to satisfy the vassals, but his soul is filled with deadly bitterness against his father. He confesses his feelings to Batín; Lucindo and Albano guess them because he failed to preserve this appearance. The later error of the Duke and others consisted in assuming that his feelings were unaffected by the circumstances of his meeting with Cassandra and by her charm and beauty. After muttering his bitter complaints to Batín he is told by his servant to bear his afflictions patiently, to simulate happiness, pleasure and trust so that his obvious envy should not give occasion for vengeance (313-18). He rejects this advice, but he was in fact trying to some extent to carry it out. Until Cassandra arrives Federico shows that he is afraid of what may (or may not) happen in the future – the birth of legitimate heirs who will displace him; in fact he is afraid of what never happens, and his fear soon gives way to emotions of a very different kind, once he has met Cassandra. The melancholy remains, though it now has another cause. No wonder that the others all continue to attribute it to the original source.

Federico does not mention his former love for Aurora until rather later in the play. Aurora, as we have seen, tells the Duke about it while they wait together for the arrival of Cassandra. Aurora thinks that Federico's love for her is permanent, and she asks the Duke to make him her husband for that reason. The meeting with Cassandra makes Federico forget all about Aurora, just as it banishes his chagrin at his father's marriage. Neither the Duke, nor Aurora, nor the courtiers observe these changes in his attitude. They all assume that he remains in love with Aurora and angry because of the marriage; they take a transient mood and a fleeting affection to be permanent and enduring. Federico does not consciously deceive them here; they all make mistakes.

At the end of the first act he tries to take stock of his position. If life is a dream, he has a waking dream which could not even occur in the mind of a man in delirium (928-35). He calls on God to help him (958) and refers to his strange madness. Batín guesses that his stepmother's beauty is the cause of his plight. Federico admits that this is so. He now begins to 'die of an impossible love, to feel a jealousy that is possible enough (992-3). Despite the invocation of God's name, he makes no attempt to fight this new and sudden passion. He realises the danger he is in, only to succumb completely to it.

'Quando Lope quiere, quiere'

After Federico has disgusted his father by casting doubts on Aurora's honour, Batín exclaims:

> ¡Oh qué bien has negoçiado
> la graçia del Duque!

The Count replies:

> Espero
> su desgraçia, porque quiero
> ser en todo desdichado;
> que mi desesperaçión
> ha llegado a ser de suerte
> que sólo para la muerte
> me permite apelaçión.
> Y si muriera, quisiera
> poder boluer a viuir
> mil vezes, para morir
> quantas a viuir boluiera.
> Tal estoy, que no me atreuo
> ni a viuir ni a morir ya,
> por ver que el viuir será
> boluer a morir de nueuo.
> Y si no soy mi omiçida,
> es por ser mi mal tan fuerte,
> que porque es menos la muerte,
> me dexo estar con la vida.   (1196–1215)

This speech is not to be dismissed as so much quibbling and conceits. Federico is revealing his condition so that the audience may judge it. He shows that even if his love for Cassandra was, in the first place, involuntary, he has chosen to accept it. He not only wallows in misery; he chooses misery and prefers it to death. '*Espero* su desgraçia'; '*quiero* ser en todo desdichado'; 'si muriera, *quisiera* poder boluer a viuir... para morir'. His will is fixed in his fatal, unhappy love; he is in despair – a word which does not mean mere hopeless gloom, but the state of the damned souls in hell – and he longs for death.[4] He will not help himself. He is glad that his father has quarrelled with him, he refuses to tell Batín the cause of his trouble and he even drives away this faithful servant in order that he may luxuriate in solitary woe:

> Vete, si quieres, tanbién,
> y déxame solo aquí,
> porque no aya cosa en mí
> que aun tenga sombra de bien.   (1244–7)

His evil is his own choice. He has not struggled against it or tried to escape from it. Lope has shown us this victory of passion over reason convincingly enough; that does not mean that he meant us to approve of it. Federico is seen as potentially a lost soul, and he himself thinks that he is lost; he has voluntarily accepted damnation. He perversely accepts this fate before he has had any sensual satisfaction or enjoyed any emotional requital from the woman who has caused it all. He is at best over-dramatising a situation that other men have successfully overcome; but if we take his words literally – and Lope may well have meant us to do so – we can only assume that Federico would have rejected salvation from any quarter from which it might have come. He is glad to have fallen out with his father; he drives away Batín.

The scene with Cassandra serves to repeat the fact that he is not in love with Aurora and that he bears no grudge against his stepmother. He goes on to expatiate on his 'death':

> Yo me muero sin remedio,
> mi vida se va acabando,
> como vela, poco a poco,
> y ruego a la muerte en vano
> que no aguarde a que la çera
> lleg[u]e al v́ltimo desmayo,
> sino que con breue soplo
> cubra de noche mis años.   (1416–23)

Cassandra still thinks he is referring to Aurora, but he disillusions her. Then he invokes the myths of Phaeton, Icarus, Pegasus, the wooden horse of Troy and Jason to assert the impossibility of his love. Finally the fable of how hunters catch pelicans enables him to declare himself to Cassandra. He again finishes by mentioning his death:

> porque es tanto mi peligro,
> que juzgo por menos daño,
> pues todo ha de ser morir,
> morir sufriendo y callando.   (1528–31)

In this scene we see the man who knows what he wants and who believes he cannot get it. He has not seen that she is attracted to him, that the unfaithfulness of his father has made her ready enough to accept the love of another, and so he continues to indulge in self-pity and death-wishes. He is so much absorbed by the impossible sin in thought, that the sin in act will make little difference to his mental state.[5]

Aurora's efforts to rouse Federico's love by making him really jealous of her favours to the Marquis Gonzaga are completely unsuccessful. Batín draws his attention to what is happening and tries to awaken his interest too. The Count remains unmoved:

> Eso fué entonzes, Batín,
> pero es otro tiempo agora.   (1745–6)

'Quando Lope quiere, quiere'

The servant soon lays his finger on the source of the trouble. If swans and cocks cannot bear rivals, how can men? Federico's reply that the best punishment for a faithless woman is to leave her with her new pleasure completes Batín's conviction that his master now loves another woman. Federico calls Batín 'bachiller' and sends him away to see how the Duke is faring. As he leaves Batín says:

> Sin causa neçio me nombras,
> porque abonar tus tristezas
> fuera más neçia lisonja. (1794-6)

Federico then sees Cassandra again. She has now largely overcome her scruples. In an aside he talks of her as 'desnuda la dulce espada por quien la vida perdí' (1859-60). She asks about his melancholy and provokes a declaration by reciting the history of Antiochus. Then comes his avowal, the gloss of a fifteenth-century *quintilla*,[6] which proves how he has lost his soul, his fear of God and his respect for his father. His impossible love holds him in despair:

> En fin, señora, me veo
> sin mí, sin vos, y sin Dios:
> sin Dios, por lo que os desseo;
> sin mí, porque estoy sin vos;
> sin vos, porque no os poseo. (1916-20)

He fully reveals to her how his love for her is unrequited, yet it has made him forget his duty to himself, to others and to God. She urges him to flee, but he can only die. He asks for her hand to kiss in farewell. He takes it, and the kiss does its work and undoes her as well as him. She struggles half-heartedly, but the kiss has ended her resistance. Both leave the stage by opposite exits, none the less the spark has been kindled; events will take their course. Federico's final conceit is to rejoice that his soul is immortal, so that he can enjoy his guilty love throughout eternity (2027-30).

In the development of the affair there is a curious progression in the use of ceremonies between stepson and stepmother. '*Federico sale con Cassandra en los brazos*' (339), runs the stage direction for their first entrance together. A chivalrous man rescues a helpless woman; we see the human beings, not the courtiers. When he learns who she is, he kneels to her (398); she asks for an embrace (407), but he kisses her hand. She is more unceremonious than he. Later on at the reception, she asks why the Count must stand while she and the Duke remain seated (862). She is told that Federico will be the first noble to kiss her hand as a vassal. In the first scene between the two in the second act, we have the following lines:

Cassandra. Federico.
Federico. Mi señora,

	dé vuestra Alteza la mano	
	a su esclauo.	
Cassandra.	¿Tú en el suelo?	
	Conde, no te humilles tanto;	
	que te llamaré exçelençia.	
Federico.	Será de mi amor agrauio.	
	Ni me pienso lebantar	
	sin ella.	
Cassandra.	Aquí están mis brazos.	(1296–1303)

Later in the scene she thous him, while he addresses her as 'señora' and 'vuestra Alteza', but as his feelings become increasingly engaged, he returns the thou to her. And in the last scene of the second act her action in allowing him to kiss her hand involves the surrender of all her moral and religious scruples:

>   que por vna mano sube
>   el veneno al corazón.   (2014–15)

The love affair is externalised in these gestures of etiquette; the conventions of court life can be as good poetic symbols as Peribáñez's tools and stock. Cassandra is friendly, condescending, informal; Federico, led deeper into the morass, abandons formality for boldness and finally conquers with a sign of respect and good manners.

There is little need to follow Federico's part in the third act. He has had four months of illicit love, and Aurora has learned his secret. The Duke's return fills him with consternation, and he loses any sympathy that we may have felt for him, by his decision to court Aurora again to distract suspicion from his incestuous love affair. Aurora, knowing the truth, refuses to play her part. Cassandra is offended and threatens to betray both herself and her lover to the Duke. Federico perseveres with his plan, but finally he is deceived by the disillusioned Duke, kills his love whom he thinks a vulgar conspirator and is himself killed – 'no shriving time allowed' – by the Duke's orders. There is a terrible appropriateness in this ending: the Duke's trumped-up accusation might have been true, because Federico had originally been angry at the prospect of being deprived of the succession; the secret murder of Cassandra by her lover repays the secret sins they had committed together; and perhaps he is given no opportunity to repent because he has already surrendered his soul.

Van Dam considers that Cassandra is the most important character in the play; he calls her 'la heroína... cuyo carácter está pintado con el mayor esmero'.[7] It is hard to say that Lope intended her to be more important than the Duke or Federico, but her part is well thought out and brilliantly written. Her reactions are more comprehensible to a modern reader than are those of the two men, and perhaps for that reason her part has been considered more important than theirs. Lope, perhaps, judged her less harshly than he did Federico. In the spirited scene in the last act when she rates her lover for his desire to marry Aurora, her outspoken words seem superior to Federico's pusillanimity on that occasion or than the neurotic moodiness with which he declared his illicit passion. She is not swept into sin as he is; she gradually accepts it, but puts up some kind of struggle against it. Nevertheless, the fact that she is more easily credible to us today does not mean that Lope meant the whole play to revolve round her rather than the others. Her part is important, but the Duke and Federico are possibly more important still.

Cassandra is a stranger to Ferrara. She does not recognise the man who saves her life, and he does not recognise her (363–402). The introductions put the two on a friendly footing, and Cassandra goes on to say that she has more pleasure in having the Count as her son than in being Duchess of Ferrara (495–7). A scene later we hear how she is worried about the Duke's irregular life (603–6), and her presentiments are bitterly fulfilled by his cold welcome of her, by his subsequent discourtesy and unfaithfulness. The second act opens with her long speech to Lucrecia in which she wishes she were of humble rank and more happily married. The Duke, she says, takes no more notice of her than of a chair, bureau or portrait, and she throws out a hint of the possible consequences when she says:

> y es mexor, si causa es
> de algún pensamiento extraño,
> no dar ocasión al daño,
> que remediarle después. (1070–3)

Lucrecia sympathises but cannot help her. A husband cannot be roused, as a gallant can, by favours to another man. Has she told her father of her sufferings? No, she has not done so. Lucrecia then refers to the moodiness of Federico, and her mistress says that there is no real cause for it, because she will not bear children to the Duke. The Duke and Federico then come in; neither man appears to notice Cassandra. As she leaves the stage she says bitterly:

> Bamos, Lucreçia; que, si no me engaño,
> deste desdén le pesará algún día. (1136–7)

Aurora tells Cassandra that the Count is upset at his father's marriage and that he has refused to speak to her because of it. Cassandra has accepted the story told by Federico to the Duke that his disdain for Aurora is due to her favours to the Marquis. Aurora leaves her after remarking that Federico's sadness 'ni es amor ni zelos es' (1295). This statement is not quite true, but it is nearer the truth than either of the two women suspect. Cassandra then explains to him that he need not fear the Marquis as a rival or that she will bear children to her husband. She begins by scolding him and ends by weeping at her own plight. Her stepson is soon in tears himself as he explains that he is in the grip of a very different passion, that he is not jealous of unborn children, that he is not in love with Aurora but with another woman who is inaccessible as the sun. Cassandra, in all innocence, tries to cheer him by telling him:

> Las almas de la mugeres
> no las viste jaspe elado;
> ligera cortina cubre
> todo pensamiento humano.
> Jamás amor llamó al pecho,
> siendo con méritos tantos,
> que no respondiese el alma:
> 'Aquí estoy; pero entrad paso.'
> Dile tu amor, sea quien fuere;
> que no sin causa pintaron
> a Venus tal vez los griegos
> rendida a vn sátiro o fauno.
> Más alta será la luna,
> y de su çerco argentado
> baxó por Endimïón
> mil vezes al monte Lathmo.
> Toma mi consejo, Conde;
> que el edificio más casto
> tiene la puerta de çera.
> Habla, y no mueras callando. (1482–1501)

She is in fact revealing herself in spite of herself. The curtain, the wax doors are frail, as she says, but their preservation and inviolability are all that separate reputable behaviour from selfishness, lust and passion. Thanks to the strength of Federico's feelings and to the Duke's churlishness, she is doing what Federico accuses her of doing: fanning the flames of his passion. All that she has said about other women applies only too well to herself. Federico's speech about the pelican makes her discover the truth: she is the sun if Aurora was only the dawn. She is left to struggle: here is the tool for revenging herself on her noble but boorish husband,[8] moreover 'las partes del Conde son grandes' (1572–3). She feels herself carried away, but she struggles a little against a sin in thought.

> Salid, çielo, a la deffensa,
> aunque no yerra quien piensa;
> porque en el mundo no hubiera
> honbre con onra si fuera
> ofensa pensar la ofensa.

> Hasta agora no han errado
> ni mi honor, ni mi sentido,
> porque lo que e consentido
> ha sido vn error pintado.
> Consentir lo ymaginado,
> para con Dios es error,
> mas no para el desonor;
> que diferençian yntentos
> el ver Dios los pensamientos
> y no los ver el honor.   (1577–91)

She says that though she has entertained thoughts of adultery, she has not sinned by act or offended honour. She has, however, taken the first steps towards both.

In the last scene of the second act she gives way in spite of her conscience. Her husband's ill-treatment of her continues, and she is out for revenge. Federico is 'galán' and 'discreto' (1826). If she should let herself go, other women have done as much before. So out comes the story of Antiochus, and he tells her how he is 'sin mí, sin vos, y sin Dios'. This speech is a last warning to her; she thinks again of God, of her husband, of divine and human warnings. The only remedy is for them not to see one another; he must fly from her. He craves a last boon, to kiss her hand in farewell. Weakly she gives it to him, and she finds that she is in his power. Although the lovers leave by opposite exits, we know now that they cannot remain apart.

When the Duke returns from the war he is a new man. The sudden reformation of his nature through taking arms at the behest of the Pope has been censured as untrue to life by some critics. The change is admittedly sudden, but the Duke had shown his hatred of his old vices while he still pursued them (165–73). The fact that he was called on to subordinate his own convenience and ambition to serve the symbol of Christian unity might well lead a man to control his baser instincts when he returned. At its lowest, the conversion may be taken as an example of how added responsibilities sometimes lead a man to an increased self-control: a phenomenon that is observed frequently enough in daily life, as well in plays such as *Peribáñez*. Nothing is to be heard against his reputation now; Ricardo says:

> El Duque ha ganado vn nonbre
> que por toda Ytalia suena;
> . . .
> con que ha sido tal la enmienda,
> que trahemos otro Duque.
> Ya no ay damas, ya no ay çenas,

> ya no ay broqueles, ni espadas,
> ya solamente se acuerda
> de Cassandra, ni ay amor
> más que el Conde y la Duquesa.
> El Duque es vn santo ya.   (2351–63)

The Duke is pleased that Federico governed his state with discretion and prudence (2310–15). Hardly has he greeted his family after his return than he settles down to study the petitions of his subjects (2467, etc.). In all this we can see that there has been a real change in the man; but Lope drops several hints that the conversion was not quite complete.

After the Duke has greeted his wife and his son, he thanks them for their good care of his realm and briefly refers to his victories. He then says:

> Y assí, pienso trocar de aquí adelante
> la ynquietud en virtud, porque mi nonbre
> como le aplaude aquí, después le cante,
> que quando llega a tal estado vn ombre,
> no es bien que ya que de balor mexora,
> el viçio más que la virtud le nombre.   (2322–7)

A little later, talking of his wife, he says to Batín:

> Yo pienso de oy más quererla
> sola en el mundo, obligado
> desta discreta fineza
> y cansado juntamente
> de mis mozedades neçias.   (2438–42)

Batín replies:

> Milagro ha sido del Papa
> llebar, señor, a la guerra
> al Duque Luis de Ferrara,
> y que vn hermitaño buelba.
> Por Dios, que puedes fundar
> otra Camáldula.   (2443–8)

The Duke then says: 'Sepan mis basallos que otro soy' (2448–9). In all these speeches the Duke seems to look on his conversion as a public, rather than as a private, matter: 'sepan mis basallos', 'mi nonbre le cante'. There is a suspicion of self-righteousness, of being righteous overmuch, in what he says and in the way he says it. Batín, who throughout this scene is speaking with his tongue in his cheek, compares the Duke to a hermit and to the founders of the Camaldula; hermits had not always a very good reputation in seventeenth-century Spain, and that of the Camaldula was also doubtful.[9] Later on we shall see that Batín calls the Duke a 'santo fingido' (2800). So that there are indications that the Duke, though he has changed very considerably from what he had been in the first scene of the play, is not quite the good man he thinks he is.

We can now summarise the mistakes made by the three principal characters before the moment in which the Duke in Act III reads the anonymous letter.

The Duke is a man who lives in the past. He leads a licentious life before he marries and after. He neglects the fact that his marriage involves new responsibilities, that when he pursues his old courses he compromises his own honour and insults his bride. He has some sense of public duty; he wants his state to be well run; he is anxious to do his best for Federico and for Aurora. But he never realises that his vices are disreputable as well as sinful, that he is really giving his proud-spirited wife cause to seek revenge and that he is in fact the artificer of his own dishonour. He never suspects duplicity in his son, whom he treats frankly (1688). He is not perspicacious, and in fact Federico deceives him, consciously or unconsciously, in a number of ways. The Duke thinks:

1. that Federico's melancholy was caused by his own marriage. Here he is living in the past, for Federico had been angry about being dispossessed before he met Cassandra.

2. that Federico was still in love with Aurora after Cassandra had arrived in Ferrara.

3. that Federico was in earnest when he talked of Aurora's favours to the Marquis Gonzaga.

4. that Federico and Cassandra will have disagreed with each other (2415) or misgoverned (2486–7) during the time he was away fighting for the Pope.

5. that no matter how he behaved towards her, Cassandra would always be a good wife to him.

Federico lives in the present without thought of the past. He falls in love, criminally, with Cassandra, and he never attempts to struggle with his illicit passion but allows it to dominate him completely. He lets his love for Aurora die when the new love comes; he never thought of his father with the respectful affection and gratitude that he owed him. He cherishes his neurotic moods instead of trying to see himself as one who had lived and loved before Cassandra came to Ferrara. He too makes a number of assumptions about those around him which are all proved false as the play progresses:

1. Before Cassandra arrives he assumes that she will bear children to the Duke who will dispossess him.

2. When he begins to fall in love with her he assumes that she will never return his passion.

3. He assumes that the affair with Cassandra can be terminated at will, that she will react as he does when the Duke returns from the wars.

4. He assumes that Aurora will be willing to marry him after he has left her for his stepmother and ignored her completely for a number of months.

5. He considers that he is able to keep all Ferrara in ignorance of his affair by the pretence of marrying Aurora.

Cassandra's errors are not unlike Federico's, but she sees with clearer eyes and is less superficial. A stranger to Ferrara, she inevitably assumes what she is told: that Federico bears her a grudge because she will bear children to the Duke, that Federico is in love with Aurora, but that he is madly jealous because Aurora has shown favour to the Marquis. Federico clears away all these misconceptions in the second act. She, more excusably than Federico, cuts herself off from her past. He quarrelled with his father; she refused to write to hers to tell him how the Duke treated her. Her great mistake, however, was to assume that the Duke would always continue to treat her as though she were a piece of furniture. She made no effort to detect those aspects of his nature which Lope shows us and which foretell his reformation on his return from the wars. She was so much angered by his slights that, in spite of human respect, honour and religion, she seized on the temptation that Federico offered to her. Her struggle was more prolonged than his, and her love for him, once awakened, was more profound, less purely emotional and of the moment, than was his for her. She falls as deeply as he does, and she is determined to pursue the incestuous affair after the Duke returns. In doing this she is more courageous than her lover, whose cowardice is more repellent than his earlier moodiness. Her will is now fixed on the evil thing as his was before. He tries to retreat; she refuses to do so. The discreet Count does not understand the woman he has chosen:

¡O qué mal me conozes! (2283)

she exclaims as she threatens to reveal all that has passed to the Duke.

The Duke does not learn the truth until he receives the anonymous delation. He is struck with horror, and an instant's reflection persuades him that the letter is probably true. He has deserved punishment for his sexual excesses.[10] As Cassandra and Federico had seen their predicament in classical anecdote or fable (Phaeton, Icarus, Endymion, Antiochus, Myrrha and so forth), so he thinks of Absalom's rebellion that was David's punishment for the murder of Uriah the Hittite and the adultery with Bathsheba. The fictions of the poets lead to sin; the true Scriptures bring self-knowledge. Although he has not committed murder like David, his conscience convicts him. He deserves the punishment; the letter told the truth. He then goes on to wonder how he can avenge his outraged honour without publishing the fact that it has been outraged.

The scene between father and son follows this soliloquy. Federico asks for Aurora's hand while he pretends that his feigned jealousy was the imaginary consequence of the strength of his love. The Duke simulates approval, and then he says that he must discuss the matter with Federico's 'mother'. Then follows a series of speeches in which Federico hopes to deceive the Duke by hinting at disagreements between himself and his stepmother, but which the Duke, who now suspects the truth, rightly interprets as a sign that Cassandra is now more than a 'mother' to his son.

Federico.	No siendo su sangre yo ¿para qué quiere dar parte vuestra Alteza a mi señora?	
	. . .	
Duque.	¿Sientes que madre la llame? Pues dízenme que en mi ausençia, de que tengo gusto grande, estubistes mui conformes.	
Federico.	Eso, señor, Dios lo sabe; que prometo a vuestra Alteza, aunque no açierto en quexarme, pues la adora, y es razón, que aunque es para todos ángel, que no lo ha sido conmigo.	
	. . .	
	A vezes me faboreze, y a vezes quiere mostrarme que no es posible ser hijos los que otras mugeres paren.	
Duque.	Dizes bien, y yo lo creo.	(2582–2606)

Federico thinks that he is deceiving his father but he is not. The Duke deceives him by pretending to be deceived. So the wheel turns full circle, and Federico condemns himself by the means that he thought would have saved him. The scene is full of irony: the mutual deceit of father and son, of husband and lover, of avenger and victim.

The scene between Cassandra, Aurora and the Duke is more obvious. Here the Duke deceives Cassandra, who unconsciously gives herself away by remarking that the Count 'vn retrato vuestro ha sido' (2656). Van Dam has noted the cruel sarcasm with which the Duke says:

> Si bien del Conde y de vos
> ha sido tan bien regido,
> como muestra, agradezido

> este papel, de los dos.
> Todos alaban aquí
> lo que los dos merezéys.[11] (2644–9)
>
> Ya sé que me ha retratado
> tan ygual en todo estado,
> que por mí le habéys tenido;
> de que os prometo, señora,
> deuida satisfaçión. (2657–61)

After this we see that the Duke needs no more to be convinced of the truth of the accusation. He makes sure, however, by eavesdropping when Cassandra and Federico are quarrelling about the future of Aurora. The Count is now absorbed with his own personal danger, whereas Cassandra is fully prepared to fling discretion to the winds.[12] The Duke need wait no longer; his suspicions have been amply confirmed.

The Duke now devises a way of punishing the guilty lovers which avoids publishing the exact nature of their guilt and his own dishonour. He deceives Federico into assassinating the gagged, bound and hooded Cassandra, who, he is told, is the leader of a conspiracy against the state. When she is dead the Marquis kills Federico because, so the Duke says, he murdered his stepmother for fear her unborn child might deprive him of the succession. Federico who had before deceived his father, is now deceived by him and killed. In part the play is the story of how the engineer is hoist with his own petard.

All through the play there are metaphors, comparisons, images and remarks about the difference between appearance and reality, the name and the thing, the supposed causes of obvious effects. Lope constantly stresses how confused things are, how easily a wrong judgement may be arrived at. When Federico rescues Cassandra from her real danger in Act 1, Albano says 'Pienso que es burla', and Floro replies 'Y yo lo mismo digo' (334), but the cries for help were genuine. When the Marquis begins to court Aurora seriously he is told by Rutilio:

> Con el contrario que ves,
> en vano remedio esperas
> de tus locas esperanzas. (1618–20)

Yet the Marquis finally wins Aurora, for Federico is not really his rival. Aurora talks of the 'confuso laberinto çiego de mis fortunas tristes' (709–10); Cassandra in her long soliloquy (1532–91) finds her imagination in such confusion that she cannot see clearly; such are the 'escuros yntentos' and 'claras confusiones' that she has listened to and now feels. Aurora's favours to the Marquis were originally an invention of Federico's (1164–6), later they are a deliberate policy of Aurora (1612–17), then they are again referred to as a fact by Federico (2161–4), only to be explained away again to the Duke (2565–8). The favours are disowned by their inventor, but in the end they are a reality; Aurora accepts the Marquis's proposal and almost certainly goes off with him to Mantua. Cassandra congratulates herself on having lost the way to Ferrara because she was thus able to meet her stepson earlier (478–81), but this was the beginning of the other *yerro* that was to bring her to her death. (There are many such ironies in the play: we need not notice them all, but this one shows the fallibility of Cassandra's judgement as well as it ironically foreshadows the conclusion.) Cassandra also complains that the Duke turns day into night (1376) and that he regards his wife as a piece of furniture (1054–8); the Duke reproves Federico for talking about Aurora as though she were the night (1193); Federico tells the Duke he is using treatment fitter for a maiden than for a man when the marriage with Aurora is first discussed (1129–30). And there are other passages that show how easily the life of impulse can replace civilised behaviour. When Batín describes how he feels tempted to hit gentlemen on the head in a crowd or bite their necks (936–41), he describes in burlesque terms what Cassandra more poetically describes in the metaphor:

> ligera cortina cubre
> todo pensamiento humano.   (1484–5)

Where error, confusion and wrong deductions are so frequent, there must be some kind of attempt to guard against being deceived.

In this Ferrara where the deceived deceiver boasts of his dissimulation (1120) and the Duke, who had no secrets from his son (1688), tricks him into his death, the words *discreto, discreción* and *prudencia* are used in a worldly sense. When Batín tells Federico that men who are 'cuerdos y discretos' exercise patience in unavoidable misfortune, he goes on to say that they must pretend to be happy, pleased and trustful (313–18). The Duke calls Federico 'discreto' because he supposes that Federico is dissimulating chagrin and inventing empty, but convincingly worded, compliments (889). Cassandra twice refers to Federico as 'discreto', but she attaches no precise meaning to the word, which here seems merely to convey that he shows wit in a gentlemanly manner (1438, 1826). When Batín tells the Duke that she is 'mui discreta, y mui virtuosa y santa' (2418–19) he is lying shamelessly. The Duke is certainly deceived when he praises Cassandra's 'prudençia' after he returns from the war (2428). If we remember that prudence is one of the cardinal virtues and that discretion was originally the quality exercised in distinguishing truth from falsehood,[13] we can see that the words are being deliberately distorted by Lope. Federico is not really *discreto*, nor is Cassandra, nor is the Duke. The word is used ironically, not loosely.

The part played by Aurora does not require much comment. She tries to discover what the facts are and to act as the situation demands. Like everyone else she believes that Federico's melancholy was caused by the fear of dispossession by the Duchess's children, and Aurora finds it hard to believe that his love for her is extinct. Lope implies a contrast with Cassandra when Aurora decides to make Federico jealous of the Marquis. She can do this legitimately as a single woman (1616–17); Cassandra, as a wife, does it criminally (1092–3). Federico gives Aurora this idea; she pursues it without result. Still in love with him, her jealousy makes her suspicious, enables her to see with the eyes of a lynx (2064); she discovers the truth: Federico has rejected her love for an incestuous relation with his stepmother. She then refuses to act as a cloak for this crime; when he again approaches her, she almost tells him what he is doing:

> Conde, ya estás entendido;
> déxame casar, y aduierte
> que antes me daré la muerte,
> que ayudar lo que as fingido.   (2193–6)

But he does not understand what she is saying. So she joins with Cassandra to prevent this marriage from taking place. The Duke seems to think differently about it, but he is not serious; for he now knows, or at least strongly suspects, that he has been cuckolded by his bastard son. After the tragedy Aurora probably goes to Mantua with the Marquis. On the whole she behaves well. Her love for Federico has been destroyed, and she decides to make a new start. She has endeavoured to see what lies behind appearances, and she finally learns the truth. She has our sympathy when she refuses to become the tool of the man she had loved; and we feel that she is really fortunate when she chooses the Marquis to be her husband.

Batín's part is also important. The *gracioso* is often to be taken seriously even if he provides obviously comic relief at the same time. The stories he tells to Federico to cheer him up show the ridiculous aspects of his master's melancholy as well as being funny in themselves. We have already noticed how he gave Federico good advice about what to do in adversity (313–18). Here he is like the other moral *graciosos* in *El caballero de Olmedo*, *La verdad sospechosa* and *El burlador de Sevilla*. His clowning with Lucrecia after the rescue has no particular significance until he admits that he would like to be famous as a *sabio* (455–67). In his speeches to Federico he consistently tries to make Federico conscious of what he really feels or of what is going on around him. He is not too strict a moralist, but in his indications we can see that he has his master's good at heart. He praises Cassandra's beauty, and, a few scenes later, guesses that Federico is in love with her (977–9). It is worth noting that a short while before, he had told

'Quando Lope quiere, quiere' 177

the Duke and Aurora that the rescue of Cassandra had completely removed Federico's disgust at his father's marriage (775–81). They forget this, and continue to imagine that the marriage is the sole reason for the Count's melancholy.

We have already noticed how Federico sent Batín away after the quarrel between father and son. Batín had threatened to leave him for another master (1225–31), and later he asks Aurora to take him with her to Mantua. He stays with Federico for some time however, and tries to make him interested in Aurora's favours to the Marquis. Federico remains moody, remarks that times have changed and finally insults him as he sends him off to see what the Duke is doing. We see that the relation between master and servant is worsening as the former rejects the path that will lead him back to sanity and morality. Batín is careful not to go too far, but if Federico had taken the hints the other let fall, there might never have been a tragedy of punishment without vengeance.

In the last act Batín knows that his master is carrying on an affair with the Duchess. Federico now tries to confide in him, but he merely tells a series of funny stories about unobservant or absent-minded men. He remains on the stage while Cassandra and Federico have a violent dispute about Aurora, a dispute that involves shouting and that implies that stepson and stepmother are indeed lovers. This scene must have shown him all, even if his master had concealed this from him up to this moment. A few seconds later he tells the Duke that Cassandra is very discreet, virtuous and saintly (2418–19), that the Duke is holy as a hermit (2446). We see that he must be lying; perhaps he wished to prevent the Duke from forbidding him to go away. Afterwards – when the Duke has heard of the adultery, but before he acted on his information – Batín asks Aurora to take him with her to Mantua. He has worked hard and prospered little.

> Fuera desto, está endiablado
> el Conde. No sé qué tiene:
> ya triste, ya alegre viene,
> ya cuerdo, ya destenplado.
> La Duquesa, pues, tanbién
> insufrible y desygual;
> pues donde va a todos mal,
> ¿quieres que me baya bien?
> El Duque, santo fingido,
> consigo a solas hablando,
> como honbre que anda buscando
> algo que se le ha perdido.
> Toda la casa lo está.   (2792–2804)

These lines are a half-burlesque but telling description of the three principal characters in the play: Federico mad, the Duchess intolerable, the Duke a hypocrite. Batín, who has prided himself on being a faithful servant, leaves an undependable master. He passes judgement on the Duke, who is not really the saint he pretends (or perhaps tries) to be. The departing servant is speaking mysteriously to another who also knows the truth. His speech is rich in innuendoes. He and Aurora both know what the Duke is looking for, as well as what was the matter with the Duchess and the Count. The phrase 'santo fingido' was probably an afterthought;[14] it would be unwise to dogmatise too strictly as to what Batín meant by it. But there is at least a hint that we should not accept the Duke at his own valuation. The half-serious comments of the *gracioso* imply criticism of the punisher as well as of his victims.[15] Did Lope put these ideas into the mouth of the clown so that they could, if necessary, be explained away?

The last scenes of the play, the execution of this punishment without vengeance, written with superb skill and great dramatic power, are not easy to interpret. Lope's judgement is concealed and never made explicit. His attitude seems to be: this is what happened; make what you can of it! You can take the Duke to be a saint (as Ricardo does) or a hypocrite (as Batín does). Is he, like Tamburlaine, the scourge of God, who punishes the erring with another sin? Or is he God's anointed, who impartially dispenses God's justice? The Duke of the final scenes has been claimed as God's representative and as a maniac by different critics.[16] This much is certain. He punishes the guilty lovers without giving either of them a chance to make their peace with God, and the punishment is brought about by means of two terrible falsehoods.[17] It seems difficult to reconcile these facts with his supposed saintliness, however much dissimulation was supposed to be justified when reasons of state or the laws of honour demanded it.

What are the consequences of the vengeance? The crime of the lovers was as black as could well be imagined. We feel for them, but we cannot hope that they will escape the consequences. Federico surrenders his will without a struggle and then tries to conceal his actions by a vile kind of cunning. He is killed, and his good name is lost for ever. The reputation he leaves behind him is almost worse than if the true facts had been generally known: the Duke proclaims that his son murdered a defenceless pregnant woman in case her son deprived him of the duchy. Cassandra however, presumably goes down to history as the innocent victim of a horrible murder. Her good name survives her, despite her real guilt. Did Lope mean us to think that her crime was less grave than her lover's; that she deserved death, but not dishonour? Or is this just another instance of how a secret vengeance preserves the wife's honour as well as the husband's?[18]

There has been a good deal of argument about the precise significance of the title of the play.[19] Arguments based on the fact that Lope started to head the second act: *2º acto de v* and the third *3º acto de ve* lead nowhere.[20] We have seen that Federico and Cassandra were justly punished in fact, but that does not mean that the Duke was necessarily right to punish them as he did. Obviously the Duke thought he was doing the right thing. It may, then, be necessary to draw a distinction between what he thought he was doing and what he actually did. After the discovery of his dishonour, he remarked:

> Castigarle no es vengarme,
> ni se venga el que castiga. (2546–7)

He made a distinction between punishment and vengeance which made the one exclude the other. This becomes clear later on when he calls on Heaven to help him punish the sin, not merely avenge his dishonour:

> Cielos,
> oy se ha de ver en mi casa
> no más de vuestro castigo.
> Alçad la diuina vara.
> No es venganza de mi agrauio;
> que yo no quiero tomarla
> en vuestra offensa, y de vn hijo
> ya fuera bárbara hazaña.
> Éste ha de ser vn castigo
> vuestro no más, porque balga
> para que perdone el çielo
> el rigor por la tenplanza.
> Seré padre, y no marido,
> dando la justicia santa
> a vn pecado sin vergüenza
> vn castigo sin venganza. (2834–49)

Punishment of sin belongs to Heaven; vengeance is a private act for a private wrong. His wife and son deserve both the punishment of God and the private vengeance of the Duke. He, however, thinks that he can separate the two. He says the punishment is to be 'vuestro no más', that it is to belong to God exclusively, that in fact, the title of the play means 'Divine punishment, not human revenge'. The Duke is God's instrument for justice upon earth. His duty is to punish where punishment is required. Federico and Cassandra deserve punishment. The Duke decides to enforce God's will, which he cannot refuse to execute.

The Duke, then, rightly decides to punish the crime, not merely to avenge himself. If he had pardoned the lovers he would not have been acting as a father to his realm. We must now see whether the means he chose can also be defended. The Duke is the representative of Divine Justice, and he must uphold his own dignity or the office of judge – and hence Justice itself – will be brought into disrepute. It may well be that Lope condoned on these grounds the Duke's 'Machiavellian' deceptions. Nevertheless there remains another attitude towards them which shows that they are not quite so admirable as the Duke himself thinks.

The Duke claims that he abandons vengeance for justice, that he is fulfilling the duties commanded of him by God. Yet the thought of private vengeance and the laws of honour are not absent from his soliloquies. After he made his first distinction between punishment and vengeance he finished his speech by saying:

> que mal que el honor estraga,
> no es menester que se haga,
> porque basta que se diga. (2549–51)

After vowing a punishment without vengeance to a sin without shame, he added:

> Esto disponen las leyes
> del honor, y que no aya
> publiçidad en mi afrenta,
> con que se doble mi ynfamia.
> Quien en público castiga,
> dos vezes su honor ynfama,
> que después que le ha perdido,
> por el mundo le dilata. (2850–7)

Honour, he remarked a little later, wishes to give the verdict in this lawsuit, and shame and infamy plead against love and blood (2897–2909). Lope hardly conceals the fact that the Duke is trying to get the best of both worlds at the same time and by the same means. The Duke tries to separate punishment from vengeance, but he cannot do so. Despite his good intentions, he could not keep the one separate from the other. This ambiguity in the Duke's mind as he brings about the final catastrophe is not a blemish on the play. Had he acted either as an entirely just judge or as a commonplace avenging husband, we could not have seen so well the consequences of his previous sins and public conversion.

The Duke loses almost everything that he valued. He married in order to secure his vassals from a war of succession at his death: Cassandra bore him no children, and he had Federico killed. He returned from the war, determined to lead a good married life, and now his marriage is at an end. Federico had been his chief joy while he lived, and Federico is dead, dishonoured and must be forgotten. Aurora will almost certainly go to Mantua with Gonzaga and Batín. He is left with Ricardo, Floro, Febo and the rest, to snatch what consolations he can from the ruins of his life.

The only victory he has won is to have upheld justice and to have disguised his marital dishonour from his subjects, but at what a cost! He has little to look back on with pleasure, nothing to look forward to, except, perhaps, more military successes in the Pope's wars. If a tragedy needs a tragic hero, the Duke is the hero of this play; his frailty was the failure to realise that, as a married man, he could not go on living the life of a licentious gallant. An Elizabethan dramatist might have made him commit suicide at the end of the play; Lope lets him live on, disillusioned, and with a secret that cannot be told.

There are other implicit ironies about the Duke. The man who did not care too much about his private, personal honour as a respectable, married man – who preferred his *libertad viciosa* and the *mugerçillas viles* to his good name – acts to repair his honour only when it is compromised by the actions of his wife. The tender father ruthlessly sacrifices his beloved son. His cold-blooded savagery shows itself, not only in his ironical remarks to Federico and Cassandra before the final deceptions (2589–92, 2657–61) and in the way he chooses to devise their deaths, but also in the satisfaction that he shows when his son murders his wife:

> Aquí lo veré; ya llega;
> ya con la punta la passa. (2972–3)

The attitude is understandable enough, but Lope can hardly have meant his audience to approve unreservedly of this expression. As soon as the Duke is aware of the guilt of the lovers he is stricken with horror at his son's lack of filial feeling, but he acts as a father only in that he employs another hand to strike him down.

We must remember that Lope, if he wished to criticise the actions of the Duke, had two difficulties to contend with. Any criticism of the cruelty of the code of honour had to be made indirectly; and reflection on the conduct of the head of a state (particularly in the reign of Philip IV, who also sought the company of *mugerçillas viles*) had to be implied rather than expressly stated. The censor of *El castigo sin venganza* wrote: 'Este tragico suceso del Duque de ferrara, està escrito con verdad, i con el deuido decoro a su persona, i las introducidas, es exemplar, i raro caso. Puede representarse.'[21] Lope satisfied the censor, but the play ran for only one day.[22] Was the short run due to the fact that Lope's criticisms were felt to be too explicit? We do not know, but the mystery has never been satisfactorily explained.

There may also be an additional irony in the fact that the 'punishment without vengeance' does not deceive everybody. The Duke acts a part in front of a number of people who already know enough of the truth to understand exactly what he is doing. Lope shows us that this secret vengeance (or punishment) is not really so very secret. The Duke obtained his information from an unidentified ragged man who was much disturbed when he handed in his paper (2481-2); this man would understand what had happened when he heard of the deaths of the Duchess and Federico. Aurora had already witnessed the Duke's dishonour, and she confided the truth to the Marquis (2040-2110), who later killed Federico; they also must have understood. Batín and Lucrecia were the confidential servants of the lovers; each of them had seen the beginnings of the affair and had been present on the stage at the moment when Cassandra exclaimed:

> Quíteme el Duque mil vidas,
> pero no te has de cassar. (2287-8)

They too knew what was happening. Batín whispered to Aurora:

> que no es sin causa
> todo lo que ves, Aurora. (3005-6)

Federico tells Cassandra that rumours unfavourable to him and to her are circulating in the palace; he must marry Aurora to silence evil tongues:

> Quiero fingir desde agora
> que sirbo y que quiero Aurora
> y aun pedirla por muger
> al Duque, para desbelos
> dél y de palaçio, en quien
> yo sé que no se habla bien. (2270-5)

At least five people (the ragged man, Aurora, the Marquis, Batín and Lucrecia) know that Federico and Cassandra have committed incestuous adultery together; others have their suspicions. Whom did the Duke deceive? Federico, the unobservant in the palace and the outside world. This was a 'castigo sin venganza' for the ordinary Ferrarese and the Mantuans; the inner circle knew that there was dishonour, treachery, adultery and murder behind the façade. But the façade was preserved, the Duke's dishonour remained hidden, because he did not know that Aurora, Batín and the others knew about it as well.

Certainly this is one of Lope's finest plays. The psychological acuteness of the love affair, the brilliant dramatisation of the final climax have been appreciated by critics of all nations. In this essay I have tried to show that Lope's treatment of the whole subject is detached. He does not apologise for Duke, Count or Duchess; here, he says, is what happens when we do not recognise the confusions and deceptions that lie around us and when passion overcomes the restraints of polite behaviour, traditional wisdom, morality and religion. Public virtue is no good unless it is supported by private virtue. Our hope is to be guided by truth and integrity, to be patient in adversity and not to let our passions dominate our conduct.

The Duke's womanisings provoke Cassandra's revenge; her desire for vengeance on him leads to his on her; Federico's melancholy is cultivated by himself, leads him to unnatural crime and death. And in spite of the heroic action of the Duke at the end of the play, his triumph is at his own expense, and it is an empty victory that deceives nobody of importance. Vanity of vanities, all is vanity.

11
The exemplary nature of *El caballero de Olmedo*

Menéndez y Pelayo, replying to Schack's criticism that the tone of the third act of *El caballero de Olmedo* was out of keeping with the light-heartedness of the first and second, pointed to the brilliance of 'el arte del poeta en la manera de preparar y de vencer esta dificultad'. He went on:

> Una especie de *sombra fatídica* pesa sobre los personajes, y ahoga con frecuencia en sus labios la voz del placer: se comprende que están *predestinados para algo siniestro*; que su juventud, su amor, su gallardía no serán parte a detener *la inexorable suerte*; viven entre presagios y agüeros, aunque se rebelan contra su influjo: las malas artes de la hechicería alternan con las del lenocinio. Amor que comienza con mágicos cercos y conjuros; que se fragua en las tinieblas por el ministerio de una bruja... tiene mucho más de trágico que de cómico, y no puede anunciar un final muy placentero. *Un fatalismo tétrico*, pero que no carece de poesía a su modo, y que además está templado por las escenas de donaire y por la mórbida y suave manera del poeta, es el alma de la composición.[1]

Don Marcelino's argument seems to be well founded, for the first two acts do indeed prepare us for the final tragedy in a very subtle way, as more recent critics have pointed out.[2] Even so, the expressions printed above in italics are open to an unfortunate misinterpretation, suggesting that we are here dealing with the workings of fate; that Don Alonso and Doña Inés lack free will; and that Lope's intention was to write a sort of *Don Álvaro, o la fuerza del sino*, or perhaps a Spanish version of the story of the house of Atreus. We shall never understand the plays of Lope (who, after all, wrote this play after he had been ordained to the priesthood) if we describe them in terms of 'predestinación', 'inexorable suerte' or 'fatalismo tétrico'. Dramatic criticism ought rather to avoid these tendentious words which seem to negate what no seventeenth-century Spaniard could negate. Let us examine not only how, but also why the projected marriage between Don Alonso and Doña Inés does not take place, but without basing our argument on the *a priori* concepts used here by Menéndez y Pelayo.

In this play love is not portrayed as an instrument of good such as would remedy a young lady's foolishness (as in *La dama boba*) or cure a young man's infirmity of mind (as in *El vergonzoso en palacio*). Blecua has perceptively observed how the three main characters, as they each make their first entrance, speak of the love which possesses them. His observations are apposite and important, and he shows us how Don Alonso, Doña Inés and Don Rodrigo are all victims of love's passion.[3] The hero and heroine both make their entrances discoursing on the universality of love, whilst Don Rodrigo complains of the suffering it inflicts on him. These entrances establish clearly the relationships of the characters to each other; we see how Inés and Alonso will love each other, and how Rodrigo will be miserably unhappy. Following this line of approach, let us examine the nature of the passion which afflicts the lovers, and how they describe it.

On the lips of Alonso and Inés, love is associated with fire and with death. When he saw her in the streets of Medina this love 'encendió' Don Alonso with 'fuegos...excesivos' (lines 13–14); some lines later he describes Inés as a 'fuego que me abrasa y arde' (71). Even in the light-hearted, bantering *romance* in which Alonso describes the meeting to Fabia, he calls his beloved a basilisk whose burning poison was scarcely to be tempered by the holy water of the stoup in the church (143–6). 'Vime sentenciado a muerte', he goes on, because 'hoy / te meten en la capilla' (155–8). Later he recounts to Tello how death would be preferable to all this 'vivir sin ver' (887–8), how love burns him incessantly, never giving him respite (903–6); it is a lion (907), and he would have to be a salamander if he were always to be where he might see Inés (911–14). Inés, he says, 'mi dueño es / para vivir, o morir' (995–6). She is that 'hermosa homicida' who 'da vida a cuántos mata', in the words of Tello's gloss (1142, 1154). Inés imagines herself as a moth, or rather a phoenix, in Alonso's flame (1057–62), and for Rodrigo, love and death are the arbiters of existence (461–90), and Inés is his 'homicida' as she is Alonso's. Any one of these images, if taken by itself, may be considered as an example of the conventional language of seventeenth-century lovers. In two or three cases the context is happy, witty and even playful. What cannot be denied, however, is that in this play love is generally presented in metaphors of death and destruction, which not only prepare us for the portents and omens that foreshadow the final tragedy, but also seem to indicate that love is in itself a harmful and destructive thing rather than the secure bond that links two lives in conjugal felicity.

Such, then, is the way love is spoken of by the lovers, its victims. But what of those who look on? Fabia is the key here. Speaking to Alonso, she tells him that

        Todos los medios humanos
        tengo de intentar por tí.   (202–3)

She calls upon the devil's fire to burn Inés's heart:

        Apresta,
        fiero habitador del centro,

> fuego accidental que abrase
> el pecho desta doncella. (393–6)

Her arguments induce Tello to accompany her on her sinister mission, because 'importa a la brevedad / deste amor' (595–6). Before the end of Act I she says:

> ¡Oh qué bravo efeto hicieron
> los hechizos y conjuros!
> La vitoria me prometo. (816–18)

These details give us some of the traits of Fabia's character. They also demonstrate how she believes Inés's passion to be the direct consequence of her spells. Alonso claims that he does not believe in the effectiveness of magic; Fabia does believe, and perhaps Lope too believed. I do not think it necessary to seek any further for a diagnosis of the lovers' passion. Their love affair began as a normal effect of the laws of nature, which are invoked by both lovers to explain it; it was aggravated by the direct influence of the devil, whose attributes are flames and eternal death. In this play the passion of love is in a large measure diabolical.

Before studying Don Alonso, let us examine the impression he leaves in the minds of the other characters in the play. Inés sees him only as her beloved; such a witness cannot be impartial, yet her words arouse in us a sympathy for him, a sympathy which helps us to understand her infatuation. The words of Fabia at the end of the first act may be venal, but they are also eloquent:

> Armado, parece Aquiles
> mirando de Troya el cerco;
> con galas parece Adonis. (859–61)

Although we cannot believe anything that is said by a woman who has her mind on the gold chain she has been promised by Alonso, her description is borne out by Alonso's courage in the skirmish with Don Rodrigo, and in the bullfight. The most favourable testimony is that given by the King and the Constable, in two scenes which have hardly any other function in the structure of the play:

> Es hombre
> de notable fama y nombre. (1596–7)

Condestable. Galán y bizarro ha estado
el Caballero de Olmedo.
Rey. ¡Buenas suertes, Condestable!
Condestable. No sé en él cuál es mayor,
la ventura o el valor,
aunque es el valor notable.
Rey. Cualquiera cosa hace bien. (2093–9)

The exemplary nature of *El caballero de Olmedo*   187

The supreme authority of the King sets the seal on the fundamental virtue of our hero. One must emphasise *fundamental*, for there is no question of seeing in Don Alonso a man without flaw.

Don Rodrigo is far from being a calm and impartial enemy of Don Alonso, but there may be a basis of truth in his diatribes. In the skirmish outside Don Pedro's garden, after Don Alonso's challenge, Rodrigo asks:

> ¿Quién es
> el que con tanta arrogancia
> se atreve a hablar?
> . . .
> Pues hallará quien castigue
> su locura temeraria.   (695–700)

In the second act he discovers who his rival is, referring to him as

> don Alonso, aquel de Olmedo,
> alanceador galán, y cortesano,
> de quien hombres, y toros, tienen miedo.   (1348–50)

In the first scenes of the last act we see the jealousy of Rodrigo, who has become aware of Don Alonso's contempt for him, as well as his good fortune and his bravery. When he vows to kill Alonso, Rodrigo refers to him as the 'hidalguillo loco' (2068). His friend Don Fernando saves his insults until the last, when he calls Don Alonso

> El de Olmedo,
> el matador de los toros,
> que viene arrogante y necio
> a afrentar los de Medina;
> el que deshonra a don Pedro
> con alcagüetes infames.   (2437–42)

He had described him as a 'mozo temerario' some scenes previously (2333). Don Alonso's enemies call him 'arrogante', 'loco', 'temerario', 'necio', and, shortly before his death, a *labrador* says to him: 'Muy necio valor tenéis' (2409). Perhaps his enemies give us important clues, even though we do not share their jealousy and ingratitude.

Alonso calls on Fabia's help with no thought for the consequences of his action. As far as he is concerned she is a 'peregrino dotor', an 'Hipócrates celestial' (44, 46). Although Fabia assists him as far as she is able, she twice warns him of the risk he runs: 'Alto has picado' (72), she tells him, and 'a gran peligro te pones' (184). Don Alonso pays her no heed when she warns him. When she returns from visiting Don Pedro's house she pretends that her mission was a complete failure. The scene is a comic one, with the author portraying the credulity of Don Alonso, the slyness of Tello and Fabia's ability to deceive. But this is merely a secondary aspect of the scene; what is fundamental is that, for a few moments, Don Alonso realises how imprudently he has gone about his love affair:

> Ello ha sido disparate
> que yo me atreviese al cielo. (536–7)

> ¡Oh, qué necio fui en fiarme
> de aquellos ojos traidores,
> de aquellos falsos diamantes,
> niñas que me hacían señas
> para engañarme y matarme! (550–4)

This nascent feeling of disillusion passes at once, for Fabia tells what actually happened: Inés received her favourably. Alonso had no cause to despair of his love. But Lope seems to underline how, for a few moments, the hero of the play accuses himself of excessive and ill-founded confidence in his beloved Inés's feeling for him.

In the scene outside Don Pedro's garden Don Alonso's words are as proud as his actions are brave. He is the hero of the play, and we, whether audience or readers, look on him with sympathy and a certain admiration. The quarrel with Don Rodrigo, however, is an act of imprudence, and the words spoken before the challenge by a man who also knows how to speak with his sword (698) are arrogant:

> Mal conoce a don Alonso,
> que por excelencia llaman
> el Caballero de Olmedo. (685–7)

From time to time Alonso chides Tello for his lack of prudence:

> Mira lo que haces, Tello;
> no entres adonde no salgas. (673–4)

Tello, according to his master, acted with 'gran necedad' (934) when he wore in the streets of Medina the cloak 'stolen' from Don Rodrigo. In these two cases Lope shows how Alonso reproves in Tello his own faults. On other occasions it is Tello who attempts in vain to show his master that his conduct is indiscreet and unwise. In the first scene between Alonso and Fabia Tello's comments merely interpose a question-mark when Don Alonso calls the old woman's hands holy (200); later he makes cruel fun of the supposed beating she has suffered in Don Pedro's house. Tello (like Pármeno in *La Celestina*) is aware of the old bawd's immoralities, deceits and sorceries; although he tries to help her get the hanged man's tooth, he is incapable of carrying out the deed. He collaborates with her in spite of himself, he is on his guard with her, and at the same time tries to woo her to get from her the chain presented by his master. Such is the attitude of

The exemplary nature of *El caballero de Olmedo* 189

the *gracioso*, who nevertheless shows himself to be a faithful servant and the voice of Don Alonso's conscience.

We have already noted Don Alonso's imprudence in the garden scene. Tello had warned him: 'No hagas / algún disparate' (690–1), and Don Alonso paid no heed. These details prepare us for a series of warnings in the first scene of the second act, in which the servant tries to restrain his master. Tello warns him that so much coming and going between Olmedo and Medina will not go unnoticed, that Don Alonso ought to conceal his visits to Inés's house and his conversations with her, that Don Rodrigo is aware of all that has been happening, that he is in a strong position on his own ground and that it is impossible to foresee the outcome of a love affair begun with spells and sorceries (887–974). Alonso answers these arguments, pleading the violence of his passion: if Leander 'pasaba un mar / todas las noches' (919–20), what is his journey from Olmedo to Medina in comparison? Finally he says:

> Tello, un verdadero amor
> en ningún peligro advierte.
> Quiso mi contraria suerte
> que hubiese competidor,
> y que trate, enamorado,
> casarse con doña Inés.
> Pues ¿qué he de hacer, si me ves
> celoso y desesperado?
> No creo en hechicerías,
> que todas son vanidades;
> quien concierta voluntades
> son méritos y porfías.
> Inés me quiere.   (975–87)

Tello's scruples are of no avail. Don Alonso does not understand them, he does not believe in magic, but what he does believe is that the true love of himself and Inés will overcome all the threats posed by Don Rodrigo. After such words we cannot doubt but that the end which Don Alonso has in view is marriage; but the means he employs are reprehensible, and the man himself is careless, not to say foolhardy.

The last scene of this act also consists of a dialogue between master and servant. Tello gladdens his master's heart by bringing him Inés's letter, which is read in instalments so that the pleasure will last longer – this is in one respect comic, and in another a desperate ploy to hide the anguish of a lover who fears an unhappy outcome. Don Alonso confesses that he is uneasy after a dream in which he does not believe:

Tello.   ¿Agora en sueños reparas?
Alonso.   No los creo, claro está,
              pero dan pena.   (1746–8)

The 'dream' is the same as that dreamt by Doña Alda in the old ballad: 'En París está doña Alda', misinterpreted by her ladies-in-waiting, and fulfilled by the death of Roland. Don Alonso is in a state of depression; Tello tries to cheer him, telling him he is making poor return for the 'heroica firmeza' of Inés, and that he should turn his attention to the *fiestas* in Medina. This scene contrasts with the other: now it is Tello who pays no heed to fears of the outcome. We also see how a man who had no scruples about employing a witch to help him in his love affair is depressed by a dream, an omen, the import of which, as is the duty of every good Christian, he tries to dismiss. The dramatist's technique is deliberate: the dream is that of Doña Alda which foresaw a fatal event, and he thus leads us to expect another eventual catastrophe, as has been noted by other critics; in this way the act finishes with a juxtaposition of contradictory ideas, but which all lead to the tragedy of the last act. We see a bold man, discouraged by an omen in which he ought not to believe; a servant who had been cautious, but who now tries to encourage his foolhardy master; and both confronted with a portent which ought not to be considered as such, but which is one nevertheless.

In this way Lope prepares the eventual catastrophe. The bravery of Don Alonso in the bullring is the logical consequence of what we already know of him from the scene outside Don Pedro's garden. This chivalry towards his enemy fits in well with all that has been revealed before the moment when the hero displays a certain disdain towards Don Rodrigo whilst still saving his life. The mad insistence on returning by night to Olmedo reminds us of Tello's warnings quoted above about local rivalries and the imprudence of 'tanto ir y venir'. The apprehension he feels as he takes his farewell is the culmination of the images of the first two acts and of the reaction of Don Alonso when confronted with the omens revealed in his conversation with Tello. The farewell takes the form of an old *copla*, already cited by Cervantes in the dedication of the *Persiles* (written in 1616, published in 1617) and printed some years previously in the *Flor de romances, y glosas, canciones y villancicos* (Saragossa, 1578):[4]

> Puesto ya el pie en el estribo,
> con las ansias de la muerte,
> Señora, aquesta te escribo,
> pues partir no puedo vivo,
> cuanto más volver a verte.

And in the gloss we find lines such as these:

> Aquí se acabó mi vida,
> que es lo mismo que partirme. (2249–50)

We can understand how such a man dares to return to Olmedo after

The exemplary nature of *El caballero de Olmedo* 191

Fabia's warnings, how he manages to conquer his own fears and how he believes that he will not be killed by the ungrateful man whose life he himself had saved. He lives in an unreal world of love and bravery, he has set in motion malevolent forces which he cannot control and continues to think that because he himself is a man of honour, Don Rodrigo must be also. Even when the assassins stop him on the road, he thinks that they are ordinary bandits who mean to rob him (2427–34). The end comes. While he dies, he passes judgement on himself, telling us the causes of his tragedy:

> ¡Qué poco crédito di
> a los avisos del cielo!
> Valor propio me ha engañado,
> y muerto envidias y celos. (2462–5)

He asks for God's mercy; says that his love was 'dirigido a casamiento' (2473–5); and finally pleads:

> Tello, Tello, ya no es tiempo
> más que de tratar del alma. (2497–8)

Death teaches him the reason for his downfall: 'valor propio', not merely valour, but temerity. The character which his enemies saw in him is confirmed by his own lips at the moment of death. He never loses our sympathy in the course of the play, but we see how his defects make him the instrument of his own ruin. Here, at least, Lope follows fairly closely the precepts of Aristotle recommending a 'tragic frailty' in the character of a tragic hero.[5]

Don Pedro, who is far from being a perspicacious man, makes an acute and amusing comment on feminine psychology when Inés declares to him her intention to become a nun:

> Pero porque suele ser
> nuestro pensamiento humano
> tal vez inconstante y vano,
> y en condición de mujer,
> que es fácil de persuadir,
> tan poca firmeza alcanza
> que hay de mujer a mudanza
> lo que de hacer a decir. (1224–31)

Tello is later to praise the 'heroica firmeza' of Inés (1789), and here, as at other points in the play, Don Pedro is mistaken. Doña Inés is not fickle, or inconstant, or vain. What is true – and here her father is right – is that she allows herself to be carried along by the impulse of the moment. Blecua notes how Fabia convinces her more quickly than Celestina does

Melibea,[6] because (leaving aside the bawd's spells) she admits her love for Alonso from the very beginning:

> y en el instante que vi
> este galán forastero
> me dijo el alma 'éste quiero',
> y yo le dije 'sea ansí'. (223-6)

In spite of Fabia's bad reputation, the two sisters admit her to the house, out of curiosity. And when the matter of a letter from an unknown man is brought up, Doña Inés replies to it at once, an impulse telling her that it must be Don Alonso who has written it. In the second act her father faces her with the prospect of marriage to Don Rodrigo, whom she hates; to gain time she replies, without any reflection, that she wishes to take the veil. Later she will say to her lover:

> Bien sabes que breves males
> la dilación los remedia. (1262-3)

She acts on impulse, without thinking that she could tell the truth to Don Pedro, who would not have rejected such a son-in-law. She shows the same quick-wittedness in getting herself out of an immediate difficulty in the laundry-list scene, but her supposed vocation is in the last analysis counter-productive. She manages to convince her father, but Don Rodrigo soon recognises the deception.

There is a parallel between the roles of Don Alonso and Doña Inés. The former's rashness is reproved by Tello, and Alonso himself admits it for a few moments, thanks to Fabia's deceit. Leonor is here a Tello to Inés, and Inés too has a moment of disillusion when she believes that her love is in vain. The principal function of Leonor in the play is to criticise the impulsiveness and rashness of her sister:

[Inés.]	¿quién concierta y desconcierta este amor y desamor?
Leonor.	Tira como ciego amor; yerra mucho, y poco acierta. (227-30)

After Don Rodrigo's *décimas*, in which he declares how his life is a struggle between love and death, Doña Inés says:

	¡Qué de necedades juntas!
Leonor.	No fue la tuya menor.
Inés.	¿Cuándo fue discreto amor, si del papel me preguntas?
Leonor.	¿Amor te obliga a escribir sin saber a quién? (491-6)

The exemplary nature of *El caballero de Olmedo*

And when Leonor is told that Alonso will come to the window, she asks her sister:

	¿Quién te aconseja, o qué desatino es ése?
Inés.	No es para hablarle.
Leonor.	Pues, ¿qué?
Inés.	Ven conmigo y lo sabrás.
Leonor.	Necia y atrevida estás.
Inés.	¿Cuándo el amor no lo fue?
Leonor.	Huir del amor cuando empieza.
Inés.	Nadie del primero huye. (523-30)

Before the end of the first act there is another exchange between the sisters which sums up this fundamental relationship:

Inés.	Leonor, ¿no me das consejo?
Leonor.	Y ¿estás tú para tomarle? (878-9)

Leonor represents Inés's conscience, as Tello does Alonso's. In spite of some moments of doubt, she too collaborates in the deception of their father. So here we have another example of the good sense of one person overcome, against their better judgement, by the passion and impulses of another. Leonor sees the danger that these feelings may lead to her sister's downfall, warns her accordingly and then allows herself to be carried along by the forcefulness of Doña Inés.

The episode of the ribbon shared between Don Rodrigo and his companion outside Don Pedro's house does not seem on first reading to be essential to the construction of the play. It serves to introduce the conflict between Don Alonso and his enemy, but does not lead to a series of errors which might result from the taking by others of a ribbon destined for Don Alonso. Perhaps this is partly a device of the author's to put his audience on the wrong track, giving them a suggestion of a possible line of development before immediately (and unexpectedly) cutting it short. We have already observed how this scene serves to underline Don Alonso's bravery and arrogance, but if it were no more than that, why does he fail to obtain the ribbon? The fact is that, if the challenge reveals the virtues and defects of the hero, the affair of the ribbon throws light on the character of Doña Inés. The exchange of the ribbon makes us notice that she too has a moment of disillusionment when she sees how her supposed love affair may be nothing more than an insubstantial dream. Don Rodrigo and Don Fernando wear in their hats what she had left for another; she sees this, and exclaims:

¡Qué vana fue mi esperanza!
¡Qué loco mi pensamiento! (787-8)

Fabia consoles her, persuading her that her fears are groundless. It is no more than a brief pause in her enthusiastic passion, a pause at once forgotten. Like Don Alonso, she does not learn from the lesson; nor does she heed the advice of her companion and sister. The characters of the intrepid gallant and his impulsive lady are developed in the same way.

Don Rodrigo is a poor wretch, condemned by his own lack of confidence. He makes his first entrance discussing the difficulties of love, and Doña Inés spurns disdainfully what he says in his *décimas* on love and death. Outside Don Pedro's garden, he mentions the lack of confidence which leads him to doubt whether Inés could have left the ribbon for him (647–52). In spite of a valiant gesture, he is routed by his rival, and leaves his cloak behind. In the second act he is wild with jealousy, and after putting to Don Fernando the idea of killing Don Alonso, he exclaims:

> Mortal desmayo
> cubre mi amor de celos y de enojos. (1382–3)

In the third act he reveals himself in the same terms:

> Es imposible acertar
> un hombre tan desdichado. (1817–18)

> a mí
> me esperan para que yo
> haga suertes que me afrenten,
> o que algún toro me mate
> o me arrastre, a me maltrate
> donde con risa lo cuenten. (1873–8)

Unhorsed by the bull, and helped by his enemy, he comments:

> Mala caída,
> mal suceso, malo todo. (2029–30)

> ¡Estoy loco!
> ¡No hay hombre tan desdichado,
> Fernando, de Polo a Polo!
> ¡Qué de afrentas, qué de penas,
> qué de agravios, qué de enojos,
> qué de injurias, qué de celos,
> qué de agüeros, qué de asombros! (2038–44)

Lack of confidence goes hand in hand with cowardice. In all of this Don Rodrigo is shown in eloquent contrast to Don Alonso. But in one thing he resembles him: in the lack of prudence in his actions. If Alonso forgets the importance of the facts pointed out by Tello, Rodrigo never forgets them. He is preoccupied by so much coming and going between Olmedo and Medina, and by the presence of a bawd and witch in the house of the woman he loves. Because of this preoccupation Rodrigo reaches the fatal decision that he must do away with Don Alonso by violent means. In doing so he becomes cowardly and dishonourable, for Alonso is a noble and generous adversary who has saved his life. Moreover, the decision is dangerous, but being in such a desperate state he has no thought for the possibility that it may also bring about his own death.

In the play a threefold construction may be observed. Alonso takes no notice of the advice of Tello, who eventually has to follow his master. Doña Inés pays no heed to that of Leonor, who becomes her accomplice. In like manner Rodrigo has his counsellor in Fernando. Though prudent, Fernando has in the end to acquiesce in the criminal plans of his friend. Let us look at some examples of his advice. In the first act he asks Rodrigo:

> ¿De qué sirve inútilmente
> venir a ver esta casa? (623-4)

He knows the real nature of Rodrigo's fears:

> Efetos son de amante verdadero,
> que en viendo otra persona de buen talle,
> tienen temor que si le ve su dama
> será posible, o fuerza, codicialle. (1335-8)

After a marvellous poetic definition of jealousy Don Rodrigo asks him:

Rodrigo.   Yo me quiero casar; vos sois discreto.
           ¿Qué consejo me dais, si no es matalle?
Fernando. Yo hago diferente mi conceto. (1366-8)

He sees Rodrigo's madness, and tells him so at the end of this scene (1390). During the bullfight he tries to encourage his friend:

> Volvamos, Rodrigo, a entrar,
> que por dicha nos esperan,
> aunque os parece que no. (1869-71)

And when at last Don Rodrigo reaches his decision, Fernando interposes:

Fernando. Él [Don Alonso] sabrá ponerse en cobro.
Rodrigo.   Mal conocéis a los celos.
Fernando. ¿Quién sabe que no son monstruos?
           Mas lo que ha de importar mucho
           no se ha de pensar tan poco. (2070-4)

He also tries to advise him in the last scenes of the play, but Don Rodrigo does not listen to him.

There is a corresponding threefold responsibility for the final catastrophe: the arrogance of Don Alonso, the impulsiveness of Doña Inés and the cowardice of Don Rodrigo bring the first to death, the second to a convent and the third to the gallows. Each of the three has a counsellor–accomplice, who sees clearly the essentials of the situation. But the counsellors are disregarded and finally carried along by the stronger spirit of a master, a sister or a friend. Three parallel cases of temerity, impulsiveness and lack of confidence, when taken together, lead to the climax of the tragedy.

Don Pedro is the *barba*, that decent old fool whom we find in many of the plays of Lope, Tirso and Calderón. His role, nevertheless, has its importance in the construction of the play, however unoriginal it may appear. He does not understand his daughter, nor has he the slightest notion of what is going on, even under his own roof. He does not know that she finds Don Rodrigo repugnant:

Fernando.	Hame [Rodrigo] puesto por tercero para tratarlo con vos.
Pedro.	Pues hablaremos los dos en el concierto primero.
Fernando.	Aquí está [Rodrigo], que siempre amor es reloj anticipado.
Pedro.	Habrále Inés concertado con la llave del favor. (751–8)

Nor does he know what kind of man the prospective son-in-law is. When his daughter tells him that she wants to become a nun, he believes her, although he realises that it may be a short-lived whim. He never believes that the supposedly pious old woman is the same bawd who provided him with girls when he was a bachelor; and he takes at face value the assertion that Tello is a graduate of Corunna called Martín Peláez (Corunna never had a university, and Martín Peláez was a friend of the Cid's). He is eventually told by his daughters what for so long he was ignorant of: that Inés and Alonso are in love, and that all Inés's strange behaviour – the pretended desire to become a nun – was due to her hatred of Don Rodrigo. Don Pedro's reply shows us that the whole business of pretence, deceit and lies was foolish and unnecessary; if Doña Inés had been frank with him from the start, there would have been no need of Fabia, nor of the supposed religious vocation. And in all probability Don Rodrigo would have had no occasion to execute his sinister plans. Don Pedro reproaches his wayward daughter:

> Mi amor
> se queja de tu rigor;
> porque a saber tu disgusto,
> no lo [marriage with Rodrigo] hubiera imaginado.
> (2547–50)

The scene is one of pathos. Don Pedro approves of the new marriage because Don Alonso is a man of great valour; but a few moments before this scene we saw Tello find his dying master in the countryside between Medina and Olmedo. The lovers acted in a manner which was at once clever, rash and unexpected, in order to deceive a decent old man. Without their knowing it, he was well disposed towards the wedding if only they had told him. The ignorance of Don Pedro, impetuosity of Doña Inés, temerity of Don Alonso and cowardice of Don Rodrigo are all responsible for the final catastrophe.

The role of Fabia is complex. In the early scenes she acts like a Celestina or a Gerarda, a bawd and witch at one moment, witty and amusing at the next. In her are combined loquacity and great knowledge of the feminine soul; Inés is won over by the arguments she employs – and we also know that she is a witch aided by the devil. Since we see the Celestina in her, we expect a secondary plot in which Tello will work alongside her to swindle his master while they fan the flames of his love affair. But Lope cheats us. Tello, compared at one point to Sempronio (1005), proves more loyal than Pármeno; and Fabia herself has good motives when she warns Don Alonso not to return to Olmedo that night. In the second act she is less sinister than in the first; her stick, rosary and spectacles make her a comic figure – not a witch so much as a hypocrite. She also appears in humorous vein when she and Tello exchange quips outside the bullring. With her warnings in the last act she loses all her malevolent character. With regard to Don Rodrigo and Don Fernando she is a well-meaning adviser.

	Los de Medina hacen riza porque tienen ojeriza con los lacayos de Olmedo.	(2004–6)
[*Alonso.*]	O embustes de Fabia son, que pretende persuadirme porque no vaya a Olmedo, sabiendo que es imposible. Siempre dice que me guarde, y siempre que no camine de noche, sin más razón de que la envidia me sigue.	(2277–84)
[*Alonso.*]	Volver atrás, ¿cómo puedo? Invención de Fabia es, que quiere, a ruego de Inés, hacer que no vaya a Olmedo.	(2379–82)
Fabia.	Yo pienso que mayor daño te espera, si no me engaño,	

>   como suele suceder,
>   que en las cosas por venir
>   no puede haber cierta ciencia.   (2527–31)
>
> *Fabia.*   El parabién te doy,
>   si no es pésame después.   (2584–5)

Fabia begins the play by praying to the devil and swindling Don Alonso. At the end she still brings about more or less supernatural portents, but with an entirely beneficent intention. Throughout the whole play, however, she is for Don Rodrigo the infamous bawd who dishonours Don Pedro's house.

The echoes of the *Celestina* in the play are frequent and intentional. Alonso is Calisto; Inés, Melibea; and Fabia, Celestina herself. In early editions of the *Celestina* we are told that the work was composed 'en reprehension de los locos enamorados: que vencidos en su desordenado apetito a sus amigas llaman y dizen ser su Dios. Assimismo fecha en auiso de los engaños de las alcahuetas y malos y lisongeros siruientes.'[7] At times modern criticism does not take these words seriously. Often the *Celestina* is read as if it were *Los amantes de Teruel* or another romantic drama. This problem of interpretation does not here concern us for its own sake; suffice it to say that, for the seventeenth century, before Rojas's masterpiece was put on the Index, the prefatory words were taken at face value. For Salas Barbadillo, the work was an extremely moral one: 'Entre aquellas burlas, al parecer livianas, enseña una doctrina moral y católica.'[8] I believe that Lope, to whom the amorous plaints of Calisto could not have been unknown, also took seriously the moral found there by his contemporaries. We know too that Cervantes, in *El celoso extremeño*, warns us of the dangers of *dueñas* 'nacidas y usadas en el mundo para perdición de mil recatadas y buenas intenciones',[9] although the modern reader is more likely to be struck by Mari-Alonso's humorous gossip than by her dubious morals. The *Celestina* was on the one hand a work of entertainment, and on the other a moral treatise. Something of this duality is inherited by Lope's new Celestina. In spite of the change which Fabia's role undergoes in the third act, she reminds us of the witchcraft and immorality of her literary antecedent. She invokes the devil, she dishonours Don Pedro's house. For the groundlings and gentlemen who attended the first performance of this play, in spite of the humour of the dialogue and her well-meaning warnings, Fabia would continue to be an infamous figure, and Alonso would seem mad to employ her to further his love affair. They would share the indignation of Rodrigo when he exclaims:

>   ¡Qué honrada dueña recibió en su casa
>   don Pedro en Fabia! ¡Oh, mísera doncella!   (2309–10)

The exemplary nature of *El caballero de Olmedo* 199

And for all Lope's good humour, and for all the sympathy we feel towards Inés, we must pronounce judgement against her when we hear her utter words such as the following:

> ya que a mi padre, a mi estado,
> y a mi honor pierdo el respeto... (807–8)

and

> Fabia será mi maestra
> de virtudes y costumbres. (1291–2)

The joke makes one laugh, but at bottom it is bitter.

In play after play Lope quotes, or at least alludes to, some happy lines from the old ballad, *El conde Claros*:

> que los yerros por amores
> dignos son de perdonar.[10]

The errors of Alonso and Inés lead to death for the former and to the convent for the latter. The lovers are worthy of forgiveness, but they are the agents of their own downfall. There is nothing in the play of any 'sombra fatídica' or 'fatalismo tétrico'. As for the other characters – Leonor, Fernando and Tello – they call to mind the adage of Ovid:

> Video meliora proboque,
> deteriora sequor. (*Metamorphoses*, VII, 20)

Those who do not die are left to begin a new life after a terrible warning.

The play, then, is a kind of parable on the dangers of temerity. The whole dramatic construction is manipulated towards this end. But such is the richness of the drama, so rich and so varied the succession of scenes very different in character, that very often the moral and didactic purpose is forgotten, and we enjoy instead the humour, the beauty or the mystery of Lope's poetic gifts, nowhere so profuse as in this work. Here are some examples:

Fabia.
> La fruta fresca, hijas mías,
> es gran cosa; y no aguardar
> a que la venga a arrugar
> la brevedad de los días. (315–18)

[*Alonso.*]
> No se vio florido almendro
> como todo parecía;
> que del olor natural
> son las mejores pastillas. (111–14)

[*Fernando.*]
> Son celos, don Rodrigo, una quimera
> que se forma de envidia, viento y sombra;
> con que lo incierto imaginado altera;
> una fantasma que de noche asombra,
> un pensamiento que a locura inclina,
> y una mentira que verdad se nombra. (1357–62)

[*Tello.*]	¿Toros de Medina a mí? Vive el cielo que les di reveses, desjarretando de tal aire, de tal casta, en medio del regocijo, que hubo toro que me dijo: Basta, señor Tello, basta. No basta, le dije yo; y eché, de un tajo volado, una pierna en un tejado.
Fabia.	Y ¿cuántas tejas quebró?
Tello.	Eso al dueño, que no a mí. (1956–67)
[*Tello.*]	Ya la destocada noche, de los dos polos en medio daba a la traición espada, mano al hurto, pies al miedo. (2662–5)

In short, *El caballero de Olmedo* has a moral argument which is well developed and carried through, and at the same time an unrestrained *joie de vivre* which occasionally bewitches us and makes us forget the moral preoccupations which are implicit in the work. Lope saw clearly that the *Celestina*, interpreted in the light of Counter-Reformation ideas, could be adapted to make an exemplary play; but at the same time his great poetic gifts, and perhaps his own temperament, led him sometimes to forget the moral and to express the pleasures of life and its beauties.

12
A Hispanist looks at *Othello*

The code of honour is fundamental to the Spanish theatre.[1] Lope de Vega said that cases of honour made good subjects for plays, because people felt them so strongly.[2] Honour demanded that you should be loyal to your prince, that you should uphold your religion, that you should stand on your dignity, that you should protect the weak, that you should fulfil your promises, and so forth. Honour was as precious as life itself; some would have said more precious. And any real loss of honour could be restored only by killing those responsible for it. Honour was fragile and precarious; it could be lost by the direct lie or by a physical blow. These characteristics of honour were probably accepted in many countries. The Spaniards further maintained that a man's honour depended on the behaviour of his womenfolk. A daughter or sister who was publicly suspected of immoral behaviour deprived her father or brother of his honour as well as herself of her own honour. She could remove the injury by marrying her lover; otherwise she was liable to be killed by her guardian. In the same way, a wanton wife completely destroyed the honour of her husband. If he was to remove the dishonour of cuckoldry, he had to kill her and her lover; only by so doing could he become honourable again in the eyes of his fellows. This idea is characteristic of many Spanish seventeenth-century authors; but there is no reason to suppose that it was exclusively Spanish.[3]

The notion of honour was complex in another way also: it could be regarded as an individual thing or as something that was kept by other people. It was equivalent to 'virtue' in certain contexts, to 'reputation' in others.[4] It is often referred to as reputation, opinion, fame, good name, credit, etc. Some Spanish moral writers approved of honour in so far as it approximated to virtue, but they were less sure about the cult of reputation (a worldly thing) and wholly opposed to vengeance.[5] The notion of honour as reputation is more frequently represented on the Spanish stage;[6] it gave an opportunity for illustrating the old notion that things are not what they seem, that appearance often contradicts reality. Guilty wives appear to be innocent until the matter is searched out;[7] occasionally an innocent wife appears to be guilty and is slain by an outraged, but deceived man,[8] the situation which destroys Othello after the murder of Desdemona.

Calderón's famous play *El médico de su honra* was printed in 1637. It is based on an earlier play of uncertain authorship, of which the plot is almost the same. In both plays an innocent woman is slain because she seems guilty to her husband. The avenging hero makes a surgeon bleed her to death, and after that he marries again. The most respected critics all assume that Calderón stood one hundred per cent behind this savage husband.[9] They assume that this Christian dramatist completely approved the sacrifice of an innocent life on the altar of the code of honour. I am unable to accept this view. The hero has brought dishonour on himself and on another woman by promising marriage to her and then deserting her before the play begins; the final marriage merely makes an honest woman of a poor creature whom he had betrayed. The dishonour he had brought to another was thus repaid on him. Further, throughout the play there are resemblances between this cruel but punctilious man and his cruel but just King. The play is set in the reign of Peter the Cruel, whose death is foreshadowed as the play proceeds. All through the play there is a parallel between the hero and the King. Calderón implies that both men have the same defects and that they will perish together. Furthermore, in the heroine Calderón shows us an example of rash conduct, and in the hero, another of rashness in thought. As a Catholic Christian, Calderón believed in the cardinal virtue of prudence. The preoccupation with this virtue and its opposite (rashness) is important in his two other plays of wife murder.[10] I therefore believe that Calderón dramatised the vengeance of honour because it made a suitable medium for portraying prudence in conduct and prudence in understanding the world around us. I believe that he no more approved of wife murder than anyone of us does. He gave his savage husbands some good qualities, but we are meant to admire them only up to a certain point.

As far as I am aware, no one has tried seriously to trace this theory of honour in English drama. Our critics talk of honour – in the sense of punctiliousness – but they do not often consider whether, or to what extent, a man's honour was thought to consist in the behaviour of his wife or of his daughter.[11] The behaviour of the brothers of the Duchess of Malfi is regarded as unmotivated; Leontes's desire for vengeance is equally a puzzle. Knowledge of the Spanish code helps to make their behaviour comprehensible. There were no clear-cut solutions for lost honour in England as there were in Spain, but the Spanish code seems implied, though not always approved of, in several plays. The rash husband in Middleton's *The witch* thinks he murders his wife immediately after the sister has accused her of adultery with a man-servant; but in

Massinger's *The parliament of love* would-be adulterers were beaten or drenched by husbands, not murdered by them. Cuckoldry was a preoccupation both in England and in Spain. But the English attitude was less precise than the Spanish. *A woman killed with kindness* could hardly have been tolerated in Spain, and *The parliament of love* might have been thought crude and brutal, or at least in bad taste there. Nevertheless there was some common ground: Cervantes's tale of *El curioso impertinente* (*Don Quixote*, part I, chs 33-5) was three times used as a plot in Jacobean times,[12] and it was imitated in a couple of *novelle* by Gayton.[13] In fact the notorious cuckold could never have been a man of reputation in early seventeenth-century England. Though the theory may never have been formulated in England (as it was so often formulated in Spain),[14] I suspect that many Englishmen would have accepted Spanish ideas of marital honour without difficulty. Could anyone have respected Macbeth if Lady Macbeth had had a lover? Are there any cuckolds in the Jacobean theatre who are not meant to be laughed at?

In the pages that follow, *Othello* is examined in the light of the Spanish code of honour. A few general assumptions underlie the argument. One is that the Spanish theory that man's honour largely consisted in his womenfolk's conduct was understood (even if not believed in) by Shakespeare and his audience. Another is that though Spain was thoroughly Catholic and England nominally Protestant, there was still much in common between English and Spanish religious thought during the reign of James I.[15] The interpretation seems to account for the dramatic importance of the first act, which some critics hardly seem to notice. My intention is to show:

1. how the idea of honour binds the play together, and
2. that Shakespeare was also concerned with the importance of the cardinal virtues (prudence, justice, temperance and fortitude) and the evils of rashness, cunning and injustice.

Othello is usually regarded as a tragedy of jealousy, although one or two critics have refused to accept this view. A nineteenth-century critic wrote: 'Not jealousy, but love and honour are the ruling emotions of Othello's soul.'[16] A more recent critic considers that 'We cannot call a man jealous who is convinced of his wife's unfaithfulness.'[17] Jealousy can hardly be ruled out because it does not fit into a modern definition when it was covered by a sixteenth-century one. Lily Campbell's account of the play is entirely concerned with jealousy, and she finds in it the four kinds of jealousy postulated by Varchi, whose work was translated by Robert Tofte and published in 1615. According to Varchi, honour was one of the four causes, and it may be noted that Spanish playwrights distinguished between the 'jealousy of love' and the 'jealousy of honour'.[18] The jealousy of honour is applicable to a man who is convinced of his wife's unfaithfulness, for it is characteristic of Lope's and Calderón's outraged husbands. But to regard jealousy as the main subject of the whole play is to misunderstand the play. Lily Campbell allows honour a place because honour is a cause of jealousy; her statements sometimes coincide with those given below. The play, however, becomes a finer thing if it is regarded as the story of a man destroyed by the exploitation of his sense of honour than if it were merely a pathological study of jealousy. The jealousy of honour is part of the play, an important part, but not the whole of it. Campbell's remarks that 'honour is the keynote of Othello's jealousy', that Shakespeare 'harps the note in Cassio, Iago, Othello' are true;[19] the claim made here is that the sense of honour is the foundation of the play and that jealousy, so ably treated by Campbell, is only part of the design.

Othello kills Desdemona because he believes that she has committed adultery with Cassio. He believes that his honour as a married man has been compromised by her conduct. *Nihil magis honore*. A man's honour was as precious as life itself.[20] If blood called for blood, dishonour called for blood too. According to the popular Spanish notions, the husband ought to kill his wife if she betrayed him and thereby destroyed his (as well as her) honour. If Desdemona had really destroyed Othello's honour – which to some extent depended on her conduct – then, as honour was so precious, his honour could be restored only by killing her. Othello's conduct seems to fit the Spanish pattern.

Othello made clear his conception of different sorts of honour in his speech to Desdemona in the 'brothel' scene:

> Had it pleas'd heaven
> To try me with affliction; had they rain'd
> All kinds of sores and shames on my bare head,
> Steep'd me in poverty to the very lips,
> Given to captivity me and my utmost hopes,
> I should have found in some place of my soul
> A drop of patience; but, alas, to make me
> The fixed figure for the time of scorn
> To point his slow unmoving finger at! – O, O!
> Yet could I bear that too; well, very well:
> But there where I have garner'd up my heart,
> Where either I must live or bear no life,
> The fountain from the which my current runs,
> Or else dries up – to be discarded thence!
> Or keep it as a cistern for foul toads
> To knot and gender in !   (IV, ii, 48–63)[21]

He makes a distinction between his honour as a public man – an officer and a gentleman – and as a husband. He claims that he has fortitude enough to bear the loss of the first kind of honour. He would have had patience to endure the scorn of his fellows if he had lost wealth and position and become a prisoner. But he could not stomach the idea that his wife was unchaste. He had to kill her for the sake of his self-esteem.[22] Later on he says to her:

> O perjur'd woman! thou dost stone my heart,
> And mak'st me call what I intend to do
> A murder, which I thought a sacrifice. (v, ii, 66–8)

He sacrifices her to his honour, reputation or good name, because he is convinced of her guilt. (She makes it murder, because she denies her guilt at the moment of death.) In his final disillusion, when Iago's villainy has been made obvious even to him, he asks:

> But why should honour outlive honesty? (v, ii, 248)

Iago's honesty[23] – now proved to be worthless – is equal to Othello's honour – which had made Othello commit a crime, when he thought he was executing an act of justice. Life might as well end for both the 'honourable' man and the 'honest' one. Later he calls himself 'an honourable murderer', who did 'all in honour' (v, ii, 292–3). But he was tricked and deluded by false appearances. Othello acts in the same way as Calderón's savage husbands, except that he finally admits he did wrong to murder an innocent woman. His honour, he considers, consists chiefly in Desdemona's virtue, and when he thinks that she has lost it he kills her. Spencer remarks that Othello, when he strangles her, sees himself 'as the instrument of universal justice';[24] of course he does. Every vengeance of honour so appears to its perpetrator. Menéndez Pidal pointed out that the Spanish avengers, no matter how much they protested, were compelled to murder their wives, because these murders were a tribute to society as a whole.[25]

There is an obvious link between Othello and Brabantio. Iago reminds Othello:

> She did deceive her father, marrying you. (III, iii, 210)

This is the sequel to Brabantio's couplet:

> Look to her, Moor, if thou hast eyes to see:
> She has deceiv'd her father, and may thee. (I, iii, 292–3)[26]

Brabantio's part can be explained by the fact that he has been robbed of a daughter whom he had loved and who had loved him well, by a son-in-law he did not approve of. There seems, however, to be another idea which makes the link between the two men closer. Othello will imagine that his wife's conduct has prejudiced his marital honour; Brabantio imagines that his daughter has destroyed his honour as a father. In Spain the behaviour of an unmarried woman affected the honour of her guardian (father or brother) to a slightly less degree than the behaviour of a wife affected the honour of her husband.[27] Brabantio's anger at Othello's marriage seems due to outraged honour as well as to outraged fatherly feeling. And his death, later reported by Gratiano (v, ii, 202–4), was probably as much the result of the former as the latter.

At the beginning of the play we hear the following lines spoken by Iago and Roderigo:

Roderigo.   What a full fortune does the thick-lips owe,
               If he can carry 't thus!
Iago.   Call up her father.
               Rouse him, make after him, poison his delight,
               Proclaim him in the streets; incense her kinsmen,
               And, though he in a fertile climate dwell,
               Plague him with flies; though that his joy be joy,
               Yet throw such changes of vexation on 't
               As it may lose some colour.   (I, i, 67–74)

The pronouns are ambiguous. Roderigo mentions the 'thick-lips' – Othello; Iago, 'her father' – Brabantio. H. C. Hart and John Dover Wilson assume that the pronouns in the following lines all refer to Othello. But the two malcontents proceed to 'rouse' Brabantio and to 'proclaim him in the street'. 'His delight' may be Othello's pleasure in his young bride; it may also be Brabantio's joy in the company of his daughter. Othello, of course, dwells 'in a fertile climate' and is to be plagued with flies. The first three lines of Iago's speech can apply to either father or husband; the three 'hims' are better suited to the former, the 'his' and the 'he' (in line 70) to the latter. Argument about this passage is possible; but the words seem to have a possible inclusive reference to both men. The double meaning is perhaps a sign that we may connect Brabantio with Othello as we hear Iago speak. The proclamation seems intended to cause Othello some pain by means of the purposeful humiliation of Brabantio. In other words, the attack on Othello's marital honour begins by an attack on Brabantio's honour as a father.

Iago tells Brabantio 'you have lost half your soul', (I, i, 88), that an 'old black ram is tupping your white ewe' (lines 89–90), that the devil will make him a grandfather (line 92). These and the later insults (lines 110–18) seem gratuitous and pointless unless Iago intended to proclaim Brabantio's dishonour as loudly as he could. Honour is reputation. What will Brabantio's reputation become when words like these are shouted in the street? 'Half your soul' may be referred to Desdemona[28] but honour was often regarded as a spiritual thing in the seventeenth century. When Cassio, later, says: 'I have lost the immortal part of myself' (II, iii, 255), he means his reputation, his honour. Iago tells Brabantio that he has lost his honour; he also makes sure that it is lost by the coarse way in which he publishes the news of Desdemona's flight.

Roderigo's speech, with its prolix iterations and pompous absurdity of manner, supplies the reinforcements for Iago's foulmouthed attack:

> your fair daughter,
> At this odd-even and dull watch o' th' night,
> Transported with no worse nor better guard
> But with a knave of common hire, a gondolier,
> To the gross clasps of a lascivious Moor –
> If this be known to you, and your allowance,
> We then have done you bold and saucy wrongs;
> But if you know not this, my manners tell me
> We have your wrong rebuke. (I, i, 123–31)

The rhetoric is perhaps ridiculous, but the speech conveys facts that Brabantio does not want to hear.[29] Roderigo brings out the details in such a way that the case is made to look as bad as possible. This language is strong: 'knave of common hire...gross clasps...lascivious Moor'. A little later Roderigo talks about her 'gross revolt' (line 135). Brabantio, carried away by his anger, calls for a light and, in fact, proclaims himself in the streets (lines 141–5). Iago's first plot succeeds well enough.

How did Shakespeare mean his audience to judge the Brabantio scenes? The question is not easy to answer. Brabantio puts himself in the wrong by his rash accusations of witchcraft and by his refusal to forgive his daughter. But he has been intolerably insulted by Iago, and Roderigo's more restrained declarations were harshly uttered and delivered from the street to an upper window. Othello and Desdemona were lovers; they presumably had some sympathy from the audience for that reason. But they behaved furtively and without consideration to an old man who was her father. We cannot assume that Shakespeare, or his audience, would have been as whole-heartedly on the lovers' side as a modern audience would be. Respect for parents was probably stronger in the early seventeenth century than it is today. If we are meant to feel some sympathy for Shylock after Jessica ran away with Lorenzo, we cannot help feeling it for this less repulsive, if unforgiving, old man. He too is a pitiable figure.

Brabantio is of course concerned at his daughter's apparent treachery. His expressions of anger, petulance and shame:

> Mine's not an idle cause. The Duke himself,
> Or any of my brothers of the state,
> Cannot but feel this wrong as 't were their own (I, ii, 95–7)

take on an added force if they are regarded as the outpourings of a dishonoured man. Desdemona, 'in spite of...her...credit' (I, iii, 96–7), has fallen 'in love with what she fear'd to look on'. The Duke excuses Othello and Desdemona; Brabantio leaves her to her black lover and utters a warning to him. Some few lines before, he had asked for 'Destruction on my head' (I, iii, 176–8) if he had unworthily blamed Othello. Brabantio then invoked his own death, of which we hear towards the end of the play. Grief at his daughter's treachery, shame at his own dishonour, the punishment of Heaven for an unjust and hasty accusation, all may be supposed to bring about his death.

Iago's next plot concerns the downfall of Cassio. It involves Roderigo and Montano. Roderigo, the 'gull'd gentleman' of the folio, is a man of substance to whom honour ought to have meant something.[30] He sells his land, follows Iago to Cyprus and acts as his accomplice. Iago tells him to 'find some occasion to anger Cassio, either by speaking too loud, or tainting his discipline' (II, i, 260–3), or by any other convenient means. Obviously he is to defy Cassio as an officer, to try to provoke a quarrel by making Cassio lose face. Roderigo agrees. Iago continues: 'Sir, he's rash, and very sudden in choler, and haply with his truncheon may strike at you; provoke him that he may' (II, i, 266–8). Roderigo complies: 'I will do this, if you can bring it to any opportunity' (II, i, 275–6). To bring Cassio into disrepute, Iago urges 'this poor trash of Venice' to dishonour himself by allowing the other to strike him. The dishonour of Cassio is to be contrived by the dishonour of Roderigo, who raises no objections. After it all he grumbles: 'I have been to-night exceedingly well cudgelled' (II, iii, 352–3). He does not even mention the disgrace.

Iago makes Cassio drunk. Cassio strikes Roderigo and threatens to knock Montano 'o'er the mazzard' (II, iii, 159). Montano's part in the play is not very prominent, but we are told three times about his sense of honour. Iago says he is one of the

> Three else of Cyprus – noble swelling spirits,
> That hold their honours in a wary distance,
> The very elements of this warlike isle. (II, iii, 51–3)

Emilia tells Cassio that

> the Moor replies
> That he you hurt is of great fame in Cyprus
> And great affinity. (III, i, 44–6)

And when Othello interrupts the brawl he says:

> Worthy Montano, you were wont be civil;

> The gravity and stillness of your youth
> The world hath noted, and your name is great
> In mouths of wisest censure – what's the matter
> That you unlace your reputation thus,
> And spend your rich opinion for the name
> Of a night-brawler? Give me answer to 't. (II, iii, 182–8)

These remarks are later substantiated, for it is Montano who deprives Othello of his sword in v, ii. In the second act Montano defends himself, and calls on Iago to speak for him. Iago does so, and Montano's honour is vindicated. It was, however, in danger.[31] Cassio realises that he has lost both position and honour: 'Reputation, reputation, reputation! O, I have lost my reputation! I have lost the immortal part of myself, and what remains is bestial. My reputation, Iago, my reputation!' (II, iii, 254–7). Iago speaks words of comfort: 'As I am an honest man, I thought you had receiv'd some bodily wound; there is more sense in that than in reputation. Reputation is an idle and most false imposition, often got without merit, and lost without deserving. You have lost no reputation at all, unless you repute yourself such a loser' (II, iii, 258–65). Iago talks like Falstaff at Shrewsbury;[32] the difference is that Falstaff is talking to himself whereas Iago is persuading Cassio that all is not lost. The common factor in both speeches is the reminder that base men despise what noble men like Prince Henry, Hotspur, Othello and Cassio esteem. In its context Iago's speech to Cassio is part of the plan to ruin Othello's honour in his own eyes. Cassio's reputation with Othello has been deliberately destroyed, but Cassio must not think that all is lost, or he will be of no further use to Iago. There is additional irony in the fact that Iago later says to Othello the exact reverse of what he has said here. 'Good name in man and woman, dear my lord . . .'.

In the first act of Othello we see the destruction of a father's honour. In the second we have a little drama of military honour as a prologue to the last acts which show the loss of the hero's marital honour. The second act consists of the schemes of a man who is beyond honour and dishonour: he makes a man of no honour dishonour an honourable man and imperil the honour of another.

The stages of Othello's downfall have so often been described that we need not follow them all here. Iago's famous speech on good name occurs at the start of it.[33] Othello must be reminded of the value and the precariousness of his honour (which consists so largely in the honour of his wife) before he can be made to believe it has gone. The speech also reminds the hearer of what Iago had said to Cassio about reputation in the previous act; it thus links Othello's case with those that have just been examined. His doubts begin, and they are expressed in a series of remarks that keep harking back to this speech about honour and good name:

> He that is robb'd, not wanting what is stol'n,
> Let him not know 't and he's not robb'd at all. (III, iii, 346-7)

> Her name, that was as fresh
> As Dian's visage, is now begrim'd and black
> As mine own face. (III, iii, 390-2)

Then, as her guilt seems to grow more obvious, the thought of the revenge for lost honour becomes more and more evident:

> If there be cords or knives,
> Poison, or fire, or suffocating streams,
> I'll not endure it. (III, iii, 392-4)

The solemn oaths made by Iago and Othello on their knees ('Arise black vengeance from thy hollow cell...'), which recall the emotional turbulence of the 'revenge' plays, show that there can be no turning back from this vengeance.[34]

The fourth act opens with Iago's crude words about kisses in private, being naked with her friend a-bed and the handkerchief. Othello then mentions honour, but this time it is Desdemona's honour:

Othello.   She is protectress of her honour too:
               May she give that?
Iago.   Her honour is an essence that's not seen;
               They have it very oft that have it not.
               But, for the handkerchief – (IV, i, 14-18)

Honour, in a woman, is chastity and her reputation for chastity. Iago's words mean that a woman may be chaste and have an immoral reputation, or that she may be sinning secretly. Othello takes the words in their second sense, as Iago intended. Iago is now saying words like those he said to Cassio in Act II. But his intention is different: he means Othello to think that Desdemona only appears to be chaste. His words imply that Othello should come down from the high-falutin' world of honour to the supposed hard fact of the missing handkerchief. Then Iago is able to work his general into mental incoherence and a physical swoon. When he recovers Iago continues his talk about cuckoldry and makes Othello desperate. The eavesdropping scene completes the moral degradation; Othello is now an object of ridicule. To the outside world, however, he is still the man of honour; the others do not yet know how far he has fallen away from his noble nature. When the Venetian envoys arrive, the man who thought himself dishonoured at last dishonours himself by publicly striking his wife, by calling her 'Devil' and by offering her to Lodovico. Othello thought that Desdemona had destroyed his honour; he was mistaken. He himself destroyed it utterly and completely by his behaviour to her in front of the envoys.[35]

Othello's vengeance is a mixed business. He enters talking about 'the cause' (v, ii, 1), and goes on to say that he must kill her 'else she'll betray more men' (line 6). The cause is presumably honour; but the other remark is hard to understand. Does it mean that if he does not kill Desdemona, his dishonour will kill him, and she will betray other husbands after he is dead? Or has she 'betrayed' Cassio and will she ensnare other lovers later? Perhaps these words are not intended to have a precise significance; Othello may be stammering out excuses for an action he feels impelled to commit. Then he expresses the sensuality and love which accompany and cannot be stifled by jealousy or the just revenge of outraged honour. 'This sorrow's heavenly; / It strikes where it doth love.' Shakespeare here hints that what Othello thinks is justice is in part perverted sensuality, for Desdemona says:

> That death's unnatural that kills for loving.   (v, ii, 45)

Othello's pity for her soul can be paralleled in many Spanish plays.[36] When Desdemona denies her guilt, he exclaims:

> O perjur'd woman! thou dost stone my heart,
> And mak'st me call what I intend to do
> A murder, which I thought a sacrifice.
> I saw the handkerchief.   (v, ii, 66-9)

He had meant to kill her body but allow her to save her soul; now he thinks that he must murder both. The audience, however, sees in his words the true nature of his deed: what he thinks a sacrifice to honour and justice is really murder. He kills Desdemona. Then the truth is gradually revealed to this 'murderous coxcomb', and he is driven to take his own life because he has lost not only Desdemona but his good name too: 'That's he that was Othello', he replies to Lodovico, just before the end.

We see, then, that Othello's dishonour is the sequel to the dishonour of Brabantio and of Cassio by Iago and Roderigo. Roderigo has no honour. Iago pretends to esteem or despise honour as best suits his plans. The critics usually say that when Iago talks about how Emilia may have lain previously with Othello or will lie with Cassio (I, iii, 381-4; II, i, 288-93, 301), he is merely hunting for a motive for his malignity. Possibly this is a correct diagnosis. But at least one thoughtful critic of the play has taken Iago's words as though they were spoken in earnest.[37] In the first passage Iago says that 'it is thought abroad' that Othello slept with Emilia. In the second he says 'For that I do suspect the lusty Moor', and he expresses fear only of what Cassio may do, not of what he has done. Such rumours and fears were cause enough for murder by some Spanish husbands. Iago says only that he has *heard that some people say* he was cuckolded by Othello, and a little later he says that he *suspects* him and *fears* Cassio. Even if Othello had not seduced Emilia, Iago had reason to suppose that his marital honour was tarnished by an untrue rumour.[38] A man of honour would have tried to save the situation, either by silencing the rumour-mongers or by investigating the fact secretly and closely and killing Emilia if he was sure of her guilt. Iago did nothing of the kind. He treats honour as he treats religion: he plays with it and gives it lip-service, but never thinks of applying its principles to his own case. So this man, who leads Othello by the nose after his honour, has no care for his own. He is a 'critical' man (II, i, 119) who accepts a current notion for his own purposes without believing in any way in the notion itself.

Honour of the Spanish kind seems to underlie the vengeance of Othello and the rage of Brabantio. The soldier's honour is depicted in various ways in the scene of the brawl in the second act. Iago plots against the honour of all and sundry, not for the sake of exposing an absurd notion, but in order to destroy Othello.

'The concept of the difference between outer show and inner truth is not only important as a part of Iago's character; it permeates the whole play. The essence of Othello's tragedy is that he judges wrongly by appearances.'[39] Not only Othello, but Desdemona, Cassio, Roderigo, Emilia... They all think that Iago is their friend; they are all deceived in other ways too. The difference between appearance and reality, between seeming and being, between outer show and inner truth, is brought out in many minor details in the play.[40] The idea of honour added powerfully to these contrasts. Othello thought he was dishonoured when he was still a man of honour; he dishonoured himself by insulting and killing his innocent wife. He destroyed the reputation he wrongly thought destroyed. The 'honourable murderer' was his own judgement on himself; it fully expressed his fall and his deception.

Honour made a convenient means for dramatising the difference between appearance and reality. How far did Shakespeare intend to criticise the idea in itself? Othello's tragedy is partly the consequence of his belief in honour. Perhaps honour also hardened Brabantio's heart. We must beware of assuming that because a theory is misapplied or misunderstood, it is therefore discredited. Othello made mistakes about honour which led to horrible results. But that does not mean that Shakespeare thought the whole conception of honour as reputation was a monstrous absurdity. In *I Henry IV* – the play of military honour – Falstaff's speech about honour is not to be taken as Shakespeare's own view, for the heroic figures of Prince Henry and Hotspur express themselves without irony. Military honour was, however, a simpler thing than marital honour. The first depended on a man's own efforts, the second on his wife's. We cannot say whether Shakespeare would have approved of the vengeance of honour if Desdemona had been guilty; for there is no play which shows the combination of an honourable husband and an unfaithful wife. Iago's speech on good name, though it is like the devil's quoting scripture, is in itself an eloquent plea for the cult of reputation. Iago's malice is most devilish when he uses an acceptable idea for a wicked end. The best interpretation of these lines (which have been quoted hundreds of times for their surface meaning) is that they convey what Shakespeare believed in, but for a wrong purpose. If Shakespeare believed in the importance of reputation, he was also concerned with the way in which this belief was carried out. It is not enough to have principles: one must know how to apply them. Othello erred because he did not realise this fact.[41]

In the third scene of the first act the Duke distinguishes between the discrepant estimates of the size of the Turkish fleet and the fact that any of these estimates may mean danger to Cyprus. We see a prudent statesman in action. Brabantio's entrance and appeal make him promise rigorous justice. Othello offers his 'round unvarnish'd tale', and Brabantio accuses him of using witchcraft to seduce Desdemona. The Duke then says:

> To vouch this is no proof –
> Without more wider and more overt test
> Than these thin habits and poor likelihoods
> Of modern seeming do prefer against him.   (I, iii, 106–9)

These words apply well enough to Brabantio's unfounded and rash accusation. They also apply to Othello's later rash and unfounded suspicions of Desdemona, which also were arrived at without certain and overt tests, by the thin habits and poor likelihoods of modern seeming adduced by Iago and by no one else. The Duke's reproof to Brabantio is a prophetic warning to Othello.

After Othello's eloquent account of his wooing, the Duke again appeals to Brabantio:

> I think this tale would win my daughter too.
> Good Brabantio,
> Take up this mangled matter at the best.
> Men do their broken weapons rather use
> Than their bare hands.   (I, iii, 171–5)

Brabantio rejects this advice also. He curses himself if he unjustly blames Othello and asks his daughter where she owes obedience. Her reply makes him disown her. Whereupon the Duke tries to mend matters:

> Let me speak like yourself, and lay a sentence
> Which, as a grise or step, may help these lovers
> Into your favour.
> When remedies are past, the griefs are ended
> By seeing the worst, which late on hopes depended.
> To mourn a mischief that is past and gone
> Is the next way to draw new mischief on.
> What cannot be preserv'd when fortune takes,
> Patience her injury a mockery makes.
> The robb'd that smiles steals something from the thief;
> He robs himself that spends a bootless grief. (I, iii, 199–209)

He gives plenty of sound advice, and it is disregarded. Brabantio casts scorn on it by suggesting that it be applied to the loss of Cyprus. But his reply does not cancel out the Duke's distichs. Verify facts, make the best of a bad job, face the worst that can happen, do not cry over spilt milk, patience subdues fortune, do not let adverse fate lead you to purposeless grief. All these remarks by the Duke, in smooth blank verse or in gnomic couplets, show us the course that man should take when he is in adversity. The Duke variously counsels prudence or patience. Brabantio rejects this good advice; Othello fails to act on it, though he sometimes thinks he does; Iago listens and adapts it to his own ends.

As the temptation of Othello proceeds, the ideas of patience and prudence occasionally assert themselves in his speeches. Obviously he is neither prudent nor patient in fact.[42] He utters distortions of these sentiments which make his fundamental imprudence and impatience even more obvious. The prudent man tests his judgement against that of other men; but if he accepts another's opinion, he must be sure that the other man is right. Othello surrenders his judgement to Iago, because he is convinced that Iago's apparent honesty is real.[43] Had Iago been a good man, then Othello would have done right to trust him. The audience knows that Iago is bad, and that Othello's trust is self-deception. At the start of the temptation he declares that prudence will guide his decision about Desdemona's innocence or guilt:

> Nor from mine own weak merits will I draw
> The smallest fear or doubt of her revolt;
> For she had eyes, and chose me. No, Iago;
> I'll see before I doubt; when I doubt, prove;
> And on the proof, there is no more but this –
> Away at once with love or jealousy! (III, iii, 191–6)

Nevertheless, only a very few lines later he is convinced when Iago tells him:

> She did deceive her father, marrying you;
> And when she seem'd to shake and fear your looks,
> She lov'd them most. (III, iii, 210-12)

Iago is able to use with complete success the argument which Othello had guarded against. Othello's wise good sense soon deserts him. When later he speaks about patience he says:

> Dost thou hear, Iago?
> I will be found most cunning in my patience;
> But – dost thou hear? – most bloody. (IV, i, 89-91)

These words are a horrible travesty of the Duke's speech in the first act. What kind of patience is this?

Othello degenerates into rashness. Three times is he described as rash: by Desdemona, by Emilia, by Lodovico:

Desdemona. Why do you speak so startingly and rash? (III, iv, 79)

Emilia. Thou art rash as fire to say
That she was false. (V, ii, 137-8)

Lodovico. Where is this rash and most unfortunate man?
Othello. That's he that was Othello – here I am. (V, ii, 286-7)

The first two witnesses to his rashness are interested parties; Lodovico is an impartial observer, and Othello admits the accusation against himself. His deterioration from being 'all in all sufficient', from the 'noble Moor', 'the nature whom passion could not shake' (IV, i, 261-4) has been studied by many writers, who have pointed out how passion conquers reason, how his judgement is warped by Iago's suggestions.[44] There is a double effectiveness in Iago's comments on his emotional condition; they tell the audience how Othello is degenerating and speed on the actual degeneration. Iago judges him as he corrupts him.[45] Othello's horrible exclamations make the process still more obvious.[46] Anything in the way of revenge can be expected from a man who cannot reason and who expresses himself in words like these. Prudence, temperance, fortitude have been replaced by rashness, violence and passion. Justice, too is distorted into a treacherous scheme of murder (which is foiled) and another brutal murder which succeeds.

The four cardinal virtues are destroyed in Othello. Iago appears to possess them.[47] Iago remains sober through the drinking-bout, but his apparent temperance is false, because he tries to make Cassio and Montano drunk; he stays sober to further his purpose, not through love of virtue. He complains to Roderigo of his lack of promotion, but to no one else; he can pass as a patient man. When he pretends to be just, he advocates murder. These qualities, however, are less obvious in his part than is his false prudence.

When Iago reflects that he is giving Cassio good advice, but with a bad object, he also says:

> Divinity of hell!
> When devils will their blackest sins put on,
> They do suggest at first with heavenly shows,
> As I do now. (II, iii, 339–42)

This remark describes the temptation of Cassio aptly enough, but it also applies to the temptation of Othello. Iago deceives Cassio with good advice; he reminds Othello of the obligations of honour. Every appearance of virtue comes out in his words to conceal the colour of his real intentions. The 'Good name in man and woman, dear my lord' speech is only the most obvious instance of it. His cunning is devilish because it appears so well intentioned, so 'honest', so virtuous. That this cunning is false prudence hardly needs any illustration: think what good advice he gives Cassio, how plausible are the analyses of Desdemona which he gives to Roderigo and to Othello, and how loyal a friend he seems to be to all three of them. However, there is one aspect of his part which seems to me to be especially remarkable in this respect: his concern with time.

Much has been written about the problem of time in *Othello*. Perhaps all that business of the two clocks is less important than the way Iago thinks about time in itself and how his plans are to be adjusted to it. The literature of the sixteenth and seventeenth centuries contains many references to time as a succession of crucial moments in which good or bad choices could be made. The prudent man made good use of time. Calderón called one of his plays *Dar tiempo al tiempo* – 'give Time time to work.' Gracián extolled the importance of waiting ('la espera') in his treatise *El discreto*. Philip II said that he and time were a match for any man; the first viceroy of Mexico told his successor that the secret of good government was to do little and to do that slowly – only by this could we be sure that we were not deceived.[48] Man should not try to impose his will on the world or on the course of events; instead, he should try to fit his desires into the course of events, to swim with the tide, not against it. So Iago, though his purpose is evil, acts at first in such a way that time is made his ally:

> If consequence do but approve my dream,
> My boat sails freely, both with wind and stream. (II, iii, 58–9)

He values time, and would not waste it with 'such a snipe' as Roderigo, but for his 'sport and profit' (I, iii, 391–2). When Iago advises his gulls – Roderigo, Cassio and Othello – wise saws about time, patience and the dangers of rashness are often heard from his lips. To Roderigo he says: 'There are many events in the womb of time which will be delivered' (I, iii, 366–7), and

> How poor are they that have not patience!
> What wound did ever heal but by degrees?
> Thou know'st we work by wit, and not by witchcraft;
> And wit depends on dilatory time.
> . . .
> Though other things grow fair against the sun,
> Yet fruits that blossom first will first be ripe. (II, iii, 358–65)

He repeats to Cassio almost the same advice that the Duke had given to Brabantio:

> Since it is as it is, mend it for your own good. (II, iii, 291–2)

And he tells Othello:

> Leave it to time. (III, iii, 249)

> Nay, but be wise; yet we see nothing done;
> She may be honest yet. (III, iii, 436–7)

> Patience, I say; your mind perhaps may change. (III, iii, 456)

And when Othello says he will be cunning and bloody in his patience, Iago says:

> But yet keep time in all. (IV, i, 92)

The Duke spoke words of comfort to heal the breach between father and daughter. Iago speaks words very like the Duke's to rouse angry passion and to bring about murder.

All seems to go well with Iago's plans until the fifth act. The murder of Cassio is to crown his plot with success. Iago enters with Roderigo, and in his words there is urgency and daring, but nothing now of caution or prudence:

> Here, stand behind this bulk; straight will he come.
> Wear thy good rapier bare, and put it home.
> Quick, quick; fear nothing; I'll be at thy elbow.
> It makes us or it mars us; think on that,
> And fix most firm thy resolution. (V, i, 1–5)

The plot miscarries; Roderigo is killed, but not Cassio. Iago tries to incriminate Bianca, and then – a fatal mistake – he tells Emilia to run to the citadel to tell Othello and Desdemona what has happened. Then he repeats to himself what he had said to Roderigo at the beginning of the scene:

> This is the night
> That either makes me or fordoes me quite. (V, i, 128–9)

As long as Iago acts cautiously, acts with worldly prudence, his schemes succeed; he is able to deceive Othello with the truth,[49] Cassio with apparently good advice and Roderigo with fair promises. When he has to stake all on a single throw – the death of Cassio – he comes to grief. True prudence can learn from the false prudence of Iago.

Desdemona is well intentioned but impulsive. Her conduct in the first act was precipitate: her marriage was the result of passion rather than reflection; her plea to accompany Othello to Cyprus – a dangerous place – was not necessarily to be regarded as wise. When Cassio asks for her help she replies:

> my lord shall never rest;
> I'll watch him tame, and talk him out of patience;
> His bed shall seem a school, his board a shrift;
> I'll intermingle every thing he does
> With Cassio's suit.   (III, iii, 22–6)

She carries out her threat. We need not follow her speech and actions in the following scenes; she never pauses to think that her husband might not be favourably impressed by a young wife's pleas for a good-looking young officer.[50] Shakespeare means us to sympathise with her in her sufferings – she is patient – but he does not expect us to admire her imprudence.[51] Her part seems very similar to Doña Mencía's in Calderón's *El médico de su honra*: she is a virtuous woman, who never fails to do the wrong thing.

There are other imprudences committed by Cassio, Roderigo, Emilia. There is no point in listing them. Real prudence belongs to the onlookers: the Duke in Act I, Lodovico, Gratiano and Montano in Act v. Their judgements are right. The Duke states the laws of virtue which the actors in the tragedy break; the three spectators in the last act assess the actors' merits: Iago is a 'hellish villain', the murder of Desdemona was a 'monstrous act' and Othello was a 'rash and most unfortunate man'. No one can counter these judgements; they are clear to all who see or read the play. They give no final judgement on Othello himself whether his 'solid virtue' was shattered to pieces or still survived when he took his own life. Either view is perhaps compatible with the interpretation of the play in terms of honour and prudence.

Othello is a tragedy of honour. In it Shakespeare has shown how a man who allows himself to be deceived by appearances fatally deceives himself. He is surrounded by others who are also deceived and by one man who is an arch-deceiver. The advice of the Duke would have saved Othello if he had followed it, but passion destroyed his judgement. Othello's care for his reputation was as estimable as his love for Desdemona; he went wrong because he allowed Iago to pervert it. What happens to Othello is foreshadowed in Brabantio's sterile rage at the dishonour which needed only a word of reconciliation to be removed. The first act of *Othello* is important, not merely because it gives us the background of the Cyprian tragedy, or the excuse for the beginning of Iago's temptation ('She did deceive her father, marrying you'), or psychological insight into the chief characters, but because it shows how Brabantio ruins his honour and how respect for Christian moral teaching can save men from disaster in this world as well as in the next. Othello and the others fail to learn this lesson.[52]

13
Tragic themes in Spanish ballads

> Let me say againe, [quoth Sancho] If your Lady-ship will not giue mee the Iland, as I am a foole, Ile refuse it, for being a wise-man: for I haue heard say, The neerer the Church, the further from God; and, All is not gold that glistereth; and that from the oxen, plough and yokes, the Husband-man *Bamba* was chosen for King of *Spaine*: and that *Rodrigo*, from his tissues, sports, and riches, was cast out to be eaten by snakes (if we may beleeue the rimes of the old *Romants*, that lye not.)
>
> Why, no more they doe not (sayd *Donna Rodriguez*, the Waytingwoman, that was one of the Auditours) for you haue one *Romant* that sayes, that *Don Rodrigo* was put aliue into a Tombe full of Toades, Snakes, and Lizards, and some two days after, from within the Tombe, he cryed with a low and pitiful voyce, *Now they eat, now they eat me in the place where I sinned most*: and according to this, this man hath reason to say, he had rather be a Labourer then a King, to bee eaten to death with vermine.
>
> *The second part of the history of the Valorous and witty Knight-Errant, Don Quixote of the Mançha*. Written in Spanish by Michael Ceruantes: and now translated into English (London, printed for Edward Blount, 1620) (p. 222).

Anyone who talks about Spanish ballads today must recognise two debts. One is to W. J. Entwistle, whose great book *European balladry*[1] placed the subject in a European setting; the other is to the most venerable of Spanish scholars, Don Ramón Menéndez Pidal, who, in his eighty-eighth year, saw his life's work rewarded by the publication of the first volume of the great corpus of Spanish balladry.[2] These two men have rendered enormous services to the study of Hispanic culture, and in a sense much recent work is already implicit in theirs; later generations of critics will often dot their *i*s and cross their *t*s. I want therefore to say at once that I owe much to them and to recall that the one gave the first published lecture at Canning House[3] and in every way he could helped forward the younger generation of Spanish scholars in this country; while the other, who was one of the great men of our time, not only trained a brilliant generation of scholars to follow him but also revealed mediaeval Spain to intellectual Europe. In what follows my debt to Don Ramón will be obvious and explicit; my debt to Entwistle is less obvious and more personal. For I received from him encouragement and stimulus when I much needed them, and his book on ballads helped me rather to crystallise my ideas than to give me new ones. I can only hope that what I now put forward will not be proved false by any of the authoritative statements of these two great scholars.

Ever since I began to read ballads I have found them puzzling. Why is this poetry so moving? For, it seemed to me, ballads, if they are good poetry, break the rules of all other good poetry. Some of the finest poems by Donne or by Quevedo exist in different versions, but we can usually tell from a comparison of these versions that one is better than the others. Ballads, as Menéndez Pidal says, live in their variants, and one version is not necessarily better than another. When we read Donne or Quevedo we are impressed by the originality of their highly charged language, the way in which familiar words, yoked together, produce new feelings in us; ballads, on the other hand, often seem composed of clichés that are to be found in other ballads. Yet these poems continue to move us, sometimes more deeply than quite good poems of a more original kind. I cannot claim to have explained this puzzle, but I think that something can still be found out by considering together some of the Spanish ballads which I have most frequently reread.

Before I do this, however, it seems worth while to remember that ballads are the product of a social system that has now almost disappeared. They were recited and sung in what were very often illiterate communities, and their language may well echo the language habits of their reciters. It is well known that the old countryman spoke vividly and in proverbs,[4] whereas modern urban men speak in vague abstractions and dead metaphors. Can we say that the clichés of ballads are in any way superior to the clichés of our twentieth-century newspapers and public speeches? Possibly this may be so. Our blueprints and bottle-necks, targets and headaches often cover up a lack of exact thought or help to conceal a meaning by overlaying it with verbiage. Ballad clichés often pad, but they do not conceal. And from time to time come phrases and sentences of startling directness which perhaps recall the graphic idioms of old-fashioned country speech. It does not much matter if these are repeated in different ballads, or even in the same one, provided that they are apposite, appropriate to their context.

Country metaphors were drawn from the objects with which the countryman worked: the land, crops, animals, tools. Working with these objects, he usually kept the metaphors within bounds. He did not 'iron out bottle-necks' or say that 'the process of dilution has reached saturation point'. Occasionally there were Sancho Panzas who were carried away by their love of proverbs and used them wrongly, but these were exceptions.

The daily use of the object or the sight of it kept the metaphor within bounds, so that country speech made its effects through its vivid suitability to the context. The suitability exists even when the statement is hyperbolical. I remember a Westmorland man who told me how a neighbour had married for money but lived to regret it: 'Aye, he went to t'midden for muck, an' he was poisoned by t' stink.'

We can find a good deal of this idiom in literature before European prose was emasculated by good taste, Renaissance literary theory and the polite ideals of the age of Louis XIV. The wealth and vigour of Spanish popular idiom is itself almost proverbial. I need mention only the titles of two modern Spanish collections of proverbs: *More than 21,000 Spanish proverbs* and *12,600 more Spanish proverbs*.[5] Country idioms have reinforced some of the finest Spanish narrative and dialogue: in the *Celestina*, in *Lazarillo de Tormes* and in the *Quixote*. It is hardly necessary to illustrate this well-known fact, but perhaps I may be forgiven if I quote Teresa Panza's remarks about the absurdity of her becoming a lady:

> I will not haue folke laugh at mee, as they see mee walke in my Countesses apparell, or my Gouernesses, you shall haue them cry straight, Looke how stately the Hog-rubber goes, she that was but yesterday at her spindle, and went to Church with the skirt of her coat ouer her head in stead of an Huke, to day she is in her Varthingale and her buttons, and so demure, as if we knew her not: God keepe mee in my seuen wits, or my fiue, or those that I haue, and Ile not put my selfe to such hazards; Get you, Brother, to bee a Gouernement or an Iland, and take state as you please, for by my mothers *Holy-dam*, neither I nor my daughter will stirre a foot from our village: better a broken ioynt then a lost name, and keepe home, the honest mayd, to bee doing is her trade, goe you with *Don Quixote* to your aduentures, and leaue vs to our ill fortunes; God will send better, if we be good.[6]

Teresa's speech is effective not merely because it is picturesque but because her proverbs are appropriate. Even when she is absurdly muddled about the number of her wits or the nature of islands, her statements remain clear. She uses a vivid metaphor to reflect an unexpected light on the subject it stands for. Folk idioms like these helped prose writers in earlier centuries than ours – I think of Bunyan and Nashe in England – and they contrast with our modern educated speech and our shallow, turgid prose.

This rich idiomatic kind of language can sometimes be found in ballads, but not always. In fact ballads are seldom metaphorical, and even similes are rare in them. Nevertheless the directness of their language and their mentions of the everyday things that 'art-poetry' often ignores sometimes remind me of the way in which old country people talk. Two passages from British ballads may illustrate the point (Spanish parallels exist, but I want to quote an original here, not a translation). First, the direct vigour of the murder of Clerk Saunders:

> Out he has taen a bright long brand,
>   And he has striped it throw the straw,
>   And throw and throw Clarke Sanders body
>   A wat he has gard cold iron gae.[7]

And although metaphors are few in ballads, there is often that same sense of the validity of the everyday object which underlies country metaphor. Here is how Johnie Armstrong pleaded for his life to the king of Scotland:

> Grant me my lyfe, my liege, my king,
>   And a bonny gift I'll gie to thee;
>   Gude four and twenty ganging-mills
>   That gang throw a' the yeir to me.
>
> These four and twenty mills complete
>   Sall gang for thee throw all the yeir,
>   And as mekle of gude reid wheit
>   As all their hoppers dow to bear.[8]

And sometimes we find this homely, definite imagery of hoppers, corn, meal and malt, beef and mutton, side by side with steeds shod with silver and gold and fantastic creatures, beautiful or terrible, from the supernatural world. Such contrasts are often prominent. The world of faery and fantastic splendour exists side by side with life as ordinary men know it: life among things which were known, valued or feared, and in terms of which ordinary men and women expressed the problems of their daily lives. This is one of the ballad contrasts which seems to me to be revealing.

Our English and Scottish ballads, fine as some of them are, remain curiously outside our cultivated literature, poetic and dramatic. Shakespeare quotes them incidentally, and a few romantic poets imitate them, but they are far from being a dominant influence in the history either of our poetry or of our drama. In Spain and in the Spanish-speaking world the ballad has exercised a much stronger influence.[9] The oral ballads were imitated by culivated poets in the sixteenth century and in the twentieth; they were dramatised in the theatre of the Golden Age by some of the greatest Spanish playwrights. Not only that. At times the work of great poets in Spain has become traditional and been handed down orally as were the older poems. So that ballads form, as it were, a more homogeneous part of Spanish literature, they 'belong' more there, than do ballads in England and Scotland. I would not say that Spanish ballads are superior to ours, but that – largely because their metre appealed strongly to great Spanish poets – they more consistently form a part of Spanish culture than ours do. Our poets preferred the blank-verse line and the octosyllable to the ballads' sing-song stanzas. Spanish poets knew that their ballad metre could strengthen all but their most refined productions.

Much of what I am going to say here can be applied to our ballads as well as to the Spanish, but with occasional exceptions I shall refer exclusively to Spanish ballads; the chief exception will be one instance in which a Spanish ballad may have influenced a version of one of our own.

A hundred years ago the subject-matter of many Spanish ballads was pretty familiar to educated Englishmen. J. G. Lockhart, the biographer of Sir Walter Scott, was the chief among a number of their popularisers. He published a number of versions of the historical ballads in a translation of *Don Quixote* printed in 1822, and the first edition of his *Ancient Spanish ballads historical and romantic* appeared the following year. It was reprinted very many times during the next fifty years, and I believe Lord Macaulay found his versions vastly superior to the originals.[10] Times have changed. At most we can find only a period charm in Lockhart's verses, romantic evocations of an imaginary age of chivalry, such as we are shown on the engraved title-page of the first edition and in the charming illustrations by David Roberts and others to that of 1842. Lockhart gave his public what he saw in the originals, and that is something very different from what we can see in these poems today.

The Spanish ballads must be read in Spanish. The English translations are padded, indirect, over-rhetorical and diffuse. Here is Lockhart's translation of six lines of one of the Spanish ballads about Roderick the Goth, the king who lost Spain to the Moors in 711:

> All stain'd and strew'd with dust and blood, like to some smouldering brand
> Pluck'd from the flame Rodrigo shew'd: – his sword was in his hand,
> But it was hack'd into a saw of dark and purple tint;
> His jewell'd mail had many a flaw, his helmet many a dint.[11]

The Spanish original reads:

> Iva tan tinto de sangre   que una brasa parecía.
> . . .
> la espada lleva hecha sierra   de los golpes que tenía;
> el almete de abollado   en la cabeça se le hundía.[12]
>
> He went so blood-stained that he looked like a live coal.
> . . .
> He carries his sword made into a saw by the blows struck on it.
> His helmet so much dinted it sank on to his head.

Lockhart could not resist the temptation to overwrite his original. The result is not a ballad but a romantic pastiche. The direct metaphors of live coals and saws lose their force through the translator's unjustified qualifications; and the physical impact of the helmet battered down on to King Roderick's head is missed completely. In the original Spanish the immediacy of folk speech seems here at least to come through the ballad conventions. This fails to happen in Lockhart's translation.

Immediacy of this kind can be found in many Spanish ballads, but others – it must be confessed – are repetitive and diffuse. Few of them have metaphors or similes like the ones I have just quoted. At one time I thought that the early versions from fifteenth- and sixteenth-century song-books and chap-books were always more terse, more concise than those collected orally in modern Spain, Spanish America or the Jewish Spanish-speaking colonies in the Near East. But Menéndez Pidal has said – and his collection is likely to demonstrate – that beauty may creep into a ballad in any stage of its transmission. His modern material, ranging from New Mexico to the Plate and from Chile to Palestine, contains many hitherto unknown gems. Not until the whole collection is before us will it be safe to generalise. My examples, therefore, will be taken from texts written down over four hundred years ago, but that is because these have long been accessible to me whereas many modern versions are only now becoming available.

Menéndez Pidal has also shown that some of the oldest Spanish ballads about national heroes derive from the early mediaeval epics, of which only two survive completely, although others can be reconstructed. His proofs of this derivation are too complicated to be summarised here, but his conclusions are, I consider, established. Some ballads about the Cid and the savage story of the Seven Princes of Lara derive directly from these epics. The ballads of King Roderick, one of which has already been mentioned, come from an historical novel or novelised chronicle composed about the year 1440. It is possible, then, to compare some Spanish ballads with their non-ballad sources, and it might be expected that ballads – so often a form of poetry peculiar to the illiterate – would always be inferior as literature to the more artistic epics and other works from which they derive. This is hardly so. Let any unprejudiced reader examine the epic fragments of the Seven Princes and the ballads that derive from them; let him do the same with the appropriate sections of Corral's *Crónica sarracina* and the ballads of King Roderick: he will find, I think, that the ballads are more moving and more intense in their impression than are their immediate sources. Ballads are worth study for their own sake, not merely because they are, as it were, the ghosts of something earlier and more artistic.

To describe their poetry is very difficult. Some valuable atempts to do so have been made by scholars, but their criteria are sometimes too general. Concepts like vividness, narrative or dramatic power, or magical glimpses of unknown worlds do not help very much to explain why we enjoy ballads or to describe their peculiar merits. I cannot hope to be much more precise. But perhaps a few samples of what seem to me to be their best poetry may provide a tentative solution. The most helpful idea produced by Entwistle is that of the relative impersonality of the ballad as compared with the personal style or attitude of the artistic lyric or narrative poem.[13] Ballads tell us what is supposed to have happened and leave us to form our own conclusions. And the telling involves a number of conventions and stylisations which prevent our being more than sympathetic witnesses of what is going on. We may feel *for*, we do not feel *with*, those whose words and deeds are related to us.

I want now to take certain scenes and episodes in Spanish ballads which have moved me and try to explain what they seem to me to imply. I take a number of poems which end unhappily, and the same method might of course be pursued with other themes too. There are, for instance, few ballads of the supernatural in Spain that can be compared with our own ballads, and those few are inferior. But Spain is rich in poems which describe how a local hero proves himself superior in manliness and honour to a king, or even to the Pope, or which portray the dangers and anguish of love, or the heroism of Spaniards on the battlefield, or even what the Moors may be thought to have felt as the Spaniards won from them town after town. The matter I have chosen seems to me richer than these other possibilities and more revealing; and my approach to it will consist in first considering the function in some ballads of those who witness the events described. The witness stands apart from the main action, and his detachment seems to have certain implications for the comprehension of the poems themselves.

Now let us go back to King Roderick, whose lust brought about the destruction of Spain by the Moors, who escaped blood-stained and battered after eight days of battle. He reflects:

> Ayer era rey de España, oy no lo soy de una villa;
> ayer villas y castillos, oy ninguno posseía;
> . . .
> oy no tengo una almena que pueda dezir que es mía.[14]

His horse takes him up into the hills. He meets a shepherd and begs for some food. The shepherd gives him some black bread which tastes bitter; the King weeps as he eats it, thinking of the rich meats which he had enjoyed when he was really a king. The shepherd directs him to a hermit and the hermit, after he has absolved Roderick, shuts him up in a tomb with a seven-headed serpent as a penance. The King, destroyed by his sin, has to beg from a shepherd to keep alive before he can perform the terrifying penance which will finally save his soul. How are the mighty fallen!

A somewhat similar encounter takes place in a Northumbrian ballad

The death of Parcy Reed. Parcy Reed, betrayed by the three false Halls of Girsonfield, is attacked by the Scots and left for dead on the hills. The old text of this ballad ends with Parcy Reed's farewell after the Halls have abandoned him. Another version, expanded from that sent by James Telfer to Sir Walter Scott in 1824, includes a conversation between the dying noble and a shepherd who finds him. The shepherd is horrified at his discovery of Parcy Reed, the Lord of Troughend, mangled by thirty-three wounds: 'Can this be Lord Troughend?' he asks. Parcy Reed begs the shepherd to bring him some water from a spring: it does not matter now whether he be Lord Troughend or not; he is simply a helpless dying man.[15] All the extra material found in this version and not in the older one is suspiciously literary in tone, including this incident. Yet there is something moving in it, and I have often reread it. I now consider that Telfer found the story of Roderick and the shepherd in Lockhart and rewrote the old text adding this episode to it. The *Ancient Spanish ballads* were printed in 1823, and Telfer sent his first version of *Parcy Reed* to Scott the following year. The seeming authenticity of his conclusion is due to the fact that he imitated a Spanish ballad situation.

Parcy Reed's nobility is a fine and splendid thing, but it is no use to him when he lies wounded and thirsty awaiting death. Roderick has lived to command others and is now the slave of the whim of his horse, another helpless man, who hopes somehow to save his soul before he dies. The shepherds emphasise these facts. They have no nobility, but they are unlikely to meet such unpleasant misadventures as befall their betters. They are the sort of men who will sing ballads about their betters' fates when they themselves are not shepherding. They are double witnesses to the great man's pride and fall: those of higher rank fall even lower than they. Roderick is forced to accept the shepherd's crusts, Parcy Reed begs his shepherd to fetch him a drink of water from a beck. The noble or king finds that he cannot do without something that is free to any commoner.

Not all the ballad witnesses are so significant as these two shepherds. The porter who tells Count Dirlos that a rival is about to marry his wife, the other porter who tells the supposed palmer that Charlemagne is at Mass – these men have little relevance to our enquiry, except that both see the hero as what he pretends to be (an unknown stranger or a humble palmer) rather than as what he is (a great noble or Charlemagne's son). The huntsman who spies on the Count Claros and the Princess is a despicable Paul Pry and no more; the peasants who accuse the two Carvajales of ravaging their lands and raping their wives are merely malevolent perjurers. These men, like the Christian slave in Saragossa questioned by Don Gaiferos, whose griefs prevent him from thinking of anything else, are mentioned here lest I be accused of omitting them. They are what I would call insignificant witnesses; they help on the story, but what they have to say does not reveal anything important about the attitude of the reciter or of the audience to the events that are described. The two shepherds, however, seem to me to do exactly this.

There are also onlookers who warn the great men of the fate that awaits them, but the king, noble or prince pays no heed and meets his death. King Sancho besieged his sister Doña Urraca in Zamora. A traitor called Vellido Dolfos left Zamora and made his way to Sancho's camp. He pretended that he could show Sancho a weak place in the city's defences, and – when Sancho was at a disadvantage – he murdered the King and ran back to seek safety in the besieged city. A sentinel on the walls of Zamora (an enemy, for he spoke from the walls while Sancho was outside them) called out a warning to the King which was disregarded. Here is the text of the ballad, which starts with the warning and ends with the murderer's escape:

>¡Guarte, guarte, rey don Sancho,   no digas que no te aviso,
>que del cerco de Zamora   un traidor había salido:
>Vellido Dolfos se llama   hijo de Dolfos Vellido;
>si gran traidor fue su padre,   mayor traidor es el hijo;
>cuatro traiciones ha hecho,   y con ésta serán cinco!
>Si te engaña, rey don Sancho,   no digas que no te aviso.
> Gritos dan en el real: ¡A don Sancho han mal herido!
>¡Muerto le ha Vellido Dolfos;   gran traición ha cometido!
> Desque le tuviera muerto   metióse por un postigo;
>por las calles de Zamora   va dando voces y gritos:
>¡Tiempo era, doña Urraca,   de cumplir lo prometido![16]

The point is not merely that an enemy sentinel shows fundamental loyalty; it lies also in the fact that the lesser man sees the danger that the King does not recognise.

Somewhat similar, but less obvious, is the situation in the ballad of the death of Don Fadrique, Master of the Knights of St James and half-brother of Peter the Cruel. Peter summons him from Coimbra to Seville. Various incidents happen en route: his mule falls as they cross a ford, he loses a gilded dagger and a favourite page is drowned. At the gates of Seville he meets a man in deacon's orders who tells him that he is now the father of a young baby and that he should return in order to baptise him. Don Fadrique does not listen but goes on to the palace, where Peter separates him from his followers and has him secretly beheaded. Fadrique's head is carried to Peter's mistress, and she throws it to a mastiff, which, however, had belonged to Don Fadrique. The dog bewails its dead master, and an old aunt earns imprisonment by scolding the fratricidal king. The words of the deacon were clearly meant to indicate a way in which Don Fadrique could have avoided his doom, but he disregarded them and was slain. The noble ignores the warning given by the commoner who cannot compel the noble to listen to him. We are not told that the deacon knew of Peter's intention; but no hearer of the ballad could help realising that this was in fact a warning to Don Fadrique of how he might have escaped death if only he had stopped to listen.[17]

There are other onlookers too. After the battle of Roncesvalles an old man goes searching for his son among the heaps of dead men. He sees a Moor in armour and asks him for news of his son. The Moor tells him: 'this knight lies dead in yonder field, his feet in the stream and his body on the bank; he was pierced by seven lance thrusts'. There the ballad ends. We are simply given a description of a search and a conversation: a Moorish witness – the old man – his dead son. The economy and restraint of this ballad – a fragment of a lost Spanish epic – is perhaps more powerful than the epic itself would have been.[18]

And – as a last example of witnesses – there is the story of a lady called Doña Alda, who dressed in her finery goes to church accompanied by other ladies, including her mother-in-law. A herdsman who sees her calls out: 'What a fine widow! a widow dressed in scarlet!' Her mother-in-law tells her that the herdsman is warning them that they will be late for Mass. But the herdsman knows what every one but Doña Alda knows: that her husband's corpse lies in the church. When she arrives there she weeps and screams. She bites and twists the golden rings on her fingers and tears to shreds the gold and scarlet dress which the herdsman had drawn attention to. And – the ballad implies – she calls on the Virgin because she is about to die.[19] This ballad is a modern text, collected this century. It makes an effective contrast with the other that I have just quoted from. But in both we find the juxtaposition of the herdsman or Moor, persons unaffected by the tragedy, who tell those concerned in it the truth that they do not know. The onlooker's function varies, but he is primarily a witness. He sees the hero's glory and his fall. He represents the humble ballad audience who admire, sympathise with and perhaps feel sorry for their heroes, but who remain otherwise unaffected by their fates.

Wealth, position, power and finery are no protection against grief, bad fortune and death. They make a change of fortune all the more noteworthy. Misfortune is constantly brought out by violent contrasts. Al-Mansour brings Gonzalo Gustios out of prison into the palace – and there presents him with the eight severed heads of his sons and their tutor.[20] The prisoner in darkness is linked to the outside world, where flowers bloom, corn ripens and lovers serve Love, by a bird's song; the bird is shot by a cross-bowman.[21] Guarinos, fettered hand and foot, up to his waist in water in his dungeon, hears the Moor Marloto's preparations for the tournament to celebrate Midsummer Day.[22] Over and over again the ballads show this contrast of health and prosperity with misery and death, in close proximity one to another.

In some English collections of ballads, tragic ballads are admitted as a separate class. How are they tragic? What do we mean by the word? Some ballad heroes deserve their fates; others are completely innocent. King Roderick had destroyed Spain by his lust, and perhaps King Sancho ought not to have taken up arms against his sister. But Don Fadrique was an innocent man, Don Beltrán who was killed at Roncesvalles and the lady who learned of her husband's death in the church were both completely innocent. The label 'tragic ballads' can be affixed to a large number of different kinds of ballad, if the word 'tragic' merely means that the hero or heroine meets disaster at the end of it. The reasons for the disaster are not always those thought proper to ancient tragedy by Aristotle or to more recent plays by the critics who have tried to follow him. Some ballad heroes had some tragic frailty (like, perhaps, Don Fadrique's trust in his murderous brother Peter) which led to their downfall; others, however, were completely innocent, had done nothing at all to deserve their fates. The word 'tragic' in these cases seems to mean no more in ballad criticism than it does in our daily newspapers.

Yet I believe that this word can have some meaning when it is used of ballads. Robert Graves gives as his eighth quality of a ballad: 'It begins in the last act of the drama and moves to the final climax without stage-directions.'[23] The remark has often been quoted – not always with acknowledgement – and I think that it is revealing. There are some comic and some romantic ballads, but the drama is often of the most sombre kind. If we are going to talk about tragic ballads we must try to find some justification of the term. It must apply to such situations as the following. Doña Alda, wife of Roland, is in her castle. She is accompanied by three hundred ladies, one hundred of whom are spinning gold thread, another hundred are weaving silks and yet another hundred are playing on musical instruments. She dreams a bad dream, which makes her scream so loudly that her cries could be heard in the city of Paris. Her court flatterers interpret the dream favourably to her, but their interpretation is false:

> Otro día de mañana   cartas de lejos le traen;
> tintas venían de fuera,   de dentro escritas con sangre,
> que su Roldán era muerto   en la caza de Roncesvalles.
> Cuando tal oyó doña Alda   muerta en el suelo se cae.[24]

Or there is the lady called Julianesa (or Moriana in other versions) in splendid captivity among the Moors. Her captor Galván is asleep with his head in her lap as she looks out of the window. Outside she sees her Christian lover, barefoot, shrieking out curses and grief at her capture.

He cannot see her; she sees him but can make no sign to him. Tears from her eyes fall on the face of the Moor.[25] In some versions this poem ends happily, but the passage summarised is the finest part of it. This is the situation that I propose to call tragic: a juxtaposition of happiness and misery.

John Housman noted how in ballads we often see the 'conflict between two contrasting worlds', for instance the supernatural as against the real one, or the contrast between parental authority and the wishes of a couple in love.[26] Perhaps what I am trying to say is part of this same idea. Life and death, happiness and misery are brought close together in contrast in all the ballads I have discussed. No matter how splendid the hero's career as soldier, noble or prince has been, death comes suddenly and extinguishes the splendour. The Scottish ballad hero Hughie Grame was able to leap fourteen feet with his hands tied behind his back, but that could not save him when his time came to die.[27] So the ballads often emphasise the splendour, luxury, strength or brave deeds of their heroes before they meet their deaths. One Doña Alda was waited on by three hundred gentlewomen, the other wore gold and scarlet. Roderick and Sancho were kings, and the ballads that tell of their deaths are preceded by others which tell of their power and might. The heroes are magnificent, but their magnificence often ends in failure, disgrace, despair and death.

These so-called tragic ballads (including some usually lumped under other categories) are in fact examples of mutability. They show how power and pride often come suddenly to a miserable end. They show how men and women can ruin themselves by their vices or by trusting the wrong people. And often they show that no matter how blameless the life of the prominent man may have been he still cannot escape the fate that more guilty men also meet. We can regard the stories as 'cases of fortune', stories of catastrophe which show the dangers of life in high places. Sometimes the catastrophe is redeemed by the virtue or at least the fortitude of the hero, but this does not always happen. Often the story is not tragic in the Aristotelian sense. But it is nearly always tragic according to the use of the word in mediaeval days. In 1444 Iñigo López de Mendoza, Marquis of Santillana, wrote: 'Tragedy contains in itself the falls of great kings and princes, such as Hercules, Panthus [?=Pentheus] and Agamemnon and others, whose births and lives began and for a long time continued happily, and at last sadly fell.'[28] Chaucer in his translation of Boethius the century before had asked: 'What other thing biwailen the cryinges of tragedies but only the dedes of Fortune, that with an unwar stroke overtorneth realmes of grete nobley?' And then he added the gloss: 'Tragedie is to seyn, a ditee of a prosperitee for a tyme that endeth in wrecchednesse.'[29] Does not this definition cover the cases that I have summarised?

King Roderick, King Sancho, Don Fadrique, Don Beltrán, the two Doña Aldas and the rest.

Spanish ballads, then, in their 'tragic' moments convey the same sort of feelings that we find in other mediaeval works about the fall of princes. You may well ask now whether in fact the ballads are any more than a sort of echo of what was expressed better in the works from which the ballads derived. The sentinel of Zamora, for instance, certainly occurred in the epic from which the ballad I quoted descended; and the pathos of Gonzalo Gustios in prison is also felt in the lay of the Seven Princes of Lara. In each of these cases I find a greater terseness in the ballad version, though comparison is hardly fair when we know the original epic sources so incompletely. With other ballads the problem does not arise. There is no shepherd who gives his bread to King Roderick in Corral's historical novel; if the ballad of Doña Alda and the death of Roland and the other ballad of Don Beltrán both come from the lost Roncesvalles epic, we have no means of knowing how that epic treated these topics. The other ballads have no predecessors that we know of. The story of Don Fadrique, that of the captive lady whose tears fell on to her Moorish captor's face and of the widow who went to church too gaily dressed – all these are ballads which have no obvious artistic predecessors. I therefore claim that ballads sometimes recreate as well as preserve a fine attitude towards mutability which can also be found elsewhere; but in the ballad it is expressed with peculiar strength. The strength is partly due to the way in which the heroic figures are isolated or stand in contrast with ordinary men and women, who often appear in the ballads as mere witnesses of the fortunes and misfortunes of their betters.

William Empson, one of the more penetrating modern English critics, has written a few interesting remarks about society as portrayed in British ballads: the contrast between those who take part in the ballads and those who transmitted them. He says: 'Most fairy stories and ballads, though "by" and "for", are not "about" ' the people. He continues:

> The Border ballads assume a society of fighting clans who are protected by their leaders since leaders can afford expensive weapons; the aristocrat has an obvious function for the people, and they are pleased to describe his grandeur and fine clothes. (This pleasure in him as an object of fantasy is the normal thing, but usually there are forces the other way.) They were class-conscious all right, but not conscious of class war.[30]

I consider that this statement, though it might be criticised in some details, is profoundly true. By 'the forces that work the other way' Empson presumably means those that bring about the hero's death. My theory is really implicit in his words. One of the most acute passages in G. H. Gerould's *The ballad of tradition* is that in which he describes the subjects that we might expect to find, but do not find, in ballads. Among these he lists class envy:

> The folk who have sung ballads for a long while past, at least, have been simple of mind and station...Apparently they have been seldom moved to envy of their betters, since envy is not a motive used. Personal jealousy, like personal pride, is common enough; but dissatisfaction with the scheme of things does not appear. Even the outlaws object only to the injustices of administration.[31]

Certainly the envy of the rich by the poor was less obvious in the seventeenth century than it is today. Perhaps the ballad was a kind of safety valve for social envy. The hero is rich, brave, admirable, strong and noble; but because of these qualities he is more likely to meet disgrace and violent death than farmers and labourers are. Lightning strikes only the high trees. So, perhaps these men thought, if we cannot shoe our horses with gold and silver or give golden combs to our wives and girls, we can at least remember that we are not likely to be shut up in a tomb with a seven-headed serpent or have our heads cut off and thrown to mastiffs. Better be humble and poor than disgraced and killed.

The attitude I have tried to define is found in early texts and in later ones of different ballads. Oral tradition has not corrupted this basic feeling about the fall of the mighty. The sense of mutability in earthly rank and fortune is contained in different texts of varying age. The poverty and hardships of the humble needed some compensation. Fantastic splendour and the mutability of fortune provided 'an object of fantasy' and a means of coming to terms with reality.

In this essay I have tried to show why some ballads have impressed me. After taking a few which show some of the quality of country speech I have examined some poems of catastrophe which emphasise the contrasts of prosperity and adversity, strength and bondage, wealth and misery, life and death. My point is that these contrasts are expressed with force and intensity even in very poor texts. I have tried also to show that the reason for this intensity of feeling about the mutability of human life may have been connected with a more general mediaeval notion of tragedy, and that this spectacle was felt to be exemplary by the humble who have continued to preserve these poems. Improved methods of communication, literacy and the mechanical pleasures of the twentieth century are engaged in destroying both the poetry itself and the attitudes that it gave rise to. In its place we now have television, the cinema and a cheap press. One may justifiably doubt whether this particular change is an unmixed blessing.

14
Spanish and English religious poetry of the seventeenth century[1]

About four hundred years ago John Knox wrote as follows in his *Comfortable epistle to Christ's afflicted Church*:

Let Wynchester, and his cruel counsell, devise and study till hys wits faile, howe the kyngdom of his father, the Antichrist of Rome, may prosper: And let him and them drink the bloudde of Goddes sainctes till they be droncke, and theyr bellyes burst, yet shall they never provide long in their attemptes. Their counsailes and determinacions shalbe like the dreame of a hungry or thyrstie man, who in his slepe dreameth that he is eatinge or drinckinge; but after he is awaked, his pain continueth, and his soule is unpacient and nothinge eased. Even so shall these tyrantes, after their profounde counsayles, long devices and assured determinations, understand and know that the hope of ypocrites shal be frustrate; that a kingdome begunne with tyranny and bloudde, can neither be stable nor permanent; but that the glorie, the riches, and manteiners of the same, shalbe as strawe in the flame of fyre. Altogether with a blaste they shal be consumed in such sorte, that their palaces shal be a heape of stones, their congregations shal be desolate; and such as do depend upon their helpe, shal fal into destruction and ignominie with them.

I quote this passage for its manner rather than for its matter. The last thing I want to do is to stimulate any kind of religious difference or bitterness, and this passage was written deliberately to stir up strife. The strife and bitterness, however, are an essential background to my subject, and I do not want to be accused of glossing over them. I do not approve of Knox's intention, but the passage has one characteristic which will underlie most of the poetry that I shall discuss in this essay. I do not refer to those admirable Biblical echoes that lie behind such phrases as 'their palaces shal be a heape of stones, their congregations shal be desolate'. Instead I would ask you to notice that extraordinary simile of the dream of the hungry or thirsty man 'who in his slepe dreameth that he is eatinge or drinckinge'. Perhaps it is a recollection of the hardships Knox himself endured in the French galleys; there he may well have had the very experience he describes. What, however, makes the simile memorable is the fact that this image of the thirsty man's dream both corresponds with the brief spell of power that Knox's enemies enjoyed and is at the same time drawn from ordinary life as we know it, whether we have had this particular dream or not. We have here an ordinary fact, taken from common life, used as an example of what Knox regarded as a higher truth. And so in his more purely devotional treatises he could say: 'Trubillis ar the Spurris to stir us to Pray', or: 'For yf God be present by assistance of his Halie Spreit, or that no dout is in our conscience, but that assuredlie we stand in Godis favour, what can corporall trubill hurt the saule or mynd? Seing the bitter frostie wind can not hurt the bodie it self, whilk is maist warmlie coverit and cled from violence of the cold.' Spurs have now gone to the wretched dump-heap of English dead metaphors, but in Knox's phrase they are still sharp; and there is a strong sense of solid comfort when he compares God's favour to a heavy warm overcoat worn in an icy gale.[2]

Language of this kind seems to have been common in sixteenth-century devotional literature. Instead of going to the famous Spanish mystics for examples I prefer to quote from a little-known book which was probably written in the same year that Knox wrote his *Comfortable epistle*. The author was Fray Domingo de Valtanas, O.P., and the book a treatise on Christian doctrine. On almost every page can be found similes like those quoted from Knox which both illuminate the truths of his teaching and bring it into close relation with everyday life. Here are a few specimens. 'Faith is like the link-boy who carries his torch by night to light his master going to the palace; the link-boy does not go into the palace, but he takes his master to the door. So Faith in this life serves only to light us to the gates of Heaven.' 'Misers are like the pig, which, while it is alive gives neither wool nor milk but only noises and trouble; but after it is dead it gives black puddings and good meat, and those who never knew it eat it. So bad rich men save their wealth for those they do not know.' 'We may liken purgatory to a prison for gentlemen debtors; for there are admitted only the friends of God who have not the money to pay their debts to Him.' 'Birds fly in order to teach their young ones to fly; and Christ prayed and did other works in order to teach us what we ought to do.' 'Until a man realises that he is a sinner he does not understand or feel how harmful a thing sin is; it is like a pitcher, which while it is in the water in the well, one cannot tell how much it weighs, until it is taken out of the well. All this air is full of motes, and they cannot be seen until the sun shines; so the sinner, while he is in sin, does not know its seriousness, until by penitence he abandons it.' And Valtanas draws on other aspects of life too: with him the habits of gamblers, dirty linen, standing on a bench to reach a high shelf, dolls, the wine-press, a sword-handle, oil and water, new fashions in clothes, as well as birds, beasts, flowers and all the phenomena of nature, all illustrate the workings of God's laws or the ways in which men defy them. Along with frequent quotations from the Bible and from the Fathers and Doctors of the Church went these homely illustrations and similes. And he himself resumed his own procedure when he exclaimed: 'All the universe, what is high and what is low, is nothing else than a love letter in which God places all the works of His almighty hands in all their beauty and finery to invite us to love Him.'[3]

This kind of writing made the mysteries of religion more intelligible to the simple. By it ordinary experience of everyday life was brought into touch with religious experience. The analogy of religion could be perceived in all places and at all times. There was no shutting off religion into an isolated compartment, from which ordinary feelings and actions were excluded. So that the sixteenth century was spared that mixture of tenuous abstractions and reverend unctuousness which afflicts much twentieth-century devotional writing. Reverence, perhaps, suffered. A writer, slightly later than Valtanas, compared Our Lord to an ass who bears our sins in His Passion, but who rises like a sturdy elephant at the Resurrection.[4] But even this lapse of taste is excusable when the effective realism of some of the other examples is considered. God was to be found everywhere as well as in church. St Theresa said that He walked among the pots and pans in the kitchen. And this awareness of Him in all that takes place around us is not the least of the merits of the religious poems we are going to discuss.

Both in the British Isles and in Spain the religious thinkers saw grave dangers in secular literature. Nicholas Ferrar, the friend of George Herbert and Crashaw, wrote as follows:

Inasmuch as all the comedies, tragedies, pastorals, etc. and all those they call heroical poems, none excepted; and likewise all the books of tales, which they call novels, and all feigned histories written in prose, all love-hymns, and all the like books are full of idolatry, and especially tend to the overthrow of Christian religion, undermining the very foundations thereof, and corrupt and pollute the minds of the readers with filthy lusts, as, woe is me, I have proved in myself: and in this regard therefore, to shew my detestation of them to the world, and that all others may take warning, I have burned all of them, and most humbly have, and do beseech God, to forgive me all my misspent time in them, and all the sins that they have caused in me, which surely, but for His infinite grace, had carried my soul down into hell long ere this. And I profess to be of Mr. Gallatius his opinion, that the having an Orlando in the house is sufficient ground to have burnt it down over their heads, that truly fear God. I beseech all that truly fear God, that love Jesus Christ, to consider these things well. Amen. Amen. Amen.[5]

In the same way Fray Pedro Malón de Chaide (the writer whose simile of the ass and the elephant I quoted a moment ago), compared the novels of chivalry, pastoral novels and the beautiful poems of Garcilaso de la Vega to a dagger in the hands of a madman and to a slow poison working through the veins of a healthy man. In England religious literature was less prominent in the total sum than it was in Spain. In Spain the men who protested most against profane literature set themselves to provide pious books which should rival the poisons and daggers. So that much of the writing of the Counter-Reformation in Spain had a double purpose: to touch the heart of and convert the ordinary man, and to provide agreeable reading matter for those whose hearts had already been touched. Thus, in the late years of the sixteenth century, we find Malón de Chaide himself, whose life of St Mary Magdalene reads almost as well as a novel, Diego de Estella, whose book of the *Vanity of the world* contains a chapter on the vanity of writing works of theology, and Fray Luis de Granada, as well as the more famous Luis de León – all these men writing the most vigorous and readable prose – included in the modern histories of Spanish literature.

As far as poetry is concerned, there were different attempts to turn the worldly muse into the handmaid of religion. Luis de León and Malón de Chaide produced fine poetical translations of the Psalms and other poetical portions of the Old Testament. Other poets simply adapted the secular techniques to sacred subjects: instead of writing odes to princes and great ladies, they wrote them to Christ, to the Virgin and to saints. But the process reached its most extreme expression in the literature 'a lo divino', that is to say holy parody of the different profane genres. As early as the late fifteenth century we can find a number of examples of pious words to worldly tunes – the same procedure as that used by the modern Salvation Army. We find rubrics like this: 'Fray Ambrosio Montesino made up these verses about the birth of Christ on the order of the most excellent lady the Marchioness of Moya. They can be sung to the tune of: Who is it who made you angry, my good love? Who is it who made you angry?' Or: 'Fray Ambrosio made up these verses about St John the Evangelist at the order of our Queen Donna Isabella to be sung to the tune of: Mother, the shepherd hasn't come yet; something must be the matter in the country.'[6] In both these poems the traditional poetic refrain has been skilfully adapted to give it an edifying, pious meaning. The fact that in Spain an oral tradition of lyric poetry had existed, probably since the beginning of the eleventh century, made these attempts successful. Sometimes only very small changes needed to be made in the refrain, and a pious gloss easily replaced a profane one. So the pious refrains became traditional too, sometimes reminding their hearers of the old words as the new ones were sung. We have half a dozen or so fifteenth-century specimens, but the number rapidly increased towards the end of the sixteenth century; they were taught to children, printed in chap-books, repeated from anthology to anthology, transmitted orally. Nowadays many have been collected from oral tradition by folklorists in Spain, Spanish America and the Canary Islands.

Besides the popular lyric tradition there was a ballad tradition too. Poems in the ballad manner, but on sacred subjects, were composed in the sixteenth century and also found their way into oral tradition. In a recent collection made in the province of Santander[7] there are included many versions of ballads about the lives of Christ and the Virgin, and a few more about saints, and about Old Testament stories. I suspect that nearly all of them were composed and became current in the years immediately following the Council of Trent.

There were, then, two largely oral currents of poetry, one lyric, the other narrative, which were consciously diverted into religious channels. The lyric is by far the more important from the literary point of view. Nearly all the shorter lyrics of St John of the Cross arise from this tradition. It affected also many of the religious poems of the two greatest religious poets of the seventeenth century: Lope de Vega Carpio and José de Valdivielso. This current cannot be neglected by any student of Spanish poetry; in England there was practically nothing to correspond with it. Not because the English had an insuperable aversion to divine parodies, but because there was no oral lyric tradition in England remotely comparable to that in Spain.

The process that had been so successful with popular poetry was also applied to written works of literature. The moralists and preachers had attacked pastoral novels and novels of chivalry; the new writers set to work to make these edifying too. To counter the baleful novels of chivalry such works as the *Knight of the Sun or the pilgrimage of man's life in battle*, the *Knight of the Clear Star or man's battle and triumph against the vices* and the *Christian Militia of the Pilgrim Knight, conqueror of Heaven* appeared during the years 1552–1601. The works of Garcilaso de la Vega were adapted line by line by Sebastián de Córdoba in a pious fashion, and though this work is artistically negligible in itself, it influenced the poetry of St John of the Cross.[8] Lope de Vega wrote a divine pastoral novel called *Los pastores de Belén*, a work which contains some of the finest Christmas carols in Spanish. And the habit continued for many years. The results were often wretched from a literary point of view, but every now and again a work of some originality came out of them. As with the divine parodies of popular poetry, pious writers trained themselves to use the profane techniques and ways of feeling for a holy purpose. And the result was that the religious poetry of Spain became capable of expressing itself in completely human terms. Religion and life thus remained to an extraordinary degree in contact with one another.

The most famous divine parody in England was one supposed to have been used by King Charles I. It is included among the *Praiers used by His Majestie in the time of his sufferings*, delivered to Doctor Juxon, Bishop of London, immediately before his death. These prayers were included in some editions of the *Eikon Basilike*, though not in all. The first prayer is in fact taken almost verbatim from Sidney's *Arcadia*, and Milton denounced the profanity of Charles's devotional use of a worldly novel. But there were many other examples, though they take more finding than Spanish ones do. Professor Martz has shown how Robert Southwell adapted lines by Sir Edward Dyer and how George Herbert with greater subtlety similarly used thoughts of Sir Philip Sidney.[9] In both cases we can see the same process at work as we find in contemporary Spain: the pious borrower is not content with mere verbal borrowings; he incorporates into his religious poem ways of feeling which had hitherto been associated with those whom Donne called his 'profane mistresses'. As we shall see later, this gives some of Lope de Vega's religious pieces their greatest strength.

Together with the divine parody went an extension of the divine analogy which we have already noticed in John Knox and in Domingo de Valtanas. In fact these phenomena are closely related. Divine parodies are perhaps only a special kind of divine analogy. In most of the examples I mentioned earlier there is a double similarity between the simile and what is compared to it. Knox saw the brief state of the Bishop of Winchester as a hungry man who dreams he is enjoying a good meal; when the dreamer wakes he is still hungry, and so too the bishop, when his spell of glory is over, will wake up to find himself starved of all the splendour which he thought permanent and was only transient. Valtanas's pig is like a miser because it yields no good thing in life; but after death, each provides for others in spite of it or himself. These similes are mostly double or continued comparisons, and as time goes on and later writers try to say the same things even more forcefully the comparisons turn into double or continued metaphors. What literary historians call conceits are usually continued metaphors which are given an ingenious twist. And despite differences of language and religion there is often a general similarity between English and Spanish conceits in the seventeenth-century poems of the two nations.

The chief artificer of Spanish continued metaphors was a man named Alonso de Ledesma, whose *Conceptos espirituales* – spiritual concepts or conceits – came out in 1600. These poems were very popular indeed, and their author produced two more sets of them within the next twenty-five years. The original edition was also reprinted several times. His technique was simply to take some such analogy as those that we have already discussed and work it out in detail. The majority of his *Conceptos* are religious, and the device was much imitated by his followers, who included great poets though he could hardly have made such a claim himself. Here are some examples of the kind of thing he did. He constructs a sonnet on the virtues of St Ignatius Loyola by comparing him with Vulcan, who you will remember was also lame; the iron that the smith works is the souls of his fellow men, prayer supplies the bellows, obedience the pincers, conscience the hammer and anvil and Christ Himself the fire. In another poem on St Stephen, that saint is compared to a jeweller, who set the stones – precious because they were the instruments of his martyrdom – in his own body. In another, Christ is a visitor to a university which is in need of reform. Or there is yet another poem in which man lets out his house – really of course his soul – to a tenant named Sin who leaves it in such bad repair that he is shocked and takes on another tenant, this time a more satisfactory one, named Disillusion.[10]

Ledesma's recipe underlies much seventeenth-century poetry. In Spain, at least, he helped greater men than he to realise what the continued metaphor was capable of. Most English conceits consist of a continued metaphor paradoxically exploited, and so do a very large number of Spanish ones. You may remember Thomas Carew's epitaph on Mary Wentworth, whose body was made of such purely tempered clay that it easily broke:

> Else the soul grew so fast within
> It broke the outward shell of sin,
> And so was hatch'd a Cherubin.

And later in the poem:

> So though a Virgin, yet a Bride
> To every Grace, she justifi'd
> A chaste Polygamie, and dy'd.[11]

These lines are agreeably ingenious, but hardly great poetry. The continued metaphor was, however, capable of much grander and more tender religious uses. George Herbert is our great English exemplar of them. His sonnet, *Redemption*, sees man's relation to God as that of a complaining tenant to a landlord:

> Having been tenant long to a rich Lord,
>   Not thriving, I resolved to be bold,
>   And make a suit unto him, to afford
> A new small-rented lease, and cancell th'old.
>
> In heaven at his manour I him sought:
>   They told me there, that he was lately gone
>   About some land, which he had dearly bought
> Long since on earth, to take possession.
>
> I straight return'd, and knowing his great birth,
>   Sought him accordingly in great resorts;
>   In cities, theatres, gardens, parks and courts:
> At length I heard a ragged noise and mirth

Of theeves and murderers: there I him espied.
Who straight, *Your suit is granted*, said, & died.[12]

The basic idea is one that Ledesma could easily have used. But Ledesma could never have matched the simple magnificence of the climax or the homeliness of the language which leads up to it: thriving, be bold, afford, small-rented lease and so on. The 'ragged noise and mirth of theeves and murderers' would also have been beyond his grasp. Herbert was possessed of an extraordinary sensitivity to detail which is the mark of a great poet. There are some fine double meanings in such expressions as 'knowing his great birth' and even in 'I resolved to be bold', which to me recalls the *audemus dicere* preceding the Lord's Prayer after the Consecration at Mass. Herbert easily stimulates such religious reverberations; Ledesma hardly ever does, because his metaphors are merely ingenious and superficial.

Ledesma, artistically, was a failure, but he showed greater poets the way. He had a host of imitators who like himself were mere versifiers, but José de Valdivielso and Lope de Vega were great religious poets. Before the end of this chapter I hope to be able to show how this was the case, but meanwhile I want to deal with a peculiar Spanish manifestation which is largely glossed over by the official histories of Spanish literature. I refer to the seventeenth-century *villancico* or carol, sung in church on great festivals as a kind of vernacular parody of the monastic office.

The *villancico* was already formed when this practice started, but its liturgical use was so unexpected that I cannot forbear describing it. On the eve of important feast-days the office consisted of three nocturns, each of which consisted of three psalms and three lessons. So these collections of carols were put together in three sets of three and performed for the benefit of those who could not follow the service in Latin.[13] The result was a strange medley of religion and seeming profanity which most critics and most religious people find extremely shocking. I must confess that I do not share their feelings. These carols were for public rejoicings. They did not, could not, express intimate, highly refined states of mind. Instead the poets strove to display the simple sense of joy which all could share. The feelings of a bishop or grandee towards the central mysteries of Christianity are not necessarily different from those of a charwoman or a bricklayer, but they will be differently expressed. To express religious joy so that all men and women could share in it, these poets put their words into the mouths of the humblest; supposed gipsies, slaves and even criminals are made to express the basic feelings which others could have expressed with greater verbal refinements. The fact that such men spoke with a peculiar accent or in broken Spanish or in thieves' cant added a humorous piquancy to their words. The congregation could, at the same time, share the feelings of the speaker and laugh at the way he spoke. The apparent incongruity of the situation increased both its edification and its humour. Christ was born for all men, shepherds as well as Magi; need we scold these poets for including also gipsies, negresses, Portuguese and bravoes?

A few years ago I published a set of these poems which I found among the chap-books which Pepys brought back from Seville in 1684. The carols themselves seem to date from about sixty years before. They include a dialogue between two negresses in negro Spanish, of a deliberate *naïveté*. The women bring to Christ as gifts all that they in their simplicity particularly enjoy or prize: shirts, sweetmeats, toys and finery for the Virgin Mary. In another the speaker is a ruffian. He apostrophises Christ in the manger; his speech is full of oaths and bragging, but the oaths, taken literally, are a tribute to the Baby, and the boasts are meant to do Him honour. The poem almost topples over into farce, but the tenuous balance is, I think, precariously preserved.[14] There is a great mass of this poetry which has never been investigated seriously. It went on until the last third of the eighteenth century, when it was suppressed by law. The subject deserves much fuller treatment than it has yet received; I can only mention it here and pass on. Its nearest English equivalent is to be found in some of Crashaw's more extravagant poems, but even these lack the extreme character that so many of the Spanish poems display.

This extreme expression of Counter-Reformation popular religiosity could not be expected to be found in the world of Lancelot Andrewes and Jeremy Taylor, even if there is something rather like it in Crashaw. But I have already hinted that other Spanish seventeenth-century religious poems are very like George Herbert's. How could this similarity have come about? One answer is, of course, that though the Anglican Church had separated from Rome, suppressing the Mass, prayers to saints and the cult of the Blessed Virgin Mary, yet many Anglicans still retained much from mediaeval times. How much George Herbert used the Holy Week reproaches in his great poem *The sacrifice* has been established by Miss Rosemond Tuve in her book: *A reading of George Herbert*.[15] Still, even so one may doubt whether the old roots of Anglicanism remained sufficiently strong to produce such fruits after so many years of bitter controversy and doctrinal change. Something else seems implied, some stronger and more direct influence of Roman Catholic Europe on England.

The direct influence of Spanish religious verse on English remains a possibility. William Drummond, Richard Fanshawe, Thomas Ayres and Thomas Stanley all translated or adapted known Spanish originals into English. None of these poems were, as far as I know, religious poems, but if Góngora, Lope, Pérez de Montalván and Quevedo appeared in English in the seventeenth century, why should not religious poems also have been translated, as long as they did not deal with controversial subjects?

Gondomar reported to Philip III his astonishment at finding Spanish books on religious topics for sale in London bookshops.[16] We know that many Spanish books found their way into English libraries at that time. Bishop Ken's library contained many Roman Catholic books of devotion and meditation, including several Spanish ones, whereas it was – according to his nineteenth-century biographer – deficient in the controversial writings of the continental reformers. Many of the old books in Emmanuel College library were the legacy of Archbishop Sancroft; among them are an edition of Ledesma, Valdivielso's poetical life of St Joseph, the *Rimas sacras* of Lope de Vega and Hojeda's magnificent *Christiada* – an unjustly neglected epic poem about the life of Christ. Many of these poems are marked by the archbishop himself, and I am sure that at least some of his markings indicate that he found some poems edifying. Here, then, were two seventeenth-century English bishops who could read Spanish enough to find edification in it; they may not have been the only two. And if bishops, why not also a good many of the lesser clergy and pious men generally? John Donne, George Herbert and Richard Crashaw, at least, almost certainly knew and read Spanish. Direct influence, therefore, of Spanish devotional poetry on English remains a possibility, even if it cannot be proved. There is, however, another continental influence which is certain and of greater importance; to discuss it it will be necessary to go back a little.

The poems of Luis de León lie outside the original scheme of this chapter but I must refer to one of them. It is his ode on the Ascension. This poem consists of only five stanzas in most editions, but four additional stanzas occur in one manuscript. The authenticity of the four stanzas has been much discussed, and most editors reject them. Professor E. Sarmiento, in the notes to his edition of León's poems, made an interesting plea for them. He pointed out that the fuller version of this ode, as well as making a successful artistic whole, provided an orthodox religious meditation, according to the scheme of meditations popularised in the many books of devotion of the period. The scheme is that of the famous *Spiritual exercises* of St Ignatius Loyola. The shorter version of the poem, on the other hand, provided merely a truncated version. The first duty of the meditator is to fix in his mind the scene of the action on which he is to meditate, and this was called the 'composition of place'. After this he was to develop the theme by applying to it the different powers of the soul, in a way I shall explain shortly. The full scheme can be followed in this fine poem in the nine-stanza version.[17] And if the Ignatian plan of meditation can be seen in this one poem of León's, something like it may have been followed in other religious poems by other writers. Whether the poem's extra stanzas are authentic or not, Professor Sarmiento's analysis is extremely important. The precepts of St Ignatius were followed by clergy, religious and many lay Catholics in the sixteenth century and since. May we not expect to find the same technique employed in very many other religious poems by Roman Catholics outside, as well as inside, Spain?

John Donne was born and brought up in the old religion. Though in 1611 he wrote a satire against Jesuit Machiavellianism called *Ignatius his conclaue*, there is evidence that he too practised the Ignatian method of meditation. Perhaps I ought to add that the satire against the Jesuits is almost as virulent (though it is rather more humorous) as the passage from John Knox with which I started. The copy I read belonged to Archbishop Sancroft, who had underlined the following lines:

And he [Lucifer] had long obserued that the *Clergie* of *Rome* tumbled down to *Hell* daily, easily and voluntarily, and by troupes, because they were accustomed to sinne against their conscience, and knowledge.[18]

Neither Donne nor Sancroft were in any sense crypto-Romans, but both of them found some profit in post-Tridentine methods of meditation.

The evidence about Donne has been detected by two modern scholars who have worked independently: Miss Helen Gardner of Oxford and Mr Louis L. Martz of Yale. Mr Martz has followed out the patterns in the two great *Anniversaries*[19] and has shown also that some aspects of it apply to the other poems too, even apparently irreligious poems. Miss Gardner found that a dozen of the *Holy sonnets*, rearranged, formed a meditation of the Ignatian type on the four last things.[20] Her rearrangement of the order is also the order of the first edition of Donne's poems, and this fact seems to me conclusive. Her revised arrangement has seventeenth-century authority.

The Ignatian scheme consists roughly of the following method. After some short preparatory prayers the meditator prepares for the body of the meditation in two preludes. The first consists of the 'composition of place' in which the subject of the meditation is visualised – say the Temple or the mountain where Christ was speaking, or a metaphorical sight if the meditation is of a more abstract kind. The second prelude consists of a prayer appropriate to the subject-matter of the meditation. The body of the meditation follows: in turn the three powers of the soul (the memory, the understanding and the will), are applied to the Biblical scene or to the more abstract subject. The memory calls the scene up before the eyes of the mind, the words spoken or things done; the understanding enters into its meaning; and the will then makes the decision according to the lessons learned by the understanding. The exercise ends with prayers that take the form of colloquies with God Himself. The scheme can be followed out in Donne's poems with the aid of the two guides mentioned.

The case of John Donne does not seem likely to be controverted. Mr

Martz has also shown that something similar can be found with George Herbert, Richard Crashaw and even the puritan Richard Baxter. He argues that a large number of continental treatises on devotion were translated into English at Antwerp, Douay and St Omers, and that these were read in many besides recusant circles in Jacobean and Caroline England. There are also Protestant translations of many continental divines such as Luis de Granada and Diego de Estella. His case might be made stronger still were he to take into account the contents of libraries such as those of Bishop Ken and Archbishop Sancroft, which I have already referred to: there we find a large number of these treatises in their original languages: Spanish, Italian, French, as well as Latin. American scholars often assume that seventeenth-century Englishmen at best knew a very little French; but I think that there is no doubt at all that a great many men of learning knew Italian and Spanish too. Here, then, is the reason for the similarities that I have called attention to between English and Spanish religious poetry – it is not just because of a common climate of opinion or because of the fact that both are eventually derived from a common mediaeval heritage; they are, in fact, both the results of the same tradition of religious meditation, which largely derives from the *Spiritual exercises* of St Ignatius.

The following anonymous English seventeenth-century poem shows clearly the influence of this work:

> Yet if his majesty, our sovereign lord,
> Should of his own accord
> Friendly himself invite,
> And say, I'll be your guest to-morrow night,
> How should we stir ourselves, call and command
> All hands to work! Let no man idle stand!
> Set me fine Spanish tables in the hall;
> See they be fitted all;
> Let there be room to eat,
> And order taken that there want no meat.
> See every sconce and candlestick made bright,
> That without tapers they may give a light.
> Look to the presence; are the carpets spread,
> The dais o'er the head,
> The cushions in the chairs,
> And all the candles lighted on the stairs?
> Perfume the chambers, and in any case
> Let each man give attendance in his place.
> Thus if the king were coming would we do,
> And 'twere good reason too;
> For 'tis a duteous thing
> To show all honour to an earthly king,

> And after all our travail and our cost,
> So he be pleased, to think no labour lost.
> But at the coming of the King of Heaven
> All's set at six and seven;
> We wallow in our sin;
> Christ cannot find a chamber in the inn.
> We entertain him always like a stranger,
> And as at first still lodge him in the manger.[21]

This poem can be considered in terms of meditative procedure. The memory calls up the imaginative picture of the earthly king's visit in a lively 'composition of place', and then with the words: 'Thus if the king were coming would we do' the understanding gets to work and examines the situation. The duty of the will is clearly implied at the end. But in a sense, the whole content of the poem is taken from the meditation of the second week in the *Spiritual exercises*: 'The call of the earthly king helps in the contemplation of the life of the Eternal King.' I add a few extracts in rough translation:

Consider what a good subject should say to so liberal and humane a king; and if a man were not to accept his requests how he would deserve the vituperation of every man and the name of a false knight...If we consider the vocation of the earthly king to his subjects, how much more worthy of consideration is it to see Christ our Lord, the eternal King, with all the universe before Him, to whom and to each one of whom He says: My will is to conquer the whole world and all my enemies and so to enter the glory of My Father.[22]

These very passages may well have been the source of the anonymous poem. Now the source from which a particular poem derives has little to say to the merit of the poem. But here we can see that its liveliness of language is closely allied to the imaginatively visual and auditory composition of place. To consider Christ as King awakens a recreation of house-proud splendour which contrasts with the manger and the miserable heart of man. The calls 'All hands to work! Let no man idle stand!', the visual image:

> See every sconce and candlestick made bright,
> That without tapers they may give a light

imply a powerful contrast with the human laziness and apathy in the presence of God. The poem is as vivid and its language is as lively as the bits from Knox and Valtanas with which I began this chapter. From which fact it seems as though we might say that the Ignatian method of meditation – in the way in which it combined the supernatural with the natural, in the way that it saw the divine in terms of the human – was at one with the controversialists and popularisers. Here again religious poetry

Spanish and English religious poetry

is seen in completely human terms; religion and ordinary life remain in contact.

No words could be more urgent than those that Donne used to God in his twelve Holy Sonnets:

> Batter my heart, three person'd God; for you
> As yet but knocke, breathe, shine, and seeke to mend;
> That I may rise, and stand, o'erthrow mee, and bend
> Your force, to breake, blowe, burn and make me new.

Or in his picture of his soul as a condemned prisoner:

> Oh my blacke Soule! now thou art summoned
> By sickness, deaths herald and champion;
> Thou art like a pilgrim, which abroad hath done
> Treason, and durst not turne to whence hee is fled,
> Or like a thiefe, which till deaths doome be read,
> Wisheth himselfe delivered from prison;
> But damn'd and hal'd to execution,
> Wisheth that still he might be imprisoned.[23]

Even in the *Songs and sonnets* we hardly find language as direct and unliterary as this. Is there any way, I wonder, by which this kind of thing can be justified according to Renaissance literary theory? Does not this sort of writing burst open all the bonds and bars of Italianate elegance, Scaliger and the doctrine of the three styles? It is well known that the language of the Bible shocked some men of letters at this time. They must often have found the language of religious poetry almost equally shocking.

I know of nothing in Spanish that is exactly of the same kind as these Holy Sonnets of Donne. But at its best, in Lope and Valdivielso, there is a sensibility like that of George Herbert. As an example I will take a well-known sonnet from Lope's *Rimas sacras* – one that was underlined also by Archbishop Sancroft.

> Pastor, que con tus siluos amorosos
>   me despertaste del profundo sueño,
>   tú, que hiciste cayado dese leño
>   en que tiendes los braços poderosos;
> Vuelue los ojos a mi fe piadosos,
>   pues te confieso por mi amor y dueño,
>   y la palabra de seguirte empeño
>   tus dulces silbos y tus pies hermosos.
> Oye, Pastor, que por amores mueres,
>   no te espante el rigor de mis pecados,
>   pues tan amigo de rendidos eres;
> Espera, pues, y escucha mis cuidados;
>   pero, ¿cómo te digo que me esperes,
>   si estás para esperar los pies clauados?[24]

Christ is seen as the Good Shepherd who has a Cross for his crook and who whistles to his flock to guide it. Except for the references to Faith and to the Cross – which even then is referred to as *leño* (wood) – Lope uses no specifically Christian words in the octet of this sonnet. He is a sheep who loves and follows his shepherd – and that is all, except for the hints conveyed by Faith and the wooden crook. But the shepherd is soon revealed as being less the flesh and blood shepherd of the Spanish countryside than the literary shepherd of post-Renaissance fiction – the pastoral shepherd of Garcilaso, Sannazaro and Montemayor. The line 'Oye, Pastor, que por amores mueres' might occur in any sixteenth-century eclogue. Its full effect can only be gained when we remember these poets as we read. The literature so criticised by Nicholas Ferrar and Malón de Chaide is essential to the full appreciation of this sonnet, which makes its religious effect by means of profane reverberations. Lope's own sinful life and love affairs – perhaps as well known to his contemporaries as they are to too inquisitive modern scholars – and his own profane compositions – which included an imitation of Sannazaro – are only just hidden around the corner. The conventional reference, however, when we remember who this Shepherd really is and how He died, is fused in a great religious truth. After this surprise we are lifted on to a religious level: the hideousness of Lope's sins is no obstacle when we remember that Christ never rejects those who submit themselves to Him. There is a hint of a profane allusion here too – for 'probar la espada en un rendido' (to try your sword on one who has surrendered) – was a proverbial expression for an ungentlemanly action. And finally the sonnet ends on a profound pun. But perhaps pun is too strong a word. At least it seems to me that two meanings are conveyed in the last line of the sonnet. I think one can say in modern Spanish 'Allí me esperaba, los pies clavados' – there he was waiting for me rooted to the spot. And so Lope says: (1) but how can I tell you to wait for me, when you are there with your feet motionless, rooted to the ground, and (2) how can I tell you to wait for me when you are there with your feet nailed to the Cross. It is not quite a pun, but the use of a word in its extended meaning and in its literal meaning at the same time. It is certainly a powerful phrase that brings home the physical horror of the Atonement. The poem makes its effect by the controlled alternation between the shepherd, the pastoral shepherd, the Good Shepherd and our crucified Lord. The contrast is made partly by the contrast between the beautiful feet at the end of line 8 and the nailed feet at the end of the poem.'How beautiful upon the mountains are the feet of him that bringeth good tidings, that publisheth peace.' And 'they pierced my hands and feet'. The poem is justly renowned as one of the best religious poems in Spanish.

So this rambling survey comes to an end. I want to say what the comparison I have made seems to imply. In spite of the differences between England and Spain in religion, the similarities in their respective religious poems seem to me to be more important than their differences. That the differences existed I have tried to prove. But the main thing is the fact that in each country there was a common way to express religious truths in vivid everyday terms. This was partly due to the fact that both countries had a mediaeval heritage in common, but still more to the fact that a devotional literature spread from Spain through Roman Catholic Europe into England, in spite of fundamental differences of religious belief and practice. This seems important in the history of Protestant piety, but its results are alone important as a critical fact. Nevertheless the fitting of Donne's sonnets into a meditative pattern makes them rather different from what they seemed before, and the realisation that many of these poems arose from a composition of place and the exercising of the senses and the three powers of the soul increases our awareness of what the poet was doing. I think that these facts, merely instrumental as they are, were useful to the poet in that they stopped him from useless divagations and enabled him to concentrate on his object. Perhaps they also helped to free himself from the shackles of Renaissance theory, the sense of what is fit or appropriate, which I think did much harm to secular lyric poetry in the sixteenth and seventeenth centuries. (I even wonder, sometimes, whether Petrarch makes up for his intolerable followers.) I myself would rather read yards of the inferior religious lyrics of Golden-Age Spain than the same quantity of amorous sonnets. And this preference is not so much due to the subjects of the poems as to the namby-pamby refinement of so much of the love poetry. The religious poets seem to deal with a much greater variety of mood, a greater range of experience, a wider metaphorical breadth and at least as great an intensity of feeling. I think that they are worth more attention than profane critics usually give them.

Notes

I THE FOUR ELEMENTS IN THE IMAGERY OF CALDERÓN

1 Felipe Picatoste, *Calderón ante la ciencia. Concepto de la naturaleza y sus leyes, deducido de las obras de Calderón de la Barca* (Memoria premiada por la Real Academia de Ciencias Exactas) (Madrid, 1881).
2 *Obras poéticas de D. Luis de Góngora*, ed. R. Foulché-Delbosc, 3 vols. (New York, 1921), vol. I, no. 33; hereafter referred to as F.-D.
3 From *El condenado de amor*, of uncertain authorship, but among Calderón's plays in the Biblioteca de Autores Españoles.
4 Bances Candamo's *loa* to Calderón's *El gran teatro del mundo*; see the preface to *Poesías cómicas, obras póstumas de D. Francisco Bances Candamo* (Madrid, 1722).
5 From the first act (by Calderón) of the *comedia* by three wits, *El privilegio de las mujeres*.
6 *Calderón ante la ciencia*, p. 69.
7 *Pastoral 3: Autumn*, lines 59–60.
8 From Northup's edition in *Revue Hispanique*, XXI (1909), lines 3–10.
9 *Soledad primera* (F.-D., vol. II, no. 263), line 44.
10   El náufrago...
                que halló...
                más tormenta en las peñas que en las ondas,
                cuando pisó por estos horizontes
                montes de agua y piélagos de montes.
                                    El mayor encanto, amor

              Cuya surtida desagua
              sus fossos en horizontes,
              que dudan quando les fragua
              si son piélagos de montes,
              o si son montes de agua.   *El viático cordero*
11 Luis Veléz de Guevara, *Autos sacramentales*, ed. A. Lacalle (Madrid, 1931): *Auto del nacimiento*, lines 21–30.
12 *Panegírico* (F.-D., vol. II, no. 318), lines 249–52.
13 F.-D., vol. I, no. 221, lines 12–14.
14 *Ibid*. no. 214, lines 8–11.
15 *Soledad segunda* (F.-D., vol. II, no. 264), lines 214–15.
16 F.-D., vol. II, no. 297, lines 1–2.
17 *Panegírico*, line 112.
18 *Obras de don Iuan de Tarsis, Conde de Villamediana* (Madrid, 1635): *La gloria de Niquea*, p. 46.

19 *Polifemo*, (F.-D.), vol. II, no. 261), lines 261-4.
20 *Soledad primera*, lines 603-6.
21 *Soledad segunda*, lines 745-6.
22 *Soledad primera*, lines 2-6.
23 *Soledad segunda*, lines 303, 304-7.
24 Eugenio de Ochoa (ed.), *Tesoro del teatro español* (Paris, 1838), vol. I, p. 517a.
25 *Soledad segunda*, lines 816-19.
26 *Panegírico*, lines 59-62.
27 *Obras líricas y cómicas de Don Antonio Hurtado de Mendoza* (Madrid, 1728), p. 256.
28 *Soledad primera*, line 20.
29 *Ibid.* line 44.
30 *Ibid.* lines 369-71.
31 *Soledad segunda*, line 489.
32 *La gloria de Niquea*, ed. cit., p. 42.
33 *Antología poética en honor de Góngora desde Lope de Vega a Rubén Darío* (Madrid, 1927), p. 44.

2 FERNANDO: THE CONSTANT PRINCE

1 Edward M. Wilson and W. J. Entwistle, 'Calderón's *Príncipe constante*: two appreciations', *Modern Language Review*, XXXIV (1939), 207-22 (p. 219).
2 I am thinking of such plays as Lope's *El remedio en la desdicha*, and Cervantes's *Los baños de Argel*.
3 Alonso de Ercilla, *La Araucana*, Canto I, stanza 2.
4 The part of Tarudante is relatively unimportant in the pattern of the whole play. Entwistle notes: 'Alfonso to some extent duplicates his uncle, and Tarudante is a more farouche duplicate of the Rey de Fez' (*Modern Language Review*, XXXIV (1939), 220).
5 Critics often tend to assume that the influence of scholasticism on the literature of the Spanish seventeenth century was a bad one; that the 'wrangling of the school-men' led merely to word-torture and quibbling superficial conceits. It is in such passages as these that the value of the careful distinctions of scholasticism makes itself felt. To us *melancolía* and *tristeza* might be used almost interchangeably; Calderón uses them precisely, to show that the Infanta does not realise what is grieving her. The 'Sólo sé que sé sentir' passage is not a quibble but the most terse way of conveying this confusion to the audience: it is not realistic language, but it is effective and serves its purpose magnificently.
6 The German critic F. W. V. Schmidt put this contrast in a different manner. He explains that the play is impressive because of the extraordinary depth and power in the relationship and contrast between Fénix, who represents the 'living-dead', and Fernando, the 'dead-living'. *Die Schauspiele Calderóns dargestellt und erläutert* (Elberfeld, 1857), pp. 381-2.
7 See pp. 5-6, 11-12, above.
8 I think that 'aliento' is not only meant to mean 'courage', 'spirit' here. Remember what Muley has told the King earlier in the play:

> Los cautivos (¡pena fiera!)
> en una mísera estera

> le ponen en tal lugar,
> que es, ¿dirélo? un muladar;
> Porque es su olor de manera,
> que nadie puede sufrille
> junto a su casa. (III, i)

3 ON *LA VIDA ES SUEÑO*

1 I wrote this sentence in 1946.
2 Line-references throughout this chapter are to A. E. Sloman's edition (Manchester, 1961).
3 *Calderón y su teatro*. I quote from the edition of Madrid, 1910, p. 108.
4 *Ibid.* p. 272.
5 *Ibid.* p. 394. My italics.
6 *Ibid.* p. 276.
7 *Ibid.* p. 278.
8 'Sognare e operare ad un tempo, porre nel sogno la vigilanza ed accortezza dell'uomo desto, quest'è un assurdo, di cui ride la logica del poeta, al solito sì chiara e sì ferma. Ma quest'assurdo è pur necessaria conseguenza della sovrapposizione delle due tesi, che s'annunciano e appena si svolgono nel drama, quella scettica, e quella religiosa. La condanna delle vanità mondane e del gioco delle apparenze e delle illusioni conduce al nirvâna buddhistico. Ma il mondo disciolto bisognava pur ricostruirlo, ricrearlo a immagine di Dio. Col vuoto e il nulla in cuore non si accede al trono dell'Altissimo. Generalizzando il sogno, come il poeta faceva, ruisciva egli veramente a sollevare colle opera buone, il nuovo edificio al suo Dio? Possibile non si rendesse conto della nessuna responsabilità che l'uomo ha nel sogno?...Dalle strette della logica il poeta poteva salvarsi, ammettendo un sognare particolarissimo, non compreso dal sognar comune, una specie di "soñar despierto", a cui è un' allusione fugace nell' "auto"...Più doveva stargli a cuore la bontà della dottrina che la congruenza dell'opera sua d'arte e di fantasia.' Arturo Farinelli, *La vita è un sogno*, 2 vols. (Torino, 1916), vol. II, pp. 283-4.
9 'Il dramma, che si disse sgomentevolmente serio e di vertiginosa profondità, offre gli strappi più vivi ad ogni seria e profonda riflessione. Corra il pensiero da una parte, e corra dall'altra l'azione drammatica, il poeta non se ne preoccupa. Ditegli che nel mondo del sogno e dell'illusione deve porsi anche l'onore, ed egli si ribellerà al vostro e al suo proprio giudizio. Nulla di chiaro riesce a veder l'uomo nell'universale fantasmagoria, anzi non vede punto; gli si confonde ogni cosa nell'indistinto del sogno; e Calderón obbliga tuttavia a chiaramente distinguere il raggiar dell'onore nella vita morale degl'individui e della società. E, in conclusione, trasmuta il dramma del sogno della vita nel dramma dell'onore restaurato. L'apre col lamento e la sorpresa di Rosaura, venuta nella terra di Sigismondo a vendicarsi dell'oltraggio subìto; e lo chiude col trionfo della causa santa di Rosaura e la riparazione del torto, la salvezza dell'onore. Debbon disfarsi al soffio più tenue le maestà e le pompe; e non v'è soffio, non v'è sogno che valga a dissolvere l'onore. Onore, lealtà, fedele sommessione al sovrano, gentilezza, cortesia, convenienza sociale, ordine, compattezza di vincoli nella famiglia e nello stato, misura, vedete quanto si salva dal complesso delle larve

vane che costituiscono il mondo e la vita terrena. Nell'oscillar di tutto, ammirate tanta stabilità di principi. Se il mondo scompare, rimane la legge' (*Ibid*. vol. II, p. 285).

10 *Ibid*. vol. 1; Félix G. Olmedo, S. J., *Las fuentes de 'La vida es sueño'* (Madrid, 1928); Blanca de los Ríos, *'La vida es sueño' y los diez Segismundos de Calderón* (Madrid, 1926); Ángel Valbuena Prat, *Historia de la literatura española*, 2 vols. (Barcelona, 1937), vol. II, p. 405n; L. P. Thomas, 'La Genèse de la philosophie et le symbolisme dans *La Vie est un songe*', *Mélanges offerts à M. Wilmotte*, 2 vols. (Paris, 1910), vol. II, pp. 751–85. Of the last work Farinelli acutely remarked: 'Ed è follia pensare raffigurino nel dramma, interamente ed esattamente, quello che raffigurano nell' "auto" i personaggi trascelti per la storia della rigenerazione umana; e significhi così Basilio il divino "Poder", Clotaldo l'intelligenza, Clarín la volontà o l'arbitrio, i servi i sensi, ecc. *La vita è un sogno*, vol. II, p. 182.

11 Farinelli, *La vita è un sogno*, vol. II, p. 279, and note on p. 415.

12 I am reminded here of some ideas of Bishop Butler: 'Upon the whole, if the generality of mankind were to cultivate within themselves the principle of self-love; if they were to accustom themselves often to set down and consider, what was the greatest happiness they were capable of attaining for themselves in this life, and if self-love were so strong and prevalent, as that they would uniformly pursue this their supposed chief temporal good, without being diverted from it by any particular passion; it would manifestly prevent numberless follies and vices. This was in a great measure the Epicurean system of philosophy. It is indeed by no means the religious or even moral institution of life. Yet, with all the mistakes men would fall into about interest, it would be less mischievous than the extravagances of mere appetite, will, and pleasure: for certainly self-love, though confined to the interest of this life, is, of the two, a much better guide than passion, which has absolutely no bound nor measure, but what is set to it by this self-love, or moral considerations.' *Sermons* by the Right Reverend Father in God, Joseph Butler, D.C.L., late Lord Bishop of Durham (Oxford, 1850), pp. xxvi–xxvii. (From the Preface.)

13 Compare: 'Thus saith the Lord, Let not the wise man glory in his wisdom, neither let the mighty man glory in his might, let not the rich man glory in his riches: But let him that glorieth glory in this, that he understandeth and knoweth me that I am the Lord' (Jeremiah, ix, 23–4).

14 Epictetus, *The enchiridion, or manual*, VIII.

15 See also the dialogue between Clarín and Rosaura before the battle in the last act:
Rosaura.   ¡Ay, Clarín! ¿Dónde has estado?
Clarín.   En una torre encerrado,
               . . .
Rosaura.   ¿Por qué?
Clarín.   Porque sé el secreto
               de quien eres, y en efeto,
                   Dentro cajas.
               Clotaldo...Pero ¿qué ruido
               es éste?   (3021–32)

16 L. P. Thomas pointed out that certain attributes of the Trinity were present in the part of Basilio. Starting from the *auto* of *La vida es sueño* he detected in

Basilio's long speech the working of the Trinity in it; he pointed out how certain passages exemplified Power, others Wisdom, others Love. I do not wish to deny that there is in Basilio, along with other characteristics, the germ of the notion of the Trinity found in the *auto*. This has some importance in the consideration of Segismundo's attitudes towards his father, for when Segismundo rebels he is rebelling against a divinely established order. But for the comprehension of the part of Basilio in the *comedia* we must see primarily a human being led astray by the presumption of wisdom. In interpreting any of Calderón's plays that he afterwards made into *autos*, we must be careful not to read too much of the *auto* back into the *comedia*. The play is nearly always simplified in the process of conversion. See note 10 above.

17 The misery, that is to say, of those who are dominated by their passions and are not guided by reason; this of course is not the same as the pessimistic misery of the romantic poets.

4 THE DISCRETION OF DON LOPE DE ALMEIDA

1 I had hoped to be able to revise the quotations in this article by taking into account the readings in MS. 14.297 of the Biblioteca Nacional, Madrid. Unfortunately I have not been able to do so. I have therefore kept the quotations and page references to the third Astrana Marín edition of 1945 – a book still to be found in many libraries – and to the arbitrary scene-divisions in that of Hartzenbusch. I have, however, emended one or two quotations in accordance with the readings of an early *parte* and with those adopted in the editions of Ángel Valbuena Briones. (25 October 1972).
2 The setting of *El pintor de su deshonra*.
3 Tirso de Molina: *Comedias II. El amor médico y Averígüelo Vargas*, ed. Alonso Zamora Vicente and María Josefa Canellada de Zamora (Madrid, 1947), pp. xi–xii. See also M. Herrero García, *Ideas de los españoles del siglo XVII* (Madrid, 1928).

4 *Tello.*   Estamos en tierra ajena;
          el recato portugués
          con las mujeres, ya ves
          que libertades enfrena.   (lines 2751–4)
   Jerónima. ¿Segunda vez, Don Gaspar,
          en mi barrio, y a estas puertas?
          Si en Castilla están abiertas,
          dando ocasiones lugar
          que logren sus intereses,
          acá los cierra el honor,
          porque del modo que amor,
          son los celos portugueses.   (lines 2779–86)
   Jerónima. La castellana llaneza
          permite allí ociosidades,
          que por acá lleva mal
          la gente menos sencilla.
          Mientras no estéis en Castilla,
          vivid como en Portugal,

> y hayámonos bien los dos:
> que entre libros y recetas,
> guarda también escopetas
> mi estudio.   (lines 2801–10)

5 D. Francisco Manuel de Melo, *Carta de guia de casados*, ed. Edgar Prestage (Oporto, 1923).
6 E.g. 'Esto se tendrá en Portugal por soltura y liviandad; mas, supuesto ser en corte y en esta ocasión, pregunto: Estas señoras ¿en qué ofendieron a Dios, a su prójimo o a su opinión? Ellas se huelgan hacer esta honra a los extranjeros, que lo preciaron harto, vuélvense a sus casas; holgara de saber en qué está el mal en esta facilidad y llaneza, tan contraria a la hipocresía y cautiverio de Portugal.' Tomé Pinheiro da Veiga, *Fastiginia o fastos geniales*, trans. Narciso Alonso Cortés (Valladolid, 1916), p. 85a.
7 'The four elements in the imagery of Calderón', *Modern Language Review*, XXI (1936), 291–8; reprinted in this volume, pp. 1–14.
8 In *La garduña de Sevilla* by Castillo Solórzano, when Sarabia discovers that his wife was unfaithful to him, the author tells us that: 'Bien sabía Sarabia que lo que le tocaba era buscar a los adúlteros y quitarles primero la vida, y luego a su mujer' (ed. F. Ruiz Morcuende, Clásicos Castellanos (Madrid, 1942), p. 26). It is interesting to note that Lope kills Luis before he kills Leonor.
9 Milton, *Paradise lost*, Book iii, line 108.
10 The contrast with *El médico de su honra* in this respect is notable. Both plays date from the same year, and their plots are very similar. I think that *A secreto agravio* was probably written after *El médico* and that Calderón purposely avoided the clash between Christian morality and the code of honour (which makes the death of Doña Mencía so disquieting to many persons) in the later play by deliberately excising all but the most superficial religious references from it.

5 TOWARDS AN APPRECIATION OF *EL PINTOR DE SU DESHONRA*

1 *Theatro de los theatros de los passados y presentes siglos*, ed. Duncan W. Moir (London, 1970), p. 34.
2 See A. A. Parker, *The approach to the Spanish drama of the Golden Age*, Diamante VI (London, 1957), several times reprinted.
3 There are curious details about the revived Carnival at Barcelona after the conquest of that city by the second Don Juan of Austria in Miguel Parets, 'De los muchos sucesos dignos de memoria que han ocurrido en Barcelona y otros lugares de Cataluña: crónica escrita por...entre los años de 1626 a 1660', tomo v, noviembre 1641 hasta junio de 1652, in *Memorial Histórico Español*, XXIV (1893), 221–9; XXV (1893), 147–8, 153–4.
4 Compare these lines from Juan Boscán:
> Dezí: si véys baylar, no oyendo el son
> de los que baylan, ¿no staréys burlando
> y no os parecerá que locos son?

'Respuesta de Boscán a don Diego de Mendoça', lines 61–3, in Juan Boscán, *Obras poéticas*, ed. Martín de Riquer, Antonio Comas and Joaquín Molas, vol. I (Barcelona, 1957), p. 354.

5   ¿Quién fue aquél tan riguroso
    que nos dejó introducido
    un gravamen tan enorme
    y fuero tan esquisito:
    que el honor de los varones
    justamente merecido
    restribe en un fundamento
    fácil de ser combatido?

   Juan Rufo, *Romance de los comendadores*, lines 321–8, in Rufo's *Las seiscientas apotegmas y otras obras en verso*, ed. Alberto Blecua (Madrid, 1972), p. 255.

6 'Escollo armado de hiedra'; see B. J. Gallardo, *Ensayo de una biblioteca española de libros raros y curiosos*, 4 vols. (Madrid, 1863–89), vol. I, col. 1048; vol. II, col. 176. Also Edward M. Wilson and Jack Sage, *Poesías líricas en las obras dramáticas de Calderón: citas y glosas* (London, 1964), no. 78. The poem is also reprinted in José Fernández Montesinos's *Romancerillos tardíos* (Salamanca, 1964), no. 75, pp. 128–30.

7 Baltasar = 'tesoro escondido'; Daniel = 'juicio de Dios' in *La cena de Baltasar*. Nearly all the *autos* contain similar examples. A study of Calderón's use of proper names might make clear a good many problems of interpretation in the *autos* and in the *comedias*.

8 See note 6 above.

9 When the Prince gives Belardo a diamond he comments:

   Poco entiendo de diamantes;
   que no valen, si se venden,
   lo que si se compran valen.   (III, xx)

10 Belardo was one of Lope de Vega's pen-names. Perhaps in naming his character Calderón had in mind Lope's famous *romance*: 'Hortelano era Belardo'.

6 THE CLOAK AND SWORD PLAYS

1 F. Bouterwek, *History of Spanish and Portuguese literature*, translated from the original German by Thomasina Ross (London, 1823), vol. I, p. 506.

2 *Calderón y su teatro* (Madrid, 1910), p. 364.

3 *A handbook to the study and teaching of Spanish*, ed. E. A. Peers, with chapters by W. J. Entwistle and W. C. Atkinson (London, 1938), p. 175.

4 'Studies in literary decadence. II: *La comedia de capa y espada*', *Bulletin of Spanish Studies*, IV (1927), 80–9.

5 E. J. Hasell, *Calderon* (Edinburgh and London, 1879), p. 39. [The typescript shows that E. M. W. toyed with the idea of correcting this misquotation from *Hamlet*; I have let it stand.]

6 Some interesting observations on various aspects of these plays are to be found in Ángel Valbuena Prat's *Calderón, su personalidad, su arte dramático, su estilo y sus obras* (Barcelona, 1941), pp. 149–68. The pages in which the author shows how Calderón ironically comments in these plays on the conventions and tricks that he exploits are particularly to be noted.

7 Menéndez y Pelayo, *Calderón y su teatro*, p. 358.

8 [E. M. W. left the source of these quotations blank; so I quote from and refer to the page and column in *Obras completas*, 3 vols., II: *Comedias*, ed. A.

Valbuena Briones (Madrid, 1956). Misprints have been corrected in one or two places.]

9 A. Farinelli treats extensively of Calderón's conception of love in his chapter 'Amore e natura' in *La vita è un sogno*, 2 vols. (Torino, 1916), vol. II, pp. 89–117. His treatment is relevant to this section of this chapter, e.g.: 'Calderón vede il raggiar d'amore in ogni manifestazione di vita. L'amore è somma di tutte le scienze' (p. 89). 'L'amor vero è possesso della divinità, accensione dello spirito in Dio; ed ha pietà del corpo, del gaudio e tripudio dei sensi' (p. 92).

10 M. B. García Suelto in the preface to his *Comedias escogidas de Calderón* (Madrid, 1826); quoted by Hartzenbusch in Calderón, *Comedias*, vol. IV, pp. 707–8 (Biblioteca de Autores Españoles, XIV) (Madrid, 1850).

11 [See *Obras completas*, vol. 1: *Dramas*, ed. A. Valbuena Briones (Madrid, 1959), p. 1594b.]

12
>   Mirad, Lisardo, que a veces
>   aun el mismo sol engaña,
>   tomando de los colores
>   reflejos y luces varias.
>   (Félix in *Antes que todo es mi dama*, 882a)
>
>   ejemplo sea
>   el cielo, el sol y el cristal.
>   Tocad de apariencia igual
>   la verdad.   (Beatriz in *Mañana será otro día*, 784a)
>
>   no os dé lo demás desvelos;
>   que damas que piden celos,
>   darán favores mañana.
>   (Captain Clavijo in *Mañana será otro día*, 778b)

13 A. Lasso de la Vega, *Calderón de la Barca. Estudio de las obras de este insigne poeta, consagrado a su memoria en el segundo centenario de su muerte* (Madrid, 1881), pp. 201–3.

14 *Ibid.* pp. 219–20.

15 Quoted by R. B. Merriman, *The rise of the Spanish Empire*, 4 vols. (New York, 1918–34), vol. III: *The Emperor*, p. 650.

16 *The imitation of Christ*, I, 4.

17 *Ibid.* I, 14.

18 *El astrólogo fingido, El maestro de danzar, La dama duende, Casa con dos puertas mala es de guardar, La desdicha de la voz, Los empeños de un acaso, Peor está que estaba, No siempre lo peor es cierto, No hay burlas con el amor, Antes que todo es mi dama, Con quien vengo, vengo, Cada uno para sí, No hay cosa como callar, Dar tiempo al tiempo, Mañana será otro día*.

7 A KEY TO CALDERÓN'S *PSALLE ET SILE*

1 Emilio Cotarelo y Mori, *Ensayo sobre la vida y obras de D. Pedro Calderón de la Barca* (Madrid, 1924), pp. 292–3.

2 *Psalle et sile*, ed. L. Trénor Palavicino and J. de Entrambasaguas (Valencia, 1936–9); quoted by Entrambasaguas, pp. 80–1.

3 *Ibid.* preliminaries and pp. 81, 57–63.

4 *Ibid.* pp. 54, 62, 52.
5 'Septena versuum retiacula in capitelo uno, et septena in capitelo altero.'
6 All my quotations are taken from Trénor's facsimile edition. I have modernised the text and numbered the lines.
7 'Quasi stercus auribus vestris immitunt. Chrisost. homilia 38. in Matth.' (marginal note). See also J. Sage, 'Calderón y la música teatral', *Bulletin Hispanique*, LVIII (1956), 275–300.
8 'Salue, ô Ciudad Metropoli de Hespaña' (line 2174); in *Obras poéticas*, ed. R. Foulché-Delbosc, 3 vols. (New York, 1921), vol. 1, p. 423. Cf. Dámaso Alonso, *Poesía española, ensayo de métodos y límites estilísticos* (Madrid, 1950), pp. 96–9; Enrique Moreno Báez, in *Ínsula*, 15 May 1950.
9 'Aufer à nobis cor lapideum, et da nobis cor carneum, quod te amet, te diligat... S. Ambros. *in praeparatione ad Missam*, Feria 4' (marginal note).
10 Cf. Calderón's play *La Virgen del Sagrario*, in *Obras completas*, 3 vols., 1: *Dramas*, ed. L. Astrana Marín, 3rd edn (Madrid, 1951), p. 1035a. Also Cristóbal Lozano, *Los Reyes nuevos de Toledo* (Barcelona, 1792), pp. 56, 84.
11 I must thank Professor A. A. Parker for explaining this passage to me. Calderón refers also to Psalm 131 (Vulgate): 'Adorabimus in loco ubi steterunt pedes ejus.'
12 Cf. the remarkable note of Professor E. Sarmiento to Fray Luis de León's ode *En la Ascensión*, in *The original poems of Fray Luis de León* (Manchester, 1953), p. 87. Also Louis L. Martz, *The poetry of meditation: a study in English religious literature* (New Haven and London, 1954), *passim*.
13 I Kings, xix, 12.
14 *Soledad primera*, line 197.
15 'El primer puncto es poner delante de mí un rey humano, elegido de mano de Dios nuestro Señor, a quien hacen reverencia y obedescen todos los príncipes y todos hombres christianos', etc. *Obras completas de San Ignacio de Loyola*, Biblioteca de Autores Cristianos (Madrid, 1952), pp. 178–9.
16 *El alcalde de Zalamea*, in *Dramas*, ed. L. Astrana Marín, pp. 519b–520a.

8 CALDERÓN'S DRAMATIC POETRY

1 The following attempts to gather together Calderón's non-dramatic poems have a limited usefulness: J. E. Hartzenbusch, *Comedias de don Pedro Calderón de la Barca*, vol. IV, pp. 724–34 (Biblioteca de Autores Españoles, XIV) (Madrid, 1850); F[elipe] P[icatoste], *Calderón: poesías inéditas*, Biblioteca Universal, LXXI; these mid-nineteenth-century editions have often been reprinted. Calderón de la Barca, *Obra lírica*, prólogo de Manuel de Montoliú (Barcelona, 1943) – a selection; J. Simón Díaz, 'Textos dispersos de clásicos españoles: II. Calderón de la Barca', *Revista de Literatura*, XV (1959), 121–4.
2 The three poems mentioned in this paragraph may be found in Edward M. Wilson, 'Some unpublished works by Don Pedro Calderón de la Barca', *Homage to John M. Hill*, ed. Walter Poesse (Bloomington, Ind., 1968), pp. 7–18.
3 El Reverendissimo P. M. Fr. Miguel de Cárdenas, *Sermon en las honras del reverendissimo padre maestro fray Nicolas Baptista, predicador de su magestad* (Madrid, 1663), preliminaries.
4 See my studies: 'Calderón and the *Décimas a la muerte*', Bulletin of Hispanic Studies, XLVIII (1971), 301–13; 'Un romance ascético de Calderón: "Agora, Señor,

agora..."', *Boletín de la Real Academia Española*, LII (1972), 79–105. See Chapter 7 for the study on *Psalle et sile*.

5 Edward M. Wilson and Jack Sage, *Poesías líricas en las obras dramáticas de Calderón: citas y glosas* (London, 1964). In this and the following paragraphs I refer to nos. 166, 71, 78 and 168 in that work.

6 Margit Frenk Alatorre, 'Refranes cantados y cantares proverbializados', *Nueva Revista de Filología Hispánica*, XV (1961), 155–68.

7 The sonnet begins: 'No Fatal te construye Mauseolo' and is to be found on fol. *4r of *Sossia perseguida. Sueño, y pregunta de Cassio, a Prudencio. En que se trata del honor paterno, y amor filial, con otras cosas, y de curiosas y buenas letras de humanidad* (Madrid, 1621).

8 Gerardo Diego, *Antología poética en honor de Góngora desde Lope de Vega a Rubén Darío* (Madrid, 1927), p. 44.

9 N. Fernández de Moratín, *Desengaño al theatro español* (?Madrid, n.d.), pp. 29–30.

10 See F. Rico, *El pequeño mundo del hombre: varia fortuna de una idea en las letras españolas* (Madrid, 1970), pp. 242–59.

11 'La correlación en la estructura del teatro calderoniano', in D. Alonso and C. Bousoño, *Seis calas en la expresión literaria española (prosa, poesía, teatro)* (Madrid, 1951), pp. 115–86; see especially pp. 118–21.

12 G. Marañón, *El Conde-Duque de Olivares (la pasión de mandar)*, 3rd edn (Madrid, 1962), p. 152.

13 E. H. Gombrich, *Art and illusion* (London, 1962), pp. 187–9.

14 A. Rubió y Lluch, *El sentimiento del honor en el teatro de Calderón* (Barcelona, 1882). [I have been unable to supply the page-reference for this quotation.]

15 Lupercio and Bartolomé L. de Argensola, *Rimas*, ed. J. M. Blecua, 2 vols. (Madrid, 1951), vol. II, p. 669.

16 Wilson and Sage, *Poesías líricas*, p. ix (*Saber del mal y del bien*).

17 Here are the play titles on which I have built this paragraph: *En esta vida todo es verdad y todo mentira. ¿Cuál es mayor perfección, hermosura o discreción? Los empeños de un acaso. De una causa dos efectos. Enfermar con el remedio. El astrólogo fingido. La dama duende. El galán fantasma. El maestro de danzar. El escondido y la tapada. Peor está que estaba. No siempre lo peor es cierto. Mejor está que estaba. Saber del mal y del bien. Nadie fíe su secreto. Guárdate del agua mansa. No hay cosa como callar. Dar tiempo al tiempo. Mañana será otro día. Casa con dos puertas mala es de guardar.* [Readers will notice that E. M. W. makes similar use of Calderón play-titles in Chapter 6 (p. 103), a chapter he did not himself plan to include in this volume. But the two lists are by no means identical; they show consistency of thought, not repetitiveness, so I have left them alone.]

18 C. Pérez Pastor, *Documentos para la biografía de D. Pedro Calderón de la Barca* (Madrid, 1905), pp. 375–6.

19 E.g. in his edition of Calderón's *autos* (Madrid, 1952), p. 424.

20 I owe the addition of the word *aun* in the last line to Professor A. A. Parker, who found it in one of the manuscript texts of the play, though it does not appear in the printed editions. I think it is probably authentic.

9 IMAGES AND STRUCTURE IN *PERIBÁÑEZ*

1 Lope de Vega, *Peribáñez y el Comendador de Ocaña*, ed. C. V. Aubrun and J. F. Montesinos (Paris, 1943). Quotations and line-references are to this edition.
2 I do not want to decry the comparative method. But I propose here to interpret this play as far as I can without reference to other works by Lope himself or by his contemporaries. Coleridge remarked that a work of art should contain in itself the reason why it was so and not otherwise (*Biographia literaria*, Chapter XIV). I try to show this in my discussion of *Peribáñez*.
3 The editors remark: 'Comme dans tout art romantique, la moitié des intentions du poète ne parventait pas à se réaliser dans la comédie, mais restait à l'état d'esquisse, de suggestion abandonnée à l'imagination des auditeurs, qui devait en compléter et nuancer le sens' (p. ix). Later they add: 'Là encore (v. 762–3) Lope esquisse une situation, souligne une phrase et laisse au lecteur le soin d'imaginer. Car il crut toujours qu'il incombait à l'auditeur ou au lecteur – et non point au poète – de faire la psychologie de ses personnages' (p. xliii). Cf. my remarks at the beginning of the chapter of this book on *La vida es sueño*.
4 See especially pp. x–xiv of their edition. For the *Arte nuevo* I have used H. J. Chaytor's edition in *Dramatic theory in Spain* (Cambridge, 1925).
5 William Wordsworth, *The poetical works*, ed. E. de Selincourt (Oxford, 1944), vol. II, p. 386. Aubrun and Montesinos discuss the songs and rural background of the play on pp. xx and xxi of their edition.
6 'La solidarité paysanne n'était pas moins forte à Ocaña [qu'à Fuente Ovejuna]. Tous ceux qui entourent Peribáñez, s'ils sont de la même condition que lui, font montre de la plus grand fidélité envers sa personne; s'il avait voulu se rebeller, beaucoup auraient suivi son exemple' (Aubrun and Montesinos, p. xxxviii).
7 'Les villageois de Lope servent de décor et de chœur; mais, pour *Peribáñez*, il faut entendre chœur dans un sens rigoureux, dans un sens antique.' After a revealing quotation from Menéndez y Pelayo (his introduction to *Peribáñez* in the Spanish Academy's edition of Lope's *comedias*, vol. **x**, p. lxv) they add: 'En introduisant dans son *Peribáñez* la voix populaire sous la forme d'un *romance* [see lines 1917–28], il nous fait sentir profondément le caractère de cette communauté rurale castillane. Le protagoniste en est l'expression la plus accomplie; et les autres personnages, faits de la même argile, prolongent pour ainsi dire la conscience du héros, dont ils se savent solidaires et dont ils partagent les anxiétés.' (p. xxi). A good part of this chapter is implicit in these phrases.
8 'Don Fadrique, dans *Peribáñez*, n'a rien d'un monstre, quoiqu'en dise Menéndez Pelayo' (p. xxiii). 'Il diffère grandement des petits tyrans locaux que Lope et ses émules ont mis en scène pour que leurs propres vassaux ou le roi les châtient publiquement' (p. xxxv). 'Le Commandeur d'Ocaña n'est pas de cette lignée. Il ne méprise point systématiquement ses vassaux, il ne leur fait pas violence. Il jouit même du respect de tous. Dans l'opinion du roi, il est "el mejor soldado que trujo roja cruz". Il tombe victime d'une passion frénétique...qui dépasse le grossier appétit des personnages analogues dans les autres comédies. Sa plus grande noblesse de caractère rend sa mort plus tragique' (p. xxxvii).
9 *Romance del iuramento que tomo el Cid al rey don Alonso* ('En sancta Gadea de Burgos'), in *Cancionero de romances* (Antwerp, n.d. [?1547–8]), facsimile edn by R. Menéndez Pidal (Madrid, 1914; new edn, Madrid, 1945), fols. 153v–155r.

10 It was of this lyric that Montesinos so acutely wrote: 'el gran maestro de la palabra con dos adjetivos anima una escena y crea un carácter'. *Estudios sobre Lope* (Salamanca, 1969), p. 155.
11 Joseph Silverman, 'Peribáñez y Vellido Dolfos', *Bulletin Hispanique*, LV (1953), 378–80.
12 In their introduction the editors recall that in Lope's plays: 'Face à l'amour courtois, l'amour rustique fait valoir un de ses traits particuliers: une fidélité à toute épreuve. La villageoise, qui ne pratique point la coquetterie, est plus inabordable, plus rétive à la séduction que toute autre femme' (Aubrun and Montesinos, p. xl).
13 The editors translate *la virtud* by 'notre honnêteté'. Is it not rather the 'honnêteté' of Casilda?
14 'Qu'avait-il besoin [par ailleurs] de tant d'ornements et de hors-d'œuvre, ce poète qui savait évoquer en quelques vers, avec un prestige prodigieux, cet intérieur villageois si propre et si avenant: "...en nuestras paredes blancas..."' (Aubrun and Montesinos, p. xliv).
15 Note on line 2693, p. 152, where this passage is also mentioned.
16 'Casilda ne comprend rien à ce discours, si ce n'est que son mari lui demande une faveur (un ruban) (vers 2390); et elle l'accordera volontiers à qui fait montre de tant de faveurs à son égard' (Aubrun and Montesinos, p. 135). The difference between my interpretation and the editors' is not great. She says: 'Muchas cosas me decís / en lengua que yo no entiendo.' My interpretation, more careful, takes account of the fact that she replies with some relevance to the puns on *celos* and *soldados* already quoted. As far as the interpretation of the scene as a whole is concerned, it matters little whether she understands one or more details.
17 'Il est à la fois émouvant et comique, et charmant en sa simple vérité, ce cri de Casilda qui défend son honneur parce qu'elle est l'épouse d'un capitaine' (Aubrun and Montesinos, p. xxxiv).
18 '*Peribáñez* met en scène un plébéien qu'ennoblit son propre sentiment de la dignité' (Aubrun and Montesinos, p. xxiii).
19 The editors write: 'Les manœuvres de celui-ci [Luján] ne suffisent pourtant pas; et don Fadrique doit recourir à un homme de qualité plus relevée, quoique aussi peu scrupuleux, pour mener à bien son entreprise amoureuse. Ce détail accuse, d'une façon imperceptible aujourd'hui, le progrès de l'affection du Commandeur' (p. xliii). I am not wholly convinced that the status of Luján and Leonardo marks the development of the Commander's passion. But I owe my interpretation of the passage to thoughts prompted by these remarks.
20 The whole social question is fully dealt with by the editors in their introduction, pp. xxii, xxix–xxxiv. W. J. Entwistle also raises one or two interesting points on this topic in his review of their work in *Modern Language Review*, XLIII (1948), 281–3.
21 'Le théâtre de Lope a créé un nouveau mode bucolique, supérieur sans doute à celui des pastorales, mais guère plus vrai' (Aubrun and Montesinos, p. xx).

10 'QUANDO LOPE QUIERE, QUIERE'

1 Quotations and line-references are to C. F. A. Van Dam's edition of the autograph manuscript (Groningen, 1928). The phrase 'Quando Lope quiere quiere'

was made the subtitle of *El castigo sin venganza* when it was reprinted by Pedro Craesbeeck in Lisbon in 1647 in the collection entitled *Doze comedias las mas grandiosas que asta aora han salido de los meiores y mas insignes poetas*. See Van Dam, p. 13; J. F. Montesinos also noticed the appropriateness of the phrase.

2 In Lorenzo de Ayala's translation of Belleforest's adaptation of the novel by Bandello, which is the source of this play, we read how the Marquis of Ferrara, 'persuadido, a lo que se entiende, de algunos de sus vassallos, determino de casarse'. A few lines later we are told: 'no parecia sino que se auia casado mas por dar contento a sus vassallos, o por encubrir sus apetitos desordenados, que para abstener su desonestidad y multiplicar su linaje' (Van Dam, p. 63).

3 Cf. the well-known sonnet by one of the Argensolas: 'Yo os quiero confesar, don Juan, primero': no. 297 in *Oxford book of Spanish verse*, chosen by J. Fitzmaurice-Kelly; 2nd edn by J. B. Trend (Oxford, 1940).

4 The longing for death, which is so often on Federico's lips, is of course an omen of the final catastrophe. A. García Valdecasas remarks: 'El castigo temporal había de ser la muerte en todo caso. Casandra y Federico lo sabían muy bien. La muerte es el tema constante de sus diálogos de amor, la muerte el pensamiento que una y otra vez asalta el de Federico.' *El hidalgo y el honor* (Madrid, 1948), p. 203.

5 'Ce que j'admire le plus en ce point, c'est que, peignant une passion coupable, la passion de Phèdre partagée par Hippolyte, Lope trouve l'art de condamner cette passion en la peignant dans ses transports les plus vifs.' E. Baret, *Œuvres dramatiques de Lope de Vega* (Paris, 1874), vol. I, p. 337. Quoted by Van Dam, p. 39.

6 See J. M. de Cossío, 'El mote "sin mí, sin vos y sin Dios" glosado por Lope de Vega', in *Revista de Filología Española*, xx (1933), 397–400.

7 Van Dam, p. 104.

8 Lope took the idea of Cassandra's revenge on the Duke directly from the source: see Van Dam, p. 65.

9 Hermits are satirised or shown in unfavourable light in *Don Quixote*, part II, ch. 14, *El buscón*, ch. 10, and in many other Spanish works. For the Camaldula, see Van Dam's note, p. 391.

10 García Valdecasas, *El hidalgo*, p. 204.

11 Van Dam, p. 112.

12 Van Dam quotes an interesting paragraph by Alberto Lista, who saw in the history of the lovers the reverse of what happened to Macbeth and Lady Macbeth. 'Casandra al principio es tímida e irresoluta, tanto como Federico violento; pero cometido el crimen, la primera es más atrevida, y su amante más tímido' (Van Dam, p. 25).

13 See A. A. Parker's appendix on 'discreción' in his edition of Calderón's *No hay más fortuna que Dios* (Manchester, 1949), pp. 77–92.

14 Van Dam notes that Lope first wrote: 'El Duque, ymaginatiuo'.

15 Van Dam, who finds the Duke's conversion unconvincing, notes that Batín also is unconvinced. 'Yo me olgaré de que sea verdad', he says (2398–9) when Ricardo tells him the news. He notes too how the same scepticism is shown in the anecdote of the 'gata domínica' (2374–91).

16 See K. Vossler, *Lope de Vega y su tiempo* (Madrid, 1933), p. 283. Also J. F.

Montesinos in *Revista de Filología Española*, XVI (1929), p. 188, and García Valdecasas, *El hidalgo*, p. 203.

17 In the Bandello–Belleforest–Ayala source we read how the ruler of Ferrara sent to his wife in prison 'vno de los de su consejo con dos frayles, personas de gran doctrina y vida aprouada, el vno para que la llevase las tristes y espantables nueuas de su muerte, y los otros para que la persuadiessen que se arripintiesse de sus peccados, y rogassen a Dios tuuiesse misericordia de su anima. Y lo mismo se hizo con el Conde su hijo' (Van Dam, p. 80). Lope deliberately suppressed this incident when he dramatised the story. In the source there is no deception by the Marquis of Ferrara; Lope made the Duke more Machiavellian in his vengeance than was the forerunner.
18 Valdecasas notes that 'en la venganza secreta no sólo se busca salvar el honor propio, sino también el mismo honor de la mujer' (*El hidalgo*, p. 201).
19 See the résumé given by Van Dam, pp. 30–3, 93–4. Also García Valdecasas, *El hidalgo*, pp. 203–6.
20 Van Dam, pp. 173, 229.
21 Van Dam, p. 281.
22 Van Dam, pp. 10, 56–7.

11 THE EXEMPLARY NATURE OF *EL CABALLERO DE OLMEDO*

1 M. Menéndez y Pelayo, *Estudios sobre el teatro de Lope de Vega*, 6 vols. (Santander, 1949), vol. v, pp. 72–3.
2 [This note was left blank in the original, but see R. D. F. Pring-Mill's introduction to Lope de Vega, *Five plays*, trans. Jill Booty (New York, 1961), pp. xxix–xxx; A. S. Gérard, 'Baroque unity and the dualities of *El caballero de Olmedo*', *Romanic Review*, LVI (1965), 92–106, especially p. 94; M. Wilson, *Spanish drama of the Golden Age* (Oxford, 1969), pp. 78–80; Edward M. Wilson and Duncan Moir, *The Golden Age: drama 1492–1700* (London, 1971), pp. 67–8 (this section is by Moir).]
3 See the interesting prologue to Blecua's edition of this play, published by Clásicos Ebro (Zaragoza, 1943). [I have not been able to supply the missing page-references to Blecua's edition. The quotations (and their corresponding line-references) in the original Spanish version of this article came from that edition. I have used instead the edition most familiar to English readers, that of I. I. Macdonald (Cambridge, 1934, and numerous reprints).]
4 See Antonio Rodríguez-Moñino's handsome reprint of this *cancionero* (Valencia, 1954), p. 258. In the same volume (p. 160) is the poem glossed by Tello in the second act: 'En el valle a Ynés'.
5 'There remains, then, the character between these two extremes, – that of a man who is not eminently good and just, yet whose misfortune is brought about not by vice or depravity, but by some error or frailty...The change of fortune... should come about as the result not of vice, but of some great error or frailty, in a character either such as we have described, or better rather than worse.' *The poetics of Aristotle*, edited with critical notes and a translation by S. H. Butler, 4th edn (London, 1911), pp. 45–7.
6 [I have not been able to supply this page-reference.]

7 See, for example, the beautiful facsimile of the edition of Seville, '1502', published by Antonio Pérez Gómez (Valencia, 1958), fol. A4v.
8 See Alonso Jerónimo de Salas Barbadillo, *La peregrinación sabia* and *El sagaz Estacio*, ed. Francisco A. Icaza (Madrid, 1924), p. 86.
9 *Novelas exemplares*, ed. R. Schevill and A. Bonilla, 3 vols. (Madrid, 1922–5), vol. II, p. 240.
10 Possibly printed in a *pliego suelto* at the beginning of the sixteenth century; the ballad became widely known in subsequent years. It appears in the *Cancionero de romances* (Antwerp, n.d.), fol. 87r. I quote from R. Menéndez Pidal's facsimile edition (Madrid, 1914; new edn, Madrid, 1945).

12 A HISPANIST LOOKS AT *OTHELLO*

1 The treatment of the code of honour in Spanish plays has been the subject of much discussion. The following are the chief works: A. Rubió y Lluch, *El sentimiento del honor en el teatro de Calderón* (Barcelona, 1882); A. Castro, 'Algunas observaciones acerca del concepto del honor en los siglos XVI y XVII', *Revista de Filología Española*, III (1916), 1–50, 357–86; W. L. Fichter in his preface to Lope de Vega's *El castigo del discreto* (New York, 1925); R. Menéndez Pidal, 'Del honor en nuestro teatro clásico', in *De Cervantes y Lope de Vega* (Buenos Aires, 1945); A. García Valdecasas, *El hidalgo y el honor* (Madrid, 1948).
2 *El arte nuevo de hacer comedias en este tiempo*, ed. H. J. Chaytor in *Dramatic theory in Spain* (Cambridge, 1925), lines 327–30.
3 See Castro, 'Algunas observaciones', pp. 14–39.
4 See García Valdecasas, *El hidalgo*, pp. 141, *et seq.*
5 The authors I have in mind are Fray Luis de Granada, Fray Diego de Estella, Mateo Alemán, Quevedo and Fr Juan Eusebio Nieremberg.
6 Castro, 'Algunas observaciones', pp. 19–21.
7 As in Lope de Vega's *El castigo sin venganza*.
8 As in Calderón's *El médico de su honra* and *El pintor de su deshonra*.
9 This assumption is made by all the writers mentioned in note 1. See also M. Menéndez y Pelayo, *Calderón y su teatro* (Madrid, 1881), and more recent studies by Ángel Valbuena Prat and E. Frutos Cortés. [The sentence which occasioned this note was true in 1952; that it is no longer is largely E. M. W.'s doing.]
10 *A secreto agravio secreta venganza* and *El pintor de su deshonra*. [See Chapters 4 and 5 of this volume.]
11 Professor Peter Alexander kindly allowed me to see the proofs of the fifth chapter of his *Shakespeare primer*. In it he deals with the importance of personal honour in *Hamlet, Coriolanus, Antony and Cleopatra* and *Macbeth*. His account implies the importance of the theme in *Othello*. William Empson has anticipated some of my ideas in his brilliant chapter 'Honest in Othello' in *The structure of complex words* (London, 1951).
12 *The second maiden's tragedy, The coxcomb, Amends for ladies*. See A. S. N. Rosenbach, '*The curious impertinent* in English dramatic literature', *Modern Language Notes*, XVII (1902), 357–67.
13 Edmond Gayton, *Pleasant notes on Don Quixot* (Oxford, 1654), pp. 202–30.

14 See Castro, 'Algunas observaciones', *passim*. The clearest dramatic exposition of it is perhaps to be found in Lope de Vega's *Los comendadores de Córdoba*.
15 Gondomar, for instance, reported to Madrid the high opinion James had of the writings of Fray Luis de Granada.
16 W. R. Turnbull, *'Othello': a critical study* (Edinburgh and London, 1892), p. 163.
17 R. Flatter, *The Moor of Venice* (London, 1950), p. 127. I hope I use this book with caution.
18 See García Valdecasas, *El hidalgo*, pp. 198, 207–8.
19 Lily B. Campbell, *Shakespeare's tragic heroes: slaves of passion* (Cambridge, 1930), p. 162.
20 'Honor, is the Reputation and Credit, or the good name and Fame of a Man, which the generous Spirit priseth, at so high a rate, as before hee will have the same eclipst, hee will loose all his wealth, yea, and his dearest life.' Robert Tofte, *The blazon of jealousie*, translated from the Italian of Varchi, quoted by Campbell, p. 162.
21 My quotations are taken from Peter Alexander's edition of the *Complete works* (London and Glasgow, 1951).
22 The same thought is perceptible in the soliloquy in the third act:
>I had rather be a toad,
>And live upon the vapour of a dungeon,
>Than keep a corner in the thing I love
>For others' uses.   (III, iii, 274–7)
23 Empson's examination of the use of the word 'honest' in this play is highly relevant. His explanation of this line differs from that given here (*The structure of complex words*, p. 228). He stresses, however, that 'honour' and 'honesty' to some extent are equivalents.
24 T. Spencer, *Shakespeare and the nature of man* (New York and Cambridge, 1943), p. 130.
25 'Del honor en nuestro teatro clásico', pp. 142–4.
26 Flatter has dealt with the parallel at some length (*The Moor of Venice*, pp. 70–84). According to his theory, Iago's remark is crucial in Othello's temptation.
27 See Rubió y Lluch, *El sentimiento del honor*, pp. 144–69.
28 Mr John Crow suggested to me that this expression may have another significance: is it the application to a daughter of words usually used of a wife?
29 H. Granville-Barker (*Prefaces to Shakespeare* (Princeton, 1947), p. 205) argues that the speech is meant to be absurd. Flatter says 'When he [Roderigo] wishes to impress Brabantio, he speaks well, both with dignity and effectiveness' (*The Moor of Venice*, p. 208). The point is perhaps one to be decided by actors and producers rather than by critics.
30 Cf. Castro's paragraphs on 'El honor, patrimonio de la nobleza' in 'Algunas observaciones', pp. 21–2.
31 Empson notes that Montano and the others 'act as a faint parody of Othello's Honour, which is a much idealised version of the same kind of thing' (*The structure of complex words*, p. 229n).
32 'What is honour? A word. What is in that word? Honour. What is that honour? Air...Honour is a mere scutcheon. And so ends my catechism' (*I Henry IV*, v, i).

33 'Iago begins his attack on Othello to rouse his jealousy by talking about his good name' (Campbell, *Shakespeare's tragic heroes*, p. 161).
34 The scenes of jealousy in *The winter's tale* provide a parallel to the degeneration of Othello. When Leontes says that Hermione has sullied 'the purity and whiteness of my sheets, which to preserve is sleep' he is thinking in terms of marital honour. In I, ii, he promises Camillo that he will 'give no blemish to her honour'; in II, i, he calls her an adulteress before the lords of the court.
35 The parallel with Leontes in Act II of *The winter's tale* is obvious.
36 Lope's *Los comendadores de Córdoba*, the two *Médico* plays, etc.
37 'The hatred which he feels towards Othello demands revenge; and revenge demands not only a wife for a wife; it demands also that Othello shall feel this same gnawing jealousy which is destroying him' (Campbell, *Shakespeare's tragic heroes*, p. 160; see also Empson, *The structure of complex words*, p. 247).
38 Cassio's 'bold show of courtesy' (II, i, 99) was perhaps also meant to add to Iago's hate.
39 Spencer, *Shakespeare and the nature of man*, p. 135.
40 Desdemona fell 'in love with what she fear'd to look on'; she beguiled the thing she was 'by seeming otherwise'; Brabantio thought that Othello must have used black arts to win her; Roderigo thought that Cassio was his rival; Cassio thought that he was sober while he was drunk; Emilia could not see that Iago was the 'busy and insinuating rogue' who devised the slander against her mistress, etc.
41 See the most interesting discussion of this subject by Empson, *The structure of complex words*, pp. 245-8.
42 Most critics have drawn attention to this fact; they have not given it sufficient prominence.
43 See especially III, iii, 121-8; 261-3; IV, i, 74.
44 'With this forfeiture of self-control he ceases to be master of his fate. His entire life passes under the dominion of necessity' (Turnbull, *Othello*, p. 369). Cf. Campbell, *Shakespeare's tragic heroes*, pp. 160-73; Spencer, *Shakespeare and the nature of man*, pp. 126-8, 133-5.
45 These comments begin with 'I see this hath a little dash'd your spirits' in III, iii, 218, and reach their climax in 'I see, sir, you are eaten up with passion' in line 395 of the same scene.
46 'Death and damnation! O!' 'O monstrous! monstrous!' 'O, blood, blood, blood!' 'Damn her, lewd minx! O, damn her!' 'Pish! – Noses, ears and lips. Is't possible? Confess! Handkerchief! – O devil! (*Falls in a trance*)' (III, iii, 400, 431, 455, 479; IV, i, 42-4).
47 Spencer describes him as 'a thoroughly rational being... He knows all the right things, but he perverts the familiar doctrine to his own ends' (*Shakespeare and the nature of man*, p. 132).
48 R. B. Merriman, *The rise of the Spanish Empire*, 4 vols. (New York, 1918-34), vol. III: *The Emperor*, p. 650. [Cf. pp. 102-3, Chapter 6, above.]
49 Cf. the Spanish term 'engañar con la verdad' used by Lope de Vega, *Arte nuevo de hacer comedias*, line 319.
50 See Flatter, *The Moor of Venice*, pp. 102-4.
51 Turnbull wrote: 'The unveracity of Desdemona is a potent factor in the tragedy; with her imprudence it aids and abets the malignant stratagems of the Ancient.

In her courtship she probably practised some craft and cunning, both in word and deed. For Brabantio declares at the end of the council scene, "She has deceived her father, and may thee"...But the presumed prenuptial habit of dissimulation continues and increases after her marriage. When difficulties present themselves she evades the truth from a sort of natural timidity, and openly toys with falsehood: "I am not merry but I do beguile / The thing I am by seeming otherwise". Even her archness and coquettish rebelliousness partakes largely of false colouring. She alleges that in the days of Othello's wooing, she has often spoken dispraisingly to Cassio, who was their go-between. Again she is easily started into tergiversation, as we see from the affair of the handkerchief which she declares is not lost; and repeats the falsehood with most emphatic iteration' (*Othello*, p. 354). There is some force in this claim, but it seems a trifle over-stated. Desdemona's lies are white rather than black. Her unveracity is less important than her imprudence.

52 My thanks are due to Professor Peter Alexander and to Mr John Crow who gave me invaluable advice in the preparation of this paper.

13 TRAGIC THEMES IN SPANISH BALLADS

1 Oxford, 1939; reprinted 1951.
2 *Romancero tradicional*, colección de textos y notas de M. Goyri y R. Menéndez Pidal, vol. 1: *Romanceros del Rey Rodrigo y de Bernardo del Carpio* (Madrid, 1957).
3 W. J. Entwistle, *The adventure of Spanish*, Diamante, 1 (London, 1951).
4 See E. M. Wright, *Rustic speech and folk-lore* (Oxford, 1914), especially ch. 11.
5 Francisco Rodríguez Marín, *Más de 21.000 refranes castellanos* (Madrid, 1926); *12.600 refranes más* (Madrid, 1930).
6 I quote from Shelton's translation of 1620, p. 31. However incorrect his translation may be, no one can deny his ability to find English idioms to reproduce Spanish ones. In this respect he was one of Cervantes's most faithful translators. For the identity of Shelton see Edwin B. Knowles, 'Thomas Shelton, translator of *Don Quixote*', *Studies in the Renaissance*, v (1958), 160–75.
7 F. J. Child, *The English and Scottish popular ballads* (New York, 1957), no. 69. A 15 (II, 159a).
8 Child, no. 169. C 12–13 (III, 370).
9 See R. Menéndez Pidal, *El romancero hispánico*, 2 vols. (Madrid, 1953), *passim*.
10 I regret that I cannot substantiate this reference.
11 *Ancient Spanish ballads* (Edinburgh and London, 1823), p. 5.
12 *Romancero tradicional*, vol. 1, pp. 47–8.
13 See the introductory chapters of *European balladry*, etc. Menéndez Pidal, *El romancero hispánico*, vol. 1, pp. 60–3.
14 *Romancero tradicional*, vol. 1, p. 48.
15 Child, no. 193 (IV, 24–8). See also IV, 520–1.
16 R. Menéndez Pidal, *Flor nueva de romances viejos* (Madrid, 1943), p. 194.
17 *Romancero del Rey Don Pedro*, ed. Antonio Pérez Gómez (Valencia, 1954), pp. 100–14.
18 *Cancionero de romances* (Antwerp, n.d.), facsimile edn by R. Menéndez Pidal (Madrid, 1914; new edn, Madrid, 1945), fol. 188r.

19 'Romance de la muerte ocultada' from R. Menéndez Pidal, *Flor nueva de romances viejos*, p. 260.
20 *Silva de varios romances* (Barcelona, 1561), ed. A. Rodríguez-Moñino (Valencia, 1953), p. 10.
21 *Cancionero de romances*, fol. 251r.
22 *Ibid.* fol. 109v.
23 Robert Graves, *The English ballad: a short critical survey* (London, 1927), p. 9.
24 *Flor nueva de romances viejos*, p. 11.
25 *Cancionero de romances*, fol. 227v.
26 J. E. Housman, *British popular ballads* (London, 1952), pp. 25-8.
27 Child, no. 191 (IV, 8-16).
28 'E tingendia [sic] es aquella que contiene en sy caydas de grandes reys e prinçipes, asy como de Ercoles, Panto e Agamenon e otros tales, cuyos nasçimientos e vidas alegres se començaron, e grande tiempo se continuaron, e despues tristemente cayeron.' *Cancionero de Juan Fernández de Ixar*, ed. J. M. Azáceta, 2 vols. (Madrid, 1956), vol. II, p. 562.
29 *Boethius de consolatione philosophie*, book II, prose II. [See also the Prologue to *The Monk's tale*.]
30 William Empson, *Some versions of pastoral* (London, 1935), p. 6.
31 G. H. Gerould, *The ballad of tradition* (Oxford, 1932), p. 65.

14 SPANISH AND ENGLISH RELIGIOUS POETRY OF THE SEVENTEENTH CENTURY

1 In this essay I have attempted to show that there was unity as well as diversity in two contemporary religious literatures and to hint at the sources of that unity. My analysis of the Spanish tradition owes a great deal to my private discussions with Professor A. A. Parker. My other debt is to Mr Louis L. Martz's profound book: *The poetry of meditation* (London and New Haven, 1954). I must also thank the Reverend Professor Norman Sykes for his encouragement and for the loan of the works of John Knox, and Dr R. W. Ladborough of Magdalene College for four very helpful criticisms.
2 John Knox, *Works*, ed. David Laing, 6 vols. (Edinburgh, 1854), vol. iii, pp. 248, 89, 137.
3 Fray Domingo de Valtanas, *Doctrina christiana: en que se tracta de lo que deue cada vno creer, huyr, obrar, dessear, y que cosa es Dios: con otras cosas dignas de saber* (Seville, 1555), fols. 14r, 35v, 126r, 30v-31r, 82r. (My translation.)
4 Pedro Malón de Chaide, *La conversión de la Magdalena*, ed. P. Félix García, O.S.A., 3 vols. (Madrid, 1930), vol. ii, pp. 184-5.
5 *Nicholas Ferrar: two lives, by his brother John and by Doctor Jebb*, ed. J. E. B. Mayor (Cambridge, 1855), pp. 58-9.
6 *Cancionero de Montesino* in the *Romancero y cancionero sagrados*, ed. Justo de Sancha, in Biblioteca de Autores Españoles, xxxv (Madrid, 1855), pp. 429b, 441a.
7 José María de Cossío and Tomás Maza Solano, *Romancero popular de la Montaña*, 2 vols. (Santander, 1933-4).
8 See Dámaso Alonso, *La poesía de San Juan de la Cruz* (Madrid, 1942); *Poesía española* (Madrid, 1950), pp. 228-82.
9 *The poetry of meditation*, pp. 184-93, 259-73.

10 Many of these poems may be read in the *Romancero y cancionero sagrados*.
11 Sir John Grierson, *Metaphysical lyrics and poems of the seventeenth century* (Oxford, 1921), p. 181.
12 *Ibid*. p. 103.
13 See the excellent study by Adolfo Méndez Plancarte in the introduction to the second volume of the *Obras completas* of Sor Juana Inés de la Cruz (Mexico, 1952), pp. xi–lxxi.
14 E. M. Wilson, 'Félix Persio Bertiso's *La harpa de Belén*', *Atlante*, II (1954), 126–36.
15 Rosemond Tuve, *A reading of George Herbert* (London, 1952).
16 *Documentos inéditos para la historia de España. Correspondencia oficial de don Diego Sarmiento de Acuña, Conde de Gondomar* (Madrid, 1945), vol. IV, p. 4. 'Despacho... al Rey nuestro señor en 17 de marzo 1614.'
17 Fray Luis de León, *The original poems*, ed. E. Sarmiento (Manchester, 1953), p. 87.
18 John Donne, *Ignatius his conclaue* (London, 1611), p. 39.
19 *The poetry of meditation*, especially pp. 221–48.
20 John Donne, *The divine poems*, ed. Helen Gardner (Oxford, 1952), pp. xl–lv.
21 Text reprinted from J. W. Hebel and H. H. Hudson, *Poetry of the English Renaissance* (New York, 1932), p. 441.
22 San Ignacio de Loyola, *Obras completas* (Biblioteca de Autores Cristianos) (Madrid, 1952), p. 179.
23 *The divine poems*, ed. Gardner, pp. 11, 7.
24 Lope de Vega, *Rimas sacras* (Madrid, 1614). Modern text in *Oxford book of Spanish verse*, chosen by J. Fitzmaurice-Kelly; 2nd edn by J. B. Trend (Oxford, 1940).

INDEX OF NAMES AND TITLES OF WORKS

'Names' here refers almost entirely to authors and editors. The names of editors have not been included where this would involve needless duplication of entries under authors, or where the identity of the editor is not important. The names of literary characters have also been omitted, and references to such characters must be sought *via* the titles of the works in which they appear. References to ballads and other poems of unknown authorship are by first line, under the main heading 'Anonymous'; where variant versions of a ballad exist, I have tried to choose the version Wilson seems to be referring to. References to books of the Bible are under the main heading 'Bible'. [DWC]

Abel, Lionel, *Metatheatre: a new view of dramatic form*, 47
Alemán, Mateo, 264 n. 5
Alexander, Peter, 267 n. 52
    ed., Shakespeare, *Complete works*, 265 n. 21
    Shakespeare primer, 264 n. 11
Alonso, Dámaso
    La poesía de San Juan de la Cruz, 268 n. 8
    Poesía española, ensayo de métodos y limites estilísticos, 258 n. 8, 268 n. 8
Alonso, Dámaso *and* Bousoño, Carlos, *Seis calas en la expresión literaria española*, 122, 259 n. 11
Alonso de Soria, Fray, *Historia y milicia cristiana del caballero peregrino, conquistador del cielo*, 238
Ambrose, St, 107, 108, 109
    Precatio praeparans ad missam, 110, 258 n. 9
Andrewes, Lancelot, 242
Anonymous
    'A cazar iba don Pedro', 229, 230, 231, 232
    'Aquel pastorcico, madre', 237

'Asentado está Gaiferos', 227
'As it befell upon one time', 231
'Clark Sanders and May Margret', 222–3
'De Mérida sale el palmero', 227
'Después que el rey don Rodrigo', 226, 230, 231, 232
'En el valle a Ynés', 263 n. 4
'En los campos de Alventosa', 229, 232
'En París está doña Alda', 190, 230, 231, 232
'En sancta Gadea de Burgos', 139–41, 260 n. 9
'Estábase el conde Dirlos', 227
'God send the land deliverance', 226-7
'¡Guarte, guarte, rey don Sancho!', 141, 228, 230, 231, 232
'Las huestes del rey don Rodrigo', 224, 226, 230, 231, 232
'Mala la hubiste, franceses', 229
'Medianoche era por filo', 199, 227
'Moriana en un castillo', 230-1, 232
'Pártese el moro Alicante', 229
'Puesto ya el pie en el estribo', 190, 263 n. 4

Anonymous – *contd.*
  'Que por mayo era, por mayo', 229
  '¿Quién os ha mal enojado?', 237
  'Sin mí, sin vos y sin Dios', 165, 169, 262 n. 6
  'Sum speiks of lords, sum speiks of lairds', 223
  'Válasme, nuestra señora', 227
  'Yet if his majesty, our sovereign lord', 245-7
  'Yo me estaba allí en Coimbra', 228-9, 230, 232
Antonio de Jesús María, Fray, *Don Baltasar de Moscoso y Sandoval*, 106
Arabian nights, 28
Aranda y Mazuelo, Francisco de, 106
Argensola, Lupercio Leonardo de, *Isabela*, 12
Argensola, Lupercio Leonardo de *or* Bartolomé Leonardo de, 'Yo os quiero confesar, don Juan, primero', 126, 157, 259 n. 15, 262 n. 3
Aristotle, *Poetics*, 27, 29, 191, 230, 231, 263 n. 5
Astrana Marín, Luis, ed. of Calderón, 254 n. 1, 258 nn. 10 and 16
Atkinson, W. C.
  contrib., *A handbook to the study and teaching of Spanish*, 91, 256 n. 3
  'Studies in literary decadence', 91, 256 n. 4
Aubrun, C. V. *and* Montesinos, J. F., eds., Lope de Vega, *Peribáñez*, 130, 134, 135, 136, 142, 146, 260-1 *passim*
Ayala, Lorenzo de, 262 n. 2, 263 n. 17
Ayres, Thomas, 242

Bances Candamo, Francisco Antonio de, 90
  loa for *El gran teatro del mundo*, 3, 250 n. 4
  Theatro de los theatros de los passados y presentes siglos, 65, 80
Bandello, M., *Il marchese Niccolò terzo da Este*, 262 n. 2, 263 n. 17
Barach, 107, 109

Baret, E., *Œuvres dramatiques de Lope de Vega*, 262 n. 5
Barrios, Miguel de, 119
Baxter, Richard, 245
Beaumont, Francis *and* Fletcher, John, *The coxcomb*, 264 n. 12
Belleforest, François de *and* Boisteau, Pierre, *Premier et second thome des histoires tragiques*, 262 n. 2, 263 n. 17
Bertiso, Félix Persio, *La harpa de Belén*, 242, 269 n. 14
Bible, 107, 247
  Genesis, 1
  Isaiah, 108
  Jeremiah, 253 n. 13
  John, 113
  1 Kings, 107, 109, 113, 258 n. 13
  Nahum, 248
  Psalm 22, 248
  Psalm 131 (Vulgate), 258 n. 11
  Psalm 137, 20
  Psalm 141, 109
  2 Samuel, 172
Blecua, J. M., ed., Lope de Vega, *El caballero de Olmedo*, 184-5, 191-2, 263 n. 3
Bocángel y Unzueta, Gabriel, 118
Boethius, Anicius Manlius Severinus, *De consolatione philosophie*, 231, 268 n. 29
Boisteau, Pierre, *see* Belleforest, François de *and* Boisteau, Pierre
Boscán de Almogáver, Juan, 118
  'Respuesta de Boscán a don Diego de Mendoça', 255 n. 4
Bousoño, Carlos, 105
  see also Alonso, Dámaso *and* Bousoño, Carlos
Bouterwek, F., *History of Spanish and Portuguese literature*, 90, 256 n. 1
Bunyan, John, 222
Butler, Joseph, *Preface to the sermons*, 253 n. 12

Calderón de la Barca, Pedro, 1-129 *passim*, 154, 196, 204, 205
  Afectos de odio y amor, 7

Index of names and titles of works

'Agora, Señor, agora', 117
El alcaide de sí mismo, 6
El alcalde de Zalamea, 27, 50, 90, 114, 258 n. 16
Antes que todo es mi dama, 99, 101, 103, 257 nn. 12 and 18
Apolo y Climene, 120
A San Isidro, 6
A secreto agravio secreta venganza, 48–64 *passim*, 65, 71, 202, 264 n. 10
El astrólogo fingido, 103, 126, 257 n. 18, 259 n. 17
La aurora en Copacabana, 8
Bien vengas mal, si vienes solo, 100
Cada uno para sí, 98, 103, 257 n. 18
Casa con dos puertas mala es de guardar, 100, 103, 127, 257 n. 18, 259 n. 17
El castillo de Lindabridis, 8, 10
Celos aun del aire matan, 7
La cena de Baltasar, 32, 33, 124, 256 n. 7
La cisma de Ingalaterra, 118
Con quien vengo, vengo, 6, 93, 97–8, 103, 257 n. 18
¿Cuál es mayor perfección?, 92, 94, 101, 126, 259 n. 17
La dama duende, 90, 92, 97, 100, 103, 104, 126, 257 n. 18, 259 n. 17
Dar tiempo al tiempo, 100, 102, 103, 127, 216, 257 n. 18, 259 n. 17
Décimas a la muerte, 117, 128
Décimas a la muerte de Montalbán, 117
Décimas a una dama que desdeñaba y quería, 116, 124
La desdicha de la voz, 101, 103, 257 n. 18
De una causa dos efectos, 126, 259 n. 17
Los dos amantes del cielo, 4
Elegía en la muerte del señor Infante don Carlos, 117
Los empeños de un acaso, 93, 98, 99, 103, 126, 257 n. 18, 259 n. 17
En esta vida todo es verdad y todo mentira, 126, 259 n. 17

El escondido y la tapada, 126, 259 n. 17
'Estas que fueron pompa y alegría', 22, 117
La estatua de Prometeo, 119–20
Fuego de Dios en el querer bien, 94
El galán fantasma, 126, 259 n. 17
El gran teatro del mundo, 250 n. 4
Guárdate del agua mansa, 92, 94, 127, 259 n. 17
La hija del aire I, 4, 5–6
El hijo del sol, 10
La inmunidad del sagrado, 2
El jardín de Falerina (auto), 2
Lances de amor y fortuna, 8
Luis Pérez el gallego, 5, 9
El maestro de danzar, 100, 103, 126, 257 n. 18, 259 n. 17
El mágico prodigioso, 4, 6, 117, 121–2, 124, 125–6
Mañanas de abril y mayo, 94
Mañana será otro día, 98, 100–1, 102, 103, 127, 257 nn. 12 and 18, 259 n. 17
El mayor encanto amor, 6, 9, 250 n. 10
El mayor monstruo los celos, 118
El médico de su honra, 50, 65, 80, 118, 202, 218, 255 n. 10, 264 n. 8, 266 n. 36
Mejor está que estaba, 119, 127, 259 n. 17
Nadie fíe su secreto, 127, 259 n. 17
La niña de Gómez Arias, 5
'No Fatal te construye Mauseolo', 120, 259 n. 7
No hay burlas con el amor, 91, 94, 95, 102, 103, 104, 257 n. 18
No hay cosa como callar, 93, 103, 104, 127, 257 n. 18, 259 n. 17
No hay más fortuna que Dios, 33, 262 n. 13
No siempre lo peor es cierto, 93, 96, 102, 103, 104, 127, 257 n. 18, 259 n. 17
'Oh tú, antorcha, que en ese breve', 128–9
Las órdenes militares, 4

Calderón de la Barca, Pedro, – *contd.*
  Origen, pérdida y restauración de la Virgen del Sagrario, 111, 258 n. 10
  Peor está que estaba, 103, 119, 126, 127, 257 n. 18, 259 n. 17
  El pintor de su deshonra, 65–89 *passim*, 118–19, 202, 254 n. 2, 264 nn. 8 and 10
  Poesías inéditas, 105, 258 n. 1
  El postrer duelo de España, 96–7
  El príncipe constante, 15–26 *passim*, 117, 124, 127
  Psalle et sile, 105–15 *passim*, 117
  La puente de Mantible, 9
  Romance probando ser mejor mudable que firme, 116
  Saber del mal y del bien, 127, 259 nn. 16 and 17
  La segunda esposa y triunfar muriendo, 128–9
  La selva confusa, 5, 7, 250 n. 8
  La sibila del oriente, 8–9
  También hay duelo en las damas, 99–100, 101–2
  Una dama da satisfacciones a tres galanes a un tiempo, 116
  El viático cordero, 250 n. 10
  La vida es sueño (auto), 2, 29, 31, 252 n. 8, 253 n. 10, 253–4 n. 16
  La vida es sueño (comedia), 25, 27–47 *passim*, 90, 91, 116, 121, 122–3, 124, 125, 127, 260 n. 3
Calderón de la Barca, Pedro, Mira de Amescua, Antonio *and* Pérez de Montalván, Juan, *Polifemo y Circe*, 9
Calderón de la Barca, Pedro, Pérez de Montalván, Juan *and* Coello, Antonio, *El privilegio de las mujeres*, 3, 9, 250 n. 5
Calderón de la Barca, Pedro, Vélez de Guevara, Luis *and* Cáncer de Velasco, Jerónimo, *Enfermar con el remedio*, 126, 259 n. 17
Calderón de la Barca, Pedro José, 128
Camoens, Luis de, *Babel e Sião*, 119
Campbell, Lily B., *Shakespeare's tragic heroes: slaves of passion*, 203–4, 211, 265 nn. 19 and 20, 266 nn. 33, 37 and 44
Cáncer de Velasco, Jerónimo, *see* Calderón de la Barca, Pedro, Vélez de Guevara, Luis *and* Cáncer de Velasco, Jerónimo
Cárdenas, Fray Miguel de, *Sermon en las honras del reverendissimo padre maestro fray Nicolas Baptista*, 116–17, 258 n. 3
Carew, Thomas, 'And here the precious dust is layd', 240
Castillo Solórzano, Alonso de, *La garduña de Sevilla*, 255 n. 8
Castro, Américo, 'Algunas observaciones acerca del concepto del honor en los siglos XVI y XVII', 264 nn. 1, 3 and 6, 265 nn. 14 and 30
Cervantes Saavedra, Miguel de, 154
  Los baños de Argel, 18, 251 n. 2
  El celoso extremeño, 198
  El curioso impertinente, 203, 264 n. 12
  Don Quijote de la Mancha, 28, 203, 220, 221, 222, 224, 262 n. 9, 264 n. 13, 267 n. 6
  Los trabajos de Persiles y Sigismunda, 190
Chapman, George (attrib.), *The second maiden's tragedy*, 264 n. 12
Charles I, of England, *see* Gauden, John; *and* Juxon, William
Chaucer, Geoffrey
  The Monk's tale, 268 n. 29
  trans. of Boethius, *De consolatione philosophie*, 231, 268 n. 29
Chaytor, H. J., *Dramatic theory in Spain*, 260 n. 4, 264 n. 2
Child, F. J., *The English and Scottish popular ballads*, 267 nn. 7, 8 and 15, 268 n. 27
Chrysostom, St John, 107, 108
  In sanctum evangelium secundum Matthaeum commentarii, 109, 258 n. 7
Coello, Antonio, *see* Calderón de la Barca, Pedro, Pérez de Montalván, Juan *and* Coello, Antonio

Coleridge, S. T., *Biographia literaria*, 260 n. 2
El condenado de amor, 3, 250 n. 3
Córdoba, Sebastián de, *Las obras de Boscán y Garcilaso trasladadas en materias cristianas y religiosas*, 238
Corral, Pedro del, *Crónica sarracina*, 225, 232
Cossío, J. M. de, 'El mote "Sin mí, sin vos y sin Dios", glosado por Lope de Vega', 262 n. 6
Cossío, J. M. de *and* Maza Solano, T., *Romancero popular de la Montaña*, 268 n. 7
Cotarelo y Mori, E., *Ensayo sobre la vida y obras de D. Pedro Calderón de la Barca*, 257 n. 1
Crashaw, Richard, 236, 242, 243, 245
Crow, John, 265 n. 28, 267 n. 52
Cruickshank, D. W., *see* Wilson, Edward M. *and* Cruickshank, D. W.
Cubillo de Aragón, Álvaro, 119

David, King, 107, 109, 172
Deborah, 107, 109
Diego, Gerardo, *Antología poética en honor de Góngora*, 14, 120–1, 251 n. 33, 259 n. 8
Diego de Estella, Fray, 245, 264 n. 5
Libro de la vanidad del mundo, 237
Donne, John, 221, 239, 243, 244
Anniversaries, 244
Holy sonnets, 244, 247, 249
Ignatius his conclaue, 244, 269 n. 18
Songs and sonnets, 247
Drummond, William, 242
Dunn, P. N., '*El príncipe constante*: a theatre of the world', 26
Dyer, Sir Edward, 239

Empson, William
Some versions of pastoral, 232, 268 n. 30
The structure of complex words, 264 n. 11, 265 nn. 23 and 31, 266 nn. 37 and 41

Entrambasaguas, J. de, ed., Calderón, *Psalle et sile*, 105, 257 nn. 2 and 3, 258 n. 3
Entwistle, W. J.
The adventure of Spanish, 220, 267 n. 3
European balladry, 220, 226, 267 nn. 1 and 13
review, edn of Lope de Vega, *Peribáñez*, 261 n. 20
Entwistle, W. J. *and* Wilson, Edward M., 'Calderón's *Príncipe constante*: two appreciations', 17, 24, 25–6, 251 nn. 1 and 4
Epictetus, *The enchiridion*, 36, 253 n. 14
Ercilla y Zúñiga, Alonso de, *La Araucana*, 18, 251 n. 3
Escrivá, el comendador Joan, 'Ven, muerte, tan escondida', 118

Fanshawe, Richard, 242
Farinelli, Arturo, *La vita è un sogno*, 29–30, 31, 35, 252–3 *passim*, 257 n. 9
Fernández de Azevedo, Antonio, 106
Fernández de Ixar, Juan, Cancionero de, 268 n. 28
Fernández de Moratín, Nicolás, *Desengaño al theatro español*, 121, 259 n. 9
Ferrar, John *and* Jebb, Dr, *Nicholas Ferrar: two lives*, 236, 268 n. 5
Ferrar, Nicholas, 236, 248
Fichter, W. L., ed., Lope de Vega, *El castigo del discreto*, 264 n. 1
Field, Nathaniel, *Amends for ladies*, 264 n. 12
Fitzmaurice-Kelly, J., ed., *Oxford book of Spanish verse*, 262 n. 3, 269 n. 24
Flatter, R., *The Moor of Venice*, 203, 265 nn. 17, 26 and 29, 266 n. 50
Fletcher, John, *see* Beaumont, Francis *and* Fletcher, John
Foulché-Delbosc, R., ed., Góngora, *Obras poéticas*, 250–1 *passim*, 258 n. 8

Frenk Alatorre, Margit, 'Refranes cantados y cantares proverbializados', 119, 259 n. 6
Frutos Cortés, E., 264 n. 9

Gallardo, B. J., *Ensayo de una biblioteca española de libros raros y curiosos*, 256 n. 6
García Suelto, M. B., ed., *Comedias escogidas de Calderón*, 94–5, 257 n. 10
García Valdecasas, A., *El hidalgo y el honor*, 262 nn. 4 and 10, 263 nn. 16, 18 and 19, 264 n. 1, 265 n. 18
Garcilaso de la Vega, 236, 238, 248
Gardner, Helen, ed., Donne, *The divine poems*, 244, 269 nn. 20 and 23
Gauden, John, *Eikon Basilike*, 239
Gayton, Edmond, *Pleasant notes on Don Quixot*, 203, 264 n. 13
Gérard, A. S., 'Baroque unity and the dualities of *El caballero de Olmedo*', 263 n. 2
Gerould, G. H., *The ballad of tradition*, 232–3, 268 n. 31
Gombrich, E. H., *Art and illusion*, 124, 259 n. 13
Gondomar, Don Diego Sarmiento de Acuña, Count of, *see* Sarmiento de Acuña
Góngora y Argote, Luis de, 111, 116, 118, 120, 242
  Las firmezas de Isabela, 110, 120, 258 n. 8
  'Ni en este monte, este aire, ni este rio', 3
  'No son todos ruiseñores', 11
  'Pallida restituie a su elemento', 11
  Panegírico al duque de Lerma, 11, 12, 13, 250 nn. 12 and 17, 251 n. 26
  El Polifemo, 12, 120, 251 n. 19
  Soledad primera, 7, 12, 13, 14, 113, 120, 250–1 *passim*, 258 n. 14
  Soledad segunda, 12, 13, 120, 250–1 *passim*
  'Tres víòlas del cielo', 12

Gracián y Morales, Baltasar, 154
  El discreto, 216
Granville-Barker, H., *Prefaces to Shakespeare*, 265 n. 29
Graves, Robert, *The English ballad: a short critical survey*, 230, 268 n. 23
Grierson, Sir John, *Metaphysical lyrics and poems of the seventeenth century*, 269 nn. 11 and 12
Guerra y Ribera, Fray Manuel de, 90

Hart, H. C., 206
Hartzenbusch, J. E., 90
  Los amantes de Teruel, 198
  ed. of Calderón, 105, 106, 254 n. 1, 257 n. 10, 258 n. 1
Hasell, E. J., *Calderon*, 91–2, 256 n. 5
Hebel, J. W. *and* Hudson, H. H., *Poetry of the English Renaissance*, 269 n. 21
Herbert, George, 236, 239, 242, 243, 245, 247
  Redemption, 240–1
  The sacrifice, 242
Hernández de Villalumbrales, Pedro, *Libro intitulado peregrinación de la vida del hombre puesto en batalla debaxo de los trabajos que sufrió el caballero del sol*, 238
Herrero García, M., *Ideas de los españoles del siglo XVII*, 254 n. 3
Herrero Salgado, F., *Aportación bibliográfica a la oratoria sagrada española*, 115
Heywood, Thomas, *A woman killed with kindness*, 203
Hojeda, Diego de, *La Christiada*, 243
Housman, J. E., *British popular ballads*, 231, 268 n. 26
Hudson, H. H., *see* Hebel, J. W. *and* Hudson, H. H.
Hurtado de Mendoza, Antonio, 118, 119
  Querer por solo querer, 11, 13, 251 n. 27

Ibáñez de Mendoza, Joseph Félix, 106
Isidore of Seville, St, 107

Originum seu etymologiarum libri XX, 109

Jebb, Dr, *see* Ferrar, John *and* Jebb, Dr
John of the Cross, St, 238
Jones, R. O., ed., *Studies in Spanish literature of the Golden Age presented to Edward M. Wilson*, 26
Juana Inés de la Cruz, Sor
Obras completas, 269 n. 13
Sueño, 114
Juan de la Cruz, San, 238
Juxon, William, *Praiers used by his Majestie in the time of his sufferings*, 238–9

Ken, Thomas, 243, 245
Knowles, E. B., 'Thomas Shelton, translator of *Don Quixote*', 267 n. 6
Knox, John
Comfortable epistle to Christ's afflicted Church, 234–5, 239, 244, 246
Works, 235, 268 nn. 1 and 2

Ladborough, R. W., 268 n. 1
Laguna, Fray José, 115
Lasso de la Vega, A., *Calderón de la Barca*, 100, 102, 257 nn. 13 and 14
Lazarillo de Tormes, 222
Ledesma, Alonso de, *Conceptos espirituales*, 239–40, 241, 243
Liñán de Riaza, Pedro, 118
Lista, Alberto, 262 n. 12
Lockhart, J. G., *Ancient Spanish ballads historical and romantic*, 224–5, 227, 267 n. 11
López Aguirre, Manuel, 106
López de Mendoza, Íñigo, Marquis of Santillana, 231
Losa, Andrés de la, *El caballero de la clara estrella o batalla y triunfo del hombre contra los vicios*, 238
Loyola, St Ignatius, 240
Ejercicios espirituales, 113, 117, 243–6
Obras completas, 269 n. 22
Lozano, Cristóbal, *Los Reyes nuevos de Toledo*, 111, 258 n. 10

Luis de Granada, Fray, 237, 245, 264 n. 5, 265 n. 15
Luis de León, Fray, 237
En la Ascensión, 243, 258 n. 12
Luzán y Claramunt, Ignacio, 90
Poética, 27

Macaulay, Thomas Babington, first Baron, 224
Malón de Chaide, Fray Pedro, 236, 248
La conversión de la Magdalena, 236, 237, 268 n. 4
Manrique, Jorge, *Coplas por la muerte de su padre*, 128
Marañón, Gregorio, *El Conde-Duque de Olivares*, 123, 259 n. 12
Marlowe, Christopher, *Tamburlaine the great*, 178
Martínez de Toledo, Alfonso, Archpriest of Talavera, 111
Martz, Louis L., *The poetry of meditation*, 239, 244, 244–5, 258 n. 12, 268 nn. 1 and 9, 269 n. 19
Massinger, Philip, *The parliament of love*, 202–3
Maza Solano, T., *see* Cossío, J. M. de *and* Maza Solano, T.
El médico de su honra ('Lope de Vega'), 266 n. 36
Melo, Francisco Manuel de, *Carta de guía de casados*, 49, 255 n. 5
Méndez Plancarte, Adolfo, ed., Sor Juana Inés de la Cruz, *Obras completas*, 269 n. 13
Mendoza, Antonio de, Viceroy, 102–3, 216
Menéndez Pidal, Ramón
Del honor en nuestro teatro clásico', 205, 264 n. 1, 265 n. 25
ed., *Cancionero de romances*, 260 n. 9, 264 n. 10, 267 n. 18, 268 nn. 21, 22 and 25
ed., *Romancero tradicional*, 220, 221, 225, 267 nn. 2, 12 and 14
Flor nueva de romances viejos, 267 n. 16, 268 nn. 19 and 24
El romancero hispánico, 267 nn. 9 and 13

Menéndez y Pelayo, Marcelino, 90, 97
  Calderón y su teatro, 28–9, 31, 38,
    46, 90–1, 92, 252 nn. 3–7, 256
    nn. 2 and 7, 264 n. 9
  ed., Lope de Vega, *Comedias*, 260
    nn. 7 and 8
  *Estudios sobre el teatro de Lope de
    Vega*, 184, 263 n. 1
Merriman, R. B., *The rise of the Spanish
  empire*, 102–3, 257 n. 15, 266 n. 48
Middleton, Thomas, *The witch*, 203
Milton, John, 239
  Paradise lost, 61, 255 n. 9
Mira de Amescua, Antonio, *see* Calderón
  de la Barca, Pedro, Mira de
  Amescua, Antonio *and* Pérez de
  Montalván, Juan
Moir, D. W., *see* Wilson, Edward M.
  and Moir, D. W.
Molina, Tirso de, *see* Téllez, Fray
  Gabriel
Montemayor, Jorge de, 248
  'Ven, muerte, tan escondida', 118
Montesino, Fray Ambrosio de,
  Cancionero, 268 n. 6
Montesinos, J. F., 262 n. 1
  Estudios sobre Lope, 261 n. 10
  review, Van Dam edn of Lope de
    Vega, *El castigo sin venganza*, 262–
    3 n. 16
  Romancerillos tardíos, 256 n. 6
  see also Aubrun, C. V. *and*
    Montesinos, J. F.
Montoliú, Manuel de, ed., Calderón,
  Obra lírica, 128, 258 n. 1
Moscoso y Sandoval, Cardinal Baltasar
  de, 106, 111

Nashe, Thomas, 222
Nieremberg y Ottin, Fray Juan Eusebio,
  264 n. 5

Olmedo, F. G., *Las fuentes de 'La vida
  es sueño'*, 30–1, 253 n. 10
Ovid, *Metamorphoses*, 1, 3, 199

Parets, Miguel, 'De los muchos sucesos
  dignos de memoria que han
  ocurrido en Barcelona y otros
  lugares de Cataluña', 255 n. 3
Parker, A. A., 47, 88, 258 n. 11, 259
  n. 20, 268 n. 1
  *The approach to the Spanish drama of
    the Golden Age*, 255 n. 2
  'The father–son conflict in the drama
    of Calderón', 47
  'The meaning of "discreción" in *No
    hay más fortuna que Dios*', 262
    n. 13
  'Towards a definition of Calderonian
    tragedy', 88
Paterson, A. K. G.
  'Juan Roca's northern ancestry: a
    study of art theory in Calderón's *El
    pintor de su deshonra*', 88–9
  'The comic and tragic melancholy of
    Juan Roca: a study of Calderón's
    El pintor de su deshonra', 88
  'The traffic of the stage in Calderón's
    La vida es sueño', 47
Peers, E. A., *A handbook to the study
  and teaching of Spanish*, 256 n. 3
Pepys, Samuel, 242
Pérez de Montalván, Juan, 242
  see also Calderón de la Barca, Pedro,
    Mira de Amescua, Antonio *and*
    Pérez de Montalván, Juan; *and also*
    Calderón de la Barca, Pedro, Pérez
    de Montalván, Juan *and* Coello,
    Antonio
Pérez Gómez, Antonio, 115
  ed., Rojas, *La tragicomedia de
    Calisto y Melibea (La Celestina)*,
    264 n. 7
  ed., *Romancero del Rey Don Pedro*,
    267 n. 17
Pérez Pastor, C., *Documentos para la
  biografía de D. Pedro Calderón de
  la Barca*, 128, 259 n. 18
Petrarca, Francesco, 249
Philip II, of Spain, 102, 216
Picatoste, Felipe
  Calderón ante la ciencia, 2, 4, 250
    nn. 1 and 6
  ed., Calderón, *Poesías inéditas*, 105,
    258 n. 1

Index of names and titles of works 279

Pinheiro da Veiga, Tomé, *Fastiginia o fastos geniales*, 49, 255 n. 6
Poema de mio Cid, 225
Poesse, W., ed., *Homage to John M. Hill*, 258 n. 2
Pope, Alexander, *Pastorals*, 5, 250 n. 7
Pring-Mill, R.
  'Los calderonistas de habla inglesa y *La vida es sueño*', 47
  introduction to Lope de Vega, *Five plays*, 263 n. 2

Quevedo y Villegas, Francisco Gómez de, 128, 221, 242, 264 n. 5
  El buscón, 262

Reichenberger, A. G., 'Calderón's *El príncipe constante*, a tragedy?', 26
Rico, F., *El pequeño mundo del hombre: varia fortuna de una idea en las letras españolas*, 259 n. 10
Ríos, Blanca de los, '*La vida es sueño* y los diez Segismundos de Calderón', 31, 253 n. 10
Rivas, Duque de, *Don Álvaro, o la fuerza del sino*, 184
Rodríguez Marín, Francisco
  Más de 21.000 refranes castellanos, 222, 267 n. 5
  12.600 refranes más, 222, 267 n. 5
Rodríguez-Moñino, Antonio, 114
  ed., *Flor de romances y glosas, canciones y villancicos*, 263 n. 4
  ed., *Silva de varios romances*, 268
Rojas, Fernando de, *La tragicomedia de Calisto y Melibea (La Celestina)*, 188, 191-2, 198, 200, 222, 264 n. 7
Rosenbach, A. S. N., '*The curious impertinent* in English dramatic literature', 264 n. 12
Rousseau, J.-J., 154
Rubió y Lluch, A., 97
  El sentimiento del honor en el teatro de Calderón, 125, 127, 259 n. 14, 264 n. 1, 265 n. 27
Rufo y Gutiérrez, J., *Romance de los comendadores*, 76, 256 n. 5

Ruiz de Alarcón y Mendoza, Juan, 119
  La verdad sospechosa, 176
Sage, Jack
  'Calderón y la música teatral', 258 n. 7
  see also Wilson, Edward M. *and* Sage, Jack
Salas Barbadillo, Alonso Jerónimo de, *La peregrinación sabia, El sagaz Estacio*, 198, 264 n. 8
Salinas, Count of, 118
Sancha, Justo de, ed., *Romancero y cancionero sagrados*, 268 n. 6, 269 n. 10
Sancroft, William, Archbishop, 243, 244, 245
Sannazaro, Jacopo, 248
Santayana, George, 127
Santillana, Marquis of, 231
Sarmiento, Edward, ed., Luis de León, *The original poems*, 243-4, 258 n. 12, 269 n. 17
Sarmiento de Acuña, Diego, Count of Gondomar, 265 n. 15
  Correspondencia oficial, 243, 269 n. 16
Scaligero, Giulio Cesare, 247
Schack, Adolf Friedrich von, 90, 184
Schmidt, F. W. V., *Die Schauspiele Calderóns dargestellt und erläutert*, 251 n. 6
Seneca, 108
Shakespeare, William, 223
  Antony and Cleopatra, 264 n. 11
  Coriolanus, 264 n. 11
  Hamlet, 92, 256 n. 5, 264 n. 11
  1 Henry IV, 209, 212, 265 n. 32
  Macbeth, 203, 262 n. 12, 264 n. 11
  The merchant of Venice, 207
  Othello, 201-19 *passim*
  The taming of the shrew, 28
  The winter's tale, 202, 266 nn. 34 and 35
Shelton, Thomas, 267 n. 6
Sidney, Sir Philip, 239
  Arcadia, 239
Los siete infantes de Lara, 225, 232
Silva y Mendoza, Diego de, Count of Salinas, 118

Silverman, J., 'Peribáñez y Vellido
  Dolfos', 141, 261 n. 11
Silvestre, Gregorio, 118
Simón Díaz, José, 'Textos dispersos de
  clásicos españoles: II. Calderón de
  la Barca', 258 n. 1
Smith, James, 47
Socrates, 108
Sosa, Juan Bautista de, *Sossia perseguida*,
  120, 259 n. 7
Southwell, Robert, 239
Spencer, T., *Shakespeare and the nature
  of man*, 205, 212, 265 n. 24, 266
  nn. 39, 44 and 47
Spitzer, Leo, 'The figure of Fénix in
  Calderón's *El príncipe constante*',
  26
Stanley, Thomas, 242
Sykes, Norman, 268 n. 1

Talavera, Archpriest of, 111
Tassis Peralta, Juan de, *see* Villamediana,
  Count of
Taylor, Jeremy, 242
Telfer, James, 227
Téllez, Fray Gabriel, 90, 130, 196
  El amor médico, 49, 254 n. 3, 254–5
  n. 4
  Averígüelo Vargas, 254 n. 3
  El burlador de Sevilla, 29, 176
  El vergonzoso en palacio, 184
Theresa, St, 236
Thomas, L.-P., 'La genèse de la
  philosophie et le symbolisme dans
  La vie est un songe', 31, 253–4
  n. 16
Thomas à Kempis, *The imitation of
  Christ*, 103, 257 nn. 16 and 17
Tirso de Molina, *see* Téllez, Fray Gabriel
Tofte, Robert, *The blazon of jealousie*,
  203, 265 n. 20
El Toledano, 107
Trend, J. B., ed., *Oxford book of
  Spanish verse*, 262 n. 3, 269 n. 24
Trénor Palavicino, Leopoldo, ed.,
  Calderón, *Psalle et sile*, 105, 257
  nn. 1 and 2, 258 nn. 4 and 6
Truman, R. W., 'The theme of justice
  in Calderón's *El príncipe constante*',
  26
Turnbull, W. R., *Othello: a critical
  study*, 203, 265 n. 16, 266 n. 44,
  266–7 n. 51
Tuve, Rosemond, *A reading of George
  Herbert*, 242, 269 n. 15

Valbuena Briones, Ángel, ed. of
  Calderón, 254 n. 1, 256–7 n. 8, 257
  n. 11
Valbuena Prat, Ángel, 27, 90, 128,
  264 n. 9
  *Calderón, su personalidad, su arte
  dramático, su estilo y sus obras*, 256
  n. 6
  Historia de la literatura española, 31,
  253 n. 10
Valdivielso, José de, 238, 241, 247
  *Vida, excelencias y muerte del glorioso
  patriarca San José*, 243
Valtanas, Fray Domingo de, *Doctrina
  christiana*, 235–6, 239, 246, 268
  n. 3
Van Dam, C. F. A., ed., Lope de Vega,
  El castigo sin venganza, 166, 173,
  261 n. 1, 262–3 *passim*
Varchi, Benedetto, 203, 265 n. 20
Varey, J. E., ed., *Critical studies of
  Calderón's 'comedias'*, 26
Vega Carpio, Lope Félix de, 90, 91, 111,
  118, 123, 130–200 *passim*, 204,
  238, 239, 241, 242
  *Arte nuevo de hacer comedias en este
  tiempo*, 130–1, 201, 260 n. 4, 264
  n. 2, 266 n. 49
  El caballero de Olmedo, 131, 176,
  184–200 *passim*
  El castigo sin venganza, 155–84
  passim, 264 n. 7
  Los comendadores de Córdoba, 265
  n. 14, 266 n. 36
  La dama boba, 184
  La Dorotea, 197
  Fuenteovejuna, 50, 260 n. 6
  'Hortelano era Belardo', 256 n. 10
  (attrib.) *El médico de su honra*, 266
  n. 36

'Pastor, que con tus siluos amorosos', 247–8
Los pastores de Belén, 238
Peribáñez, 50, 130–54 *passim*, 169
El remedio en la desdicha, 251 n. 2
Rimas sacras, 243, 247, 269 n. 24
Vélez de Guevara, Luis, 130
Auto del nacimiento, 9–10, 250 n. 11
'Escollo armado de hiedra', 78–9, 83, 118–19, 256 n. 6
see also Calderón de la Barca, Pedro, Vélez de Guevara, Luis *and* Cáncer de Velasco, Jerónimo
Villamediana, Count of, 118
La gloria de Niquea, 11, 12, 13, 250 n. 18, 251 n. 32
Vossler, K., *Lope de Vega y su tiempo*, 262 n. 16

Wardropper, B. W.
'Christian and Moor in Calderón's *El príncipe constante*', 26
ed., *Critical essays on the theatre of Calderón*, 26, 47, 88
'The unconscious mind in Calderón's *El pintor de su deshonra*', 88
Watson, A. I., '*El pintor de su deshonra* and the neo-Aristotelian theory of tragedy'. 88
Webster, John, *The Duchess of Malfi*, 202
Whitby, W. M., 'Calderón's *El príncipe constante*: Fénix's role in the ransom of Fernando's body', 26
Wilson, Edward M.

bibliographical note on *Psalle et sile*, 115
'Calderón and the *Décimas a la muerte*', 258 n. 4
'Félix Persio Bertiso's *La harpa de Belén*', 242, 269 n. 14
'Some unpublished works by Don Pedro Calderón de la Barca', 258 n. 2
'Un romance ascético de Calderón: "Agora, Señor, agora..."', 258–9 n. 4
Wilson, Edward M. *and* Cruickshank, D. W., 'Adiciones a la bibliografía de *Psalle et sil*e', 115
Wilson, Edward M. *and* Entwistle, W. J. see Entwistle, W. J. *and* Wilson, Edward M.
Wilson, Edward M. *and* Moir, D. W., *The Golden Age: drama 1492–1700*, 263 n. 2
Wilson, Edward M. *and* Sage, Jack, *Poesías líricas en las obras dramáticas de Calderón*, 118, 120, 256 n. 6, 259 nn. 5 and 16
Wilson, John Dover, 206
Wilson, Margaret, *Spanish drama of the Golden Age*, 263 n. 2
Wordsworth, W., *The poetical works*, 133, 260 n. 5
Wright, E. M., *Rustic speech and folklore*, 267 n. 4

Zamora Vicente, Alonso, *and* Canellada de Zamora, María Josefa, eds., Tirso de Molina, *Comedias*, 49, 254 n. 3

OHIO UNIVERSITY LIBRARY

Please return this book
have finished with it
must be retu